FRANÇOIS VILLON

SIR SAMP. *Has he not a rogue's face?*
Speak, brother, you understand phys-
iognomy; a hanging look to me. He
has a damn'd Tyburn-*face, without*
the benefit o' the clergy.

FORE. *Hum—truly I don't care to dis-*
courage a young man. He has a violent
death in his face; but I hope, no danger
of hanging.   LOVE FOR LOVE.

A NOTE ON THE MAP OF PARIS IN 1530

REPRODUCED AS THE FRONTISPIECE

This Map, by G. Braun, is one of the three earliest maps of Paris, and the most beautiful. The others, both made at this time, Sébastien Munster's and the map called *de la Tapisserie,* are in no way comparable. Braun's map was made just before the hand of the Renaissance touched Medieval Paris, and therefore presents essentially the Paris Villon knew.

On such a reduced scale many street and other names are impossible to decipher: nevertheless certain landmarks are easily discoverable. The University quarter on the Left Bank is the half-moon on the right of the map, with the road from Orleans entering at the Porte St. Jacques, becoming thence the *Grant Rue St. Jacques,* the theatre of most of Villon's life, and driving across the Petit-Pont and the Pont Notre-Dame (whose houses can be plainly seen) through to the Porte St. Martin and out into the country again.

To the east of University the abbey of St. Victor and the bourgs of St. Marcel and St. Médard are plain, and to the west the great abbey and bourg of St. Germain-des-Prés, within its walls: equally plain are the fortresses of the Louvre, the Bastille, and the Temple, the prisons of the Grant- and the Petit-Châtelet, the other main thoroughfares of Medieval Paris, the *Grant Rue St. Denis,* the *Grant Rue St. Martin,* and the *Grant Rue St. Honoré;* and the other bridges, the Pont St. Michel, the Pont au Change, and the Pont aux Meuniers.

The gibbet of Montfaucon, with fruit, is seen on its hillock to the extreme left of the map, that is, to the north, outside the walls.

The walls of Paris shown in this map are of two periods: the whole wall of the Left Bank and the inner wall of the Right were built by Philippe-Auguste between 1190 and 1209. Etienne Marcel, Charles v. and Charles vi. expanded the Right Bank and built its outer wall between 1356 and 1383.

Riviere de Sainne

PARIS IN 1530

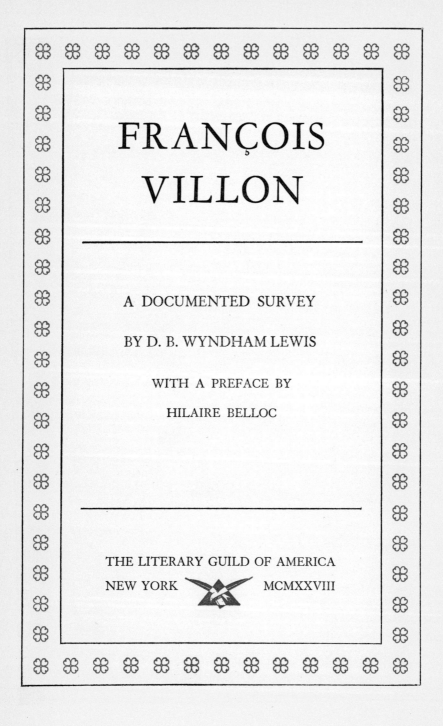

FRANÇOIS VILLON

A DOCUMENTED SURVEY

BY D. B. WYNDHAM LEWIS

WITH A PREFACE BY

HILAIRE BELLOC

THE LITERARY GUILD OF AMERICA

NEW YORK   MCMXXVIII

PRINTED AND BOUND BY J. J. LITTLE AND IVES COMPANY, NEW YORK, U. S. A.

DEDICATION.

TO

the Red-Headed Cerberus, regardant between the Pont Royal and
the Petit-Pont; to the Frothing Vorticiſt; to the Harpy behind
the Little Grille; to the Bilious but Gaitered Platonic; to
the Surgical, Hairy, yet Invisible Troll of the Dieppois; to
the Stout Love-Child of the Pierides who Believes Aquinas
to be a Mineral-Water; to the Bouncing Benthamite of
Bloomsbury who is Unaware of the Medieval; to That
Other, the Cramoisy One; to the Dodging Lutheran
of the Rue de Grenelle; to the Pythoness of Bays-
water; to the Commandant of Infantry who Babbled
of the Grand-Orient; to the Lady with the Hard
Grey Eyes; to the Levantine of London who Did
Not Think Poetry Would Do; to the Military
Character who Sacked the Lot; and to all pratt-
ling Gablers, sycophant Varlets, forlorn Snakes,
blockish Grutnols, fondling Fops, doddi-
pol Joltheads, slutch Calf-Lollies, cods-
head Loobies, jobernol Goosecaps,
grout-head Gnat-Snappers, noddie-
peak Simpletons, Lob-Dotterels,
and ninniehammer
Flycatchers,

THIS,

IN DERISION.

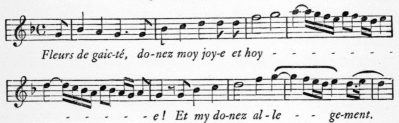

Fleurs de gaic-té, do-nez moy joy-e et hoy - - - - - - - - e! Et my do-nez al-le - - ge-ment.

PREFACE

I DO not know why I should have undertaken to write a Preface for Mr. Wyndham Lewis' *Villon*. It was a presumption, and one which perhaps I ought not to have made. I am putting these few words introductory to a work of great scholarship and research wherein the author has discovered all that Villon was, within and without. I myself can pretend to no such scholarship. I have no more position in the matter than that of the man of general education who from early youth has felt an unchanging admiration for that distinctive and typical voice of the later Middle Ages and of its France. All I could do was to put, as best I may, the effect produced by Villon upon myself; and what I believe to be the essentials of his greatness: though in this I know that I have no standing, and that Mr. Wyndham Lewis' work is there to tell the reader a hundred times more than I can.

Villon, as it seems to me, attained at once the very high place he took, has increased in the scale of European letters, stands higher now even than he did in the height of the Romantic movement, and will in the future (if we retain our culture—which is a big "If") appear as one of the very few unquestioned permanent summits in Western letters, through the quality of *hardness*.

Mr. Wyndham Lewis says it in this book (p. 297) in three words: *"clarity: relief: vigour:"*—and these are the marks of hardness: of the hard-edged stuff: the surviving.

They say that when men find diamonds in primitive fashion, they scrouch and grope in thick greasy clay till they come upon something *hard,* quite different in material from its surroundings; *that* is the stone. In the monuments of Europe, when they fall into ruin, there survive here and there what seem almost imperishable things; it is marble, it is granite which survives.

Now in letters the simile applies. I heard it well said by a great critic weighing one of the best of our modern versifiers (and "the best" is not saying much), that he liked the stuff well enough, but that it had no chance of survival because it was "carved in butter": an appreciation profound and just. It is with the production of verse as with the chiselling of a material. You handle a little figure of the fourteenth century in boxwood; it is smooth, strong and perfect. So is the cut oak of the medieval stalls. But the pine has perished.

Now this quality of hardness in any poet or writer of prose is difficult or impossible to define—more easy to feel.

It is to be discovered by certain marks which are not the causes of it, but are its accompaniments. Of these the chief is what the generation before our own used to call "inevitableness": the word coming in answer (as it were) to the appeal of the ear: the conviction, when you have read the thing, that the least change destroys it; the corresponding conviction of unity through perfection.

Villon has that. There are times when he seems to have arrived at it by heavy strain of search, "working the verse," as the French say. More often it seems to have come to him with what our fathers called "inspiration"—and after all, that is the best word. But everywhere in Villon, sought by him or discovered by him, you find it.

There goes with this, and is inseparable from it, a run, a sequence, which is not smoothness, but which is a sort of linking or leading on without the least threat of dislocation; that also is a mark of hardness. Further, carving in hard matter is alive with the power of economy, which most certainly is not an economy of excision, but the economy of direct speech. And that again you find in Villon everywhere. He puts into a phrase all that could be said to strike home:

Paradis paint, ou sont harpes et lus.

Or:

Sire, et clarté perpetuelle.

x

And again:

Emperiere des infernaux palus.

And again:

Helas! et le bon roy d'Espaigne
Duquel je ne sçay pas le nom?

Take the most famous, the Ballad of the Dead Ladies. Look
how exact and immediate are the subsidiary phrases, the sharp
arrowpoint of

Qui beaulté ot trop plus qu'humaine?

or the rise and swell of

Berte au grant pié, Bietris, Alis,
Haremburgis qui tint le Maine.

It will be said that this intensity of style—for that is "hardness"
—does not alone make up a poet. The criticism is just. It is but
the manner of the poet; were he not a poet no manner could save
him. But still it is the manner which preserves his achievement.

As for the matter, Villon has, being French, that supremely
national acquaintance with the grandeur and bitterness of reality,
and therefore the power of jesting with it; bitter sometimes, sometimes sombre, and sometimes almost genial. And he has what
goes with the bold appreciation of reality, the refuge in beauty, and
the natural (not weak) refuge in affection. But of these last he is
a little afraid—wherein again he is national.

If you desire one word to use as an antithesis to the word sentimental, use the word Villon.

Now apart from all this, Villon is also the ending of the Middle
Ages. The verse is the living voice of a man speaking right out
of fifteenth-century Paris, as though you heard him at your elbow.
But were I to follow up the fascination of the historical, of the
picture from the past, I should make this Preface much too long—
with kennels and gables, spires, black icy water, Paris under a
snowy winter of Louis XI. Since I must not make this Preface too
long, nor keep you from your author, I will end.

HILAIRE BELLOC.

xi

OPPIAN was (if I remember rightly) the first poet of the Greeks to reduce Fishing and Venery to an art; Ovid the first Latin Poet to reduce Love to an art; and the learned German Vincentius Opsopœus the first who taught the art of trowling the Bowl, buffeting the Flagon, and passing a long and merry time at table;[1] but Villon was the first, and (I believe) the only French Poet to make a profession of plunder and larceny.

—GUILLAUME COLLETET, 1650.

[1] *V. Opsopæi Victoria Bacchi seu de Arte Bibendi,* Nuremberg, 1536.

❀ ❀ ❀ ❀ ❀ ❀ ❀ ❀ ❀ ❀ ❀ ❀ ❀ ❀ ❀

FOREWORD

Nam neque adhuc Vario videor nec dicere Cinna
Digna, sed argutos inter strepere anser olores.
—V<small>ERG</small>., Buc. <small>IX</small>.

I nor to *Cinna's* ears, nor *Varus',* dare aspire,
But gabble, like a Goose, amidst the swanlike Quire.
—D<small>RYDEN</small>.

T<small>HIS</small> book began in my mind on a gray day, heavy with snow, of last winter, as I was loitering in the courtyard of St. Julien-le-Pauvre, that little hidden church which is the heart of the Latin Quarter and is so charged with memory: for it stands on the great Roman road marching from Paris to Orleans, Genabum, *and in the earlier shrine on its site St. Gregory of Tours sang the night Office in the sixth century; and much later (having been rebuilt) it became the official church of University and the scene of Rectorial elections for four centuries, and was served by the Cluniacs, and Dante himself said his prayers in it—for such was a quaint custom of the time. He came (as I had come myself that day) from Straw Street, where the Schools were, and in his great mind there still shone the refulgence of*

la luce eterna di Sigieri
Che leggendo nel vico degli strami,

though since Siger de Brabant ceased to lecture in 1277 *(as well he might, being vanquished in debate by the Angelic Doctor and asked to take his Averroism elsewhere by Estienne Tempier, Bishop of Paris) I do not see how Dante can ever have sat at his feet, Boc-*

xiii

caccio's story notwithstanding. But what has all this to do with Villon?

Here, then, in the little courtyard, contemplating the west front of St. Julien, so damnably defaced by Master-Mason Bernard Roche, pacing those stones and thinking of that winter when the wolves were abroad in the streets of Paris, I first thought of writing this book. It began in a glow of pleasure, was continued with pleasure, and is now ended; also with pleasure. Praise be to God and St. Thomas of Canterbury for the same!

On this day before this book floated into my mind, I had been wandering down the Rue St. Jacques, the docte Rue St. Jacques, and over the Petit-Pont, as I had often done before, repeating verses of this poet, whom I have revered since that day of my boyhood when I first lighted on Robert Louis Stevenson's essay, evoked (as will be easily remembered) by the great biographical study of François Villon by Auguste Longnon. Of Stevenson's essay I still think with gratitude; and indeed it must be acknowledged the best study of the medieval world (with "The Black Arrow") ever put on paper by a nineteenth-century Calvinisto-Agnostic. From the day of reading it I became eager for more of this poet, and so having passed without much hurt through the pale antechambers of the Pre-Raphaelite mysticocards and the Æsthetes ("Æsthetic: refined. (Gk.) Gk. αισθητικός, *perceptive."—*Skeat) *I came at last to the fountain-head, as joyously as ever did Pantagruel and his companions to the Dive Bouteille. It is now impossible for me ever to be alone in this ancient heart of Paris; the whole University quarter is alive with the thronging ghosts I know. I have stepped aside for the Provost Robert d'Estouteville, riding home to the Rue de Jouy in his scarlet and fur, attended by his twelve Archers, and have brushed against Master Jehan Cotart,* Promoter Curiæ, *staggering home after a stout night with the bottles: and on the Petit-Pont the voices of the fishwives are shrill.*

"Nobody," said Dr. Johnson, blowing his tea in Conduit Street, "can write the Life of a man, but those who have eat and drunk and lived in social intercourse with him." This I believe to be true, and I have done it. Villon I know now almost as I know some of my friends—or more, for how much does a man know his friends?

*I have fingered manuscripts concerning him. I know his tempera-
ment. I know his Faith, and I have at one time or another fallen
into some of his follies, excluding (at this moment) manslaughter
and burglary. His physical appearance lives in his verse. If I believed
any Oriental dribblings about transmigration I should have known
François Villon to have been a transport driver attached to a British
infantry battalion on the Western Front in the year 1915; for this
fellow resembled the poet in every way, scarred upper lip, long nose,
swarthy features, and skinny dried-up body, saving that he was no
poet, only a great rascally thief and runner after women.*

*I have traced Villon's footsteps in the banlieue and along the
Loire, in what remains of the great Innocents Charnel (it is now a
neat little, tidy little Bloomsbury square), along the Rue St. Denis,
the way of the condemned, out through the ghostly Porte St. Denis
in the vanished ramparts to the gibbet of Montfaucon, which is near
the Gare de l'Est; the way he often went to see men hanged. I have
stood on a midnight near Christmas outside the Ecole Polytechnique, which was the College of Navarre, on the Hill of St. Geneviève, and reconstructed the burglary of 1456. In the Rue des
Parcheminiers by St. Sévérin I have lingered many a night, watching for the four companions to issue from the sign of the Chariot,
all drunk, and involve themselves in that row with Master François
Ferrebourg which all but hanged Villon for the second time in
1462. I know the fellow, his habits and his haunts.*

*Of the authorities (one must have Authorities) by whose light
in varying degrees I have proceeded, I give a list in an Appendix.
It is not an exhaustive list, and the names of Bijvanck, Vitu, Schöne,
and others do not appear in it: the reason for this is that I have not
read them, or only in extracts. I have, indeed, tried to obtain one or
two of them, but with no success, since they are all long out of print
and difficult to discover, except in libraries. In my pursuit I have
been greatly hindered and discouraged by the red-haired man who
stands first in my Dedication. May St. Anthony's Fire scorch his
snout. Happily they were not essential. As for P. Champion's two
volumes on Villon's age, they are a monument of erudition, but they
are not to be possessed by me, nor will they ever be in this world.
Once I was within an ace of laying hands on them, but they turned*

into hornbeam leaves, like fairy gold. I do not doubt that they are Troll books, of the kind in which Morgan le Fay wrote the true history of the Dark Mere of Locmariaquier. They were published mortally in 1913, and became faëry shortly after.

Of the documents which enrich and adorn this book, and are not only translated but successively numbered and described with their official numbers and descriptions for the convenience of those honest men who may wish to see them in the original, the more important I have examined myself in the Bibliothèque Nationale: *but as for the deciphering of them from their crabbed originals, I have not troubled about this, but have taken them,* manibus lilia plenis, *from Longnon and Thuasne, in whose editions they appear in fair print: for only a fool goes rooting about in the stubble when harvest is laid up.*

The text of the two Testaments and the remainder of Villon's verse I have chosen, with some care, from the three best editions available, which are Longnon's of 1892, Foulet's third edition of Longnon, revised, 1923, and Louis Thuasne's Edition critique, 1923. And since in any half-dozen critical editions of Villon's verse you may find one and the same line given in three different ways, I have occasionally found the problem of choice exacting. This may seem drudgery to some, but to me—as the Landgrave of Hesse observed when assured by Luther that the rich were permitted bigamy—it is a pastime. When, therefore, one scholar has carefully amended a clear line of another scholar into something obscure, I have where possible taken the clearer line: for Life is short. As to my running translation in footnotes of the documents and passages of the text scattered throughout this book, I will say only that it pretends to no elegance, but simply to plain brevity; 'strong sense ungraced by sweetness or decorum,' as Mr. Hill said about Dr. Johnson's stage-play. Other footnotes, with the exception of a few employed for "ritual adornment and terror," [1] I have used, I hope, as sparingly as possible.

Pedantry in presenting the text I have avoided: hence I have given the Petit Testament *and the* Grant Testament *these names by which they are commonly known. But since the titles given in the*

[1] H. Belloc, *First and Last.* ("On Historical Evidence.")

most ancient manuscripts are Les Lais *and* Le Teſtament *respectively, I have placed these underneath, in brackets. Similarly, the title of the greater part of the Ballades in the ancient editions is simply* Balade *or* Autre Balade. *The more celebrated titles are the work of Clément Marot chiefly, in his edition of 1533, and also of Prompsault after him, and perhaps one more. I have therefore continued to use these—Marot's juſtly, since they are the titles of a poet—and have included the ancient titles, where they are worth including at all, in brackets also; in this way provoking neither the sneer of frantic impiety nor the screams of outraged virtue.*

As much of the Teſtaments (a considerable amount) as reveals valuable aspects of Villon's life and adventure I have used in the chapter called "The Life," and much of the same verse again, if necessary, in reviewing the Works. It is even possible that a small amount may occur a third time in that final short chapter called "The Cream of the Teſtaments," which contains a selection of the fineſt of his verse in its own pattern, not wrenched from the context: but there should be no complaint about such repetition, for great poetry can never be read too often. If there should be any fuss over this, why, I am completely indifferent; like the gentleman in the eighteenth-century poem:

> Though pleas'd to see the dolphins play,
> I mind my compass and my way.

The book is rounded off by a selection of English renderings of Villon from the hands of Rosetti, Swinburne, Henley, and J. M. Synge, though I take it to be axiomatic and Matter of Breviary that to translate great poetry into great poetry is impossible, Dryden and Pope notwithſtanding. The celebrated Rossetti rendering of the Ballade of Dead Ladies I have included, therefore, in spite of its "yeſter-year" and its "overword," and the very terrible swapping of rhymes twice which occurs in it, deſtroying the Ballade form and flying dead in the teeth of the Rubrics. The Swinburne version of the Ballade of the Hanged I have included as well, suppressing my personal feelings about "yea, perdie," which affects me in much the same manner as those books on travel called "The Lure of ——,"

xvii

which are written by maiden ladies in New England. J. M. Synge's brief prose-paraphrase of the *Ballade to Our Lady* goes in because the speech of Catholic Kerry chimes naturally with the strong and simple passion of this noble poem; and lastly, W. E. Henley's exercise in nineteenth-century London thieves' slang is a jolly thing of itself, and Villon would, I think, have grinned with pleasure at "moskeneer" and "rattle the tats."

There is no fiction in this book that I know of. I have on the other hand permitted myself occasional Legitimate Assumptions. For example, in the opening chapter, the news of the ringing of the Angelus at Sorbonne is Villon's own testimony. I have assumed (I trust not too daringly) that

(a) the bell did not ring of itself,
(b) it was therefore rung by some agency,
(c) this agency was probably mortal,
(d) the bell was probably rung, therefore, by the minor official of University appointed to ring bells, rather than by (say) the Rector Magnificus, or the landlord of the Mule tavern.

Again, in recording the death-sentence of 1462, I have assumed that it was not handed to Villon on a silver salver, but that he was brought before the Provost in the prescribed form; and during the ceremony experienced some of those feelings which a man in his position would most generally feel. And so forth. I believe such assumptions, within strict limits, to be allowable and agreeable. If I am to be damned for making them, why, then, I am damned in the excellent company of *Austin Dobson* (see his *Essay on Swift*): not to speak of the malignant Gibbon, the glittering Macaulay, and the amiable John Richard Green; all three Authorities—or so Mrs. Ramboat of Bloomsbury assures me. My own assumptions, however, have no ulterior motive.

I have to thank the following: M. Pierre Champion, for permission to reproduce the frontispiece map, which is published by the Société de l'Histoire de Paris; Dr. Théodore Gérold, of the Faculty of Letters of the University of Strasbourg, for permission to use *the music of five fifteenth-century songs from his edition of the Manuscript of Bayeux, so full of historical value, described in my Bibliography; Mr. Belloc, for permission to quote from "Avril," and also for writing a Preface; and Mr. E. V. Lucas, for bringing to my notice a letter from Marcel Schwob to Sir Sidney Colvin. Acknowledgments are also due to Mr. Charles Whibley and Messrs. Macmillan for permission to print "Villon's Straight Tip to all Cross Coves," by W. E. Henley; to Messrs. Heinemann for permission to print Swinburne's versions of the "Ballade of the Hanged" and of some stanzas from the "Lament of the Belle Heaulmière"; and to Messrs. Allen & Unwin for permission to print J. M. Synge's paraphrase of the "Ballade to Our Lady."*

And in conclusion, this is not a book for a rabble of pedants nuzzled in the brabbling-shop of Sophisters, but for those dear souls who love high poetry and the unfortunate—for if it is not in the nature of misfortune to be shoved into prison at regular intervals, to be forced to absorb huge and unreasonable quantities of water, and to be all but hanged on two known occasions at least, what is? To these, and to none other, I lovingly present this book. As for those others, vietsdazes, visaiges d'ânes, *may the Maulebec truss them all.*

St. Germain, *January* 1928.

CONSPECTUS TEMPORUM

OR

SHORT VIEW OF THE LIFE OF FRANÇOIS VILLON, A.M.

1431 (O.S.).   Birth of Villon in Paris.
[1436.   The English withdrawal.
1437.   Entry of Charles VII.]
1443 (*circa*).   Villon entered of Faculty of Arts.
1449 (N.S.).   Villon received a Bachelor.
[1451-2.   The riots of the *Pet-au-Deable*.]
1452.   Villon received Licentiate and Master of Arts.
1455.   *Corpus Christi,* June 5:
    The killing of Chermoye.
    Villon's flight from Paris.
1456.   Villon returns.
    The *Petit Testament*.
    Christmas Eve (?):
    The burglary at the College of Navarre.
    Villon quits Paris
    [Four years' wandering.]
1460.   Villon sentenced to death at Orleans: released July 17.
1461.   Villon imprisoned by Thibault d'Aussigny, Bishop of Orleans,
    at Meun-sur-Loire.

    October 20:
    Villon released by the passage of Louis XI.
    The *Grant Testament*.
1462.   Villon returns to Paris.
    November 3-7:
    Villon imprisoned in the Châtelet and released on a bond to
    the Faculty of Theology.
    Villon implicated in the stabbing of Master François Ferre-
    bourg, re-arrested, and sentenced to be "hanged and
    strangled."
1463.   January 3:
    Parliament, on Villon's appeal, commutes the death-sentence
    to banishment for ten years.
    Villon vanishes from history.

✠ *Cujus animam de morte æterna libera, Domine!*

CONTENTS

V.

VI.   APPENDICES

I

PRELIMINARY

❀ ❀ ❀ ❀ ❀ ❀ ❀ ❀ ❀ ❀ ❀ ❀ ❀

§ 1

PORTRAIT OF A MASTER OF ARTS

Cultu non proinde speciosus, ut facile appareret eum ex hac nota litteratorum esse, quos odisse divites solent.

In his appearance not over-dazzling: so that you might without difficulty recognise him as belonging to that class of men of letters who are continuously hated by the Rich.　　　—PETRONIUS, *Satiricon,* lxxxiii.

A LITTLE before nine o'clock of a bitter night in Paris, on the threshold of Christmas 1456, the sacristan or minor beadle of the University whose duty it was to ring the bell of Sorbonne for the night Angelus climbed into the rope-chamber, grasped his rope and jerked it, and set the tongue in the steeple above him swinging: *Bome. Bome. Bome.*

A pause.

Bome. Bome. Bome.

The waves of sound rolled heavily over University, over the sloping huddled roofs, down to the river, reverberating and shaking the air. In a few years onward, when a decree of Louis XI. shall have made national what is now a custom peculiar to University and to the devout Celts of Brittany, the first note of Angelus from Sorbonne will be answered by a brazen salvo, *tintamarre,* and clangour from all the bells of Paris full volley, as it were Ringing Island itself: by the deep bay of St. Germain-des-Prés, St. Séverin clamouring over the river to St. Merri, a fainter jangle coming down the wind from Notre-Dame and St. Germain l'Auxerrois, St. Peter of the Bulls chiming to St. Gervais and the Celestines by the Bastille,

3

St. Martin's Priory awaking the bells of the Chartreux and the Dominicans of the Rue St. Jacques, and joining all together in a flurry, all the three hundred churches and convents of Paris. This was the holy clamour and tintinnabulation which caused Pontanus the secular poet (as Master Janotus de Bragmardo the Sophist observed in his great Sorbonnical discourse on Bells) very profanely and wantonly to express the wish, while composing his carminiform verses, that all the bells of Paris had been made of feathers and the clappers thereof of foxes' tails. But on this December night of 1456 the University salutes Our Lady alone, and the booming of its solitary bell in the darkness is to be fixed and to echo in men's memory as long as poetry can quicken and enlarge the human spirit. For at the first stroke of the bell of Sorbonne [1] a dark young clerk sitting alone in an upper chamber of a house called the Porte Rouge in the cloister of St. Benoît-le-Bientourné, in the shadow of Sorbonne, lower down the hill towards the river, having paper and inkhorn and candle before him, looks up from his writing and, laying down his pen, with fingers stiff with cold signs himself and begins to recite hastily, half under his breath, the Salutation:

> *Angelus Domini nuntiavit Mariæ, et concepit de Spiritu Sancto:*
> *Ave Maria, gratia plena . . .*

And so to the end. The night is silent. He pauses, picks up his pen again, and contemplating for a moment his distorted shadow blackening the ceiling, with sudden resolution bends to his manuscript.

> *Finablement* (he writes), *en escripvant,*
> *Ce soir, seulet, estant en bonne,*
> *Dictant ces laiz et descripvant*
> *F'oïs la cloche de Sorbonne,*
> *Qui tousjours a neuf heures sonne*
> *Le Salut que l'Ange predit;*
> *Si suspendis et y mis bonne*
> *Pour prier comme le cuer dit.*

[Lastly, as I describe and set down these bequests in writing to-night, being alone, and in good dispositions, I hear the bell of

---

[1] The name of this bell was Mary. It bore the inscription: GALTERVS DICTVS JVVENTE ME FECIT. . . . EGO VOCOR MARIA.—(*Diarium*, Bibl. Mazarine, MS. 5323, fol. 203.)

4

Sorbonne, which rings every night at nine o'clock the Salutation brought by the Angel: and I pause to pray, as the heart directs.]

He shivers, gathers round him more closely his shabby gown, and continues writing. It is permissible, while the candle-flame ceases for a moment to flicker in the draught and throws his saturnine visage into relief, to study for a moment the appearance of this scholar: François de Montcorbier, *dit* Villon, Master of Arts in the University of Paris.

He is lean and lank, bony of arms and legs, sharp-featured, dark, secret, "dry and black as a maulkin," as he has just described himself in the verse on which he is now engaged: with eyes, as they look up at the shuddering of the flame, that have already a quick sideways glance, instinctively on guard against the leap from the shadows and the hand clapped suddenly on his shoulder. This uneasy roving of the eyes has become his normal habit. His upper lip has a permanent twist, the result of a dagger-slash received a year ago outside the church of St. Benoît-le-Bientourné in the street below. It is impossible to imagine that this improves his features. As he sits writing—he is nearing the end of his manuscript, and his teeth are chattering; the candle is beginning to gutter (he has noted it in a verse) and his ink is beginning to freeze—a chuckle breaks from him. Within the hour a select company at the *Pomme de Pin,* the *Mule,* or the *Grant Godet,* will be sniggering at some of the rhymed bequests set down in this, his *Lais,* his burlesque will and testament. It is the eve of a journey to Angers in Anjou, where he is withdrawing to ease him of the cruelty of a mistress; probably of his creditors too; and (as will appear in due time) most likely for a practical and sinister purpose also.

He rises, stuffs his papers into his breast, blows out the expiring candle, and with a natural cat-like tread passes out and down the stairs. The outer door closes gently. François Villon's night has begun.

His own works, and a sequence of documents drawn up by the officers of justice, enable the portrait to be faithfully completed. Master [2] François Villon is now, in this year 1456, in his twenty-

[2] "Master" is not tushery, but his academic right—*Dominus* (or *Magister*) *Franciscus*—and part of his *état civil.*

5

sixth year, and has already drunk deep of the cup which is to inebriate him almoſt continuously henceforth. The ſtreet, the tavern, and the brothel know and hail him as *ung bon follaſtre;* his recurring moodiness and lovesickness apart. He has already killed his man in the affair outside St. Benoît, and has only recently returned to Paris after a prudent withdrawal to the neighbourhood of Bourg-la-Reine, on the Orleans road. Of the Seven Deadly Sins known to the Medievals (for they had not yet been abolished by a Viennese Jew) he is already held firmly in bond by at leaſt five: Covetousness, Luſt, Sloth, Gluttony, and Anger. Of these Luſt most of all, I think, has him captive in her bailiwick. The *pensionnaires* of the house of Miſtress Overdone, Fat Margot, in the dark ſtreet across the river behind the Precinct of Notre-Dame, a procession of Jehannetons and Blanches and Guillemettes (their names are set in his verse), have already enslaved in turn his senses and helped to empty his lean purse: and in return he has begun (or will soon begin) to levy on one or two of them the tribute which in all ages gentlemen of imperious appetite and slender means have levied on the goodnatured fair. His own evidence a little later shows him a *souteneur.* No pimp before or since him has ever made a ballade about it.

There is no reason to doubt that during his late journey into the country Villon has affiliated himself to the company called the Coquillards, in whose secret jargon or *jobelin* he will later write half a dozen ballades. In the ranks of the Coquille, whose activities extend over a large part of France, are found the beſt card-sharpers, brigands, footpads, dice-coggers, crimps, Mohocks, mumpers, pimps, ponces, horse-stealers, confidence-men, bruisers, thugs, lockpickers, coin-clippers, housebreakers, hired assassins, and all-round desperadoes in Europe, true children of wing-heeled Mercury, patron of thieves and politicians.

> *Spelicans,*
> *Qui en tous temps*
> *Avancez dedens le pogois*
> *Gourde piarde*
> *Et sur la tarde*
> *Desbousez les povres nyois, . . .*[3]

[3] See p. 318, *A Ballade from the Jargon.*

[Light-fingered blades, who at all times go swaggering into the cabaret, drinking the good liquor, and at night issue forth to rob poor ninnies. . . .]

—so he joyously addresses them in the Third Ballade of the Jargon. And again in the Fifth, addressing particularly his *joncheurs*, sharpers, and bidding them with a whoop beware of the High Jump:

> *Joncheurs jonchans en joncherie*
> *Rebignez bien ou joncherez,*
> *Qu'oſtac n'embroue voſtre arerie*
> *Ou acolez sont vos aisnez!*
> *Poussez de la quille et brouez,*
> *Car toſt seriez rouppieux,*
> *Eschec qu'acollez ne soiez*
> *Par la poe du marieux.*

[Sharpers, sharping in sharpery, have a care, my lads, how you sharp, or you'll find yourselves hoicked and ſtrung up where your elders and betters are! Be nimble, slip out of it quickly before they clink you, and be wary, or sooner or later you're had, and the fiſt of Jack Ketch wallops down on you.] (One or two of these words of the Jargon are conjectural.)

To the same rattling boys he will also, in a sombre mood, dedicate the Ballade of Good Counsel with its shrugging refrain:

> *Car ou soies porteur de bulles,*
> *Pipeur ou hasardeur de dez,*
> *Tailleur de faulx coings, tu te brusles*
> *Comme ceulx qui sont eschaudez,*
> *Traiſtres parjurs, de foy vuydez;*
> *Soies larron, ravis ou pilles:*
> *Ou en va l'acquest, que cuidez?*
> *Tout aux tavernes et aux filles!*

[Whether you be a peddler of faked indulgences, a sharper, a dice-cogger, or a good hand at coining, you'll burn your fingers, like those false traitors landed for treason. Or be a sneak-thief, ravish and rob: where does the profit go, d'ye think? Taverns and wenches get the lot.]

which Henley so dexterously echoes in his Ballade called "Villon's Straight Tip to all Cross Coves":

> Booze and the blowens cop the lot.

It is a pleasant life in Capua while the money lasts. Flesh is cheap, and the wine flows, and the song is loud, and the Seven Deadly Sins clash their merry cymbals. There is a tavern chorus of the time which Villon and his companions must often have bellowed under the grimy beams of the *Trumelières* and the *Espée de Bois,* with the dawn, announced by the sentinel's trumpet from the high platform of the Donjon of the Louvre, oozing through the window-squares of cloudy glass or oiled linen:

Gen - tils gal - lans, com-pai - gnons du rai - sin, Be-vons d'au-tant au soir et au ma - tin, Jusqu'à cent sols, Et ho! A noſtre hos - tes - se ne paye - ron point d'ar - gent, Fors ung cre - do!

Si noſtre hoſtesse nous faisoit adjourner,
Nous luy diron qu'il fault laisser passer
Quasimodo,
Et ho!
A noſtre hoſtesse ne payeron point d'argent,
Fors ung credo!

I

[Jolly fellows, companions of the Grape, let us drink our fill night and morning, to the tune of a hundred sols—what ho! We will not pay our hoſtess a cent, save a credo! (*Credo* = a brass farthing; or alternatively, credit.)

II

If our hoſtess wants to get rid of us, we'll tell her she must wait till after Quasimodo. (= Low Sunday, the Sunday after Easter)—what ho! We will not, etc., etc.]

8

But when his recurring heaviness, "allicholy and musing," as Mistress Quickly said, seizes him, like a Quartan Ague, he can be no company, huddled in his black gown and brooding in his corner, with the empty hanap before him and his dark eyes staring into nothing. Nevertheless of the popularity of this scholar there can be no doubt. He has (in his gay or desperate moods) a quick, salt wit, and he can put his friends and enemies into verses which arouse yells of laughter, so biting and so apt they are. He can rhyme drunk or sober; and he is already acknowledged around the Halles quarter the best sneak-thief and *trompeur* of his year: so brilliant that some years hence he will have become a legend and his exploits will be written down in verse, crowning him the hero of more than one trick which rings familiar in the ears of readers of *Tyl Eulenspiegel*. Altogether this Master of Arts is in the year 1456 fairly well advanced, as we observe, along the road to Montfaucon gibbet, where the pretty gentlemen swing high, keeping their sheep by moonlight. It has been suggested, and with plausibility, that a hundred years later Rabelais drew Panurge from the figure and fame of François Villon: Panurge with his *faulx visaige*, his slim middle stature and his long nose, like a razor-handle, his misfortune of being fond of women yet subject to panic, and his other worse misfortune of being eternally short of money, and his horse-play, and swindling, and trickery, and debauchery, and rude jests— "*pipeur, beuveur, batteur de pavé, ribleur, s'il en estoit à Paris . . . et tousjours machinoit quelque chose contre les sergens et contre le guet.*" * All this is very Villon.

Finally, to round off this portrait, apologetically, and in the teeth of good taste and modern scruples, I have to suggest that this deboshed ruffian, whose companions are blackguards and trulls, has within him not only filial love and patriotism but also a glowing spark of the faith which he learned from his mother and has never lost: to which he returns, as in his verse, breaking out afterwards

---

*[A wicked lewd Rogue, a cosener, drinker, royster, rover, and a very dissolute and debautch'd Fellow, if there were any in Paris . . . and still contriving some Plot, and devising mischief against the Serjeants and the Watch.[4]]

[4] *Pantagruel*, Bk. II., xvi, Urquhart's tr., 1653. See Appendix B: *Villon-Panurge*.

and sinning, and repenting with groans, and returning once more to his vomit, like some other sinners and some saints. This faith of his flames out often in the two Testaments, so stuffed with ribaldry and laughter, most of all in the Ballade of the Hanged, in his own Epitaph, and in that great Ballade in which he casts from him for a moment the crapulous years and kneels by his mother's side, stretching out his hands with her to the compassionate Mother of God and uttering that prayer which begins,

> *Dame du ciel, regente terrienne,*
> *Emperiere des infernaux palus,*

[Lady of Heaven and earth, and therewithal,
    Crowned Empress of the nether clefts of Hell.]
                                                    (*Rossetti*).

and is his noblest work. This religion of his—I excuse myself once more: it is imperative to mention it—runs through the drab chronicle of his life like a bright gold thread, and is as much part of the essential Villon as his mocking humour and his sardonic philosophy. On the eve of being led out to be hanged he can compose a quatrain predicting that his neck will shortly discover how much another part of his body weighs: but before his wry grin, as you might say, has completely faded, he is commending himself and his doomed companions (whom he already sees swinging, sundried and blackened, on Montfaucon, with the birds stabbing at their hollow eyes) devoutly to the prayers of men and the mercy of Christ, in words which are written in the blood of his heart.

In the symphony of Medieval Paris which is Villon's poetry, in its rich tumult, its vivid colour, its cruelties and generosities and riotings and obscenities and crimes and dirt and splendour and prevailing largeness—the Middle Ages were sometimes scandalous, but never vulgar—in its strange pathos and preoccupation with Death, in all this there is mixed the brawl of the streets and the laughing loud song of taverns, the screams and giggling of daughters of joy and the everlasting disputations of the Sorbonnical Doctors, the clink of goblets and the clash of steel, the thud of flying feet and the jangle of chains and the creak of ropes on Montfaucon gallows: but under all these noises there runs, with a steady beat, permanent, like ground-bass, the chant of *De Profundis* and the *Salve Regina*.

On this night of December 1456 Master François Villon is already, I think, emptying a cup by the fire in the tavern of his choice and exchanging rude jokes with the ladies and gentlemen there assembled. It is profitable to leave him there for the moment and to turn and contemplate the University which has bred and the Town which nourishes this scholar.

❀ ❀ ❀ ❀ ❀ ❀ ❀ ❀ ❀ ❀ ❀ ❀ ❀ ❀

§ 2

THE UNIVERSITY

The alme, inclyte, and celebrate Academie, which is vocitated Lutetia.

Pantagruel, Bk. ii.

Holy God of Gods in Sion, what a mighty stream of pleasure gladdened our hearts when we have leisure to visit Paris, the Paradise of the world! . . . There are delightful libraries, more aromatic than stores of spice, there abundant orchards of all manner of books. Richard of Bury.

Of the three towns which composed Medieval Paris, the City on the islands, the Town on the right bank, the University on the left, the University was the latest to develop. It was not until the end of the twelfth century that the centre of Parisian learning began to shift from the Cloisters of Notre-Dame, St. Germain l'Auxerrois, and the monastic schools of the right bank across the river to the Hill of St. Geneviève: across the Petit-Pont, that little scholarly bridge. "The Petit-Pont," wrote Guy de Bazoches, the fine Latin poet, towards the end of the twelfth century, "belongs to the dialecticians, who walk there deep in argument." These free professors, the *Parvipontani,* had been licensed by the Chancellor of Notre-Dame to accept pupils some time before the general migration.*

By the mid-thirteenth century the University of Paris, or more properly the University (*universitas,* corporation) of the Chancellor, Masters, and Scholars of Paris,[1] was the centre of the intellectual

---

* See Appendix A: *The Earlier Schools.*

[1] The charter of 1215, in which the words *Universitas magistrorum et scolarium* occur for the first time, was drawn up by the Papal Legate Robert de Courçon, and placed the University under the direct authority of the Holy See. Philippe-Auguste had already, in

12

life of Christendom, the theological arbiter of Europe, *stupor mundi,* the darling, *filia carissima,* of the Kings of France, rich in privilege and honour and orgulously insisting on the same, recognising no overlord but the Pope: the sole master of the University of Paris from 1215 to the eve of the Revolution.[2] In the year 1453 counsel for the University, opening an interesting action before the Court of Parliament which we shall examine in due course, rehearses the ancient pride of University thus:

On scet, de l'Université de Paris, quel corps c'est en l'Eglise & en ce Royaume qui est ordonné pour introduire science & sapience, & inter mundana *n'y a autre plus grande ne plus haute que l'Université de Paris, & pour ce n'est de merveilles se les roys de France l'ont honnorée & trouvé qu'ils l'ont honnorée en deux choses,* primo: *en ce que le Roy l'appelle* filiam carissimam *&, par ce moien, ladite Université & les supportz d'elle sont en l'especial garde du Roy leur pere; la seconde chose est en grans privileges donnez par les Roys à elle & sans lesquelz elle ne peut entretenir ne pourveoir; & ont les prevostz de Paris la cure de garder lesditz privileges & autres sermens servans à la matiere, lesquelx ses lieuxtenans & sergens doivent aussy jurer.*

[It is well known, concerning the University of Paris, what position she holds in the Church and in this Realm, being ordained to impart knowledge and wisdom, and that of earthly things there is none greater or higher than the University of Paris, and on that account it is no wonder that the Kings of France have honoured and held themselves to honour her in two things, *primo:* in that the King calls her *filiam carissimam,* and therefore the said University and her members are in the especial care of the King their father; and secondly, in the great privileges accorded her by our Kings, without which she could neither flourish nor exist: and it is the duty of the Provosts of Paris to guard the said privileges and all pertaining, which is also binding on their lieutenants and serjeants.]

Before the first half of the thirteenth century sixty colleges had risen on and around the sacred Hill. The earliest, that of the Dix-Huit for eighteen destitute students, endowed by the Englishman

1200, made professors and students independent of the civil jurisdiction, and hence is the founder of University. University tradition, on the other hand, claimed (not very seriously) Charlemagne for its founder. The feast of St. Charlemagne, January 28, is still the students' and schoolboys' holiday.

[2] It is to be noted that University, so cherished by the Holy See, nevertheless on two occasions at least opposed it: in 1281, in the matter of a Bull of Martin IV. granting the Orders privileges deemed by University excessive, and again in the conflict between Boniface VIII. and Philippe le Bel, when University took the King's side.

Josse de Londres on his return from a pilgrimage to the Holy Places, was founded in 1180. The Collège de Constantinople for the Orientals followed in 1204; the Bons Enfans St. Honoré in 1209. By the end of the century the University sprawled over a great demilune of territory, beginning on the quay where the Institut de France now stands, taking a wide sweep behind the Hill of St. Geneviève and its now vanished abbey, and meeting the Seine again at the place occupied now by the Halle aux Vins, but then by the Abbey of St. Victor. To the east of the academic kingdom, outside the walls, lay the bourgs of St. Marcel and St. Médard: to the west the fortified bourg of St. Germain-des-Prés, clustered round its powerful abbey, proud with three steeples.

The map of University in Villon's time shows a huge confused agglomeration of spires and colleges and convents, lecture-halls and hostels, taverns and shops, houses for University officials, beadles, mace-bearers, apparitors, messengers, servants, and the fringes of the academic horde, open-air bookstalls, *escriptoires*, and the shops of those engaged in the academic trades, the parchment-makers, the binders, the writers, the copyists, the booksellers, and the illuminers, whose reputation had become world-wide by the time of Dante,

> *Quell' arte*
> *Ch' alluminare è chiamata in Parisi.*
>
> —Purgatorio, xi.

The *stationarii* employed the writers, the *librarii* sold the books. Both were under the strict control of University. The University's parchment was for a long time bought processionally at the great fair called the Foire du Lendit in the plain of St. Denis, the Nijni-Novgorod of its age, by the Rector himself, issuing forth from the Hill of St. Geneviève at the rear of a joyous crowd of students, and attended by banners, drum, and trumpet. Of the greater libraries open for the use of students, that of St. Victor was celebrated down to the time of Rabelais, whose parody of its catalogue every man knows: the others were the library of Sorbonne and the library of Notre-Dame. The colleges, at first simply hostels endowed by monasteries and private benefactors, became in the late thirteenth century and onwards places of education, as distinct from the schools. They took their names generally from their founders: the Collège de Lisieux, for example, from Guy d'Harcourt, Bishop of Lisieux; the Collège d'Harcourt, from Raoul d'Harcourt, Chancellor of Bayeux; the Collège de Navarre (which will enter interestingly into this history before long in connection with a very pretty burglary), from Jehanne de Navarre, Queen of Philippe le Bel; the Collège des Ecossais, from David, Bishop of Moray; the Collège de Narbonne, from Bernard de Farges, Archbishop of Narbonne; the Collège du Plessis, from Geoffrey du Plessis, a monk of Marmoutiers in Touraine; the Collège des Chollets, from Cardinal Jehan Chollet; the Collège des Lombards, from Andrea Ghini of Florence, Bishop of Arras; the Collège de Cluny, from Yves, abbot of that great monastery; the Scandinavian colleges—the Collège de Danemark, the Collège d'Upsal, the Collège de Linckôping. Out of the thick cluster of names I select one more, a celebrated one, that of the Collège de Montaigu, founded by Gilles Aycelin de Montaigu, Archbishop of Rouen, in 1314, reformed during the fifteenth century, and a byword till Rabelais' time and after for the ferocity of its discipline and the austerity of its living. "My sovereign Lord," says Ponocrates to Grandgousier, discussing the education of Gargantua, "think not that I have placed him in that lowsie Colledge, which they call *Montague* . . . for the Galley-Slaves are far better used among the Moores and Tartars, the murtherers in the criminal Dungeons, yea the very Doggs in your House, than are the poor wretched Students in the aforesaid Colledge." The learning dispensed at Montaigu was extremely sound, and the college lasted in *plein exercice* till the Revolution, Erasmus and St. Ignatius of Loyola were bred there, and Calvin,

> John Calvin, whose peculiar fad
> It was to call God murderous;
> Which further led that feverish cad
> To burn alive the Servetus.

Of all this mass of colleges the Sorbonne, late in order of foundation, had soon become the head, captain, and master-house, and then as now an occasional synonym for the whole University. It was established in 1257 and 1259 with a gift of houses to the Royal chaplain Robert de Sorbon by St. Louis the King, a college for theologians only. Popes and kings nourished and protected Sorbonne and showered privileges on it. It conferred its supreme degree, *Doctor Sorbonnicus,*[3] and under its roof in 1469 the first printing-press in France was set up. As Villon saw Sorbonne, passing it daily in the Rue St. Jacques, it was a tall Gothic pile, with towers flanking the high arch of the main door, a steeple rising above: its especial glories, its great square Hall and its Latin library, the "aromatic orchard" of Richard of Bury's panegyric, which held a thousand volumes.[4]

In 1450, when Villon was still a Bachelor of Arts, the University counted at the very least 2500 members in residence, of whom about 800 were graduates.[5] These were divided among the four Faculties of Theology, Canon Law, Medicine, and Arts; the great majority in the Faculty of Arts, although the dominant note of University had always been theology, and all dialectic bent in that direction. The Rector Magnificus ruled not only the whole University but also, directly, the Faculty of Arts; the other three Faculties had each a Dean. It is distasteful to use the word "democratic," but it rises almost inevitably as one contemplates the procedure governing the election of the Rector. His office lasted three months only, he might be a foreigner, for he was not immediately re-eligible, and he was chosen by a committee of delegates of the Faculty of Arts, meeting for that purpose in the little ancient church of St. Julien-le-Pauvre by the river: and every University historian I have read thinks it necessary to explain that the election generally took place amid scenes of turbulence. In 1524, I observe, the students forced

[3] "The Doctors of the Sorbonne are all equal. . . . For the Doctorate three disputations, *Major, Minor, Sorbonica.*"—Dr. Johnson's Paris notebook, 1775.
[4] Richelieu destroyed this building, reconstructing it 1627-1642. Of Richelieu's Sorbonne only the church now remains, with his tomb in it. The modern Sorbonne was built over and beyond the old site by Nénot, between 1885 and 1901. In the pavement of a court in the Rue de la Sorbonne traces of the medieval outline could be seen till quite recently. A print of the medieval Sorbonne, from which I have roughly described it, exists, dated 1550.
[5] Rashdall, *Universities of Europe in the Middle Ages,* Oxford, 1895. An Italian, Giovanni di Neri Cecchi, writing in 1462, places the total at that day as high as 18,000. I find the Venetian Ambassador in Rabelais' time, Maximo Cavalli, makes the total between 16,000 and 20,000. De Breul (*Antiquitez de Paris,* 1612) says that there were so many students in University in the fifteenth century that on the occasion of the annual procession to St. Denis the Rector would be still passing the Mathurins' church in the Rue St. Jacques when the head of the procession was entering the town of St. Denis, a couple of leagues away. I make no effort to reconcile all these foreigners with an English Don.

the church doors, manhandled the delegates, smashed the windows, and hooted the new Rector. The clergy of St. Julien appealed to Parliament, which ordered elections to be held elsewhere; but you cannot wave away tradition like that. In 1660, at the last Rectorial Election in the University, almost the same thing happened, at the same place.

So much, in this place, for Authority.

The students, excluding the Orientals, were grouped loosely in four Nations: the Nation of France, combining the Parisians and those of the Midi; [6] the Nation of Picardy, including the Walloons and the men of Artois; the Nation of Normandy; and the Nation of England, in which was reckoned a mixed rabble of Germans, Scots, Swedes, and Dutch. In Villon's time, when the Hundred Years' War had made the name of England poisonous, the fourth Nation had become the *Nation d'Allemagne;* but it does not seem that the new name was generally used. The Schools of the Four Nations stood in Straw Street, the Rue du Fouarre; Dante himself wrapped his chill feet in the straw there, and put Straw Street into the *Commedia.*[7] Towards the end of the fifteenth century, and much more a little later, the colleges, having completely supplanted the schools, divided themselves into two kinds: colleges *de plein exercice,* which gave the full University curriculum, excluding Law and Medicine, and colleges *d'exercice restreint,* which gave only a part. The professors lived in their colleges, which supported them, but it was not until the reign of François 1. that they began to receive a regular salary. The student came in theory under one of four headings. The *boursier* or bursar lived and was educated under the provision of the pious founder of his college. The *portioniste* paid for his board and education. The *camériste,* a gold-tuft, kept his own chamber, and often a tutor as well. The *martinet,* a non-collegiate man, paid his lecture fees directly to his professor. The standard University fees, called the *bourse* in Villon's time, were payable weekly and calculated by the authorities on the apparent

---

[6] The French Nation was subdivided into five groups, corresponding to the five ecclesiastical provinces.
[7] Certain Orders, as the Friars Minor and the Cistercians, had their own schools. The Law Schools (in which Guillaume de Villon was for a time professor) were in the Rue St. Jean-de-Beauvais, the Medicine Schools in the Rue de la Bûcherie.

resources of the student: in Villon's case they came to two sols Parisis, exclusive of graduation fees. For the bursar the *bourse* was held to cover not only books and tuition but, when necessary, food and clothing as well.[8] Long before Villon colleges had been organised, with some sort of discipline, under a principal. Doors were locked at night, and there was a necessary number of sconces and sanctions. Undergraduates had to ask leave to go out, and might only walk the streets in couples. The academic dress was the black gown falling to the heels. From a verse of the *Grant Testament*,

> *Chaperons auront enformez*
> *Et les poulces sur la sainture,*

[They will wear their hoods well over the eyes, and thumbs in the belt.]

it would seem that to wear the hood pulled well over the eyes and the thumbs tucked into the belt was the prescribed academic deportment in walking abroad. A type of the severer discipline existing in University, though not so rigorous as that of Montaigu, is the rule of the Collège de Beauvais, founded by Jehan de Dormans, Bishop of Beauvais, in 1370. Its bursars, ruled by a Master, an undermaster, and a procurator, wore a distinctive-coloured gown of violet. Meals were taken in common and in silence, and, as in a monastic house, a lector read aloud from the Bible while the community was at table. Students were forbidden to *pernocter hors du college* without legitimate reason; the roll was called every night at an early hour, and absentees were severely punished. By Villon's day, no doubt, this discipline had relaxed, like most other.

We shall look for Villon in vain among any of the pious and the well-behaved. At a time when Paris, starved and sick from the wars, saw her vagabond population reinforced alike by unpaid mercenaries and destitute priests and students of ruined colleges, and when poor scholars were forced to beg their bread from door to door—so dry was the town bled, and so openly did misery stalk everywhere—it is not to be thought that Villon and his immediate

[8] An interesting ordinance of 1309 allows poor students in extreme necessity to sell their books for food, with two strict exceptions, the Bible and the works of St. Thomas Aquinas: *Biblia dumtaxat & fratris Thomæ operibus exceptis* (Denifle, *Chartularium Univ., Paris,* ii.). In such honour was the Angelic Doctor held within thirty-five years of his death.

18

friends knew no easier way of living than by asking alms humbly of the greasy bourgeois cap in hand with the poor scholars of Madame de Navarre, whose whine was one of the notable street cries of Paris. His own method will be amply set forth as this history proceeds. There was about University in his time a large brigade of the *déclassés*, the lazy, the dissolute, and the Ishmaels, snapping up what they could. Villon himself was apparently a non-collegiate man, living at home and subject to little discipline.[9]

The battalions of lusty youth from all over Christendom—for the most part, I think, joyous, for what is an empty belly and a punishment or two when one is not yet twenty and there is wine at the *Mule?*—were naturally divided fiercely by national feuds. Jacques de Vitry has preserved from the late thirteenth century the gist of the insults buffeted to and fro from one side of the street to another:

[Because of the differences of their homes they disagree and are envious and insulting, and without shame offer insult and contumely, saying that the English are drunkards and have tails,[10] the French proud, soft, and womanish, the Germans mad and indecent in feeding, the Normans stupid and boastful, the Picards traitors and fair-weather friends. The Burgundians they hold brutish and slow, and thinking the Bretons fickle they often throw in their teeth the death of Arthur. The Lombards they call avaricious, full of malice, and unwarlike, the Romans seditious, violent, and nail-biters, the Sicilians tyrannical and cruel, the men of Brabant men of blood, incendiaries, and bandits, the Flemings prodigal, given over to feasting, and soft as butter. And because of such wrangling they often proceed from words to blows.]

And so on many a summer evening a game of tennis or a sober promenade, two by two, thumbs in belt, on the Pré-aux-Clercs [11] might develop suddenly into a battle in mass and a procession of bloody heads after it.

[9] The burglary at the Collège de Navarre is very slender evidence of Villon's having belonged to this college.

[10] This has never been true, except of the men of Kent. Observe an echo of Vitry's passage in Du Bellay's sonnet of the Fourteen Hates.

[11] The *Grant Pré-aux-Clercs*, a vast meadow bordering the river, occupying the rectangle bounded now by the Quais d'Orsay and Voltaire on the north, the Rue Bonaparte on the east, the Rue de Bourgogne on the west, and the Rue de l'Université on the south. In it the *clercs* walked or played games, the *jeu de paume*, rounders, bowls, and what not. Between the thirteenth and sixteenth century possession of the Pré-aux-Clercs was continually disputed by University and the Abbey of St. Germain-des-Prés. University finally parted with it in 1539.

The official language of University, and the language in which all lectures were delivered, was Latin. Latin was also the common communication between masters and students—an easy colloquial Latin, a *lingua franca* founded on the living tongue, and a better international language, I fancy, than the synthetic twitterings in "O" which dim persons in pince-nez try to fob off on our own apathetic age. This jargon I believe to be essentially the one which Rabelais parodies a hundred years later in the scene between Pantagruel and the Limousin scholar:

> Luy demanda, "Mon amy, d'où viens-tu à ceste heure?" L'escolier respondit, "De l'alme, inclyte, & celebre Academie, que l'on recite Lutèce."
>
> "Et à quoy passez-vous le temps, vous autres messieurs estudians, audict Paris?" Respondit l'escolier, "Nous transfretons la Sequane au dilicule & crepuscule, nous deambulons par les compites & quadrivies de l'urbe, nous despumons la verbocination Latiane, & comme verisimiles amorabons, captons la benevolence de l'omnijuge, omniforme, & omnigene sexe feminin."

> [He asked him thus: "My friend, from whence comest thou now?" The Scholar answer'd him: "From the alme, inclyte, and celebrate Academie, which is vocitated Lutetia."
>
> "Thou comest from Paris then" (said Pantagruel), "and how do you spend your time there, you my Masters the Students of Paris?" The Scholar answer'd, "We transfretate the Sequane at the dilicul and crepuscul; we deambulate by the compites and quadrives of the Urb; we despumate the Latial Verbocination; and like verisimilarie amorabons, we captat the Benevolence of the omnijugal, omniform, and omnigenal Fœminine Sexe."]
>
> (*Sir Thomas Urquhart's trans.*, 1653)

It is not difficult to perceive that deambulating thus through an Urb so rich in opportunity could lead occasionally to trouble with the secular arm, with which the University, a State within a State, lived in perpetual jealousy and conflict, although by an ordinance of Philippe-Auguste the Provost of Paris was bound by an oath, renewed every two years in St. Julien-le-Pauvre, to respect and guard all the rights and privileges of University, masters and *escholiers*. The students, being clerks—that is, holding minor Orders, for the University went hand in hand with the Church and opened the gate to office in and outside religion—were answerable only to ecclesiastical authority. A little later in this history we shall perceive a furious clash between University and the lay power, in which

20

University has (as usual) the final victory; for by virtue of statutes of 1228 and 1244 and a Papal Bull of 1231 University could always bring the lay power to its senses, if it loomed threateningly over the Left Bank, by suspending not only all lectures in hall but also sermons in all the churches of Paris.[12] In June 1452, when Villon became a Master of Arts, the Papal Legate had indeed just arbitrated in such a conflict and instituted certain University reforms and discipline, after the lecture-halls and pulpits of Paris had been closed for many months. The riots over the *Pet-au-Deable* followed. *"Pires ne trouverez que escoliers,"* says a contemporary Parisian proverb. The position of the Parisian undergraduate at this moment may be grasped by imagining an ordinary Oxford rag greatly enlarged and carried on intermittently but with gentle persistency over a couple of years; with every partaker in it joyously conscious that if he, or any of his friends, were seized or handled by the enemy in such a way as to infringe in the least any privilege, the whole of University might presently rise in deliberate majesty. A procession might be formed, silver pokers and all. Headed by the Vice-Chancellor, followed by the High Steward, the Public Orator, Bodley's Librarian, the Keeper of Archives, the Sub-Librarians, the Organist, and the Presidents, Masters, Principals, and Dons of Colleges and all their meinie, the rear brought up by the junior scout of Keble, the procession might move forth, *terribilis ut castrorum acies ordinata,* and demand the instant return of the prisoner. O frabjous Day! O happy Groves! It is true that in Paris at this period the captive might have been already despatched out of hand, as happened after the University Feast of Fools in 1304, when a student accused of stabbing a citizen in a street-brawl was given a quick trial and hanged. University rose, and the Provost was compelled to eat dust. Such a mishap does not affect the principle.

The Faculty of Arts, with which we are chiefly concerned (since it gave François Villon his letters) taught the Seven Liberal Arts— Grammar, Rhetoric (which included poetry and the elements of

[12] This tremendous power was successfully combated in 1482 by Louis xi., who obtained a Bull from Pius ii. against the suspensions. In 1499 the privilege was taken from University definitely and for ever.

law), and Dialectic, forming the *trivium*; and Arithmetic, Music, Geometry, and Astronomy, forming the *quadrivium*. In the very year, 1452, in which Villon satisfied the examiners for his Master's degree, the curriculum had been reformed. Hitherto the professor had been required to deliver his lecture extempore and in a stated manner, not drawling or draggingly, *tractim,* but briskly, *raptim*. The form of the lecture was traditional. On a selected passage in a classical author questions on parsing, scansion, and grammatical figures were followed by the lecture or commentary proper, delivered as I have said: and this was followed by an analysis and annotation of the subject-matter.[13] In 1452 it was ordered that the master was to prepare his lecture beforehand, and to read it from the manuscript, not to hand it to a student to read for dictation.

So much for the bones of learning. There was little else. By Villon's time the fire had gone out of University, the intense intellectual blaze of the thirteenth century, under which the *Summa* and the Gothic cathedrals flowered together, had faded into a twilight of lethargy and indifference. Who would not have been a student at Paris when St. Thomas Aquinas was lecturing in the vast halls of the Dominicans of the Rue St. Jacques, too small to hold his audiences? Who would not gladly have heard the Angelic Doctor, with his five guiding principles of *Claritas, Brevitas, Utilitas, Suavitas,* and *Maturitas,* expounding and commenting Aristotle? Who would not have sat at the feet of Albert the Great, or listened to Roger Bacon discussing Mathematics—disgusting as that subject must be to every man of sensibility? All this glory has vanished from the University of Paris by the mid-fifteenth century, and with it all spiritual vitality, and even some of the snarly, healthy love of combat which sustained the Doctors against the Friars two centuries earlier. Already the prestige and supremacy of University have begun definitely to totter. Among the patriotic French its name has stunk long before the day in 1431 when it is decided in full Sorbonne, at the command of the English and the Burgundians, that St. Joan is a damnable heretic and sorcerer, ripe for the fire. It has for years allied itself definitely with Anglo-Burgundian politics. *"Fille du Roy d'Angleterre,"* say the nationalists contemptuously,

[13] Evans, *Medieval France,* Oxford.

remembering the *filia carissima* of the kings of France. "University," say MM. Dubech and d'Espezel, "approved the treaty of Troyes, paid honour to the remains of Henry v., haſtened to renew allegiance to Bedford, celebrated the French defeats, took every opportunity of manifeſting fidelity to the English cause . . . and at the laſt proved ungrateful, turned completely round, and did not even mention the death of her dear Bedford in the Regiſters." [14] The days are now long paſt when Henry ii. of England wiſhed the Doctors of Paris to arbitrate in his quarrel with St. Thomas of Canterbury; when the Emperor Baldwin prayed the Pope to send maſters from Paris to reform the schools of the Eaſt, when Abelard, and St. Thomas, and Peter Lombard, and Rudolf of Cologne, Girard-la-Pucelle, Guillaume de Champeaux, Maurice de Sully, and a dozen other famous professors drew all the world to Paris, the City (so it was called, as the hiſtorian Rigord relates) of Philosophers, holding within her walls more learning than ever had Athens or Alexandria; when the panegyric of University was sung by Guy de Bazoches, by Philippe de Harvengt, by John of Salisbury (who writes early from Paris to St. Thomas of Canterbury, praising the abundance of all things of the intellect there), by Richard of Bury, and a whole cluſter of poets and scholars. The end of glory is at hand. In much less than a hundred years hence the Sorbonnical Doctors will be assailed by the Renaissance, and the splitting of northern Europe by the Proteſtant schism out of Germany, and the printing-press, inſtalled in their very bosom, and then by the huge laughter of Rabelais, rumbling like thunder over the *sorbonillans, sorbonagres, sorbonisans, sorbonigènes, sorbonicoles*. The expanding reputation of the English, Italian, and German Universities, and those of Montpellier, Orleans, and Toulouse, Prague and Vienna, will have completed the robbing of Paris of its international character. The king will have stripped the doctors of their deareſt privilege, and the Jesuits a little later will rout them with the new pedagogy. The poor duſty old men!

I have seen it affirmed that venality as well as indifference had crept into University by Villon's time, and that examiners were not invariably offended when discreetly offered a present by a candidate

[14] *Histoire de Paris*, 1926.

23

on the eve of examination. (G. Paris hints that our poet's own progress up the Schools might have been accelerated in this way. I doubt this. When had Villon money to squander on such things?) The buying of honour with gifts is a shocking thing for any man of our own age to contemplate: but the later Middle Ages were, alas! no less lax than they were superstitious.[15] Nevertheless, for all its decadence the University which bred Villon still fulfilled its chiefest end. It was still the road along which the poorest ragged student of no birth, having kept his terms by begging, might advance at last to honour in Church or State, and from rubbing shoulders with crimps and toughs in underground dens come to sitting equal with princes and rulers of the earth. This advantage the Catholic Church has always held out to the poor, along all the ages. But not all her children have accepted the Mother's gift. Villon, reviewing in a sad lovely verse the roll of his gay companions of the Schools, sees how some have advanced along the road to honour and now wear the vair and the purple, while others, the careless and the improvident, lick their sores in the gutter.

> *Ou sont les gracieux gallans*
> *Que je suivoye au temps jadis,*
> *Si bien chantans, si bien parlans,*
> *Si plaisans en faiz et en dis?*
> *Les aucuns sont morts et roidis,*
> *D'eulx n'est il plus riens maintenant:*
> *Repos aient en paradis,*
> *Et Dieu saulve le demourant!*
>
> *Et les autres sont devenus,*
> *Dieu mercy! grans seigneurs et maistres;*
> *Les autres mendient tous nus*
> *Et pain ne voient qu'aux fenestres;*
> *Les autres sont entrez en cloistres*
> *De Celestins et de Chartreux,*
> *Botez, housez, com pescheurs d'oistres.*
> *Voyez l'estat divers d'entre eux.*

[Where are the laughing gallants I ruffled with so long ago— the merry singers and talkers, so excellent in word and deed? Some are stiff and dead, and nothing remains of them. May they have rest in Paradise, and may God save those who remain!

[15] Sir Wm. Rubbage.

24

Others, praise God, are become great seigneurs and lords; and others beg their bread naked, but never see it save in shop windows. And others have entered religion among the Celestines and the Carthusians, stoutly booted, like oyster-fishers. See how diverse is their fate.]

François Villon himself might have had a benefice and died a Bishop. The Council of Bâle in 1438 ordered a certain number of livings to be reserved to Paris and all the celebrated Universities in Europe for those of their graduates whose learning, moral conduct, and poverty fitted them for the favour. The Abbé Prompsault [16] believes that Villon was actually presented by the University of Paris to the trustees, but that his character inevitably non-suited him. Villon certainly speaks of

> Item, ma nominacion,
> Que j'ay de l'Université.

[Item, my nomination, which I hold of University.]

This was the Letter, sealed with the University seal, which conferred on an approved graduate of any of the four Faculties the right of submitting his name for an ecclesiastical benefice. And again:

> Item, a Chappelain je laisse
> Ma chapelle a simple tonsure,

[Item, I leave to Chappelain my simple-tonsure benefice.]

from which one might conclude, if it were not for the incorrigible *blague* of the man and the obvious joke on "Chappelain," that he had been actually presented to a tiny benefice in the gift of University. I think he certainly had not. His reputation and his appearance would have had on any board of trustees the same electric effect as Goldsmith's scarlet breeches had on the examining bishop.

I cannot indeed see this child of the streets a country priest; nor, I think, would the alb have been to him anything but a Nessus shirt. The Church would have gained a rascal and poetry would have lost a prince. It is curious and agreeable to reflect how the circle of Villon's being touches that of Doctor Johnson at two points.

---

[16] *Œuvres de maistre François Villon, corrigées et complétées d'après plusieurs manuscrits,* etc., Paris, 1832.

Both loved the Town with a great passion and esteemed the Country death; and both might have had a country benefice, but escaped it, and so forebore to inflict irreparable loss on letters.

But they have, I imagine, nothing else in common,[17] and the Town awaits us, the roaring motley Town: I mean the whole area of Paris, north, south, east, west, and the suburbs; the inspiration and the background of Villon's life and song.

[17] This is perhaps not entirely accurate, if we accept the evidence of Dr. Percy: "I have heard from some of his [Johnson's] cotemporaries that he was generally seen lounging at the College gate, with a circle of young students round him, whom he was entertaining with wit, and keeping them from their studies, if not spiriting them up to rebellion against the College discipline, which in his maturer years he so much extolled."—Boswell's *Johnson* (Oxford edition), p. 50.

❋ ❋ ❋ ❋ ❋ ❋ ❋ ❋ ❋ ❋ ❋ ❋ ❋ ❋

§ 3

THE TOWN

Paris pour vray eſt la Maison royalle
Du dieu Phœbus en splendeur radiale,
Rozier mondain, baulme du firmament
Universel, de Sidon l'ornement.
—G. Braun's *Map of Paris.*

[Paris, in truth, is the House-Royal of the Sun-God in his splendour arrayed; Rose-Garden of the world, Balm of the universal firmament, Ornament of Sidon.]

He said it was a good Towne to live in, but not to die; for that the grave-digging Rogues of St. *Innocent* used in frostie Nights to warme their breech with dead mens Bones. —*Pantagruel,* Bk. II.

In the year 1436, when François Villon was five years old, the English quitted Paris for ever, after an occupation of sixteen years. Their dominion had been harsh, but not so entirely diabolical as some French hiſtorians make it. M. Auguste Longnon, who published a collection of 176 letters of remission selected from the archives of the Chancellery of France and covering the period of the English occupation, records only three actual cases of English barbarity.[1] Sander Russell, drinking at the sign of the Escu de Bretagne by the Porte Baudoyer, quarrels with the hoſtess over his scot and stabs the Sergeant of the Châtelet called in to arreſt him. In September 1424 the child Henry VI., by God's grace King of

[1] *Paris pendant la Domination anglaise,* 1420-1436: *Documents extraits des Regiſtres de la Chancellerie de France,* Paris, 1878.

I pass over the methodical enrichment and rewarding of the Anglo-Burgundian faction in Paris with the property of the Dauphin's friends, since this was only normal.

27

France and England—his uncle the Duke of Bedford ruling as Regent at the Tournelles—pardons Russell on the ground of his ignorance of the officer's identity, letting him off with a ſtiff term of imprisonment on bread-and-water. More serious is the case, in October of the same year, of Richard Quatre and another Englishman unnamed, who between midnight and one o'clock one night very furiously bang and batter at the door of Jehannette la Bardine, *femme amoureuse*, living by the Pont St. Michel. To the lady's requeſts that they should go away Richard and his companion reply by menaces and renewed assaults: the lady then, rising fretfully from her bed, flings ſtones at them from her window, and one of the ſtones, ſtriking Richard Quatre by accident fairly on the head, sends him to bed for eight days, and thence out of this world altogether. To Jehannette the King grants a pardon. Finally we perceive, in July 1430, two hard-bitten English men-at-arms lying in the Châtelet, Nicolas Say and Richard Geppes, under charges of shoplifting and fraud. The two warriors have a curious weakness for millinery: at the sign of the Cornet, by St. Merri, the said Nicolas Say (*par temptacion de l'ennemi*, says his letter of remission) snaps up a piece of cramoisie ſtuff. At a shop by the Palais, while Richard is amusing the mercer, Nicolas whips away with a quantity of silk; but unsuccessfully, for the mercer discovers the trick and follows them with a Sergeant, making a great howl, and so gets his money. Laſtly, after choosing *certains tissuz de soye de plusieurs couleurs* to the value of thirty livres at the shop of a woman mercer, our hearts of oak pay her with a sealed purse purporting to contain nobles, but actually containing disks of lead. They plead in defence previous good conduct and ten years' military service under Henry v.—

eu regard aussy a ce que continuelment depuis x ans ença ou environ ilz ont servy ou fait de guerres feu noſtre tres chier seigneur et pere, que Dieu absoille . . .

[Seeing also that they have continuously during the paſt ten years, more or less, served in his wars our late and very dear lord and father, whom God assoil . . .]

—and get off with a term of imprisonment. These crimes do not seem very abominable; and considering that in the countryside

28

all round Paris Armagnacs and Burgundians were pillaging and massacring at their sweet will it seems better to have been inside the walls than without, in spite of crushing taxes, insolvency, lack of food, and recurrent epidemics. Nevertheless between 1422 and 1434, as Vallet de Viriville computes, there were eight conspiracies in Paris against the English rule, and two in Normandy: from which figures a well-known firm of actuaries has deduced that the English rule was unpopular. This impression would seem to be confirmed by that very loud lament made for Olivier Basselin of the Val de Vire, which goes to such a mournful jig of a little tune in the Manuscript of Bayeux:

He - las, Ol - li - vier Vas - se - lin, N'or - ron
point de vos nou - vel - les? Vous ont les
En - gloys mys à fyn? Vous soul - li - - -
Et les bons
és gaye-ment chan - ter Et de - me - ner joy-
com - pay-gnons han - ter, Par le pa - ys de
eu - se vy - - e Jus-qu'à Sainct Lo en Co - ten - tin,
Normen-dy - - e
En u - ne com-paygn - ye moult
bel - le. Onc-ques ne vy tel pel - le - rin.

[Alas, Olivier Basselin, shall we have no more news of thee? Have the Engloys made an end of thee?

You were used to sing so gaily, to lead so joyous a life, to frequent such good companions, throughout the whole Norman land! Never was seen such a pilgrim, in such fair company, as far as St. Lô in the Cotentin!]

"Engloys" in this threnody does not primarily mean the English (for we had, God knows, no part in this poet's death) but griping usurers, skinflints, and hard-faced creditors and squeezers of blood from ſtone, to whom the name was given in Paris and all over Normandy, says P. L. Jacob in his edition of the *Vaux de Vire* of Basselin, because of the crushing taxes laid on the French during the English occupation. These were the enemy who deprived the Vire and the Cotentin of this sweet singer, good ruby-nosed drinker, and roaring companion.

> *Les Engloys ont faiɛt desraison*
> *Aux compaignons du Vau de Vire,*
> *Vous n'orrez plus dire chanson*
> *A ceulx qui les soulloient bien dire.*
>
> *Nous priron Dieu de bon cueur fyn,*
> *Et la doulce Vierge Marie,*
> *Qu'il doint aux Engloys male fyn.*
> *Dieu le Pere si les mauldye!*
> *Helas! Ollivier Basselin.*

[The Engloys have ſtruck a foul blow at the companions of the Val de Vire! Never more will you hear any songs from those who were used so bravely to sing them. We pray God with all our heart, and our sweet Lady, that He bring the Engloys to a bad end. May God the Father curse them! Alas, Olivier Basselin!]

There is another song which the Normans and the men of the Parisis were singing after the English withdrawal. It begins, derisively:

Le   roy En - glois   se   fai - soit   ap - pe - ler
Il   a   voul-lu   hors du   pa - ys   me - ner

Le roy de Fran-ce par s'ap-pel-la - ti - on. Or eſt - il mort à
Les bons Fran-çois hors de leur na-ti - on.

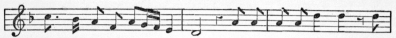

Saint - Fia-cre en Bri - - - e,[1] Du pa - ys de Fran-ce ils

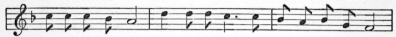

sont tous de-bou- tez, Il n'eſt plus mot de ces En-glois cou-ez.

Maul - dic - te soit tres - tou - te la li - gny - - - el

[The King of England ordered himself to be called and saluted King of France; his will was to drive good Frenchmen out of their own country, away from their land. Well, he is dead, at St. Fiacre in Brie! They are all booted out of the Kingdom of France, there's no more news of these Englishmen with tails. May all their race be damned!]

> *Ils ont chargé l'artellerie sur mer,*
> *Force biscuit et chascun ung bidon,*
> *Et par la mer jusqu'en Bisquaye aller*
> *Pour couronner leur petit roy Godon.*

[They loaded their ships with artillery, with great supplies of biscuit, and a wine-bottle apiece, and are gone over the sea to Biscay, to crown their little King Goddam; but all their effort is in vain!]

(The little King Goddam is Henry vi.)

> *Mais leur effort n'eſt rien que mocquerye!*

And once more (for the songs of a people are precious, more than fine gold and the glossy periods of pedants), this, from that roaring rural song which has been called the *Marseillaise* of the Normans:

[2] A bitter jeſt. Henry v. died at Vincennes, in the Ile-de-France, of a hemorrhoidal disease popularly called the *mal de St. Fiacre*.

Et cui - dez vous que je me jou - - - - - - - - - - e, Et que je voul-sis-se al - - ler En En-gle-ter - re de mou - rer? Ils ont u - ne lon-gue cou - - - - - - - - - - - - - - - - e.

I

["What, do you think I am such a fool as to want to go into England to lose my life? They've all got long tails!"]

II

Entre vous, gens de village,
Qui aymez le roy françoys,
Prenez chascun bon courage
Pour combattre les Englois.
Prenez chascun une houe
Pour mieux les desraciner;
S'ils ne s'en veullent aller,
Au moins faictes leur la moue.
[Et cuidez vous . . .]

[Come, then, get together, good villagers who love the King of France, raise up your courage to fight the English. Take each of you his hoe, the better to root them out of the land. And if they don't want to go, at least make an ugly face at 'em!

(Chorus: What, do you think, etc., as above)

III

Ne craygnez point à les batre
Ces godons, panches à pois;
Car ung de nous en vault quatre,
Au moins en vault il bien troys.
Affin qu'on les esbaffoue,
Autant qu'en pourrés trouver

32

Faictes au gibet mener
Et qu'en nous les y encroue.
[*Et cuidez vous . . .*]

Have no fear of getting to grips with these pea-stuffed Goddams! Any one of us is worth four of them, or at the least three.
Come, let's make game of them; find all you can of them and hoick
them up on the gallows!

(Chorus: What, do you think, etc.)]

I doubt very much, everything considered, if these sentiments,
taken for all in all, can be said to echo that respectful affection which
the English have always been accustomed to demand from foreign persons and the conquered.

Worse was to happen in Paris immediately after the English
withdrawal in 1436. They still held Pontoise, Meaux, and the Chevreuse, and thus could, and did, cut off food supplies. In 1438 it
seemed as though all the long-drawn-out miseries of the Hundred
Years' War had culminated in a final onslaught on the unhappy
town. The winter was terrible: famine raged; a plague carried off
45,000 inhabitants. The sick lay starving in the Hostel-Dieu, or
dropped in the grass-grown streets to freeze to death; and the cry
"Hélas, doux Dieu! je meaurs de faim et de froit!" * arose day and
night.[3] Bands of cutthroats prowled the suburbs. The wolves, ravening in that dreadful cold, slunk freely across the frozen Seine and
in and out of the town, and more than once carried off infants alive.
In the suburbs between Montmartre and the Porte St. Antoine
during this winter they attacked and killed fourteen grown persons.
It was not until about 1445, when François Villon was a student
of fourteen, that Paris began to raise her head again and to know
any security or comfort.

It is convenient here to pause and take a swift general survey
of events.

Charles v. ("the Wise") had died in 1380, leaving the throne

*["Alas, dear God! I am dying of hunger and cold!"]

[3] *Journal of the Bourgeois of Paris.* This state of affairs lasted till 1443, in November
of which year Pope Eugenius iv. sent out an appeal to the Christian world on behalf
of the sick in the Hostel-Dieu, St. Lazare, and the other ruined hospitals of Paris.

to a child of twelve, over whose infant head four powerful and ambitious uncles, the Dukes of Anjou, Bourbon, Burgundy, and Berry, at once began to quarrel. In March 1382 a new tax placed by the Regent Anjou on merchandise brought about the uprising of the *Maillotins*, a mob of four thousand armed with the leaden *maillets* or clubs which the Provost Hugues Aubriot had stored at the Hôtel de Ville against an English attack. There were assassinations: the rising was suppressed: the bourgeoisie had to pay the enormous fine of four hundred thousand livres. Charles vi., attaining the age to rule, did in fact begin very well, and would have continued so had he not become more or less insane in 1392, with rare lucid intervals. There began then the furious and bloody struggling of Burgundians and Armagnacs, which had by Villon's day sickened and wearied Paris and brought it to a state of deathly lassitude. After the King's final lapse into madness in 1393 the Duke of Burgundy had become Regent. His son, Jean Sans-Peur, nourished an enmity towards the King's brother, Louis, Duke of Orleans, which grew before long into a fatal feud. Among the private murders of this period that of Orleans—he was the father of Charles, the poet, Villon's patron years afterwards—by assassins in the pay of Jean Sans-Peur is such a crude melodrama that I propose lingering a moment to describe it. At eight o'clock on the night of November 23, 1407, the Duke of Orleans, issuing from a house near the Porte Barbette, where he had been to visit his mistress, the Queen Ysabeau, called for his mule. The night was very dark, and every house in the street was closely barred. His two squires, with five footmen carrying torches, came at his call. As Orleans, playing with his fringed glove and humming a love-song, prepared to mount his mule a group of seventeen armed men burst suddenly from a house near by and fell upon him. "I am the Duke of Orleans," he shouted. "We want you," replied a voice. A woman at a window screamed murder. The assassins, having hacked Orleans practically in pieces, fired the house and vanished. The next day Jean Sans-Peur went to the church of the Blancs-Manteaux to view the body of his victim, and shed tears of sensibility. He was, indeed, possessed by a vague unrest concerning the consequences; and so, after acting as pall-bearer and shedding more tears at Orleans' funeral, being

34

expelled the Council immediately afterwards by the old Duke of Berry, Jean Sans-Peur left Paris, and from a distance proved clearly (by proxy) that Orleans had been removed for twelve good reasons, political, theological, moral, social, economical, sociological, and other. The pro-Burgundian University approved the thesis. Jean Sans-Peur returned to Paris, with a victory at Hasbain behind him, obtained a letter of remission, and resumed his ordinary occupations. He had by this murder unloosed civil war. The murdered man's widow, Valentine Visconti of Milan, was dead by then of grief and anger, but her son Charles took up the quarrel, and by his marriage to the daughter of the Comte d'Armagnac was able to bring in d'Armagnac's terrible Gascons on the Orleans side. We shall meet Charles d'Orléans again in this history: a fine poet and a gentleman.

So much, then, for private enterprise. In the matter of subsequent large-scale murder there was the affair of May 28, 1418, when the Burgundians burst into Paris and slaughtered the Armagnacs, then in possession, *en masse*, so that the children in the streets played at dragging corpses up and down; and a second massacre of Armagnacs, at the suggestion of Jean Sans-Peur, in the following August. Meanwhile Henry v. of England was advancing, and had already crushed the flower of Armagnac chivalry at Agincourt. It was after the death of Jean Sans-Peur, this strong and vivacious character (*"grand dans son caractère et dans ses actions,"* writes a certain M. de Clugny of him in a *History of Costume*, 1836, into which I have been looking, *"mais trop porté à croire que sa domination était nécessaire au bonheur de la France"*), himself hacked to pieces at the bridge of Montereau in 1419 by Tanneguy du Chastel, that the weary citizens of Paris let the English in.

Henry v., with the treaty of Troyes behind him, rode into Paris on December 1, 1420, and was welcomed by the Parisians, who would have welcomed the Devil at this period. He had on his side the Burgundians, the University, and the Parliament. Eleven years later, on December 16, 1431, the year of Villon's birth, Henry vi. was crowned at Notre-Dame by the Cardinal of Winchester, the six Great Companies of Paris, the Drapers, the Grocers, the Moneychangers, the Goldsmiths, the Mercers, and the Furriers, bearing his canopy. The largesse showered on the populace at the coronation was remarkable for economy. "A bourgeois marrying off one of his daughters would have done the thing better," observes a contemporary critic. Before 1435, when the Regent Bedford died, the Parisians were remembering themselves once more to be Frenchmen and recollecting the Martyr-Maid who had made France a nation. "In the year fourteen-twenty-nine," says the rhyme in the *Myʃtere du Siege d'Orleans,* celebrating the deliverance of the city by St. Joan,

> *L'an mil quatre cent vingt neuf*
> *Reprint a luire le soleil.*

> [In the year fourteen hundred and twenty nine,
> The sun began once more to shine.]

It was ʃtill but watery sunshine, breaking with difficulty through heavy clouds; but it was a promise and a sign. In September 1435 the Duke of Burgundy and Charles VII., St. Joan's Dauphin, were reconciled at Arras. Early in 1436 Charles and his army lay at St. Germain. In May of that year Willoughby was forced to withdraw his garrison of 1500 men from the Baʃtille and fall back, sped by the hoots of the populace, on Rouen, the King's men entered, and Paris was free. The retaking of Pontoise in 1441 burʃt the iron ring around the capital. The truce of 1444 ended the nightmare. Finally in 1450 the victory of Formigny wiped out for the French the bitterness of Crécy, Poitiers, and Agincourt, and the English were at laʃt (as St. Joan had prayed) *boutez hors de France.*[4]

This, then, was the condition of Paris when François Villon ran a child about its ʃtreets: a town bled dry,[5] ravaged by misery, hunger, and disease. Yet flowers grew on the dunghill. The masterpiece of the French miniature school, the Breviary of Salisbury, with its forty-five miracles of painting, was designed and executed for Bedford towards 1430. All through the Hundred Years' War new churches rose intermittently in Paris, new convents, new houses of the high bourgeoisie, like the house of the banker Jacques Ducy in

---

[4] Calais excepted.
[5] Notre-Dame Chapter began to sell the Cathedral treasury in 1435. The number of houses empty and abandoned in Paris by 1423 is given in a contemporary document as exceeding 20,000.

the Rue des Prouvaires, which contained a courtyard with peacocks and *maints aultres oyseaulx,* a chapel, an arsenal, a picture-gallery, a music-gallery, an aviary, and rich carved doors. At the time the war ended there was a fresh late flowering of Gothic Flamboyant, a little Renaissance on the eve of the greater. Of this flowering the painted and sculptured portail of St. Germain l'Auxerrois (1439), the lovely Hôtel de Cluny (begun 1480), and the town house of the Archbishops of Sens, are still preserved. But it is not to Paris that we should look in general during the fifteenth century if we were concerned here exclusively with the arts, and activities of the spirit, and government, and religious vitality, but rather to the Burgundian court and lands of Philip the Bold, and the court of Jehan Duke of Berry. In the miniatures of that noble Book of Hours called *Les Très Riches Heures du Duc de Berry* (it can be seen to-day at Chantilly: I rank it very near the Book of Kells) the splendour of that great house rises up, flaming like a thousand jewels, and puts to shame the dingy meanness of our time.

So filled is the spirit of Villon with the Town and the love of what that other devout Parisian Baudelaire calls the *paysage de métal et de pierre,* that his verse alone re-creates his Paris, with its cries and its colours and its bustling life. To a stranger of our age who could ascend the centuries and stand by the Petit-Pont on a winter day about the year 1447, when roving bands of men-at-arms without pay had ceased to prey on the citizens and the English no longer cut off food-supplies before the gates, the aspect of Paris would seem stunning, dazzling, bewildering as a dream: the grey sky, the grey unseen river rushing under the bridges, with their double line of tall sharp-gabled houses springing from the cobbles and leaning crazily together, storey thrusting out above storey; the narrow winding streets of the Quarter, a pell-mell of ascending gables and tinted roof-tiles, the lower storeys of wood sculptured with fantastic shapes of warriors or joyous quaint animals, as in old houses still preserved at Chinon of Touraine, at Bourges, and elsewhere, in every twist and turn of fancy revealing that love of beauty in common and ordinary things which distinguishes the Middle Ages from our advanced era; the gaily-scrolled and painted signs, creaking in the wind; the ſtone fountain, with its canopy, at the crossing; the arched shrine at the ſtreet-corner, with the lamp swinging and burning before it; the chain-sockets at the ſtreet end, whereby the streets were, till the English left, closed at night; the various colours of the shifting crowd, changing and melting like figures in a phantasmagoria; the cries. Of the *Crieries de Paris* a list is given by Guillaume de la Villeneuve a century or so before Villon's day. Some of them, like the cries of old London, were in rhyme; for example, the cry of the *eſtuveur,* or hot-bath keeper:

> *Seignor, qu'or vous alez baingnier*
> *Et eſtuver sans delaier;*
> *Li bain sont chaut: c'eſt sans mentir.*

[Gentles, come to the baths, without delay. The baths are hot: I tell no lie.]

I seleĉt this cry particularly because there is a modern impression that the Medievals, being careless of public hygiene, were personally unclean. This is erroneous. At the end of the thirteenth century there were twenty-six public hot baths in Paris for a population of less than 200,000; not counting baths of the Seine.[6] London, I believe, was also reasonably well equipped. Villon himself has among his minor pieces a little "Yah, yah!" rondeau urging one Jenin l'Avenu to take a hot bath:

> *Jenin l'Avenu,*
> *Va t'en aux eſtuves,*
> *Et toy la venu,*
> *Jenin l'Avenu,*
> *Si te lave nu,*
> *Et te baigne es cuves.*
> *Jenin l'Avenu,*
> *Va t'en aux eſtuves.*

[Jenin l'Avenu, away with you to the baths! And when you're there, Jenin l'Avenu, wash yourself all over and soak in the boiler. Jenin l'Avenu, away with you to the baths!]

The real age of dirty men is the Age of Reason, which contained Frederick the Great, who is known never to have washed himself

---

[6] H. Lemoine, Archiviſte de la Seine, *Manuel d'Histoire de Paris.*

in any way for years. So much for that.[7] The *estuveur* was forbidden to cry his hot baths before dawn, because of the perils awaiting early bathers in traversing the streets. Among other cries that of the *crieur de vin*, who announced arrivals of wine at the Grève, the river-port of Paris, was justly esteemed, and in his funeral procession a cup of wine was handed round ceremonially every time the bearers stopped at a cross-road. Another good cry was the cry of the seller of a cheese,

> *J'ay bon fromaige, bon fromaige de Brie!*
> [I have good cheese, good cheese of Brie!]

which is still a glory and a comfort to mankind. I pass over a score more, especially those of the Halles quarter, which arose and rent the skies all day long. "They never finish braying in Paris," observes Villeneuve, "till night."

> *Ja ne finiront de braire*
> *Parmy Paris jusqu'a nuyt.*

I pass over, too, the cries of the Royal criers, who had at one time their own house, the Maison de la Crierie, by St. Jacques-la-Boucherie, and went about the city like so many Gargantuas, crying *comme tous les diables. Stentor n'eut oncques telle voix à la bataille de Troye.* They were chosen for their brazen lungs, and cried all Royal, governmental, and municipal announcements at every cross-road, laying money down for this concession. But there is one more cry I must not omit to mention, since it rings out for ever in Villon's Ballade of the Women of Paris: the shrill yelping of the fishwives, the *harangieres* of the Petit-Pont.

And so, proceeding, we may add finally to all this noise and colour impinging on the dazed modern senses of our visitant (though I doubt, after all, everything considered, if this racket was a tenth part as devilish as the iron racket of Paris or London to-day: it was of a different timbre, and human) the oaths of men-at-arms, the drumming and bawling of cheap-jacks and mountebanks, the clatter of hooves, the sudden jangle and flurry of a hundred bells; and above all, louder than all, possessing and overflowing and em-

---

[7] I have not touched on the undoubted fact that knights in the Middle Ages took a bath as part of the ceremony of initiation. I believe this is no longer insisted on.

bracing all, the smell, the famous smell of Paris. The town stank more bitterly than any other large town of Europe. Its drainage system had, it is true, been much bettered since the time of St. Louis, when it could be summed up in four words: *Tout à la rue*. Since then the authorities, alarmed by the pests which swept Paris at intervals, and particularly by the bubonic plague of 1348, had attempted to grapple with the problem. Jean ii. in 1350 drew up a general police regulation for cleaning the streets Charles vi. in 1388 improved and extended its scope. Charles vii. divided Paris into seven sectors for sanitation. But though the Parisians were no longer wholly dependent on the periodical overflow of the Seine to cleanse their streets, the stink of Paris remained, and was famous. The Gauls and Latins have ever been indifferent alike to loud noises and strong smells. One should not forget, considering this, the stench of Chapel Lane which (according to Sir Sidney Lee) destroyed Shakespeare, or the evening stinks of Edinburgh which so offended the nose of Dr. Johnson.[8] Community Plumbing is one of the very modern fine arts, like Criticism; but useful.

The town, then, smelt. The mud of Paris was proverbial for its property of sticking and fouling, though some of the principal streets had been paved with *pierres grosses & fortes* as far back as the reign of Philippe-Auguste. Years onward from the period we are contemplating Montaigne will be complaining mildly of the acrid stench of it, and Boileau putting it into his verse. "A smell as if sulphure were mingled with the mud," writes Evelyn in his Parisian diary in 1643. It was mud viscous, mud evil, mud inevitable, mud enduring, mud absolute. At the cry *"A la malle tache!"* the wives of the bourgeois, disconsolately gazing at their skirts, turned to buy a phial of stain-eradicator from the grinning vendor: and as they did so a brisk horseman spurring past would send up fresh fountains of the gluey stuff from the kennel to bespatter them. Coaches, which were soon to make life a hell for the foot-passenger in Paris and in London alike, were not yet. Catherine de Medicis brought them from Italy in the Renaissance.[9]

[8] Boswell's *Journal of a Tour to the Hebrides,* Aug. 14, 1773.
[9] A manuscript of 1317 shows a distinct omnibus, drawn by two horses in line and holding five travellers, crossing the Petit-Pont. Whether these carriages still existed, I do not know. I find them nowhere mentioned. Carts for merchandise were of course common.

It is not difficult to perceive, lingering on the Petit-Pont on a winter day about this time, the slim figure of a saturnine young student of the University, cutting his lecture for the day. He sees across the river, rising above the roofs, the tops of the twin towers of Notre-Dame de Paris cutting the sky, and the birds crying and circling round: Notre-Dame in its mingled majesty and grace as we see it now; but in his day the Parvis is smaller, and to the base of the Metropolitan cling the little churches of St. Jean-le-Rond and St. Denis-du-Pas. To the north of Notre-Dame spread the Cloisters and the Canons' Precinct, where the Schools of Notre-Dame were, a little town in itself: to the south a flight of thirteen steps leads down to the Seine. His quick eye glances over the massy walls of the Petit-Châtelet by the bridge, and he looks away with a light grimace, turning to argle-bargle with a stout fishwife, tossing her back as good as she gives in the matter of obscene repartee. He contemplates the passers-by: the gowned, furred burgess, the Sorbonnical Doctor, the beggar whining and dragging, showing his sores, the fiddler in the cross-lane, the quack gesticulating and mouthing to the idle crowd, "*sot par nature, par bequarre & bemol*" (the gibe is Rabelais'), on the bridge; the knot of truculent men-at-arms, ragged and bearded; the Royal courier clattering by with his white wand; the tight-waisted, square-bodiced wives of the bourgeois, with their heart-shaped headdress, the *bourrelet*; the prancing cavalcade escorting a lady of quality, her hair coiffured in high *atours*; the cloaked pair of elegants wearing soft boots of fawn Cordova leather, *fauves botes*, falling lackadaisically over the instep and proclaiming, like the carefully ill-arranged neckerchief of the Werther period, their love-bondage. He sees a Dominican friar pass, in his black-and-white habit; a couple of earth-coloured, rope-girdled Franciscans; a tramping squad of foot-Sergeants; a juggler leading a mule with cymbals; a file of pilgrims from the country plodding to the tomb of St. Geneviève. The crowd on the bridge falls back and divides at a clatter of trotting hooves and a barked command: it is Messire Robert d'Estouteville, Provost of Paris, with his body-guard of twelve Archers, riding home to his house in the Rue de Jouy. A glint comes into the student's eye, answering the sidelong glance of a couple of town mopsies carrying on their sinful

41

heads a version of the high *hennin* which Friar Thomas Couette and Friar Pierre des Gros some time before so roundly denounced from the pulpit.[10] Friar Thomas was a man of action, as I perceive from a History of Costume, and would urge little derisive boys to follow the wearers in the street crying *"Au hennin! au hennin!"*— and which has since gone out of fashion for the virtuous. . . . And of a sudden the student observes a ragged, hag-like figure shuffling past him, and turns his curious gaze on her. The old woman is known throughout the Quarter as the Belle Heaulmière. She was a famous beauty and courtesan in the early part of the century and the mistress of Messire Nicolas d'Orgemont, Master of the Chambre des Comptes, who very scandalously installed her in his house in the precinct of Notre-Dame, whence she was evicted by the Canons. In Villon's day she is a mumbling witch of eighty; her lover has died long ago, in 1416, in the prison of Meun-sur-Loire, where Villon himself will be cast in due course. In the Lament for her hot, sweet youth which Villon will write in a few years, the figure of this poor old scarecrow is preserved like a mummy for ever and ever.

But she is gone, shuffling round the corner, muttering, sucking her withered gums, hugging the shadow. A troop of pack-asses laden with corn from a farm outside the walls takes her place; a grimacing showman leading a learned pig succeeds them; and a leper rattling his *tartarelle,* or clackdish (unless it is a Monday, in which case he is confined by a regulation of Charles v. to the Grand-Pont); and a scarlet judge riding to the Palais with his retinue; and a pair of secular priests; and a quartet of tumblers; and a file of linked prisoners driven by Sergeants to the Châtelet; and after them a wedding procession, two by two, like a parterre of flowers for colour, preceded by the nodding minstrelsy scraping and blowing music from rebeck and cithole, *vielle* and flute and *trompe,*

> . . . mirth and melody
> With harp, gytron and sawtry,
> With rote, ribible, and clokard,
> With pipes, organs, and bombard,[11]

[10] Compare Lydgate's diatribe on Horns.
[11] Some of these instruments deserve a note. The rebeck and cithole, rote, ribible, and clokard are all, I think, stringed, and variants of the lute, sawtry (psaltery), gytron, or

stopping at the baker's to buy and scatter among the crowd the flat cakes called *flamiches* and *fouaces,* and again at the open window of the *cervoisier* to pass round the ceremonial flagon of thin beer brewed from corn; and so, with a thousand quips and bursts of laughter, to the parish church, where the long train of promiscuous followers, loungers, beggars, ragamuffins, and idle fellows drops off, since all the fun is over. All this the young Villon, a child of the town and a *parigot* to the teeth, observes, sniffing up the rich tumult and tasting it with zest; and waking at length from his abstraction shivers in the nip of the late afternoon. Where now?, This side of the Pont Notre-Dame, in the Rue de la Juiverie, is the *Pomme de Pin,* Robin Turgis' place, where there will be a blazing log-fire and company he knows.[12] From there it is but a step across to the *Trou Perrette* for a throw with the dice; and thence one may comfortably go on to the *Grant Godet* by the Grève, or the *Plat d'Estain* and the *Trumelières* by the *Halles,* or the *Homme Armé* by the church of the Blancs-Manteaux, or the *Espée de Bois* by St. Merri. Nearer home, in 'the Rue St. Jacques, opposite the Mathurins, is the *Mule;* or across the two bridges, in a coy darkish court behind the Precinct of Notre-Dame, is the house of Fat Margot, where his quick tongue and readiness to sling a verse have made him welcome more than once or twice.

The wind rises. The rushing of the river under the Petit-Pont can be heard mingling more loudly with the perpetual scrape and creak of swinging signs; for in that age houses and taverns alike bear signs,[13] and in reading a list of the house and street names

guitar. The *vielle* is a stringed hurdygurdy: one of the gargoyles of Chartres Cathedral is an ass playing a *vielle*. It has affinities with the Balkan *guzlak,* and I have seen it played in Paris streets to-day. Villon refers to the *vielle* in the *Great Testament*. The bombard is a bagpipe. The organs are portable, and are shown in many medieval manuscripts.

[12] The *Pomme de Pin,* most celebrated of Paris taverns (Guillebert de Metz, writing at this period, says there were 4000 taverns, wineshops, and alehouses in the town), stood in the Cité, opposite the Madeleine Church, where the Rue de la Juiverie met the Rue de la Lanterne, late into the seventeenth century, still flourishing and notable. Rabelais drank there, and Molière, and Racine, and La Fontaine. Rabelais knew the *Mule* as well.

[13] The streets generally took their names from a prominent house or tavern sign, but also from the trades which they sheltered: for example, the Rues de la Tixanderie, de la Draperie, de la Vieille-Poterie, des Lavandières, de la Tonnellerie. Several groups of trades had their own quarter: the Money-changers and Goldsmiths on the Grand-Pont, the Butchers near the Châtelet, the Lombards off the Rue St. Denis, the literary trades around University, the Apothecaries in the City. The houses on the Pont Notre-Dame, celebrated for their beauty, were numbered in 1463: the first experiment in Europe of this kind.

of fifteenth-century Paris one hears the noise of them all: the Stag, the Tin Plate, the Nun-Shoeing-the-Goose, the Striped Ass, the Harp, the Swallow, the Popinjay, the Helmet, the Bear, the Rose, the Image-of-Our-Lady, the Two Red Apples, the Golden Lion, the Three Kings of Cologne, the Spinning Sow, the Monkeys, the Scarlet Hat, the Arquebusiers, the Fleur-de-Lys, the Goblets, the Armed Man, the Wooden Sword, the Four Sons of Aymon, the Three Chandeliers. . . .

The wind rises. At the corner of the Rue de la Huchette a smoky cresset is already burning. A squad of the Guet Bourgeois, the citizens' watch, going on night duty, tramps paſt. The ſtudent shivers and makes up his mind, judging possibly, like Mr. Swiveller, which ſtreets are passable to him on this date. He turns on his heel; is elbowed roughly aside by a black-avised man-at-arms with a shade over one eye; hurls after the warrior the appropriate comment; and is loſt in the gathering dark.

The town held other amusements than the tavern and the brothel. There was the Fair of St. Germain, which in Villon's day was held not near the Abbey but at the Halles; [14] the popular and elegant fair of Paris. It opened in February and closed on Palm Sunday, and combined pleasure with commerce in the most agree-able manner; in its booths was born, a century after this time, the Parisian theatre. There was Gingerbread Fair, the *Foire au Pain d'Epices,* that kind and honourable fair, ſtill (by God's grace) flourishing at Eaſter every year under a Third Republic. There was the Fair of St. Laurent, opening on St. Laurence's Day, August 10, and laſting a week. In all these a slim ſtudent with a sharp eye might find entertainment. But on any fine evening, summer or winter, there was recreation and adventure to be had in the great Charnel of St. Innocent, or the Innocents, by the Halles. In 1186 Philippe-Auguſte had walled round this vast cemetery, with its church, and given it four gates. By the thirteenth century a Gothic arcade ſtretched along the four inner sides of the wall, and its four galleries were covered over. A high octagonal tower and lantern, with a shrine of Notre-Dame du Bois, ſtood among the tombs in

Louis XI. reſtored it to the Abbey ground in 1482.

the centre of the square. Long before Villon's time the Innocents had become the fashionable Parisian promenade, a Ranelagh, a rendezvous of gallantry: the arcades were lines with shops and stalls; above them, in the surrounding *charniers,* open charnel-vaults, each with its trefoil arch, was massed a great jumble of human skulls and bones, tumbled out of the way to make room for new arrivals in the square below. At certain seasons sermons were preached there. In 1424, finally, a fresh attraction was added: the Dance of Death, painted along the whole length of one wall. *"Item,"* writes the Bourgeois of Paris, from whose Journal I have already quoted, *"l'an mil CCCCXXIIIJ, fust faicte la Danse Macabré aux Innocens, & fust commencée environ le mois d'aoust & achevée au Karesme ensuyvant."* [15] In this long pageant, executed under Dominican inspiration and soon popular all over Europe—Holbein's series is the most notable—one saw that there is no escape from the hand of Death.[16] He stood stiff and grinning behind the Lord Pope and the Emperor on their thrones: he clutched the Abbess by the hand as she left the convent chapel: he tapped the Canon on the shoulder before the end of sermon: he postured grimacing and mowing before the Doctor at his books, the Astrologer among his alembics, the Usurer fumbling his gold, the Drunkard swigging in the pothouse. The tall Sergeant fighting in the field suddenly saw that his antagonist was Death. The Blind Man, tapping with his stick, felt himself led away by a bony hand. The Judge looked up from delivering sentence to be frozen by that awful grin. The Priest carrying the Sacred Host through the street perceived that it was Death who tinkled the little warning bell before him. The Old Woman painfully gathering sticks in the wood felt an icy grasp on her wrist, and found Death's finger nudging her. The Merchant loading his goods saw suddenly a hideous visage mopping at him over his bales, a lank hand extended. Even the Imbecile, chuckling to himself and sticking straws in his hair, discovered that he had

[15] [*Item,* in the year 1424 the *Danse Macabré* was made at the Innocents, being begun about August and finished in the following Lent.]

[16] A Dance of 47 figures, with accompanying verses in Gothic letter, may still be seen at the chapel of Kermaria-an-Isquit in Brittany.

a companion in his gambols. In a fifteenth-century MS. at Valenciennes the moral of the new pictures is thus explained:

Ainsy que les poissons sont prins par l'aine prestement, ainsy prent la Mort les hommes, car la Mort ne espareigne nully, roy ne empereur, riche ne pouvre, noble ne villain, saige ne fol, medecin ne cyrurgien, jeune ne viel, fort ne foible, homme ne femme. Yl n'est chose plus certaine, elle les fait venir à la Danse.

[As fish are taken readily by the hook, so does Death take mankind, for Death spares none, neither king nor emperor, rich nor poor, noble nor churl, sage nor fool, doctor nor surgeon, young nor old, strong nor weak, man nor woman. Nothing is more certain than that Death carries them all to the Dance.]

The Parisian sinner, familiar with all the physical aspects of death and corruption, shuddered and was amused at this new picture-gallery. Pacing the galleries of the Innocents, flagged with tombstones, the gallant paused to contemplate the image of mortality, and intercepting a glance from a passing girl renewed the chase. On the mind of Villon, who frequented the place for his own purposes, mainly undevotional, the *Danse Macabré,* and even more the masses of piled-up bones and skulls carelessly heaved aside to make room for more—in three centuries, it is calculated, about a million dead had been buried in the Innocents, mainly plague victims—made a profound impression. This same reality for once sobered the rattling Muse of John Skelton also:

> Your ugly token
> My mind hath broken
> From worldly lust.
> I have well espied
> No man may him hide
> With sinews witherèd
> From Death hollow-eyed . . .
> Our eyen sinking,
> Our bodies stinking,
> Our gummys grinning
> Our souls brynning,
> To whom then shall we sue
> For to have rescue
> But to sweet Jhesu? [17]

[17] *The Gift of a Skull.*

Nearly a century before Langland had cried:

> At Church and in charnel-vault   churls be hard to tell,
> or whether one be Queen or quean,   knight or knave.

So Villon:

> *Quant je considere ces teſtes*
> *Entassees en ces charniers,*
> *Tous furent maiſtres des requeſtes,*
> *Au moins de la Chambre aux Deniers,*
> *Ou tous furent portepanniers:*
> *Autant puis l'ung que l'autre dire,*
> *Car d'evesques ou lanterniers*
> *Je n'y congnois rien a redire.*

"See how they lie," he says, ſtanding at gaze, "all in a heap, pell-mell, the powerful and the cringing together!"

> *Et icelles qui s'enclinoient*
> *Unes contre autres en leurs vies,*
> *Desquelles les unes regnoient*
> *Des autres craintes et servies,*
> *La les voy toutes assouvies,*
> *Ensemble en ung tas peslemesle:*
> *Seigneuries leur sont ravies,*
> *Clerc ne maiſtre ne s'y appelle.*

> [These ladies all, that in their day
>   Each againſt each did bend and bow,
> Whereof did some the sceptre sway,
>   Of others feared and courted,—now
> Here are they sleeping all a-row,
>   Heaped up together anydele,
> Their crowns and honours all laid low
>   Maſters or clerks, there's no appeal.]
>   (Trans., John Payne.)

> *Or sont ilz mors, Dieu ait leurs ames!*
> *Quant eſt des corps, ilz sont pourris.*
> *Aient eſté seigneurs ou dames,*
> *Souef et tendrement nourris*
> *De cresme, fromentee ou riz.*
> *Leurs os sont declinez en pouldre,*
> *Auxquelz ne chault d'esbatz ne ris.*
> *Plaise au doulx Jhesus les absouldre.*

47

[When I consider the skulls piled pell-mell in these charnels, that were all once Maſters of Requeſts of the Chambre aux Deniers [part of the King's household, equivalent to the Privy Purse] at least—or else ſtreet-porters, I cannot tell one from the other: whether bishops or lamplighters I can tell no difference.

Well, they are dead; God have mercy on their souls. Their bodies are rotted that were once those of great lords or ladies, so delicate, so tenderly nourished on cream, and frumenty, and rice; and their bones are waſted into powder merely. Little do they reck now of frolic and laughter. Sweet Jesu, assoil them.]

It is this same melancholy fit which leads him at length to compose his Epitaph, which I have transcribed later in this book: a sad, exquisite chaunt.

The tale of the town's pleasures is not yet exhauſted. Executions were frequent—sixty-two bandits were hanged in Paris, the Bourgeois notes, in the five days April 30 to May 4, 1431—and besides the gibbets ſtanding outside the Porte St. Denis, the Porte St. Jacques, and the Porte Baudet, at the Place de Grève, the Place Dauphine, the Croix du Trahoir, at Montigny, and elsewhere, there were numerous private *echelles* belonging to the Provoſt, the Bishop, and to various abbots and chapters and other authorities having the right of adminiſtering juſtice. The moſt superb and ancient of all, the great gibbet of Montfaucon, is worth a passing glimpse, since its shadow looms so heavy and permanent over Villon's life and verse. Its base was a flat oblong mound fifteen feet high, thirty feet wide, and forty feet long. In a colonnade around three sides, on a raised platform, rose sixteen evenly-spaced square pillars of unhewn ſtone, each thirty-two feet high, linked together at the top by heavy beams, with ropes and chains feſtooned at short intervals. In the centre of the platform gaped an immense pit covered by a grating, for the ultimate disposal of the hanged. Montfaucon, which never lacked fruit dangling from its black boughs, ſtood outside the walls where the Rue Louis-Blanc now cuts the Quai de Jemmapes, a ſtone's-throw from the Eſt railway ſtation, and two secondary gibbets ſtood near it in the plain to receive the overflow. The condemned, setting forth from prison roped and tied in their carts, accompanied by the Provoſt and his bodyguard of twelve mounted Sergeants and attended by Maſter Henry Cousin,

48

Executioner of Paris from 1460 onwards,[18] and his assistants, made a brief station at the convent of the Filles-Dieu by the Porte St. Denis. Here the good sisters comforted them for their last journey with a manchet of bread and a cup of wine. The slow procession then continued its way, through the St. Denis Gate and into the country, preceded and followed by the spectators. The Sergeants spurred a lane through the mob; the Provost, magnificent in fur and scarlet, reined in and took up his position near the gibbet, with the birds swooping and crying around. The creaking carts reached the platform and halted, while Master Henry and his men busied themselves with the ropes, and the friar in attendance recited in a loud voice the last prayers for the dying. An official of the Prévôté unrolled a parchment and read the sentences, the nooses were fixed, the carts moved on, the condemned swung briskly into space, and the ceremony was over. They would hang there, twisting and rotting, pecked by the crows and spun like tops by the winds, until most of the flesh was off their bones. On summer nights it was the fashion for gallants of the kind since known as Apaches, or chevaliers of the *fortifs,* to bring their girls out from Paris for a midnight frolic by the Montfaucon gibbet; and in the seventh and last of the *Repues Franches* ("Free Feeds"), a collection of rascally adventures in verse glorifying Villon and his band and published some years after his disappearance from history, it is described how a couple of hungry *escholiers* broke up such a pleasure-party. The revellers having met to discuss the night's arrangements,

> . . . *Fut conclud, par leur façon,*
> *Qu'ilz yroyent ce soir-là coucher*
> *Prés le gibet de Montfaulcon,*
> *Et auroyent pour provision*
> *Ung pasté de façon subtile,*
> *Et meneroyent en conclusion*
> *Avec eulx, chascun une fille.*

[It was decided that they should go out to sleep that night by the gibbet of Montfaucon, and that they should take for their repast a pasty of quality, and also each one his doxy.]

[18] The complete duties of this official are set forth in a contemporary document. He must be able to "*faire son office par le feu, par l'espée, le fouet, l'ecartelage, la roue, la fourche, le gibet, couper oreilles, desmembrer, flageller ou justiger, par le pilori ou escha-*

The party assembled, having at their heels, unobserved, the two prowling *escholiers,* who had scented a meal from afar off and had decided to be of the company.

> *Et allerent vers Montfaulcon,*
> *Où estoit toute l'assemblée.*
> *Filles y avoit à foyson,*
> *Faisant chere desmesurée.*

[And so to Montfaucon, where every one was assembled. There were girls there in plenty, making great cheer and devilment.]

On the merry scene, late at night, the *escholiers* suddenly descended like a thunderbolt, disguised horribly as devils, flourishing clubs and hooks and yelling *"A mort! à mort, à mort!"* and dispersed the startled company in a rout, helter-skelter.

> *Se vous les eussiez veu fuyr,*
> *Jamais ne vistes si beau jeu,*
> *L'ung amont, l'autre aval courir;*
> *Chascun d'eulx ne pensoit qu'à Dieu,*
> *Ilz s'enfuyrent de ce lieu*
> *Et laisserent pain, vin, & viande,*
> *Criant sainct Jean & sainct Mathieu,*
> *A qui ilz feroyent leur offrande.*

[If you had seen them skedaddle it would have been the best joke you ever saw. One dashed up, the other dashed down, thinking of nothing now but their God; and so vanished from the spot, leaving there the bread, the wine, and the meat, crying to St. John and St. Matthew, vowing them offerings.]

The raiders then sat down to the feast and finished everything with considerable pleasure. It is clear from the whole of this adventure that the essence of a Montfaucon picnic was a good provision of bodies swinging overhead, preferably, I imagine, in full moonlight. All that a later Paris has had to offer the *gobemouches* of Thomas Cook in place of this amusement is the dreary imbecility of the Cabaret de l'Enfer.

What is now called the "legitimate" theatre was, in Villon's Paris, represented by three troops of actors, of which the most

faud, par le carcan, & par telles aultres peines semblables selon la coustume, mœurs ou usages du pays, lesquelz la loi ordonne pour la crainte des malfaicteurs."

important was the Confraternity of the Passion, whose performances took place at the Hospital of the Trinity, outside the St. Denis Gate. In the years following the withdrawal of the English, and as peace and order were gradually restored, the Confraternity's repertory of Mysteries ("mystery," properly "mistery," from *minister-ium*, or so I have seen it derived), which had dwindled a great deal, revived, became more splendid, and were more frequently performed. In 1450 Arnoul Gréban wrote for them a *Passion*—it had 244 acting parts—which became immensely successful and was played all over France. Villon, who loved all the sights of the town, must have attended some of these performances. From a sentence of Rabelais, indeed, it has been supposed (even by Gaston Paris) that he wrote a Mystery himself:

Master Francis Villon, in his old Age, retir'd to St. Maixent in Poitou, under the Patronage of a good honest Abbot of that Place. There to give Pleasure to the People he undertook to have the *Passion* enacted in the Way and Language of the Poitevin Country.[19]

But this cannot possibly mean more than that the poet undertook to "produce" (*entreprit faire jouer*) the play, in the theatrical term. His youthful taste probably led his feet more often to the performances of the Basoche or the Enfans de Sans-Souci than to the religious and dignified Mysteries of the *Passion*. The Basoche, or commonalty of clerks of the Parliament and the law, formed their own company as a rival attraction to the theatre outside the St. Denis Gate, confining themselves to the allegorical drama. The still more popular Enfans Sans-Souci played *soties,* satires mixed with farce and horseplay. At stated feasts, again, some of the Gilds and Confraternities performed their own Mysteries or Moralities, and the University had its Feast of Fools, that Saturnalia, often condemned and now declining, with its huge roaring procession of students disguised as grotesque animals, as women, as monks, as devils, their elected bishop gambolling at their head, holding up all Paris for the day, battling with the police and burghers, and invading even the cloisters and the churches, to the great scandal of modern agnostics and twittering Nordics with their neat little

[19] Bk. iv., xiii.

minds like (as the Irish poet so admirably said) sewing-machines. The Mystery was a different matter. The Mystery, as with our own English cycles, was derived from the Mass, from which the whole spiritual life of the Middle Ages all over Europe radiates.

Rabelais' full story of Villon at St. Maixent in Poitou, with its ruffianly ending, I shall discuss in its proper place. It is more likely, if Villon ever wrote anything solid for the theatre, that it was the admirable bit of buffoonery called the *Monologue du Franc-Archier de Baignollet,* which the more pontifical editors reject absolutely: and indeed the evidence for attribution to Villon is slight, and purely internal. But if this sharp and comic satire is not Villon's then, as I perceive after long study of it (we shall come to it in due course), it is the work of one steeped in his style and mannerism, some one who had lived very near the rose. That Villon mixed freely with farce-players and strolling mummers and occasionally played himself there can be no doubt. In the first place this was a habit of *escholiers,* as is shown in the case, quoted by P. Champion, of a certain Poncelet de Monchauvet, student, charged with murder in 1416. His defence was:

> *Qu'il n'est* buffo *ne gouliart, ne jongleur ou basteleur, & s'il a esté a jouer a aucunes farces,* comme ont acoustumé faire escoliers & jeunes gens, *ce a esté par esbatement & sans gain, & n'a point esté maistre jongleur.*

[He is neither buffoon nor mummer, minstrel nor showman, and if he has played in any farces, as is the custom of students and young persons, it has been for a frolic and not for profit; and he has certainly not been a master-minstrel.]

It is to the mummers of his day that Villon directly and personally addresses himself in the Ballade of Good Counsel:

> *Farce, broulle, joue des fleustes,*
> *Fais, es villes et es citez,*
> *Farces, jeux et moralitez . . .*

[Rhyme, rail, wrestle, and cymbals play,
    Flute and fool it in mummers' shows;
Along with the strolling players stray
From town to city, without repose. . . .]
(*Translated by John Payne*)

52

And it is quite likely that he on occasion would ſtring together burlesque verses or a *sotie* for them. His more or less contemporary Eloy d'Amerval passes down the tradition in his *Grant Deablerie*:

> *Maiſtre Françoys Villon jadis,*
> *Clerc expert en faictz & en diz,*
> *Comme fort nouveau qu'il eſtoit,*
> *Et a farcer se delectoit.*

[Maſter François Villon was formerly a clerk expert in word and deed, moſt enterprising, delighting in farces.]

As does Philippe de Vigneulles also in his Memoirs, praising a certain tailor of Metz, a playboy of his time: *"Ce fut ung second Françoy Willon de bien rimer, de bien juer fairxe & de tout ambaitement."* *

But it must be remembered that Villon was a comic legend within fifty years of his disappearance.

In this swift survey of Villon's Paris the general government of the town needs nothing more than a reference. The Municipality, ruled by the Prévôt des Marchands and four Aldermen, sat in the Parloir aux Bourgeois, or Maison aux Piliers, in the Place de Grève.[20] Bedford had reformed it (as they say) during the English occupation, and with his appointed Provoſt of Police, Simon Morhier, had kept the citizens comparatively calm during St. Joan's attack in 1429. The river traffic and commerce of Paris generally were under the Municipality's control. Their jurisdiction occasionally clashed with that of the Provoſt, who had absolute power over not only the police service but also all the prisons, pillories, gibbets, town-criers, and barber-surgeons of Paris. And here we may resume in more detail, since the bareſt sketch of the career of François Villon could hardly afford to ignore the police of Paris, the Chorus in his tragic comedy. The main body was the Guet Royal, the Royal Watch, commanded by a Chevalier du Guet (Villon twice makes

* [Truly he was a second François Villon for his excellence in rhyming, playing farces and every kind of jollity.]

[20] There was another "Parloir aux Bourgeois" againſt the ramparts by the Dominicans of the Rue St. Jacques, and incorporated into their house: but this had nothing to do with the Municipality, as its position should sufficiently show. It was probably part of the Clos aux Bourgeois given to Paris by Philippe-Auguſte, think de Rochegude and Dumolin.

53

this officer a sardonic bequest) appointed by the King. Its *cadre* on being reorganised a hundred years before by Provost Hughes Aubroit in the reign of Charles v. was twenty mounted Sergeants and forty foot-Sergeants, and remained so till 1559. The Watch was assisted by the Sergeants of the Châtelet, who in Villon's time numbered 220, divided into two equal companies of horse and foot· as Villon well knew.

Item, aux Unze Vings Sergens . . .

[*Item,* to tne Two Hundred and Twenty Sergeants.]

The Provost's bodyguard was twelve mounted Sergeants. The Guet Royal was assisted also by the Guet des Métiers, a night watch found by various corporations of tradesmen and artisans, and occupying fixed posts. To this watch belonged the draper Guillaume Bouin, whose case is included by Longnon in his papers illustrating Parisian life during the English occupation. The draper Guillaume Bouin had occasion to correct his wife Macée, a scold, with the flat of his *bazelaire,* the short sword which he was *acoustumé de porter ou guet de nuyt a la Porte Saint-Jacques.* In her fury Macée jumped from an upper window into the street and died, and Guillaume had need of a letter of remission.

There was finally a third body (often fused with the Guet des Métiers), the Guet Bourgeois, supplied by the citizens when necessary, and corresponding broadly to the Trained Bands of London.[21] A function often performed by the Guet Bourgeois, say MM. Dubech and d'Espezel in their History of Paris, was to get in the way of the Guet Royal.

Of the common prisons of Paris the three most important were the Grand Châtelet, the seat of the *Prévôté royale,* commanding the Pont au Change; the Petit-Châtelet, commanding the Petit-Pont; and the Conciergerie in the Palais, which was to have a bloody halo three hundred years after Villon. The poet himself was probably shoved in all three: certainly in two. He reserves for himself, in the lesser Testament, tongue in cheek, the chamber in the Grand Châtelet called the *Troys Lis,* or Three Beds. He was in this prison

[21] From which, as from the other irksome duty, the citizens naturally escaped whenever possible by paying substitutes.

positively at the end of 1462, when he received his second death-sentence, and later in the Conciergerie, and his whooping Ballade of joy at the remission is addressed to Eſtienne Garnier, Clerk of the *Guichet* there. Whether Villon was ever in the prison of the Bishop of Paris attached to the For-l'Evesque (*Forum Episcopi*) on the quay near the Châtelet, is not known. The Petit-Châtelet, which received the criminals and unruly characters of the Left Bank, no doubt enfolded him occasionally to cool his heels after a night's brawling. In a print of 1550 the piles of the Grand and Petit Châte-lets ſtand as they ſtood when Villon knew them. The huge, tre-mendously thick round towers with their pointed turrets, the yawn-ing archways, the machicolations, the overwhelming mass of masonry need no signpost.

> *Veſtibulum ante ipsum primisque in faucibus Orci*
> *Luctus et ultrices posuere cubilia Curæ.*

[Juſt in the Gate, and in the Jaws of Hell,
  Revengeful Cares, and sullen Sorrows dwell.]
            (*Dryden,* Vergil, Æneid VI.)

Yet the prisoner of that age was relatively fortunate, for he could share in human intercourse, and the humanitarians had no power over him.

It was, I think, at the end of the Victorian period in England, when François Villon was so extensively taken up by the lily-handed (*"ces âmes singulières,"* says Gaston Paris, *"ouvertes à la fois aux inspirations d'un myſticisme lilial et aux suggeſtions perverses d'une dépravation au moins intellectuelle."* * He means Rossetti and his school. I can see from here Villon's expression in Purgatory on learning of his adoption)—it was then that the bluff Victorian con-tempt for the fount and mainspring of the life of the Middle Ages became tinged with a sad, voluptuous guſto, like that of Stiggins shaking his head over a glass of Wanity. Certain defects in the human machinery of a Divine inſtitution which are so obvious to any observer of fifteenth-century life, the monaſtic ideals relaxed

* [These singular souls, susceptible alike to the inspirations of a lily-white myſticism and the perverse suggeſtions of a pravity at leaſt intellectual.]

and broken, relapsed priests swigging in a Paris tavern, the Abbess Huguette du Hamel and her scandalous behaviour, Friar Baulde de la Mare rioting with thieves and prostitutes, the companions of Villon—all this was strangely attractive to minds a little dazed with the fumes of lilies and languors, and in a cloudy sort of way renewed their belief in Art-fabrics.

It is no intention of mine to glide over these defects, any more than to gloat over them. All the poetry of medieval Europe is hot with satire against unworthy servants of the Church: for it has been observed that where the faith is strong the laity strongly resent failures to preserve the clerical standard. In an age when the Church was the ruling factor in men's lives from the cradle to the grave, and beyond it, when they derived from her not only consolation and succour, both bodily and ghostly, but also learning, music, drama, painting, sculpture, and every work of the mind, when (as before, and since, and ever) she was the fortress of the poor, and then solely responsible for their relief, when she at every turn fed the soul and glorified the understanding with beauty—in such an age the rascalities of those among her myriad children who forswore their vows and disgraced their habits do not seem of overwhelming account. But what! The Catholic Church needs no human praise. *Ego mater pulchræ dilectionis, et agnitionis, et sanctæ spei.** As for human blame, she is indifferent to it; for her eyes are fixed elsewhere. The debaucheries of such as Friar Baulde and his kind, who mixed freely with the vagabond populace of thieves, crimps, gipsies, beggars, and assassins thrown on the Paris streets by the wars, will occupy in these pages no more than their proportionate place. It is necessary to consider that for every quartet of lapsed Carmelites such as that quartet arrested in a Paris tavern in 1488, dressed not in the habit of their Order, but in gowns, hats, and shoes, with daggers at their belt, there were all over France, and all over the rest of Europe, other religious who lived, or attempted to live, by the Rule. It would naturally be ridiculous on the other hand to believe that the majority of religious houses at this period kept the standard of (for example) Citeaux under St. Stephen Harding of

*[I am the mother of fair love, and of knowledge, and of holy hope.] (Ecclesiasticus, 24.)

56

Sherborne, in the fullest discipline of the Rule, when, except for one frugal meal, twelve hours' manual and intellectual labour and the duties of the Liturgy filled each day from two in the morning till Compline. In an age and in a country weakened and wearied by a hundred years of war and continuously ravaged and oppressed by a thousand evils, some slackening of human fibre is no matter for surprise, even sincere.

The fifteenth century was the bitter and violent age of Jean Sans-Peur, and Gilles de Rais (though research has greatly, I believe, shorn his gambols of their Satanic splendour), and the Comte d'Armagnac, whose pleasures ranged from pæderasty by way of murder to coining, who had his confessor flogged for refusing him absolution. The great feudal lords and vassals, like Charles the Rash of Burgundy, called the Grand Duke of the West, the Bourbons and Nemours, were seditious and enemies to order. The great captains passed their time normally in slaughter, pillage, and rapine, treason, torture, and assassination, dividing the unhappy land; and justice was not always strong or courageous enough to stand up to them. Arbitrary judgments were not rare, nor the division of a defendant's goods among his accusers, his judges, and the King's favourites; nor did conditions improve until Louis xi., that silent, shabby, pensive, admirable person, demonstrated, by executing Charles de Melun and the Constable of St. Pol for treason, that there was law in France and that it applied to the great. In such a time, and considering the wasted lands, the destroyed and abandoned churches and religious houses,[22] the ruined benefices left in the track of civil wars, the general lassitude and misery which cries out in that Ballade of Charles d'Orléans to Our Lady praying desperately for peace:

> Priez pour paix, doulce Vierge Marie,
> Royne des cieulx, et du monde maistresse,
> Faites prier, par vostre courtoisie,
> Saincts et sainctes, et prenez vostre adresse
> Vers vostre Filz, requerrant sa haultesse
> Qu'il luy plaise son peuple regarder . . .

[22] For one example, the great Abbey of St. Victor, with its park and library, for which the Rector of University was appealing in 1449.

[Pray for peace, sweet Virgin Mary, Queen of Heaven and Mistress of this world; and of thy courtesy call on all the saints for prayers, and present our petition before thy Son, imploring His high majesty that it would please Him to look down on His people . . .]

and continues, showing Her the misery of the land and calling for more and more prayers:

> Priez, prelatz et gens de saincte vie,
> Religieux, ne dormez en peresse,
> Priez, maistres et tous suivans clergie,[23]
> Car par guerre fault que l'estude cesse:
> Moustiers destruiz sont sans qu'on les redresse,
> Le service de Dieu vous fault laissier . . .

[Pray, all ye prelates, and men of holy life. Monks, be not idle, and sleep not. Pray, learned masters, and all who pursue knowledge; for because of war all learning must cease. See, the religious houses are destroyed, and no man rebuilds them, and you have perforce to desist from the service of God. . . .]

—considering all this, the defection of the Bauldes of the age, still less of those secular clerks driven by hunger on the streets of Paris and the large towns to mix with the riffraff already there, becomes not so monstrous inexplicable and horrible a thing as it seems (and especially to some glad observers) detached from its background. It is well observed by L. Thuasne that the attitude of the Middle Ages towards misdemeanour and crime must be strictly remembered. At this time the civil and the religious ethos were one and the same; that is, men generally, even high officials, believed in the infinite mercy of God and in the Church's assurance, then as now, that a sin, however enormous, may be forgiven and effaced by God's pity after sincere remorse, repentance, and reparation. "Lord!" cries Robert de Sorbon, chaplain to St. Louis, in one of his *Propos,* "however great the sinner who has come to me, I have always loved him a hundred times more after confessing him than before." Remembering this, and considering the principle of a Letter of Remission accorded by the King to the criminal awarding him forgiveness, on confessing his crime and making satisfaction to the civil party, it

---

[23] *Clergie:* scholars, doctors, students. *Moustiers,* monasteries.

becomes clear that the Royal power acted in practically the same manner as the Church; but with more bureaucratic obligations attached to the form (for these Letters were not by any means scattered broadcaſt, and certain conditions had to be complied with before they could be confirmed) and with less universal clemency; and also without the power to grant such spiritual aids as the Church could afford the weak and the backsliding.[24] Therefore in contemplating a fifteenth-century criminal this attitude of his age must be taken into account, however odd it may seem to Bentha-mites in Bloomsbury.

The people, moreover, held to the Faith. M. Longnon's docu-ments record the foundation of a cluſter of new confraternities among the gilds and trades of Paris. The Gild of Glovers in 1426 begged permission and were allowed to re-eſtablish in St. Innocent the Confraternity of St. Anne, founded long before by the Iron-mongers and ruined by the wars. In 1427 the Money-changers of the Pont Notre-Dame were authorised to eſtablish a confraternity in St. Barthélemy. In 1428 the parishioners of St. Laurent, *pour le singulier refuge & affeccion qu-ilz ont aux benois sains monsei-gneur saint Michiel l'angle, monseigneur saint Ildevert, monsei-gneur saint Lubin, & madame saincte Katherine,** eſtablished an-other in their parish church. In 1430 the Maſter Cordwainers of Paris had the privileges of their Confraternity of SS. Crispin and Crispian in Notre-Dame confirmed by Henry vi. The laſt document of the Longnon collection is a letter of Henry vi. authorising the es-tablishment in February 1435, on the eve of the English withdrawal, of a new confraternity in the Dominicans' church in the Rue St. Jacques, *en l'onneur & a la louenge & gloire de Dieu noſtre createur, de la benoiſte glorieuse Vierge Marie sa mere, et dudit benoiſt martir monseigneur sainct Pierre le martir, a l'occasion de laquele*

---

*[On account of the succour they owe and the affection they bear to the blessed saints, Monseigneur St. Michael the Archangel, Monseigneur St. Ildebert, Monseigneur St. Lubin, and Madame St. Katherine.]

[24] *E.g.* Indulgences: which are not tickets enabling the holder to sneak into Paradise, nor pardons for the guilt of sin, nor licenses to commit it, but simply remissions of the temporal punishment remaining to be worked off after a sin has been forgiven; such pun-ishment as was exacted publicly in primitive times. Compare Nathan's sentence on David the King.

confrairie & fraternité le divin service pourra eſtre augmenté a la louenge de Dieu & de toute la court de Paradis.*

The object of these works of devotion was practical: the celebration every week in the year of Masses for the good eſtate of the members, body and soul, their families, friends, and benefactors; for the souls of their dead; for the good eſtate of the King and the Royal family and their relatives, living and dead; for the peace and welfare of the City of Paris; and for other intentions.[25] Nor were the corporal works of mercy excluded.

I have quoted these inſtances because they illuſtrate the devotion of the mass of the Parisian populace in Villon's age, during the worſt years of the town's hiſtory; and because it is necessary to remember that this devotion flourished at precisely the same time that the rascal Carmelite Baulde de la Mare was tippling and roaring at the sign of the Wooden Sword.

[* To the honour and praise and glory of God our Creator, the blessed and glorious Virgin Mary His Mother, and the aforesaid blessed martyr Monseigneur St. Peter the martyr, by the occasion of which confraternity and brotherhood the Divine service may be increased, to the praise of God and all the Court of Paradise.]

[20] See Appendix F.

II

THE LIFE

If my dark heart has any sweet thing it is turned away from me, and then farther off I see the great winds where I must be sailing. I see my good luck far away in the harbour, but my steersman is tired out, and the masts and the ropes on them are broken, and the beautiful lights where I would be always looking are quenched.

SYNGE, *from Petrarch.*

THE LIFE

§ I

Un des plus bizarres personnages de ce pays où Dieu n'en a pas laissé man-
quer. C'eſt un composé de hauteur et de bassesse, de bon sens et de déraison:
il faut que les notions de l'honnête et du déshonnête soient bien étrangement
brouillées dans sa tête, car il montre ce que la nature lui a donné de bonnes
qualités sans oſtentation, et ce qu'il en a reçu de mauvaises sans pudeur.
—Diderot, Le Neveu de Rameau.

[One of the oddeſt characters in this country—which the Almighty has
not deprived of such. He is a mixture of elevated sentiment and baseness, of
good sense and folly; and it would seem that notions of honeſty and dis-
honeſty are moſt ſtrangely confused in his head, for he displays those good
qualities with which Nature has endowed him without oſtentation, and the
bad ones without shame.]

As one who sets out on foot to trace a Roman road finds after faint
beginnings a ſtretch of plain going, loses the track in paſture, or
ploughland, or bog, picks it up again, driving ahead like an arrow,
and again loses it in forthrights and meanders, so in surveying
the turbulent life of François Villon vagueness alternates with certitude, marshland with hard ground, and leagues of regular ſtriding
with sudden ſtumblings clogged with doubt. Finally the road
ends abruptly at the edge of a precipice and the traveller finds himself ſtaring into Space, with only Echo,

parlant quant bruyt on maine,

[answering when one calls aloud]

(a tedious wench) to answer his holloas.

63

Before the last quarter of the nineteenth century the map of Villon's life was, for the most part, like Africa in a Mappa Mundi. His two Testaments gave the year of his birth, the year of his imprisonment at Meun, some evidence that he was at least once in danger of hanging, the names of some of his companions, and a few indications, direct and oblique, of a criminal career. Beyond that there was nothing but conjecture. *Hic anthropophagi. Hic dracones.* In 1873 Auguste Vitu suddenly burst into this silent country, returning with his *Notice sur François Villon, d'après des documents nouveaux et inédits tirés des dépôts publiques* (May 1873), rich spoil which included, from the registers of the Chancellery of France, the two Letters of Remission which throw such light on the killing of Chermoye on Corpus Christi, 1455. Four years later Auguste Longnon, having rifled the University archives and discovered the whole story of the burglary at the College of Navarre, incorporated this document, together with a full *dossier* embracing Villon's principal companions and legatees, into his monumental *Etude biographique sur François Villon,* on which Robert Louis Stevenson, fired with enthusiasm, composed the decorative, uncomprehending, and celebrated essay in *Men and Books.* In 1884 Auguste Vitu began his struggles with the Jargon, followed by Lucien Schöne. In 1890 Marcel Schwob published the Inquiry on the Coquillards, which a modest archivist of Dijon had unearthed as far back as 1842. In 1892 Longnon brought out his great edition of the *Œuvres complètes,* which is still standard, enriching it with new-found documents concerning the University riots of the *Pet-au-Deable* and the street brawl of November 1462 in which Villon was concerned with Robin Dogis. Finally the archives of Parliament and the University yielded Marcel Schwob the ultimate precious drops of information concerning Villon's following mishaps of 1462, the death-sentence, the reprieve, and the banishment.[1]

Henceforth, though fog still hangs over many stages of the road, and though there are large gaps and patches of impassable land, the main part is clear enough. It seems unlikely that anything more can be discovered. The national treasuries have been

[1] See Appendix G: *Bibliography.*

thoroughly ransacked, and Time and the bonfires of the Revolution have no doubt accounted for the rest of the documents, whether preserved in Paris, in the Orléanais, in the Bourbonnais, or elsewhere, which could have solved all remaining problems.

The road ends, as I have said, in the air. There is nothing beyond the gulf but silence. But the journey, I promise you, is a good one.

About the year 1430 a priest originally from the diocese of Auxerre was given a residential chaplaincy in the University church of St. Benoît-le-Bientourné in the Rue St. Jacques, in the shadow of Sorbonne.[2] His name was Guillaume: he took a surname, in the medieval fashion, from the village of his origin, the still-existing village of Villon, a Burgundian fief five leagues from Tonnerre in the Chablis country, on the frontier of the Slope of Gold. Guillaume de Villon was a man of parts and honour, a Master of Arts and a Bachelor in Canon Law: he had come to Paris young, had practised for a time a professor in the Law Schools of the Rue St. Jean-de-Beauvais, and had held a small benefice at Chantilly. He was allotted, with his chaplaincy in St. Benoît, a house in the cloister, a house called the Porte Rouge, on account, so it has been conjectured by leading archæologists, of its having a red door. Here Master Guillaume de Villon, attached to the chapel and altar of *monseigneur sainct Jehan l'Evangeliste* in St. Benoît, lived the rest of his life, worthily and (except for a brush in 1434 and again in 1450 with the Chapter of Notre-Dame, suzerain of St. Benoît [3]) peacefully. He moved, moreover, in honourable Parisian society,

[2] The history of this church, so bound up with Villon's, is interesting. It was built with its cloister on the site of a Merovingian shrine in the twelfth century, and having its high altar at the west end and its main door in the Rue St. Jacques, liturgically an error, was called St. Benoist-le-Bestourné, "St. Bennet Askew." By 1349 the high altar had been moved to the east end, and the church thence was called St. Benoist-le-Bientourné, *ecclesia S. Benedicti beneversi*. It was partly reconstructed in the fifteenth century, suppressed in 1790, and sold in 1797. In 1800 Mass was said in it once more; in 1812 it was sold for a warehouse; in 1832 it became the Théâtre du Panthéon; in 1854 it succumbed at length and was pulled down. The north block of the new Sorbonne covers its site, where the Rue des Écoles crosses the Rue St. Jacques.

St. Benoît was served by one curé; six canons (without canons' privileges) nominated by the Chapter of Notre-Dame, and twelve chaplains elected by the Chapter of St. Benoît. It had eight chapels.

[3] This terrible Metropolitan Chapter thrust Guillaume de Villon into their private prison for a short space in 1450. One did not stand up to them with impunity.

65

and was a frequent guest at the table of Dom Jacques Séguin, Prior of St. Martin-des-Champs. *"Et disna avec mondict Seigneur,"* notes the Prior's secretary in October 1438, *"maistre Guillaume de Villon, demourant au cloistre saint Benoist."* * And again, in November, *"Et y disna maistre Michiel Piedefer, maistre Jehan Turquant, maistre Guillaume de Villon, & ung ou deux autres."* †[4] At the table of Dom Séguin there met many of the higher clergy, lawyers, and notable officials of Parliament, even during the worst years; he was a hospitable man and one of strong personality, *grand seigneur ecclésiastique,* and his guests no doubt keenly regretted his deprivation and excommunication for *plures & multas rebelliones & inobediencias quamplurimas* ‡ by his superior, the Abbot of Cluny, in 1452. His successor, Prior Jacques Jouvenel des Ursins, was an austere person who did not number hospitality among his sterling virtues.

Guillaume de Villon was closely linked in friendship, as it appears from various documents respecting heritages, with several good Parisian families, the Hémons, the Barons, the Bonnarts, the Drouarts. In his own Burgundian country, no less than in Paris, he was a man of substance and esteem, and at one time was *seigneur* of a little domain in the Bailliage of Sens called Malay-le-Roy; a domain carrying with it (by a singular irony, considering the career of his adopted son) the right to erect a gibbet to deal with malefactors in that countryside. He possessed a slender private income (on which he was to draw pretty heavily in behalf of his ward in years to come) derived from a vine-preserve in the Clos Bourgeois at Vaugirard and the rent of three houses in the neighbourhood of St. Benoît; and it is characteristic of him that from one of his tenants he had not collected any rent for eight years, at the date of an entry in a register pertaining.

To the house called the Red Door in the cloister of St. Benoît-le-

---

*[And there dined with my aforesaid Lord, Master Guillaume de Villon, living in the Cloister of St. Benoît.]

†[And there also dined here Master Michiel Piedefer, Master Jehan Turquant, Master Guillaume de Villon, and one or two others.]

‡[Repeated rebelliousness and innumerable acts of disobedience.]

⁺Arch. nat., LL 1383, fol. 108.

Bientourné there was brought, probably about the year 1438, on Master de Villon's return to Paris from a long journey, a fatherless child, a distant relative. The kind chaplain (the fixed epithet will recur in this history, as in Homer, as in Vergil, as in the Song of Roland, as in *Aucassin,* time and again) adopted this sharp-faced starveling, fed, clothed, sheltered, and educated him, saw him through University, forgave him the villainies of his early manhood, comforted him in his despair, reprimanded him, gave him sanctuary when hard pressed, ransomed him with influence and money, and was repaid with a life of constant anxiety and the enduring love and gratitude of the reprobate, glowing for all time in his verse towards

> *mon plus que pere,*
> *Maistre Guillaume de Villon,*
> *Qui esté m'a plus doulx que mere*
> *A enfant levé de maillon.*

[My more than father, Master Guillaume de Villon, who has been to me more tender than a mother, and raised me from swaddling-clothes.]

Master Guillaume died in his house in the quiet enclosure of St. Benoît, among its little gardens, in 1468, at the age of seventy, and was buried in his church. It has been reasonably supposed that he was carried off by a great epidemic which swept Paris early in that year, particularly the St. Benoît quarter, and carried off also the Lady Ambroise de Loré, wife of François Villon's protector Robert d'Estouteville, Provost of Paris. It is even possible to fix the date of Guillaume de Villon's death, since in 1480 his fellow-priest and old pupil Jehan le Duc caused to be increased Master Guillaume's *obit,* the modest foundation for requiem Masses left by him with the Grande Confrérie aux Bourgeois, of which he was a member.[5] The entry, written by an official of the Confraternity in indifferent Latin, stands in their *Martirologe* or anniversary-book:

EPIPHANIA DOMINI.—*In vigilia Regum, in ecclesia beate Marie Magdalene, obitus fundatus per venerabilem virum magistrum Guillermum Villon. Pro cujus fundacione habemus vingiti [viginti] libras cum*

[5] This Confraternity was distinguished: Kings and Queens of France were members of it through the ages. It was established in the little church of the Madeleine in the Cité.

octo solidis parisiensibus annui redditus. Et pro augmentacione ipsius vir venerabilis dominus Johannes Leduc, quondam frater istius Confratrie, et antea discipulus prefati magistri Guillelmi Villon, dedit nobis duodecim libras ad emendum redditus: xii l. t.[6]

[*Epiphany of Our Lord.*—On the eve before the Twelfth Night, in the church of blessed Mary Magdalen, the *obit* founded by the venerable Master Guillaume de Villon: for this foundation we have twenty livres eight sols Parisis annually. To increase this *obit* the venerable Master Jehan le Duc, formerly a member of this Confraternity and one time a pupil of the aforesaid Master Guillaume de Villon, has paid us twelve livres to amend the same: xii livres Tournois.[6]]

Twelfth Night falls on January 6, and therefore (since *obits* are observed generally on the anniversary of death) it would seem clear that Guillaume de Villon died on that feast in 1468. His will, executed by Jehan le Duc, has never been discovered, but the principal legatee has been found to be his nephew, the barber-surgeon Jehan Flastrier. It is permissible to conclude from this that the haggard rogue whom the chaplain of St. Benoît had so long protected had left behind no trace or token on his flight into the outer dark five years before; or was dead.

In 1481 the barber-surgeon Flastrier founded in St. Benoît a chantry for the recital at Guillaume de Villon's tomb on the first of each month, immediately after High Mass, of the Seven Penitential Psalms, the *Libera me, Domine,* and other prescribed prayers *au remede & salut de l'ame dudict de Vyllon, oncle dudict testateur.**

This is the last news of Master Guillaume de Villon. The honourable chaplain of St. Benoît had a heart of pure gold. I do not doubt that he has sat these many score of years in Paradise.

The baptismal name of the child Master Guillaume de Villon received into his house, who was to grow into such a great blackguard and poet, was François; his surname, or rather surnames, those of his father (to whom we shall come within a few words), de Montcorbier and des Loges. At this moment it is only necessary

*[For the good estate and salvation of the soul of the aforesaid Master de Villon, uncle of the aforesaid testator.]

[6] Arch. nat., LL 437, fol. 2.

to observe that Stevenson, making play in his best Adelphi manner with "François de Montcorbier, *alias* des Loges, *alias* Villon, *alias* Michel Mouton," creates a romantic but therefore false impression. Except in University, where his name is entered as de Montcorbier, Villon used no other name throughout his life but that of his guardian. He is named des Loges once, in a Royal pardon, and nowhere else. The "Michel Mouton" was an extempore lie told in a tight place to save his skin, and never used again: as we shall see.

There was no official fuss in Paris at the time about a poet's being born, and there exists no register fixing the date of François Villon's birth. From his own clear mention in his verse, however, the year is known—the year 1431, in the last phase of the English occupation. The house in which he uttered his first yell of dismay on entering this world was probably swept away centuries ago, with the dark and narrow street which held it. There can rarely have been a more execrable world for an infant to be born into: a world of famine, plague, and oppression, the tyrant English inside and the Burgundians and Armagnacs ravaging the country without, pale misery stalking the streets, and murder all round. For the poor of Paris, who in those years lived mainly on turnip-tops and miscellaneous refuse, life must have been a grinding torment: and the father of François Villon was poor, as his son has said.

> *Povre je suis de ma jeunesse,*
> *De povre et de petite extrace;*
> *Mon pere n'ot oncq grant richesse,*
> *Ne son ayeul, nommé Orace;*
> *Povreté tous nous suit et trace.*

[Poor I am, from my childhood, of poor and obscure extraction. My father had never great riches, nor his grandfather, whose name was Orace. Poverty follows and dogs us all.]

I see the poet's father, a gaunt, silent figure, prematurely old and worn with troubles. His Christian name (the Middle Ages cared chiefly about Christian names, and were careless of patronymics) is unknown. He took from the village of his origin, a little village long since vanished, on the edge of Burgundy and the Bourbonnais, a surname: de Montcorbier. This was a custom of his time (as we have seen, Guillaume de Villon had done the same), and implied no relationship to the *seigneur* who owned the village, or to his family: certainly François Villon never at any time claimed kin with the noble and wealthy family of de Montcorbier, whose reigning head at this time was Girard de Montcorbier, *"noble homme, escuyer."* As for the name of des Loges, in which a Letter of Remission was awarded François Villon after the killing of Chermoye in 1455 (*"maiſtre François des Loges, autrement dit de Villon"*), his father had borne it in the Bourbonnais.[7] It was the name of a little *métairie* dependent on the fief and village of Montcorbier, and no doubt it was after an unsuccessful ſtruggle to live on this ſteading, ruined by the wars, that the elder des Loges came to Paris in the hope of bettering his fortunes; possibly at the time of the wedding of Charles v. to Jehanne de Bourbon, when many of his countrymen came up to the capital. If he indeed nourished hope, he was deceived. I see him, I say, a gaunt, anxious, haggard figure, bowed with disappointment and harsh fate. He died early, leaving his poverty behind him; probably in the poet's childhood— in any case before 1461, when his son wrote in the *Grant Teſtament*,

> *Mon pere eſt mort, Dieu en ait l'ame!*

> [My father is dead, God receive his soul!]

—and is numbered with the forgotten dead. His wife, presumably a native of Anjou, her brother, François' uncle, being a religious at Angers, survived him for many years. She was ſtill alive in 1461, when her son (who loved her) wrote for her the Ballade to Our Lady: a bent and shrivelled old woman living in poverty, as he explains on her behalf.

> *Femme je suis povrette et ancienne,*
> *Qui riens ne sçay; oncques lettre ne leus.*

> [A pitiful poor woman, shrunk and old,
> I am, and nothing learn'd in letter-lore.]
> (*Rossetti.*)

Nothing more is known of her life or death. From the same glorious Ballade,

[7] It had no connection with the Parisian family of des Loges, to which belonged a certain Jehan des Loges, Procurator at the Châtelet between 1447 and 1461.

Au mouſtier voy dont suis paroissienne
Paradis paint, ou sont harpes et lus,

[Within my parish-cloiſter I behold
A painted Heaven where harps and lutes adore.]
(*Rossetti.*)

the Abbé Valentin Dufour (with him Marcel Schwob) has con-
jeétured very plausibly that the *mouſtier,* minſter, or conventual
church of her parish was the Church of the Celeſtines near the
Baſtille, one of the wonders of old Paris, and particularly celebrated
for its wall-paintings of Heaven and Hell. "*Aux Celeſtins,*" writes
Guillebere de Metz about 1434, "*eſt paradis & enfer en painéſture,*
avec autres portraiéſures de noble euvre. . . . Item, devant le cuer
de l'eglise a ung autel eſt painéſ l'ymage de Noſtre-Dame." * The
Celeſtines was dedicated to the Annunciation: this affords one more
reason for conneéting it with the Ballade to Our Lady. The old
woman, therefore, may have lived in this quarter of Paris, in which
Rabelais died. On the other hand, since moſt medieval churches
glowed with colour, her *mouſtier* might equally have been of the
Left Bank—little St. Julien-le-Pauvre, then declining,[8] or the
Dominicans' great church in the Rue St. Jacques, which held at the
Revolution the bodies or hearts of twenty-two kings and princes
of the blood, and had been loaded with treasure by every French
king since St. Louis; or the Franciscans, hardly less splendid, by
the south-weſt rampart; or further north, on the river-quay, the
Grands-Auguſtins; or even fortified St. Germain-des-Prés outside
the walls, with its vaſt enclosure, its bourg, its three ſteeples, its
rich reliquaries from Toledo and Cordova, and its Merovingian
pride. In any of these churches there would be paintings, lights,
warmth, and consolation for the poor.

The old woman shared with Maſter Guillaume de Villon his
anxieties and sorrowings over the prodigal, but her journey to the

* [At the Celeſtins there is Heaven and Hell painted, and other paintings of noble handiwork. . . . Item, in the heart of the church at an altar
there is painted a piéture of Our Lady.]

[8] The abbey of Longpont, of which St. Julien was a dependency, was itself ruined by
the Hundred Years' War, and in 1449 was served by a Cluniac prior and three monks
only.

71

grave was not all misery, for maternal love and a humble devotion to God's Mother sweetened and alleviated it. She had no other children—or if she had, the poet does not speak of them. He who remembered in his verse with such affection his mother and his protector would, I think, have remembered his brothers and sisters, had he had any. His other kinships are shadowy. His grandfather, or great-grandfather, whom he names Orace, may be a myth. Nothing is known of him. M. Longnon, whose research gives him authority for saying that the name Orace, or Horace, was extremely rare in fifteenth-century France, hesitatingly puts forward the only Horace he has discovered during his immense labours on this period. This was a sort of patriotic buffoon who incensed the English, during Henry v.'s siege of Meaux in 1421-22, by braying loudly on the ramparts through a trumpet by the side of a crowned ass which the besieged had hoisted there in derision, thumping it to make it give tongue and crying to the English that Henry their King was calling to them: a pleasantry, observes Longnon with justice, *assez dépourvue de finesse*. (Henry at this period was the common name for an ass in France, as Martin was a little later.) The patriot Horace suffered eventually for his share in this piece of artless fun, being handed over on May 2, 1422, with a batch of other defenders of Meaux, in accordance with the terms of the surrender: it is doubtful whether he existed many days after that date. If indeed Villon had an ancestor of the name, this Horace would be exactly the sort of ancestor Villon should have had. But the poet may have invented him for the sake of rhyme, or, alternatively, may have sprung from the loins, twice or thrice removed, of some obscurer hero of the name.

To Master Guillaume de Villon he was undoubtedly related; it is presumed, on his mother's side. It is clear that the priest of St. Benoît must have had relatives in a much more comfortable class than the one into which François was born: solid burgesses at the least, hurriedly disclaiming in a few years any connection with their distant blackguard kinsman and drawing round them their furred gowns. Villon refers to them, with a sort of patient scorn, early in the *Grant Testament*:

72

Lady and a dozen different saints invoked on Master Guillaume's head. A clerk! *Escoute, mon petit!* In time a priest, perhaps! After that, if God is good (the old woman's eyes are misty at the thought of it) a canon, perhaps, a prior—a Bishop, even, purple-gloved and amethyst-ringed, blessing the people in his first procession, with organs thundering and bells clashing and singing-men chanting loudly *Tu es sacerdos!* I warrant in that moment the dim eyes saw, through tears, Franciscus, Servant of the Servants of God, riding on his milk-white mule among the trumpets and the cavaliers. There was no folly in such a vision. Among our English hierarchy, up to the looting of the Monasteries, St. Richard of Wych, Bishop of Winchester, was in his youth a farm-labourer, Chichele a shepherd boy, St. Edmund Rich of Abingdon (he is not forgotten, the blessed Edmund: his relics are at Pontigny in the Yonne, in the abbey there, and are still visited once every year by pilgrims, both French and English) a small merchant's son, Archbishop Robert Kilwardby of Canterbury a Dominican friar, Reynolds a baker's son, the great Grosseteste the younger son of a poor Suffolk family. Chaucer's poor Parson, "rich of hooly thoght and werk," was brother to a ploughman. And how long is it since the bells of Rome ceased tolling for the gentle saint, the peasant Sarto?

Guillaume de Villon kept his word. About the year 1443 the boy François was entered of the Faculty of Arts in the University of Paris, at a *bourse* of two sols Parisis: he was twelve years old, the age at which children became eligible for University. His name, François de Montcorbier, stands in the Register of the Nation of France, with the amount of his *bourse* against it; and it is probably at this moment that he joined to his surname the name of his protector, by which he later became exclusively known. This would both display his gratitude and ensure him an honourable start in University. Henceforward nothing stood between him and the highest offices in Church or State but his own negligence or folly; and for the next few years at least willing hands were urging him along the high road to Learning, hands equipped with good stout switches heartily applied to his infant breech. Years later, establishing the future of three "poor children of the University," Villon remembers his whippings:

Et vueil qu'ilz soient informez
En meurs, quoy que couſte bature;
Chapperons auront enformez,
Et les poulces sur la sainture;
Humbles a toute creature;
Disans: Han? Quoy? Il n'en est rien!
Si diront gens, par adventure;
"Vecy enfans de lieu de bien!"

[I will that they be well grounded in good manners, whatever floggings it cost them; wearing their hoods well over the eyes, thumbs in the belt, and behaving politely to every one; saying "Eh? What? Don't mention it!" In this way it may be said of them, "Lord! Here are well-bred children."]

I do not suppose these ritual floggings were actually any worse than those enjoyed at any English Public School during the Victorian era. They were certainly not regarded as anything but normal and part of the curriculum. On bitter winter mornings in the Schools, with nothing on the ſtone floors but ſtraw, they may even have been welcome. The age at which the birch began to be applied was then, according to the *Livre des Proprietez des choses,* seven years.

Flogging was not the firſt ceremony on admission to the Faculty. Within a day or two of the entering of the new ſtudent's name in the University regiſters he was summoned, after a preliminary "simple" tonsuring, to one of the University churches, or his college chapel, and there received minor orders. This cuſtom laſted well over the Renaissance, and was essential. Orders up to the rank of sub-deacon have no sacerdotal significance, and the *clerc* who received them could marry if he went no further in the Church: in the meantime he was qualified to perform the duties of acolyte, doorkeeper, sacriſtan, or lećtor; and—what was important in University—became answerable for disciplinary purposes only to the ecclesiaſtical power. In noble and wealthy families there was a more definite privilege attaching to the *clerc's* tonsure: it made its wearer eligible, by birth and royal favour, to hold the nominal governorship of a religious house held in fief or endowed by his family. The divine Ronsard (as you remember) was by virtue of this cuſtom honorary Prior of St. Cosme-lez-Tours, in the Loire, where, after a life so full of beauty, letters, and high passion, he was carried to die in November 1585. To Villon the tonsure meant merely that if he were seized by the civil police anywhere in France the Bishop within whose jurisdiction the accident occurred could claim him and deal summarily with his case. If one thinks this was any advantage, one will think so only until we come, in the course of this history, to Thibault d'Aussigny, Bishop of Orleans, into whose hands the poet fell in the summer of 1461.

After admission to University Villon continued to live with Master Guillaume in his house in the cloister of St. Benoît. In every way this was advantageous. It relieved an old woman of the burden of supporting him (though it is likely that the chaplain had been assisting her for some years—the excellent man), it shielded the boy from contacts which the Paris streets were now beginning to afford him, it gave him a good home convenient to the Schools, and a governor, tutor, and foster-father in one. It is permissible to surmise that with the stirrings of adolescence came a desire to escape, when opportunity served, from the too watchful care of Master Guillaume: and since the *escholier's* familiar friend, a hardened young blackguard named Colin des Cayeulx, whose history we shall review directly, was the son of a locksmith of the quarter, it is not unlawful to assume that a skeleton key for the outer door sooner or later became one of young Villon's greater treasures.

The University curriculum I have already set forth. The *escholier* Villon may be regarded for the time being as attending vigorously, if more and more intermittently, to his books. By his eighteenth year, in March 1449, he had absorbed enough letters to be admitted a Bachelor. The Registers of the Faculty of Arts [12] give his name and *bourse* in that month and that year, under the rubric NOMINA BACCALARIANDORVM:

Franciscus de Moultcorbier parisius   .   . ij s.p.

I propose, before entering on the next phase, to turn aside for a moment to contemplate the sinister features and career of two of his dear friends, *Arcades ambo,* a couple of Mephistopheles to this

---

[12] Archives of University; *Registre des Procureurs de la Nation de France,* MS. I, fol. 97 v°.

eager Fauſt. To their influence may be attributed in a large degree the life led, at firſt no doubt secretly, but afterwards openly, by François Villon. Their names are Colin des Cayeulx and Regnier or René de Montigny.

Des Cayeulx was, as I have said, the son of a locksmith in the St. Benoît quarter. He seems to have been a friend of Villon since childhood, and probably sat with him in the early Schools. His father's choice of a craft Colin muſt have regarded as a direct interposition of Heaven on his behalf, and the elder des Cayeulx, looking up from his locks and keys, no doubt often perceived in the schoolboy's eyes a glint of something more than polite intereſt. Colin in truth ſtudied the business thoroughly: it was to become invaluable to him, and a little light pilfering of church alms-boxes and such elementary exercises showed him very early that he had a vocation. I would willingly compare him with the child Chopin, of whom M. Guy de Pourtalès wrote recently: *"On l'avait mis de très bonne heure devant le clavier et il y retournait tout seul, attiré par les touches. La musique lui arrachait des larmes, des cris. Elle devint tout de suite un mal nécessaire."* So I imagine the young des Cayeulx fingering the keys, ſtudying the intricacies of locks, practising with a kind of holy rage on all that fell under his notice, feeling, surely and slowly, his technique becoming daily more perfect, his fingers more supple. Judging himself at length qualified, in spite of his youth, to mix in the larger world with professional artiſts, he joined himself to the Brotherhood of the Coquille, whose corporation will come up for notice in due course. His department was burglary, sacred and secular. *"Larron, crocheteur, pilleur et sacrilège, être incorrigible,"* said the King's Procurator, describing him a little later. "Thief, picklock, pillager, guilty of sacrilege, incorrigible." In 1450, and again in 1452, the Bishop of Paris [13] claimed him from the secular arm for theft. In 1456 the Watch arrested him for another theft. In the same year he was concerned in the matter of robbing an Auguſtinian and took a principal part with Villon in the burglary at the College of Navarre that Christmas. He fled to Normandy then, was captured, escaped from the Bishop's prison

[13] Paris had no Archbishop till 1622.

78

at Bayeux, and picked the locks of the Archbishop's prison at Rouen. In the summer of 1460, operating in the neighbourhood of Senlis, he was caught red-handed by the officers of the Provost of Senlis in the church of St. Leu d'Esserent, in the Oise valley, handed over to the Bishop, and later conveyed under guard to the Conciergerie at Paris. In September two bishops, their lordships of Beauvais and of Senlis, contended for the pleasure of dealing with this hardened ruffian. The King's Procurator, Barbin, declared him, as we have seen, an incorrigible rogue, and claimed that he had thereby forfeited the privileges of a clerk and must be handled by the secular authority.[14] Sentence of death by hanging, "*a estre pendu et estranglé*," was passed on him, not, it seems, for the breaking into the church of St. Leu d'Esserent, but for a "frolic" (from the context robbery with violence on the highway, and also rape), at Rueil, between Paris and St. Germain, and another of the same sort at Montpipeau, three leagues from Meun-sur-Loire. It is to this double frolic, for which Colin was hanged in Paris on September 26, 1460, that Villon refers twice; first in his sombre Ballade of warning to the *enfans perduz*:

> *Se vous allez a Montpipeau*
> *Ou a Rueil, gardez la peau:*
> *Car, pour s'esbatre en ces deux lieux,*
> *Cuidant que vaulsist le rappeau,*
> *La perdit Colin de Cayeulx;*

[If you go to Montpipeau, or to Rueil, take care of your skin; for Colin des Cayeulx lost his through frolicking in both places, thinking an appeal [*i.e.* to the ecclesiastical power if caught] was worth it.]

and once more in the second Ballade of the Jargon:

> *Coquillars, arvans a Ruel*
> *Men ys vous chante que gardez*
> *Que n'y laissez & corps & pel,*
> *Com fist Colin de l'Escailler.*

[Coquillards, if you go to Rueil,[15] listen to this song—take care you don't leave your skins there, as did Colin des Cayeulx.]

[14] Archives of Parliament (X²ᵃ 28, Sept. 23, 1460).
[15] The phrase "to go to Rueil" seems also to have had a figurative meaning: to go on the highway, to rob with violence. Similarly "to go to Montpipeau" = to steal by sharping.

And that was the end of this expert, to whose skill such tribute was paid during the interrogatory by the Officiality of Paris of Master Guy Tabarie in July 1458, following the College of Navarre affair. The unfortunate Tabarie, pressed on the question of how the College was entered, whether the locks were picked or removed bodily, answered that he heard and saw nothing,

"dicit tamen quod ipse audivit quod dictus des Cahyeus est fortis operator crochetorum."

[He says nevertheless that he has heard that the said des Cayeulx is a powerful operator of picklocks.]

"A powerful operator of picklocks." It may stand for the epitaph of Colin des Cayeulx.

His friend, and Villon's, Regnier de Montigny, was a better born, more versatile, more reckless blackguard. His family was honourable, holding fiefs in the neighbourhood of Paris. He was born at Bourges in 1429. His father, Jehan de Montigny, followed the Dauphin's fortunes and entered Paris with him in 1437, receiving for his service the post of Royal Pantler. Regnier's first brush with the police occurred on a night in August 1452, when he attacked and thrashed, in company with two presumed Coquillards, a couple of Sergeants outside the *"ostel de la Grosse Margot."* [16] The Provost had him banished from Paris, and within a brief space he had been clapped into prison first at Rouen, then at Tours, then at Bordeaux. He joined the Coquille during these wanderings. At Poitiers he cheated a draper out of twenty crowns, and returning to Paris, took up as a profession the game of *Marelle* —a cross between hopscotch and halma, I believe, rich with opportunities of trickery—and was soon pursued for swindling. He was next implicated in a murder committed in a tavern by the churchyard of St. Jean-en-Grève: *meutre commis en la personne de Thevenin Pensete en l'ostel de Moton ou Cimitiere Saint Jehan en Grève.* This is the incident which gave Stevenson the central idea for the story called "A Lodging for the Night." The *ostel de Mouton*, the

[16] Not necessarily the same house as that celebrated by Villon in the Ballade. The sign of *la Grosse Margot* seems to have been common to one type of house in Paris.

Sheep tavern, is moſt likely the one to which Villon pleasantly alludes in the *Petit Testament*:

> *Item, a Jehan Trouvé, bouchier,*
> *Laisse* le Mouton *franc et tendre,*

> [*Item,* I leave to Jehan Trouvé, butcher, the fresh and tender *Sheep.*]

and was no doubt the headquarters of a criminal gang. Montigny's luck was good, and he got off with a letter of remission.[17] In 1455 he sold what was probably the laſt remaining fief belonging to his family—his father had died long ago, leaving a widow and three young children in what amounted to poverty—and got through the money within a short time. In 1457 he took up sacrilege, operating with a gang in Paris: the booty included a pair of silver cruets from the hospital church of the Quinze-Vingts, near the Louvre, and a chalice and a Book of Hours from St. Jean-en-Grève. For this series he was fairly soon arreſted, shoved once more into the Châtelet, and once more formally claimed, in Auguſt 1457, by the Bishop: but this time his lordship's claim, proffered no doubt languidly, was challenged. Montigny's record was too black, and the civil power had decided to finish with him. He was condemned to death. He appealed at once to Parliament, and secured, but only through the intercession of his mother and his family's honourable name, another letter of remission. Nevertheless Juſtice was determined that Regnier de Montigny should not slide through its fingers again. On a technical flaw in his *dossier* the King's procurator, after much long-drawn argument, succeeded in getting the remission annulled. Regnier (or René) de Montigny was hanged on the 9th of September in the same year at Montigny, the gibbet near St. Laurent.[18]

His epitaph is written by his friend Villon, with a whoop, in the second Ballade of the Jargon, following des Cayeulx's:

> *Montigny y fut, par exemple,*
> *Bien attaché au halle-grup,*

[17] Chancellery Regiſter, JJ 189 (199, fol. 96 v).
[18] Archives of Parliament (X²ᵃ 25, Aug. 21, 1452; and 28, Aug. 24, Sept. 10 and 12, 1457).

Et y jargonna-t-il le tremple,
Dont l'amboureux luy rompt le suc.

[Montigny, for example, was well attached to the Wooden Widow, and thereby had an end soon put to his song by Jack Ketch.]

"The sweet war-man is dead and rotten; sweet chucks, beat not the bones of the buried: when he breathed, he was a man." Had he lived in our time he might have been a Prince of International Finance, for he had all the qualities.

Two other companions of Villon's youth perhaps deserve a moment's notice. They are mentioned by him in both Testaments and were therefore (though of a humbler rank in the hierarchy of truands) his intimates: Jehan le Loup and Casin Cholet.

Jehan, surnamed the Wolf, was a bargee and waterman employed by the Municipality of Paris towards 1456 to dredge and weed the moats and ditches of the city: an occupation affording him almost mechanically and as a perquisite the snapping up by night of odd ducks and geese from the flocks which swam around the moats and belonged for the most part to small farmers outside the walls and certain corporate bodies. The Wolf's dexterity at snitching ducks as he paddled to and fro in his dredging-boat was the admiration of all the riverside taverns. Late in 1456 he was ordered to pay a fine to the Municipality: it is not known for what misdemeanour. Later still he became a sergeant of the Châtelet.

His companion and assistant in duck-stealing, Casin Cholet, had a more *mouvementé* career. By profession he was a wine-cooper. He is believed to have been somehow implicated in the College of Navarre burglary, but this is not clear. Guy Tabarie, in his examination by the Bishop's officers, to which we shall come in due course, mentions an obscure quarrel with Cholet in which blows were struck, and this may have proceeded from the affair. Cholet, nevertheless, was apparently not called to account for any share in the burglary, and a few years later became, like his friend, a *sergent à verge* of the Châtelet—not a rare metamorphosis at that time, nor one involving much change of character. Notoriety came to him at last on August 14, 1465, when he was thrust into prison, despoiled of his office, and ordered to be whipped at all the cross-roads of Paris on the sufficiently grave charge of raising a false alarm and spreading disorder among the populace by announcing the entry into Paris of the Burgundians, who then lay before the walls under Charles the Rash. Cholet was no doubt in Burgundian pay, and had also private plunder in his eye. The facts are preserved in the *Chronique scandaleuse* of Jehan de Roye, notary of the Châtelet, together with the words of his most severe Majesty Louis XI., who observed to the tormentor as Cholet was led forth to be whipped: *"Battez fort et n'espargnez pas ce paillart, car il a bien pis desservy."* * With these discomfortable words to speed him Casin Cholet disappears from history.

Villon, who had often accompanied the Wolf and Cholet on night expeditions around the moats, bequeaths them in the *Petit Testament* a duck, "taken late, as we used, by the walls," together with a long tabard to conceal the spoil from the eyes of the Watch. In the *Grant Testament* he bequeaths them a setter-dog for the same purpose, and again *"ung long tabart & bien cachant."* Neither was professionally of the class of de Montigny and des Cayeulx. They were merely routine sneak-thieves of no distinction, though well-meaning and no doubt respectful to their betters. The ranks of Paris night-birds and truands contained many such characters, industrious but unskilled, flitting nightly to and fro between their manor of Pickt-hatch—the ruined manor of Bicestre, or Nijon, or the Tower of Billy,[19] the riverside, and the suburbs. Let not Ambition mock their useful toil, their homely joys, their destiny obscure.

With the greater part of these, the rank and file, Villon can hardly have been on any but nodding terms. His friends were the silks.

*[Flog this scoundrel soundly, and do not spare him. He has deserved a great deal more.]

[19] Notorious rookeries. Bicestre, Vicestre, or Bicêtre is the French equivalent for Winchester. The manor of Bicestre, near Gentilly, occupied in the thirteenth century by John Bishop of Winchester, burned and left in ruins during the civil wars of Charles VI.'s reign, was now a retreat for rascals of every kind. The Tower of Billy bordered the river on the right bank, between the Rue du Fauconnier and the Rue St. Paul, on the present Quai des Célestins. Nijon or Nygeon was a district outside the walls between Chaillot and Passy, near the site of the Trocadero to-day. Its manor, presumably ruined at this period, had belonged to the Dukes of Brittany.

Louons noſtre hoſtel,
Bibimus satis,
Et l'hoste lequel
Nos pavit gratis,
Et sans reschigner,
Onerans mensas
De mets delicats.

Il nous ayme bien,
Hoc patet nobis,
Car son meilleur vin
Deprompsit cadis:
Et nous en a faict
Usque ad oras
Remplir nos hanaps!
From the Songs of Olivier Basselin
of the Val de Vire.

[Praise we our tavern, where we drank our fill, and our hoſt, who fed us for nothing, loading his table, without a cross look, with delicate dishes!

He loves us greatly, as we perceive; for he poured the beſt of his wine from the jugs, and made us fill our tankards with it, even to the brim!]

Ir I have set a couple of ſtaves of a sardonic tavern-song at the head of this section it is because we are now upon the threshold of the period in Villon's life in which hot blood, and the tavern, and the kisses of harlots possess his careless youth, before Melancholy and old Remorse claim him for their own, while ginger is ſtill sweet and fiery in the mouth.

Between the conjectural year 1443, when he entered the University a child, and the summer of 1452, when it is known that he was admitted a Maſter of Arts during the procuratorship of Maſter Jehan de Conflans, whose pupil he had been, Villon has no hiſtory. Revolving in his sad mind nine years later this part of his life, he himself sums it up in one verse:

Hé! Dieu, se j'eusse eſtudié
Ou temps de ma jeunesse folle,

Et a bonnes meurs dedié
J'eusse maison et couche molle.
Mais quoy? je fuyoie l'escolle,
Comme fait le mauvais enfant . . .
En escripvant ceste parolle,
A peu que le cuer ne me fent.

[Dear God! had I but heeded my books in the days of my flaming youth, and given some thought to good conduct, I might have had my own house, and a soft bed to lie in! But Lord! I fled the Schools like a naughty child. . . . As I write this my heart is like to break.]

Good Master de Villon's anxieties had obviously begun some time before his charge obtained his Master's licence. It is permissible to surmise that the decline in the boy's character was fairly rapid. A more accustomed ease of manipulation of the skeleton key; a growing skill in treading softly in the dead of night over creaking floorboards; a keener, more careless zest in lying; a developing tendency to take risks in exit and entrance; a new shiftiness, possibly, in the eye; an increasing impatience of reprimand; a Cockney impudence of carriage and manner—these, I should say, illustrated a change in the youth François Villon which in due time became perceptible even to the old priest his guardian. Obviously, long winter evenings in the house of the cloister of St. Benoît must have become in time intolerable to a youth of Villon's temperament. I see him sitting by the hearth, yawning over Ælius Donatus or Aristotle's *Rhetoric*, watching Master Guillaume under his eyebrows as the old man chuckles and drones over his cup of hot wine with Jehan Flastrier the barber-surgeon: before the manuscript page, with its crabbed characters and cumbrous initials, rises a girl's flushed and laughing face, and a spasm of desire shakes the youth's spare body. God! Will the old man never go to bed? At length Master Guillaume rises, and takes his candle, and lights Master Flastrier to the door, and coughing a little in the nip of the night air, laboriously closes, locks, and bars the oak door behind him; and returns, recommending sleep to the pale student by the fire; and at last, at last, laying his kind hand a moment on the boy's head, takes his candle from the table and slowly ascends the stairs. Villon listens. The door of Master Guillaume's room creaks to. Give him

85

half an hour to go to sleep, say: an extra ten minutes to make sure. In three-quarters Guillemette will be laughing on his knee: he shivers again at the sudden sting and leap of his blood. He goes up slowly to his room, closing his door with careful ostentation. He sits on his bed, counting the minutes. An occasional sigh, a wheeze from the adjoining chamber. The house is still. He lingers behind his door, listening, and going to his bed again, rumples the covering expertly and strews a book or two on the floor by the bed-head. Then, slipping off his shoes, he goes, treading like a cat, down the stairs again, noiselessly unbars the door, deftly inserts his master-key in the well-oiled lock, and has slipped across the road to the *Mule,* where Montigny and Cayeulx are waiting, before the old man upstairs has been asleep ten minutes.

Hahay! Those nights at the *Mule,* and the *Pomme de Pin,* and the *Grant Godet,* and the *Homme Armé,* and the *Espée de Bois*! They resembled in some degree the Mermaid nights, for there would be a dash of University and lettered company there, both drunk and sober, and a thick voice heard suddenly bawling and banging out with a tankard the cadence of *Namque, fatebor enim, dum me Galatea tenebat,* or choking under the table in the middle of a line from the *Metamorphoses,* would be no more uncommon there than sudden exchanges

> So nimble, and so full of subtle flame,
> As if that every one from whence they came
> Had meant to put his whole wit in a jest.

But in the main, I think, the assembly at the taverns of Villon's choice would be well leavened by the kind of company by whom Glutton in our great English poem is made so welcome.

Sisse the sempstress	sat on the bench,
Watte the warrener	and his wife, drunk,
Tom the tinker	and two of his knaves,
Hick the hackneyman,	and Hugh the needler,
Clarice of Cock's Lane,	the clerk of the church,
Sir Pierce of Pridie,	and Purnel of Flaunders,
An hayward and an heremyte,	the hangman of Tyburn,
Darew the Dyker	with a dozen hirelots,
Of porters and pickpurses	and pylede tooth-drawers,

A rybibour and a ratoner, a raker and his knave,
A reaper and a redingking, and Rose the disher,
Godfrey the garlic-monger, and Griffyn the Welchman,
Gave Glutton with glad cheer good ale to hansel.

A ribald, roaring company, ftoically endured by the furred burgesses in their corner, sipping their mulled wine and deploring the new river-dues and the decadence of the Parloir aux Bourgeois. Dawn, making livid the panes of thick glass or oiled linen, would find the survivors still boozily at it, among guttering rushlights and overturned cups and joint-ftools, the drowsy *propos des beuveurs* mingling sweetly with the rhythmic snoring of the conquered, asleep where they fell. A tavern was a tavern then.

Such escapades became for Villon in course of time, it is evident, a matter of routine. Then there muft have come inevitably the day when, slipping into the house in the dawn after a night of debauchery and riot, he found himself face to face with Mafter Guillaume de Villon, about to leave to say his early Mass in St. Benoît. As plainly as if the scene were before me I see the aftonishment on the face of Mafter Guillaume, changing swiftly to anger. I hear the sharp queftions, and see the hangdog face of Villon pale, and then flush again. I hear his answers, firft sheepish, then impudent. I see him slink up to his room as Mafter Guillaume passes out, a set grimness masking the alarm, and bewilderment, and pain of the old man's heart. He will pause and fumble more than once in saying his Mass this morning, and the thick black words in the missal will betray a surprising tendency to dance.[1]

But in time, as the night flittings of the prodigal became regular and unashamed, I think Mafter Guillaume sighed and returned to his books, realising the uselessness of remonftrance, pleading, or even fury. He prayed for the lad, no doubt, in the quaint medieval fashion. He gave him shelter, and care when he returned, slinking back to hide while some danger blew over. He paid good money out of his modeft means to bail and ransom him, and probably killed a modeft fatted calf when the wanderer knocked at the Red Door in the homing intervals of his hunted life.

[1] M. Francis Carco, in a recent novel written around Villon, has imagined this scene with effect.

87

I think Master Guillaume de Villon very much resembled what (in the superstitious ages) was called a saint.

We are now on hard level ground, with plain going before us. Between the second of May and the twenty-sixth of August 1452, in the Procuratorship of Jehan de Conflans, François de Montcorbier was admitted successively Licentiate and Master of Arts, in the twenty-first year of his age. His entry, in the same Register of the Faculty as before, runs, under the rubric *Sequitur nomen cujusdam licenciati:* *

> *Dominus Franciscus de Montcorbier de Parisiis,*
> *cujus bursa ij s.p.*†

And beneath, under the larger rubric SEQUUNTUR NOMINA ILLORUM QUI INCEPERUNT SUB PRESENTI PROCURATORIA: ‡

> *Dominus Franciscus de Montcorbier de Parisiis incepturus*
> *sub magistro de Conflans, tunc procuratore . . .   ij s.*¶

The scholarship of Dom. François de Montcorbier, such as it was, is reflected for the most part in his two Testaments. He is familiar with Ovid and on terms with the *Organon* of Aristotle (and Averroes' *Commentaries*), Vergil (especially the *Bucolics*), Cato, Macrobius, Valerius, Maximus, Priscian, Porphyry's *Introductions*, and Ælius Donatus the grammarian; in a greater or less degree with Juvenal, Martial, and Boetius. From ancient history he cites the names of Hector, Troilus, Alexander, Cæsar, Hannibal, Pompey, Scipio, and Lucretia. He knew too, it seems, the *Policraticus* of John of Salisbury, from which he took the name of the pirate Diomedes in the anecdote of verses xvii-xx of the *Grant Testament*. He also had read in divers Latin chronicles, notably in the *Gesta Pontificum Cenomannensium*, whence he quarried the

---

*[Here follows the name of a certain licentiate.]

†[Dom. François de Montcorbier, of Paris, whose burse is two sols Parisis.]

‡[Here follow the names of those who began in the present Procuratorship:]

¶[Dom. François de Montcorbier, of Paris, began under the rule of Master de Conflans, then Procurator: 2 sols Parisis.]

splendid name of Haremburgis, heiress of the Maine, for insertion in the Ballade of Dead Ladies: *Aremburgis filia comitis Heliæ, quam paterno jure comitatus Cenomannensis contingebat.* The Chansons de Geste he knew also, at least in part; probably the Song of Roland in particular, for he refers (in a lewd jest) to Ogier le Danois, one of the outstanding figures of the Song. But he may equally have got Ogier out of one of the other epics of the Carolingian cycle, for the hero appears in many of them. He certainly knew intimately Jehan Clopinel de Meung's continuation of Guillaume de Lorris' vast *Roman de la Rose,* and the thirteenth-century *Liber Lamentationum* of Matheolus, whether in the original or in its translation by Jehan le Fevre, which he quotes. He takes from the Bible (then very much read) many Old Testament names: Noë, Mathusalem, Job, David, Ammon, Lot, Absalom, Holophernes, Judith, Jacob, Samson, Nabuchadonosor, and more; citing also Psalms xci. and cviii., the Book of Ecclesiastes, and the Book of Job. From the New Testament he cites St. John the Baptist, St. Mary Magdalene, Lazarus, Judas, Herod, Malchus, and the governor (*architriclinus*) of the marriage-feast at Cana. The saints he mentions by name are few: St. Dominic, St. Christopher, St. George, St. Stephen, St. Antony, St. Victor, St. Martial, and St. Mary of Egypt. In the matter of contemporary history he knew something of the dispute between the Mendicant Orders and the seculars over a question of parochial privilege which a Bull of Calixtus III. settled about 1456; the Hussite heresy, which he mentions in the minor *Ballade des Menus Propos,*

Je congnois la faulte des Boesmes,

[I know the error of the Bohemians.]

and which had brought about civil war in Bohemia between 1415 and 1434; the ruin of the great banker Jacques Cœur, silversmith to Charles VII., in 1453; the miracle of St. Joan; and the passing of the dozen princes, at home and abroad, whom he celebrates in the Ballade of Dead Lords. Beyond all this he had sufficient of arithmetic, music, geometry, and astronomy to satisfy the examiners in Arts. The entry concerning the Master's degree is there to show it Exhibit A.

Exhibit B will be put in (as the legal jargon goes) immediately. It is the official report of the action brought by the University of Paris against the Provost, following the riots over the *Pet-au-Deable* and occupying the fourth, fifth, seventh, and fourteenth of June 1453. There is one more exhibit to follow, rounding off the whole and giving a compact, coloured, and veritable picture of Villon's life at this period. This, Exhibit C, is the collection of raffish poems called the *Repues Franches*, of which (though they appeared long after his disappearance) Villon is the hero.

On Monday, the fourth of June 1453, an action [2] was begun before the Court of Parliament (Marle, President), as between the Rector and the University of Paris, complainants, and Messire Robert d'Estouteville, *chevalier*, Provost of Paris, his Criminal Lieutenant Master Jehan Bezon, the Châtelet-Procurator Master Jehan Catin, and eleven Sergeants and officials of the Provost, all defendants. For University, Master Jehan Luillier. For the defence, Master Estienne le Fevre and Master de Poupaincourt. For the King's Procurator, Master Simon. Since the evidence turns on events which took place between 1451 and 1452, but had their root in troubles of 1444, and even earlier, I judge it convenient to compile from the documents a consecutive narrative.

It requires no great imagination to believe that the relations between the brawling, turbulent State of University, arrogant in privilege and free of the civil authority, and the Provosts of Paris, had always been strained. In this very case the King's Procurator, judiciously reviewing the past, will refer as far back as the reign of *monseigneur Saint Loys*, when University was in its infancy. There had been rich trouble in 1229 between the students and the taverners of the Bourg St. Marcel. In 1281 the Picard students and the English had bloody disagreements. In 1304, as we have already seen, a Provost hanged a student after the sketchiest of trials, and was forced to grovel. In 1407, again, the Provost Guillaume de Tignonville, having hanged two students charged with a murder—once more after a quick trial—was compelled by the outcry of University, the lay power bowing before the storm, to take down

[2] Archives of Parliament, X²ᵃ 25 (June 4-14, 1453).

their bodies from the gibbet, kiss their dead mouths, and have them solemnly interred in the church of the Mathurins in the Rue St. Jacques. The inscription on their tomb recounted all this, and was of course familiar to Villon and his friends. It was in 1444, however, that the actual present troubles began. In that year the Rector, having refused on principle to pay a tax, alleged that he (and University in his person) had been grossly insulted by the tax authorities. He retaliated by putting into operation the powers given him by Statutes of 1228 and 1244 and a Papal Bull of 1231, and suspended all lectures in University and all sermons in the churches of Paris from the fourth of September till Passion Sunday, the fourth of March 1445. The lay power replied with vigour by seizing and imprisoning a Master of Arts and certain students who had made a demonstration. University demanded that they should be handed over. The lay power, backed by Charles vii., refused, and the King had the prisoners brought before Parliament and punished, at the same time threatening University (as he will do again in 1454) with severe measures if the ban on lectures and sermons were not lifted. The situation became serious, the irresistible force having apparently met the immovable body. Some adjustment was obviously necessary, and the Papal Legate, Cardinal Guillaume d'Estouteville, of the same great Norman family as the Provost Robert, stepped into the breach at the order of Nicolas v. The difficulties took some time to adjust, and it was not till the first of June 1452, at the moment when Villon was finishing his studies at the Faculty of Arts, that the arbitration and University reforms drawn up by the Legate were accepted by both parties.

University, it is interesting to observe, by no means emerges unscathed from the Legate's handling. The Doctors of Theology were ordered to look with more care to their dress and behaviour, and to diminish the expense of the ceremonial dinners with which new graduates were expected to honour them. The Masters of Colleges were severely scourged for overcharging, for exacting too high examination fees, and for otherwise taking advantage of their charge. Some of the reforms in pedagogy I have already indicated.

University accepted this treaty, but the students did not; and a little time before the actual signing of the document by both parties the intermittent skirmishing with the lay authorities, which had gone on more or less lackadaisically, flamed suddenly into a joyous campaign. There stood outside the house of the rich widow of a notary of Charles vi., Mademoiselle de Bruyères,[3] by the church of St. Jean-en-Grève, a fixed stone of immense size, called popularly the *Pet-au-Deable*. It had stood there from time immemorial as a boundary mark, and may have been prehistoric. On a day late in 1451 the students, contemplating this stone, were visited with the admirable idea of uprooting it, dragging it in a triumphal procession across the bridges to the University quarter, and setting it up again on the Mont St. Hilaire, behind the Place Maubert, in the heart of their own territory. This they accordingly did, in an uproarious ceremonial. Mademoiselle de Bruyères, perceiving next day that the stone which was the glory of her house had been ravished, raised a shrill cry and waddled at once across to the authorities with a complaint. Accordingly, within a day or two the King's officers appeared on the Mont St. Hilaire, scattered the dancing crowd of students round the *Pet-au-Deable*, and laboriously carted the great stone for security's sake to the Palais Royal, where it was placed in the courtyard. Within the week a surging mob of *escholiers*, reinforced by a battalion of the law-clerks of the Basoche, as reckless featherheads as they, invaded the Royal precinct, lugged the *Pet-au-Deable* away, and dragged it back to the Mont St. Hilaire.

I continue with part of the evidence of the Criminal Lieutenant Jehan Bezon, at the second day's hearing. He had on the fifteenth of November 1451 been ordered by Parliament to inquire into this affair.

Derechief ont esté querir à l'ostel de ladite damoiselle une autre pierre qu'elle avoit fait mettre, l'ont nommée la Vesse, ont atachié à grosses bandes de fer & par plastre ladite grosse pierre au mont Sainte Geneviesve & toutes les nuytz y ont fait danses à fleutes & à bedons. L'autre pierre ont ataché au mont Saint-Hilaire & sur elle ont apporté & mis une autre pierre longue & aux passans, & potissime *aux officiers du Roy, ont fait sermens de garder les privileges de la Vesse, & à la grosse pierre ont baillié ung chapeau tous les dimenches & autres festes. Et quant le prevost & lui y alèrent pour l'avoir, avoit ung chapeau de romarin.*

[3] At this time *Madamoyselle* was used for single and married women of status indifferently.

92

[They then went in search of another stone that the said lady had placed by her house, named it the Vesse, and fixed it by means of thick bands of iron and plaster to the Mont St. Geneviève, and danced round it every night to the sound of flutes and drums. The other stone they fixed on the Mont St. Hilaire and placed upon it another long stone, and forced all passers-by (and especially the King's officers) to swear to preserve the privileges of the Vesse. And for the big stone they provided every Sunday and feast-day a hat: and when the witness and the Provost went to take possession of the stone it had on it a wreath of rosemary.]

It seems a harmless sort of rag, and except for Mademoiselle de Bruyères, twice bereft of her ſtone, nobody seems a penny the worse. The nightly ceremonial dance to the music of flutes and drums and the crown of rosemary are, in addition, in rather graceful contraſt to the egg-and-flour ruſticities of our own day. But this was not the only charge againſt the ſtudents. I resume with Maſter Jehan Bezon. We are now in the year 1452.

Dit que plusieurs escholiers ont fait plusiers grans excés, comme ont prins & rompu de nuyt en grant tumulte les enseignes pendans es hoſtelz de ceſte ville, en criant en ce faisant: "Tuez, tuez," pour ce que gens ouvroient leurs feneſtres pour veoir que c'eſtoit. Ont aussi oſté les crochez des bouchiers de Sainte Geneviesve, ont emblé poules à Saint-Germain-des-Prés, ont prins par force une jeune femme à Vanves. . . . Ont eſté es Hales pour avoir la Truie qui file, *& pour ce comme on dit que l'eschele eſtoit trop courte, l'escholier qui montoit en icelle pour avoir ladite* Truie *cheut à terre, dont il eſt mort, ainsi que on dit.*

[Deposes, that a large number of ſtudents have created great diſturbances, for example by stealing and breaking up at nights with great noise the signs hanging outside houses of this town, at the same time crying "Kill, kill!" in order that citizens should open their windows to see what was happening. They have also stolen hooks from the butchers of St. Geneviève and abſtracted fowls from St. Germain-des-Prés, and have taken away by force a young woman at Vanves. . . . Also, they proceeded to the Halles to take the sign of the *Spinning Sow,* but as the ladder, they say, was too short the ſtudent who climbed it to take the aforesaid *Sow* fell to the ground and was killed, as it appears.]

Here we perceive the *escholiers* joining hands with the Mohocks and Tityre Tus of Auguſtan nights in London; though it may be observed in passing that where the medieval was content with noisy howling and ſtealing of tavern signs, butcher's hooks, and fowls from the Abbey—I pass over the alleged carrying off of the young woman of Vanves, who, it appears later, put up no very virginal resistance to her ravishers—the night bully of the Age of Reason practised more sadistic sports.

We begin now to perceive where Villon gets some of his jokes for the *Petit Testament*. Master Jehan Bezon is still speaking:

Pour lesquelles choses [the Lieutenant is referring particularly to the forcible swearing ceremony of the Vesse] *qui sont detestables, & la clameur du peuple qui en estoit grandes, & que les escholiers y pululoient, & aussi pour ce qu'ilz s'estoient ventez d'avoir* le Serf *pour faire le mariage de* la Truie *& de* l'Ours, *aussi* le Papegault *pour le donner à* la Truie *quant elle seroit mariée,* le prevost, *lui qui parle, & autres examinateurs & sergens alerent au mont Saincte Geneviesve pour avoir lesdites pierre & enseignes.*

[For which acts, which are detestable, and on account of the outcry of the public, because also the students were swarming and were heard to boast that they had taken the *Stag* to marry the *Sow* to the *Bear,* with the *Popinjay* to give to the *Sow* when she was married, the Provost, the witness, and divers officials and sergeants proceeded to the Mont St. Geneviève to take possession of the said stone and signs.]

The fun, therefore, consisted in tearing down house and tavern signs at night with howls and roars, and making a fantastic marriage between the *Spinning Sow* of the Halles and the *Bear,* who lived at an important house near the Porte Baudoyer; the ceremony being performed by the *Stag,* with the *Popinjay* assisting. There is a very popular facetious prose piece of this period called the *Mariage des Quatre Filz Aymon,*[4] in which a number of Paris tavern signs figured among the wedding guests of the four bridegrooms: it is obvious that the students took their inspiration from this. In all these scenes, it is incontestable, François Villon took a part. Even if he had not left a mocking bequest to Mlle. de Bruyères and written the *Rommant du Pet-au-Deable* to glorify himself and his comrades and the whole affair, there is enough evidence in the Testaments alone.

It was this last pleasantry of the tavern signs which decided Robert d'Estouteville. After the months of nightly roaring and rioting, the thefts, the complaints of fat burghers trembling at their

[4] Its full title is: *L'Esbatement du mariaige des IIII Filz Hemon ou les enseignes de plusieurs hostels de la ville de Paris sont nommez.*

windows, the open defiance of the *Pet-au-Deable* affair, the brawling and insolence of the *escholiers*, it ſtrained too far his hitherto
admirable lenience. He resolved to aɕt. The Criminal Lieutenant,
whose evidence is so painſtaking, ſtates that on the morning before
the Provoſt's officers proceeded to remove the trophies of the Mont
St. Geneviève certain ſtudents by the church of St. Laurent in the
Rue St. Denis advised them not to go, saying they would only get
their heads bashed. The Provoſt nevertheless sent his men next
day. The great ſtone of the *Pet-au-Deable* was loaded on a cart and
taken away. The Criminal Lieutenant, after taking a morning cup
near by, then went to the *oſtel de St. Etienne*, where behind barred
doors were certain defiant persons with the ſtolen signs and butchers' hooks, and also with a little cannon, *cum maximis gladiis*.
But these laſt two items are doubtful.

From this inſtant trouble begins. It was the feaſt of St. Nicolas,
the sixth of December 1452. The Provoſt seems to have let his men
get completely out of hand, and they lost their heads, as the police
often do; and there is naturally conflicɕt between the University and
the police evidence. Counsel for University, beginning with that
solemn rehearsal of the dignities and privileges of University which
I have quoted elsewhere, and passing on to remind the Provoſt of
his oath, regularly renewed, to guard the same, and to ensure their
being guarded by his police and by the citizens of Paris, proceeds
to pile up a fairly heavy indiɕtment. The Sergeants began by
huſtling some numbers of ſtudents roughly and *indifferenter*: they
then broke into a house at the sign of St. Eſtienne, belonging to a
prieſt named Andry Bresquier (then away saying Mass for his
Nation in St. Julien-le-Pauvre), and wrecked and looted it at the
Lieutenant's orders: "*Rompez tout, prenez tout, & se aucun rebelle,
tuez tout.*" * Having sacked this house and carried off beds, bed-
apparel, books, money, clothing, plate, and other valuables, they
broke immediately into another house at the sign of St. Nicolas,
smashing windows and duors and drinking all the wine they could
find there: they next entered the hoſtel of the Collège du Coquerel,
by St. Hilaire, and finding a barred door, behind which a professor,

*[Smash down everything, take everything, and if anyone resiſts, kill
them all.]

95

Mafter Darian, *notable homme*, was presumably delivering a lecture, battered it in, threatened the mafter, and carried off forty of his pupils, deriding, menacing, and roughly handling them, and openly insulting the University in its own ftreets, one Sergeant *par derision* wearing a ftudent's gown.

It is not to be thought that University would take this lying down. After long and mature deliberation in full Sorbonne a procession issued on the ninth of May 1453 from University, headed by the Rector, composed of the Doctors and mafters of colleges and eight hundred ftudents, walking unarmed and orderly eight by eight, and proceeded across the river to wait on the Provoft in his great beautiful house, with the court and gardens round it, in the Rue de Jouy, near the Celeftines. The spokesman for University, Mafter Jehan Hue, Doctor in Theology, here addressed the Provoft soberly and at some length from the text *Omnia fiant ordinata in vobis,* placing before him the demand of University that its forty prisoners should be handed over to the proper tribunal. The Provoft could not but accede to this juft requeft. The academic procession, returning from the Provoft's house along the narrow Rue de Jouy, met the head of an advancing body of Sergeants under one Henry le Fevre: [5] all these no doubt flushed with insolence and ripe for blood. There was some inevitable joftling. Henry le Fevre cried out suddenly in a passion, "Help, in the King's name, help! Kill them!" and at once (says University counsel) his men whipped out their swords, daggers, and axes. The unarmed *escholiers* fled in terror in every direction, hiding where they might. One of them, Raymond de Mauregart, a youthful Mafter of Arts, was ftruck down and killed, and another wounded to death. The Sergeants hotly pursued the flying ftudents, throwing chains across the ftreets to prevent their escape, ftabbing and beating them, and hunting them from their temporary hiding-places. The citizens prudently banged and barred their doors againft the fugitives. The police had, in fact, gone completely mad, and the Rector himself twice by the mereft chance escaped being murdered.

Charpentier [this is the presumed slayer of Raymond de Mauregart] *non content mit la main au recteur, tenant la dague en la main, en regniant Dieu*

[5] One of the principal defendants.

96

qu'il le menrroit vers lc prevoſt, & avec luy eſtoient bien xxx autres. Le
reĉteur luy diſt qu'il avoit eſté vers le prevoſt & eſtoit content de luy, & le
seigneur du Heaulme qui survint, deſtourna le reĉteur & le convoya & ainsy
qu'il aloit en la rue de la Vennerie, ung nommé Colet venoit de la Cloueterie
aiaint son arc, qui disoit que les escholiers s'efforçoient rompre l'uis du prevoſt,
& euſt frapé le reĉteur se ung homme ne l'euſt deſtourné.

[Charpentier, not content with this, laid his hand on the Reĉtor, holding
his dagger in the other, and swearing by God that he would drag him to the
Provoſt; and with him were quite thirty others. The Reĉtor said to him that
he had seen the Provoſt and was content, and the Seigneur du Heaulme, intervening, turned the Reĉtor aside and set him on his way: and as he went
along the Rue de la Vennerie one named Colet came from the Cloueterie
holding his arbaleſt and saying the ſtudents had tried to break in the Provoſt's
door; and he would have ſtruck the Reĉtor had not some one turned the
blow.]

Another aĉt of the police for which University called for
salutary punishment was the beating and ſtabbing of Maſter Pierre
Quoque, canon of St. Jean-le-Rond, who, having the misfortune
to find himself abroad in the Sergeant's path that day, was chased,
trampled on, ſtabbed, and flung into the kennel. On taking refuge
in a harness-maker's shop he was driven out again by a number of
the lower bourgeoisie, who are always on the side of the big battalions. Reeling into a barber's shop, Maſter Pierre found other fugitives hiding in corn-bins and under beds: but the barber could not
dress his wounds, and the unhappy prieſt, after fainting away under
a ſtall, at laſt dragged himself into another barber's shop and was
bandaged.

I have given all this evidence at length for its vividness. University demanded in reparation the following sentences againſt all
the defendants except the Provoſt, who did not appear, being confined to his house with a fever. They were firſtly to proceed to a
place appointed and there, kneeling with bare feet, beltless and
hatless, each holding a lighted wax torch of four livres, humbly and
in a loud voice to confess and cry mercy and pardon of the King,
his juſtice, and University. The defendant Sergeants, and especially
those proved guilty of complicity in murder, were then to be
assembled, each with a halter round his neck, and taken in a cart
to make this same *amende* in the presence of the people before the

97

Châtelet, the Port Baudoyer, and St. Bernard's church: the Criminal Lieutenant to make his apology alone before the Châtelet and also, seeing his responsibility, in the centre of University. The rest of the sentences contained the provision of a cross and a lighted lamp at the Port Baudoyer, the foundation of four chantry chapels, each of twenty livres, and finally the payment to University of six thousand livres damages, and to the Rector two thousand. To the parents of the murdered boy Raymond de Mauregart there was to be made a public *amende*, with the foundation of a chantry of a hundred livres, and two thousand crowns damages. The whole under pain of *prinse & imprisonnement de leurs corps.**

We need not dwell at length on the defense, for it rings familiar: the mild and gentle police were provoked by the students and in some cases harshly used; and those Sergeants charged with the more serious brutalities of the day were naturally nowhere near the spot at all, but in another part of Paris. One of their more reasonable points was that several of their prisoners were not *clercs* at all, and therefore no affair of University's.

To the lesser charges raised by the Criminal Lieutenant University replied: *primo*, touching the alleged theft of fowls from St. Germain-des-Prés, it was an affair six years old, and the offending students had long ago been punished by the Bishop's Court: *secundo*, touching the theft of hooks from the butchers of St. Geneviève, the said Lieutenant had summoned the butchers, who had declared that their relations with the students were most friendly and that they knew nothing of the said thefts, but the Lieutenant had suppressed this: *tertio*, as to the young woman of Vanves, she herself had asked two or three students, who had gone to Vanves on a holiday expedition, where they lived, had suggested that she might visit them, and had done so, *mais après ilz ne la pouvoient bouter hors de l'ostel*—but afterwards they could not hoick the lady out of the place. All this, in any case, added counsel quite reasonably, was beside the point,

> *Toutes ces choses ne sont* ad propositum, *mais seulement les propose ledit lieutenant pour injurier l'Université.*

*[Arrest and imprisonment of their persons.]

[All of which things are beside the point, and the said Lieutenant brings them forward solely to injure the University.]

With regard to the *Pet-au-Deable* riots, University agreed that the malefactors had qualified for punishment, but not for bloodshed; pointing out also that two of the accused students had come to terms with the Lieutenant and his brother over *ung bon diner* at the *Pomme de Pin*: a slightly damaging point for that official. As to the night-thefts of tavern signs, finally, University agreed that those taken in the act were to be punished by the proper authority.

On the sixteenth of June the first order of the Court was made. The Sergeant Charpentier, the presumed slayer of Raymond de Mauregart and the one who had so menaced the Rector, was taken in a cart, with a rope round his neck, and forced to make the *amende* University had demanded, being also fined four hundred livres Parisis: and at the Port Baudoyer his right hand was struck off at the wrist, which taught him a proper respect for Letters.[6] The other Sergeants were banished from Paris.

But the case was not yet over: University was aiming at the Provost d'Estouteville, who, as seems evident, had hitherto been very much shielded and kept in the background by his loyal Criminal Lieutenant. In January 1454 the Court had already promised the Rector that the process against the Provost personally should be undertaken, on condition that the ban on lectures and sermons was lifted. This was not enough for University, and the ban dragged on. In June, following the sentence on Charpentier and the other defendant Sergeants, the Criminal Lieutenant was declared incapable of holding his office, and deprived: his master, it would appear, was able to ignore the academic lightning. Everything considered, University had won its cause handsomely, but it was still in no haste to relax its grip of the situation. There is a decision of the Court of Parliament [7] dated August 21, 1454, which shows that the public power was at length becoming rebellious under the continual browbeating of this cosmopolitan and turbulent State. The Court, *"pour obvier a l'esclande & inconvenient qui se sont ensuiz & pourroient*

[6] MS. Dupuy 250, Arch. nat. X²ᵃ 26, fol. 236, X²ᵃ 27.
[7] MS. Dupuy 250, fol. 31 v°; fr. 5908, fol. 79 r° et v°.

ensuivre pour le temps advenir, a l'occasion des cessations des sermons esquelles l'Université de Paris a persisté jusques a present," *
orders its ushers Guillaume Taiche and Jehan du Ruit, in the name
of the King and the said Court of Parliament, to summon University, in the person of the Rector, to resume sermons in the churches
within one week from that date; intimating at the same time to
the said University that if this order is ignored the said Court, obedient to the King's command, will take such steps to ensure the
resumption *"qu'elle verra estre a faire par raison."*† . . . But it
was not till twenty-eight years after, as we have seen, that Louis xi.
routed the Doctors with a Papal Bull, and not till 1499 that they
were deprived of this huge weapon for ever.

The name of François de Montcorbier, *dit* Villon, Master of
Arts, nowhere occurs in this trouble. I conclude that he had been
able to take to his heels when the fuss began. Had not his great
heroic-comic Romance,

> *le Rommant du Pet au Deable,*
> *Lequel maistre Guy Tabarie*
> *Grossa, qui est homs veritable,*

[The Romance of the Pet-au-Deable, which Master Guy
Tabarie—a man of truth—copied out.]

been irrevocably lost, one might have learned what he was doing
in the tumult. If I judge his character aright he was prudent in
difficulties, and like Panurge *s'enfuyoit le grand pas de peur des
coups, lesquels il craignoit naturellement*. It seems certain that the
benevolence of the Provost d'Estouteville, to whom Villon makes
two oblique respectful references in the Testaments, and for whose
bride he wrote a Ballade, was valuable to him on this occasion.

This odd bond between a disreputable student and the Provost
may have sprung from common University acquaintance, for that
was a broad age and all ranks might mingle alike in the Schools

---

*[To put an end to the scandal and inconvenience which have been
occasioned, and which may still be occasioned in the future, by the cessation
of sermons, in which the University of Paris has persisted up to the present.]

†[As will seem reasonable to the Court to be taken.]

and in the taverns; but more likely (thinks Longnon) it had something to do with Villon's connection, through Master Guillaume or through his own mother, with Anjou. In 1446 there had been a tourney held at Saumur by the good King René d'Anjou, King of Sicily, that most excellent dilettante, minor poet, musician, criticaster, painter, and patron of Arts and Letters. At this tourney Robert d'Estouteville, splendidly horsed, had "won" his bride, Ambroise de Loré, daughter of the Baron d'Ivry, in single combat with the Sire de Beauvau; as Marot's title to the dull but sufficiently intimate Ballade presented by Villon to the Provost recalls: *Ballade que Villon donna à un Gentilhomme nouvellement marié, pour l'envoyer à son Epouse, par luy conquise à Espée.*[8] It seems possible, therefore, that Villon, visiting his relatives in Anjou during his boyhood, had been present at this tourney and had there made the acquaintance, however distant, of Robert d'Estouteville. At the Provost's *grant & noble* house in Paris, *ornée de marmousetes,* frequent receptions were given, and a wide hospitality; and Villon, either with or without Master Guillaume, very probably appeared there in Society once or twice, though his taste was strongly for other company. It is very evident that there was a friendship between him and Robert d'Estouteville which may be assumed to have helped him in many a minor brush with the police. But in his greatest need, as we shall see, the Provost will no longer be there to aid him.

We now come on less obviously sure ground, though it has a firm enough substratum. The suspension of all lectures by University between 1453 and 1454 left numbers of indigent *clercs* and Masters of Arts without means of support: or at least those of them who were not fanatical on the question of earning an honourable living. Though tutorship of private pupils had necessarily to cease during the period of ban, honest graduates had a source of live-

---

*[Ballade which Villon gave to a Gentleman newly-married to present to his Bride, whom he had won by the Sword.]

[8] It is also called, in some early texts, *Ballade pour Robert d'Estouteville.* The verse introducing it refers to this tourney held by "Regnier, roy de Cecille." To King René's procurator in Paris, Master Andry Courault, Villon bequeaths in the Great Testament his *Ballade des Contredictz de Franc Gontier.*

lihood in writing for the scriveners of Paris, whose stalls were numerous: but from the *Repues Franches,* which are believed to be the work of Friar Baulde de la Mare, it is clear that Villon and his particular friends knew an easier way of living than by sweating day and night over greasy parchments. The author of the *Repues* illustrates the method in seven lessons.

Lesson I. shows forth the method of obtaining, free and for nothing, fish, tripe, bread, wine, and roast meat. First, the prelude:

> *"Sçaurions nous trouver la maniere*
> *De tromper quelqu'ung pour repaistre?*
> *Qui le fera sera bon maistre."*
>
> *Ainsy parloyent les compaignons*
> *Du bon maistre Françoys Villon,*
> *Qui n'avoient vaillant deux ongnons,*
> *Tentes, tapis, ne pavillon.*

["How can we find a way of doing somebody for a good meal? Whoever can do that will be a master." Thus spoke the companions of good Master François Villon, none of them worth a couple of onions, and lacking equally tents, carpets, and standard.]

The method of obtaining fish is then expounded. Master François, parting from his band, proceeds to the fish-market near the Petit-Pont, where he selects a panier-full of the best, saying that the bearer will be paid on delivery. He accompanies the fish-porter with his burden over the bridges and across the Parvis to Notre-Dame, where he finds, as expected, a confessor in the Cloister receiving penitents. Stepping softly aside and telling the fish-porter to wait a moment, Master François approaches the confessor, who is at the moment disengaged, and pulling a pious face explains that he has with great difficulty brought his nephew with him, a moody, negligent youth, too fond of money, whom he desires the father to confess and shrive forthwith. "Certainly," answers the confessor; and Master François, stepping out, seizes the panier of fish from the porter, at the same time telling him there is one inside who will settle with him. The simple porter enters, and Master François evaporates into thin air with his fish. The narrative trots in artless rhyme:

Et passerent par Nostre-Dame,
Là où il vit le Penancier,
Qui confessoit homme ou bien femme.
Quant il le vit, à peu de plait,
Il luy diſt: "Monsieur, je vous prie
Que vous despeschez, s'il vous plaiſt,
Mon nepveu, car je vous affie
Qu'il eſt en telle resverie:
Vers Dieu il eſt fort negligent;
Il eſt en tel mercencolie
Qu'il ne parle rien que d'argent.

—Vrayement, ce dit le Penancier,
Tres-voulentiers on le fera."
Maiſtre François print le panier,
Et diſt: "Mon amy, venez çà;
Vela qui vous despeschera,
Incontinent qu'il aura faict."
Adonc maiſtre François s'en va,
Atout le panier, en effect.

[So they went by Notre Dame, where he saw a confessor receiving penitents, both men and women; and on seeing him he said without preface, "Sir, I beg you, if you please, to confess my nephew, for I do assure you he is in a strange mood, and moſt negligent of his duties towards God. He is in such a melancholy fit that he will talk of nothing but money."

"Certainly," replied the confessor, "I will do so willingly." Maſter François took hold of the panier and said, "My friend, go over there; there is one who will attend to you, and at once." So saying Maſter François disappeared, and the panier with him, in fact.]

The ſtory ends in a loud guffaw at the mutual bewilderment of the confessor and his penitent. "What!" cries the porter, "confess? Why, sir, begging your pardon, wasn't I shriven only this Eaſter? What I want is fifty sols." "Come, my son," answers the confessor severely, "your uncle has told me about you. A little less love of money, if you please, and a little more penitence and love of God." At length comes illumination: but the fish has vanished for ever.

Le povre homme, je vous affie,
Ne prisa pas bien la façon,

[The poor fellow, I assure you, did not esteem the process highly, for on my oath, he got neither gold nor silver for his fish.]

The way of getting tripe for nothing is not gentlemanly, and I will not linger over it. The way of getting bread is as easy as selling a rubber plantation situated in Iceland to a smart Financier of Capel Court. Master François, representing himself to be the grave major-domo of a family, made up for the purpose, no doubt, by a *fripier* in touch with the band, goes to the baker and orders five or six dozen rolls. When half the number have been placed in a basket he stops the baker abruptly, saying that the bread is required at once and that the porter must deliver what he has and return for the remainder. The porter sets off with his basket, accompanied by Master François, and they come presently to the gate of a great house, where Master François orders the man to set down his load and hurry back for the rest. It is not necessary to conclude this obvious *repue.*

The method of getting free wine has for a background the famous tavern of the *Pomme de Pin,* whose landlord, Robin Turgis, is a constant butt of Villon's, and a large creditor also. Villon takes two large *brocs* or pitchers, fills one of them with fair water, and proceeds to the *Pomme de Pin,* where he orders at great length a jug of white wine. The impatient drawer, to put an end to Master François' flow of *bons propos,* fills one of the pitchers with Baigneux; which done, Master François inquires leisurely, "What wine is that?" "Baigneux," replies the drawer. Master François immediately waves it aside. "Take it away! Take it away! I won't have it. Are you a jolthead? Empty my pitcher at once, I say! I want a good Beaune, and nothing else."

> *L'ung fist emplir de belle eaue clere,*
> *Et vint à la Pomme de Pin,*
> *Atout ses deux brocs, sans renchere,*
> *Demandant s'ilz avoient bon vin,*
> *Et qu'on luy emplist du plus fin,*
> *Mais qu'il fust blanc & amoureux.*
> *On luy emplist, pour faire fin,*
> *D'ung tres-bon vin blanc de Baigneux.*

Maiſtre François print les deux brocs,
L'un emprés l'autre les bouta;
Incontinent, par bons propos,
Sans se haſter, il demanda
Au varlet: "Quel vin eſt-ce là?"
Il luy diſt: "Vin blanc de Baigneux.
—Ostez cela, ostez cela,
Car, par ma foy, point je n'en veulx.

"Qu'esse-cy? Eſtes-vous bejaulne?
Vuydez-moy mon broc viſtement.
Je demande du vin de Beaulne,
Qui soit bon, & non aultrement."

As he speaks, and subtly, Maſter François hands back the
pitcher containing the water, and thus gets away without the leaſt
trouble with a free pitcher of Baigneux.

Et, en parlant, subtillement,
Le broc qui eſtoit d'eaue plain
Contre l'aultre legierement
Luy changea, a pur et a plain.

Par ce point, ilz eurent du vin,
Par fine force de tromper;
Sans aller parler au devin,
Ilz repeurent, per ou non per.

It is evident that this trick had to be played in the semi-darkness
of the cellar, or at night.

The method of getting a roaſt for nothing is also simplicity
itself, once rehearsed. Maſter François, stopping haphazard by a
cookshop, begins cheapening a fine piece of roaſt meat. To him
presently appears a surly ſtranger, demanding of the *rostisseur*:
"What is this haggling swab playing at?" A loud quarrel breaks
out immediately. The ſtranger aims a blow at Maſter François and
takes to his heels, and Maſter François, snapping up the meat un-
perceived amid the hullabaloo, utters an indignant roar and runs
after him at top speed. Round the firſt convenient corner the chase
comes to an end, and Master François and his aggressor slink off
together,

Celuy qui bailla le soufflet
Fuyt bien tost & à motz exprés.

> *Maiſtre François, sans plus de plet,*
> *Atout son rost, courut aprés.*
> *Ainsi, sans faire long procés,*
> *Ilz repeurent, de cueur devot,*
> *Et eurent, par leur grant excés,*
> *Pain, vin, chair, & poisson, & rost,*

[The one who had given the blow ran off at great speed, without waſting words; and Maſter François, without more ceremony, grabbed the roaſt and ran after him. And thus, without making a long business of it, they feaſted devoutly and had by their outrageous operations bread, wine, flesh, fish, and roaſt.]

to where the reſt of the comrades are awaiting their dinner: a choice company of hungry *escholiers* and mixed rapscallions,

> *Les hoirs du deffunct Pathelin,*
> *Qui sçavez jargon jobelin,*
> *Capitains du Pont-à-Billon,*
> *Tous les subjetz Françoys Villon.*

[Heirs of the late Pathelin [hero of the famous cheating farce], learned in the Jargon and Jobelin, captains of the Pont-à-Billon [the Petit-Pont, headquarters of rogues and beggars]; all subjeĉts of François Villon.]

The high reputation of the poet is obvious. "He was a nursing mother to us," cries the delighted companion who composed the *Repues*:

> *Maiſtre Françoys par son blason*
> *Trouva la façon & maniere*
> *D'avoir marée à grant foyson,*
> *Pour gaudir & faire grant chere.*
> *C'eſtoit la mere nourriciere*
> *De ceulx qui n'avoyent point d'argent;*
> *Atromper devant & derniere*
> *Estoit ung homme diligent.*

[Maſter François by his skill found a way to provide fresh fish galore, making joy and good cheer. He was a nursing mother to those without coin, indefatigable in cheats, before and behind.]

It has been pointed out that at leaſt four of these cheats are described in the adventures of Tyl Eulenspiegel, that roaring farce of the Low Countries, which appeared about this time. The fish

106

trick, in addition, was already nearly three centuries old, having appeared in the *fabliau* of the Three Blind Men of Compiègne. All of them are actually as old as civilisation, and ever new in Business circles. Considering the whole, it may be judiciously said that although Villon's rascalities had become a legend in Paris within a few years of his disappearance—they had a specific name: *villon-neries*—there are obviously more than a few grains of fact in the mass of fantasy.

The picture is complete. By the year 1454 the feet of François Villon, A.M., are already well advanced on the steep flowery slope. His dear companions are rakes, players, and wantons, bullies, sneak-thieves, and criminals,

> *Ambubaiarum collegia pharmacopolæ,*
> *Mendici, mimæ, balatrones, hoc genus omne.*

[The community of doxies, quacks, beggars, mummers, rascals, and all their kind.]   (*Horace,* Satires I, 2.)

Rioting and sharp practice, lechery and quarrelling, drink and neat thieving pleasantly fill his day. I see his meagre form slipping through dark narrow alleys, his side-glancing eyes, his shabby gown. He is as yet but a Bachelor in the criminal arts. In a very short time, having passed honourably in Elementary Bloodshed and Advanced Burglary, he will be admitted a Master.

§ 3

THE fifth of June, 1455. The Feast of Corpus Christi; *La Feste-Dieu.* From an early hour Paris had been bedecked with green branches, and from every window hung rich cloths and tapestries to welcome the passage of the Body of God. Along the streets at intervals stood the *reposoirs,* the temporary altars lovingly decked with flowers, and lighted tapers, and silks. Since dawn Masses had been said and sung, and the beautiful sequence of the beautiful Office of the Feast, composed by St. Thomas Aquinas in such an ecstasy of devotion, sung in Notre-Dame, in the abbeys of Paris, and in all the two hundred churches and convents of the city.

Lauda, Sion, Salvatorem,
Lauda ducem et pastorem
 In hymnis et canticis.
Quantum potes tantum aude,
Quia major omni laude,
 Nec laudare sufficis. . . .

[Sion, lift thy voice and sing;
 Praise thy Saviour and thy King;
 Praise with hymns thy Shepherd true.
 Strive thy best to praise Him well,
 Yet doth He all praise excel,
 None can ever reach His due.]

And so at length to that mighty finale, like the surge and beat of
Atlantic combers:

Bone Pastor, panis vere,
Jesu, nostri miserere,
Tu nos pasce, nos tuere,
Tu nos bona fac videre
 In terra viventium.
Tu qui cuncta scis et vales,
Qui nos pascis hic mortales,
Tuos ibi commensales
Coheredes et sodales
 Fac sanctorum civium!

[Jesu, Shepherd of the sheep,
 Thou thy flock in safety keep,
 Living Bread! Thy life supply;
 Strengthen us, or else we die;
 Fill us with celestial grace.
 Thou who feedest us below,
 Source of all we have or know,
 Grant that with Thy saints above
 Sitting at the feast of love,
 We may see Thee face to face.]

Then in every quarter of Paris had proceeded the many-col-
oured processions of Corpus Christi through the streets; the children strewing flowers; the white-robed singing-men raising a loud
song; the Confraternities with their banners; servers bearing lighted
candles and flaming wax torches; the long line of seculars, monks,
friars, wardens, and beadles, the municipal and Court dignitaries,

crowned with roses and marjoram and white violets; then the thurifers with silver censers tossing clouds of white fragrant smoke into the summer air; then more lights; and then the Sacred Host in its precious monstrance, borne by the celebrating priest under a canopy rich with cloth of gold and tassels, festooned with roses, upheld by four burgesses in holiday dress; then more priests, and more religious, more singers, more Confraternities with banners, and the populace joining in and following, the warm air vibrating to the clamour of bells and the chanting, and heavy with the smell of flowers and incense and hot wax, and the dust stirred up by so many slow-moving feet. So the processions passed, and the long summer afternoon waned, and the tapers in the streets expired in a wisp of smoke, and the flowers nodded in the heat, and the Body of God in a blaze of light returned to the tabernacles, and the organs ceased their thundering, and the altar candles were extinguished, and the holiday crowd streamed out to the streets and the noisy taverns.

Venit Hesperus. The evening came, grateful after the heat and dust of the day; and François Villon, issuing forth after supper from the house called the Porte Rouge in the cloister of St. Benoît (for he still made his home there), sniffed the cool air approvingly. What happened towards nine o'clock on this night is precisely described in a Letter of Remission accorded by Charles VII. in January 1456 to Master François des Loges, otherwise called de Villon. The Letter [1] opens with the usual preface:

CHARLES, *par la grace de Dieu, roy de France. Sçavoir faisons à tous presens & avenir, nous avoir receu l'umble supplicacion de maistre François des Loges, autrement dit de Villon, aagié de vingt-six ans ou environ, contenant que:*

[Charles, by the grace of God, King of France. We make known to all present and to come, that we have received the humble supplication of Master François des Loges, otherwise called de Villon, showing that:]

and plunges thence straight into the matter.

Le jour de la Feste Nostre Seigneur derrenierement passée, au soir aprés soupper, il estoit assis pour soy esbastre sur une pierre située soubz le cadram

---

[1] Registers of the Chancellery of France, JJ 187 (149, fol. 76 v°).

*de l'oreloge Saint Benoiſt le Bientourné, en la grant rue Saint Jacques en
noſtre ville de Paris, ou cloiſtre duquel Saint Benoiſt eſtoit demourant ledit
suppliant, & eſtoient avecques luy ung nommé Gilles, prebſtre, & une
nommée Ysabeau, & eſtoit environ l'eure de neuf eures ou environ.*

[On the day of the feaſt of Corpus Chriſti laſt, in the evening after
supper, he seated himself for refreshment on a ſtone situate under the dial
of the clock of St. Benoît-le-Bientourné in the Rue St. Jacques in Our town
of Paris, the said petitioner being resident in the cloiſter of the said church of
St. Benoît; and there were with him one Gilles, a prieſt, and a woman named
Ysabeau; and the time was about nine o'clock, or thereabout.

M. Lacroix identifies Ysabeau tentatively with Mlle. de Bruyères, the rich
widow of the *Pet-au-Deable* affair; a monstrous assumption.]

The scene is vivid as if it were being enacted now before our
eyes. It is nearly night, and here and there among the piled gables
of the Rue St. Jacques a window glows in the dusk. From the *Mule*
tavern across the road comes the sound of careless voices talking
together, and now and then a ſtave of raucous song. The tinted air
is very ſtill and clear. A bat skims round the tower of St. Benoît.
On the ſtone bench under the clock Villon and his companions sit,
talking drowsily. Of the prieſt Gilles nothing is known, nor of the
lady Ysabeau either. They assiſt a moment mutely in this scene and
vanish for ever.

The peace of the June evening is suddenly broken, and rudely.

*Ouquel lieu survindrent Phelippes Chermoye, prebſtre, & maiſtre Jehan
le Mardi, lequel Chermoye incontinent qu'il avisa ledit suppliant luy diſt: "Je
regnie Dieu! je vous ay trouvé"; & incontinent ledit suppliant se leva pour luy
donner lieu, en luy disant: "Beau frere, de quoy vous coursez-vous?" Lequel
Chermoye, ainsi que ledit suppliant se levoit pour luy faire place, le rebouta
tres rigoureusement à ce qu'il luy convint se rasseoir. Voyans ce, les des-
susditz Mardi, Gilles, & Ysabeau, & supposans que ledit Chermoye, & la
maniere de sa venue considerans, n'eſtoit venu que pour faire noise & des-
plaisir audit suppliant, se absenterent, & demourerent seulement ledit suppliant & Chermoye.*

[In which place arrived Philip Chermoye, prieſt, and Maſter Jehan le
Mardi; and the said Chermoye perceiving the said petitioner immediately said
to him: "By God! I have found you!" and immediately the said petitioner
rose to make room for him, saying: "Sweet sir, what angers you?" On which
the said Chermoye, as the said petitioner was rising to make room, pushed
him backwards so strongly that he was forced to sit down again. Seeing which

the aforesaid Mardi, Gilles, and Ysabeau, observing the said Chermoye and considering from the manner of his approach that he had come for no other purpose than to pick a quarrel and make strife with the said petitioner, withdrew, leaving only the said petitioner and Chermoye.]

Nothing is more evident than that this was the culmination of a standing feud between François Villon and the priest Philip Chermoye. Admire the prudence of Gilles, of Ysabeau, and of Master Jehan le Mardi, who, smelling thunder in the air, slipped so quietly away and left the principals to themselves. Master Chermoye was a man of action, and came at once to the point.

Lequel Chermoye tantost apres, voulant sa mauvaise & dempnable voulenté en propos deliberé acomplir & mettre à execution, traict une grande dague de dessoubz sa robbe & en frappa ledit suppliant par le visaige sur le bolievre & jusque à grant effusion de sang, comme il apparut & appert de present. Et ce voyant ledit suppliant, lequel pour le serain estoit vestu d'un mantel & à sa sainture avoit pendant une dague soubz icelluy, pour eviter la fureur & mauvaise voulenté dudit Chermoye, doubtant qu'il ne le pressast & villenast plus fort en sa personne, traict ladite dague & frappa, comme luy semble, en l'ayne ou environ, ne cuidant point lors l'avoir frappé.

[The said Chermoye a moment after, determining to accomplish and put into execution his wicked and damnable will, drew a large dagger from beneath his gown and struck the said petitioner in the face with it, on the upper lip, causing thereby a great flow of blood, as it appeared and appears now. Seeing this the said petitioner, who on account of the evening air was wearing a cloak, having beneath it a dagger hanging at his belt, in order to avoid the fury and wicked will of the said Chermoye, and fearing that he would be more bitterly pressed and attacked in his person, drew the said dagger, as it seems, and struck him in the groin or thereabout, not thinking at that time that he had so struck him.]

The fight has begun. The first blow, a downward slash, has left Villon's upper lip gashed and bleeding profusely. Villon recoils, and groping under his cloak whips out the dagger at his belt and returns the slash, wounding the priest in the groin, "or thereabout." It must be remembered that the story of the encounter has been rehearsed in the plea for the King's clemency so as to show the petitioner in the most favourable light possible.[2] In any case Cher-

---

[2] On the other hand, a petitioner or those petitioning in his behalf dared not actually depart from the truth, for fear of consequences. See Appendix C: *The Double Remission*.

moye is the aggressor, and Villon finds himself (as the French law-phrase now goes) in a ſtate of legitimate defence. As to the prieſt's carrying a dagger at all, it was not a habit out of the ordinary. Daggers or knives were commonly worn by medieval prieſts, as by the laity; not necessarily for defence, even, but for carving meat, hunting, and other ordinary purposes. Thus in England John Wyndhill, rector of Arnecliffe, bequeaths in 1431 his green, sanguine, and murrey gowns, his copy of *Piers Plowman,* and his baselard, or knife, with the silver and ivory haft.[3]

The fight continues, and suddenly ends.

Et persistant ledit Chermoye à vouloir defaire ledit suppliant, le poursuyvant & improperant de plusieurs injures & menasses, trouva ledit suppliant à ses piez une pierre laquelle il print & gecta au visaige dudit Chermoye, & incontinent le laissa & se departit ledit suppliant & se retraiſt sur ung barbier nommé Fouquet pour soy faire habiller.

[Whereupon, the said Chermoye persiſting in his attempt to do mischief to the said petitioner, pursuing him and hurling several threats and menaces, the said petitioner finding at his feet a ſtone took it and flung it in the face of the said Chermoye, and at once the said petitioner left him and departed and retired to the shop of a barber named Fouquet to have his wound dressed.]

The barber-surgeon Fouquet, having attended to Villon's bleeding lip, had a duty to perform. He demanded, for the purpose of making his report to the Watch, the names of the parties in the quarrel: to which Villon answered that his assailant was a prieſt named Philippe Chermoye, and that his own name was Michel Mouton. Then, issuing from the barber's, he took prudently to his heels and vanished. Chermoye, after lying for a time where he had fallen, was picked up—he had chased Villon into the cloiſter of St. Benoît—and taken into a house in the cloiſter, where his wounds were washed and dressed: and next day he was removed to the Hotel-Dieu for treatment, where within the week,

à l'occasion desdiz coups, par faulte de bon gouvernement ou autrement, il eſt alé de vie à trespassement. A l'occasion duquel cas, ledit suppliant doubtant rigueur de juſtice s'eſt absenté du païs & n'y oseroit jamais retourner se Noſtre grace & misericorde ne luy eſtoit sur ce impartie.

[3] Cutts.

[On account of the said wounds, for lack of proper treatment or other causes, he departed this life and died. On account of which the said petitioner fearing the rigour of the law withdrew from the district, and would not dare ever return unless Our grace and pardon were extended to him.]

So Master Chermoye passes from this life, and his adversary flies from justice. The remainder of the Letter, after stressing the fact that the said petitioner has heretofore governed himself well and honestly, without ever being accused before—the last five words may be called the Operative Clause, and have the advantage of being at that time true [4]—proceeds to the Royal warrant remitting, pardoning, and holding the said Master François des Loges, *autrement dit de Villon,* quit of all pains and forfeits, civil or criminal, of all bans, pursuits, or appeals, and restored to enjoyment of his former good fame and renown, goods, and chattels; at the same time commanding and enjoining on the Provost of Paris, his lieutenants, and all officers of justice whatsoever, that they are in no way to deprive, molest, or forbid the said Master François des Loges, *autrement dit de Villon,* in the exercise of these rights, any of which, having been attached or sequestrated by them, are instantly to be restored. Given at Saint Pourcain, in the month of January in the year of grace 1455. (New Style 1456.)

Thus the first Letter of Remission. The second,[5] awarded by the King to Master François de Montcorbier, *maistre es ars,* guilty of the death of Philippe Sermoise, priest, differs from it in one or two details. In this second account Sermoise, or Chermoye, advances cursing and blaspheming, crying, "Master François, I have found you, and I think I will heat your ears for you (*je vous courrouceray*)!" To which Villon replies as sweetly as any lamb: "What, Master Philip, are you angry? Have I wronged you? What do you want with me? I do not think I have ever harmed you." The fight then begins, as before, but Master Jehan le Mardi, who in the first account slipped away with Gilles and Ysabeau, returns, and perceiving Villon with a dagger in his left hand and a stone in his right tries to disarm him, but cannot prevent the hurling of the stone which lays Chermoye on the pavement. A most important para-

---

[4] This, observes P. Champion, is the one and only certificate of good conduct ever obtained by François Villon.
[5] Chancellery Registers, JJ 183 (67, fol. 49 r°).

113

graph follows, explaining almost completely the Royal clemency:

Lequel Phelippe fut levé de la place & porté en l'ostel des prisons dudit Saint-Benoît & illec examiné par certain Nostre examinateur ou Chastelet de Paris; lequel Phelippe interrogué par ledit examinateur que s'il advenoit que, de cedit coup, il alast de vie à trespassement, il voulut que poursuite en fust faicte par ses amis ou autres contre ledit supliant, lequel luy respondit que non, mais, en ce cas, pardonnoit & pardonna sa mort audit supliant pour certaines causes qui à ce le mouvoient.

[The said Philippe was raised from that place and carried into the prison-house of the said St. Benoît, and there examined by one of Our examiners of the Châtelet of Paris. To whom the said Philippe, being asked by the said examiner whether in the event of his dying of the said blow he would wish a hue and cry raised against the said petitioner by his friends or others, answered no, that in that case he pardoned and forgave the said petitioner for his death, on account of certain reasons which moved him so to do.]

The raging quarrelsome priest, then, for all his *dempnable voulenté*, died a Christian man, forgiving his enemy *in extremis*. The second Letter, drawing to a conclusion, reveals also that a decree of banishment had been issued against the assassin in his absence:

Pour lequel cas advenu par la maniere que dit est, ledit supliant a esté appelé à noz drois, & contre luy procedé par bannissement de Nostre royaume, ouquel il n'oseroit plus frequenter, reperer ne converser, se nostre grace & misericorde ne luy estoient sur ce imparties, si comme il dit en nous umblement requerant que, attendu, que ledit Phelippe durant sa maladie avoit voulu & ordonné que aucune poursuite en fust faite contre ledit supliant, ainz, en tant que à luy estoit, il avoit pardonné & pardonnoit audit supliant, etc.:

[On account of which act, carried out in the manner stated, the said petitioner has been summoned by Our laws, and an order of banishment from Our Kingdom made against him; which Kingdom he would not dare to inhabit, frequent, or return to, if Our grace and mercy were not imparted to him in this matter; as he says and humbly begs of us, seeing that the said Philip during his sickness desired and ordered that no hue and cry should be made after the said petitioner, since, as far as he himself was concerned, he had forgiven and pardoned the said petitioner, etc.]

and ends in the same formula of remission as the first Letter. Given at Paris, in the month of January, etc.

114

The cause of the fight remains unknown. It has been conjectured that the girl Ysabeau, who slid away when the trouble began, may have known something about it. I am inclined to believe that she is the Ysabeau of verse cxlix. of the *Grant Teftament:*

> *Et Ysabeau qui dit: "Enné!"*
> [And Ysabeau who says "Reelly."]

This was an affirmative interjection, according to Foulet, fashionable among finicking young women of the period, equivalent to "Reelly!" or "On my honour!" Was Ysabeau at the bottom of this trouble? Or, as is more likely, was it the perennial Katherine de Vausselles, whom we shall meet very shortly?

The affair is noteworthy as being Villon's firft recorded brush with Juftice, and very nearly his laft. Had the prieft Chermoye as he lay dying not deliberately placed on record his entire forgiveness in the Châtelet examiner's presence, it is highly likely that Villon would have been forthwith pursued, tried, and hanged for manslaughter out of hand; for the only witness of the fatal blow seems to have been Jehan le Mardi, a friend of the dead man, Villon's enemy.

We should have loft thereby a considerable quantity of great verse.

§ 4

> *Ford.* One that is as slanderous as Satan?
> *Page.* And as poor as Job?
> *Ford.* And as wicked as his wife?
> *Evans.* And given to fornications, and to taverns, and sack, and wine, and metheglins, and to drinkings, and swearings, and starings, pribbles and prabbles?   —*The Merry Wives of Windsor.*

> *Quæ virtus et quanta, boni, sit vivere parvo—*
> *Nec meus hic sermo est, sed quæ præcepit Ofellus*
> *Rusticus, abnormis sapiens crassaque Minerva—*
> *Discite. . . .*   —Hor., *Sat.,* ii. 2.

We left François Villon slipping discreetly out of the shop of the barber-surgeon Fouquet, some time between nine and half-paft on the night of Corpus Chrifti, June 5, 1455. It seemed advisable to get out of reach of Justice as speedily as possible, and there is no reason to believe he lingered in Paris a moment. The cloifter of St. Benoît, where he had laft seen Chermoye ftagger and fall, was closed to him. It is permissible to suppose, therefore, that before making for the Porte St. Jacques, or its near neighbour the Porte St. Michel, and the safe country, he appeared before his old mother in her humble room, breathing a little hard and making the briefeft possible explanation; and then, with what scanty ftore she could spare him, vanished swiftly by devious ways into the dark.

I do not fancy the killing of Chermoye weighed on his conscience particularly. Whatever had gone before it, the regrettable business had been forced on him, and resolved into homicide in self-defence: though to be sure he had no single sympathetic witness to support this defence, and to be hanged by miftake is peculiarly offensive to a thinking man. Before the bells of Paris had begun ringing Prime, therefore, I see him well beyond the walls and in the open country, going ftrongly in the fresh dawn wind and making for the south: for there is a verse in the *Grant Tefta-ment* (1461) which shows where he spent at leaft a week of this voluntary exile—at the village of Bourg-la-Reine, on the Orleans road, about two leagues [1] outside the walls of Paris.

> *Item, donne a Perrot Girart,*
> *Barbier juré du Bourg la Royne,*
> *Deux bacins et ung coquemart,*
> *Puis qu'a gaignier met telle paine.*
> *Des ans y a demy douzaine*
> *Qu'en son hoftel de cochons gras*
> *M'apatella une sepmaine,*
> *Tesmoing l'abesse de Pourras.*

[*Item,* I leave to Perrot Girart, barber of Bourg-la-Reine, two basins and a pipkin, since he works so hard for his living. It is just half a dozen years ago since he boarded me in his house a whole week on fat pork—witness the Abbess of Pourras.]

The fifth line fixes it. He is referring to the year 1455, when he took the road. The fooling of the barber Perrot Girart is an unpublished *repue franche,* and the poet's chuckle at remembering it

[1] One league = four kilometres.

is audible. The kind of company he fell upon in this rural with-drawal one may judge from his calling to witness, in connection with this feat, the lady known as the Abbess of Pourras. She was Huguette du Hamel, a notorious character. She had taken the re-ligious habit in 1439, had become Abbess of Port-Royal (popularly Pourrais or Pourras), in the Chevreuse valley near Paris, about 1454, and then, by swift degrees, had gone completely to the bad. In this year 1455, when Villon knew her, or pretended to, her con-duct was not the subject of more than local gossip; but by 1463 the scandal had become such that the Abbot of Chaalis, her su-perior, who had had her placed under observation, degraded her from her office and thrust her into the prison of the abbey of Pont-aux-Dames, in the diocese of Meaux, to cool her hot blood and bring her to penitence and obedience. Among the charges brought against her were that she attended feasts and revels, disguising herself, with gallants, and behaved in such a manner that the men-at-arms put her into a ballad: for which she had one of them thrashed so se-verely that he died.[2] It is by no means to be assumed that Villon is romancing when he connects her with himself in the affair of the barber of Bourg-la-Reine, over which he so pleasantly smacks his lips.

We see Villon now, therefore, dodging about the countryside just beyond Paris to the south, living on his wits. There is every reason to assume that it was during this period that he definitely joined himself to the Company of the Coquille, that freemasonry of bandits and blackguards which infested Paris and a large part of France, and especially Burgundy, Champagne, the Orléanais, Languedoc, part of Anjou, and the Ile-de-France. For them he was later to write the Ballades in the Jargon; of their brotherhood his friends Cayeulx and Montigny were already members. Were there not the seven Ballades, one bearing his acrostic, to show Villon a Coquillard, there would still be his frank admission in a minor Ballade:

[2] Archives of Parliament, X¹ᵃ 8311, fols. 190 r° and ss.
There seems to have been another lady known popularly as the "Abbess of Poilras," or Shaven-Poll: a *maquerelle publique* who was shaved on the head, whipped, pilloried, and expelled from the district. Villon may mean this one, and the mention of the barber may hence conceal a further jest; unless they are identical.

Je congnois quant pipeur jargonne.

[I know when a sharper patters the jargon.]

Thanks to the labours of Marcel Schwob, who published in 1890 the documents of the process of the Coquillards instituted at Dijon in 1455, it is possible to recall from the shadows a company of this redoubtable militia.[3] The report of the proceedings by Master Jehan Rabustel, Procurator-Syndic and Clerk of the Tribunal of Dijon, deals with the Coquillards of Burgundy only; but they operated generally in much the same manner as modern Chinese armies, each having its own defined sphere of loot, brigandage, and murder. It is not clear whether the King of the Coquille, to whom reference is made, exercised a general suzerainty or whether he was simply *primus inter pares*: he must in any case be distinguished from the King of the Gueux, or Beggars, the *Grant Coesre,* whose writ ran from the Cours des Miracles in Paris, the resort and den of all professional beggars, mumpers, and masquerading cripples, and whose subjects paid him a tax and spoke their own jargon, the *langue matoise*.[4] The different bands of the Coquille co-operated fraternally in matters of boundary and discipline, and they had in common their own statutes, police, and the Jargon which Villon has written, which linked and assisted them in their operations. As for the composition of the Coquille, its *cadre* was that large body of prowling men-at-arms, *Ecorcheurs,* foreign mercenaries, and miscellaneous brigands who, after forming part of the Royal forces against the Anglo-Burgundians, had been thrown out of employment at the end of the wars and had taken to the road. To these, the Pistols, Nyms, and Bardolphs, there naturally adhered a strong body of the vicious, the idle, and fugitives from justice, forming one mass of armed ruffianism, representing every phase of villainy, the sweepings of the criminal population of Europe, organised and

[3] Archives of the Justiciary of Dijon (Departmental Archives of the Côte d'Or, B 360, vi.). These documents were first brought to light in 1842 by M. Garnier, archivist of Dijon.
[4] The quarter of the Grande- and Petite-Truanderie was their headquarters, particularly in the fourteenth century. Their different categories, Sabouleux, Drilles, Francs-Mitoux, Culs-de-Jatte, Capons, Courtauds-de-Boutanche, Callots, Polissons, Riffodés, Hubins, Malingreux, and others cannot be dealt with here, but are worth inquiring into in various contemporary documents. Victor Hugo in *Notre-Dame de Paris* gives a general description of the Cour des Miracles and its inhabitants. The most famous Cour des Miracles was in the Rue des Francs-Bourgeois, near the Temple.

having a pseudo-military discipline. (*Coquille,* Shell, or, derivatively, Sword-Hilt. Some authorities derive the sign of the Shell from the badge of pilgrims to St. James's shrine at Compostela.) At this period the Burgundian countryside had suffered greatly from the Coquillards, and the town of Dijon in particular, in which the citizens were held up day and night and robbed with violence. The exemplary vigour and strategy of Jehan Rabustel was to put an end to these *esbatemens.*

The headquarters of the Dijon band was a brothel kept by one Jacquot de la Mer, against whom the charge runs:

> *Item,* the said Jacquot de la Mer, keeper of the said brothel, is familiar with them all, or the greater part of them, and moreover, well knowing their procedure and government, receives them into concealment and assists them in the disposal of horses and other property stolen by them, as much for the profit he makes out of them as for his share in the booty: and it is moreover notorious that for a long time before the arrest of the said companions the said Jacquot de la Mer was wont to appear in their company at all hours about this town, familiarly, knowing their procedure and government: the which is greatly to the prejudice of the said Jacquot.

This nest of ruffians Master Jehan Rabustel raided in the manner in which the London police to-day raid a dubious night-club on a night when no important personage is present. Having carefully made his plans, he placed around the brothel of Jacquot de la Mer at one o'clock in the morning a strong cordon of the Dijon Watch; and then, taking with him a guard, approached the house and knocked loudly on the door in the name of the King. Instantly the lights within were extinguished (so it is described in his report) and there was a frantic scuffling; and then silence. Eventually Jacquot de la Mer himself opened the door cautiously, evidently expecting nothing more than a visit of the ordinary watch. Jehan Rabustel and his men at once yanked him out and swept through the house, finding not only a considerable amount of stolen goods everywhere but also, coyly concealed in cupboards, under beds, and behind doors, a number of villainous heads, cat-a-mountain looks, true gallows visages. These inmates were all arrested on the spot and conveyed to the prison in the Rue des Singes.

So much for the *coup*, and the fence himself. Now for the Companions:

Le cas eſt tel: Depuis deux ans en ça ont repairié & repairent en ceſte Ville de Dijon plusieurs compaignons oizeux & vaccabundes qui, lors qu'ilz sont arrivez & durant le temps qu'ilz se tienent en ceſte dicte Ville, ne font riens, se non boire, mengier, & mener grant despense, jouer aux dez, aux quartes, aux marelles & aultres jeux. Continuelement se tienent le plus common & par especial de nuyt au bordeaul, là ou ils mainnent orde, ville, & dissolue vie de ruffiens & houliers, perdent aulcunes fois, & despensent tout leur argent & tant font qu'ilz ne ont denier ne maille.

Et, lors après, ce qu'ilz ont prins & oſté à leurs povres filles communes qu'ilz maintiennent audit bordeaul, tout ce qu'ilz peuvent avoir d'elles se partent les aulcuns & s'en vont l'en ne sait ou, & demeurent aulcunes fois xv jours, aultre fois i mois ou vi sepmaines. Et retournent les aulcunes à cheval, les aultres à pied, bien veſtuz & habilliez, bien garniz d'or & d'argent, & recommencent à mener avec aulcuns aultres qui les ont attenduz, ou aultres qui sont venuz de nouvel, leurs jeux & dissolutions accouſtumez.

[The case is thus: For two years paſt there has infeſted, and ſtill infeſts, this Town of Dijon, a number of idle and vagabond companions who, on their entry and during their ſtay in the said town, do nothing except drink, eat, and squander money at dice, at cards, at *marelle*, and other games. Moſt usually, and specially at night, they hold their assembly at a brothel, where they lead the filthy, vile, and dissolute life of ruffians and scoundrels, often losing and squandering all their money till they have left not a single denier. And then, when they have taken all they can from the poor common proſtitutes they frequent in the said brothel, some of them disappear in directions unknown, and are absent some for fifteen days, some for a month, some for six weeks. And they then return, some on horseback and some afoot, well clothed and harnessed, with plenty of gold and silver, and once more begin, with those who await them, or with new arrivals, their accuſtomed games and debaucheries.]

The language and government of the Companions are briefly dismissed:

Eſt vray que lesditz compaignons ont entr'eulx certain langaige de jargon & aultres signes à quoy ilz s'entrecongnoissent, & s'apellent iceulx galans les Coquillars, qui eſt à entendre les compaignons de la Coquille, lesquelz, comme l'en dit, ont ung roy qui se nomme le roy de la Coquille.

[It is a faċt that the said companions use among themselves a certain jargon and other signs by which they know each other, and that the said

gallants call themselves the *Coquillards,* that is, the Companions of the Coquille; and that they have, as it is said, a king, called the King of the
Coquille.]

Elsewhere in the report the Jargon is described again as *un
langaige exquiz que aultres gens ne scevent entendre.* The name of
the King of the Coquille is not given, nor is he mentioned in any
of Villon's Ballades in the Jargon; but I am tempted to smell out
a reference to him in the sixth line of the third stanza of the First
Ballade, which has such a gallows ring:

> *Plantez aux hurmes voz picons*
> *De paour des bisans si tres durs,*
> *Et aussi d'estre sur les joncz,*
> *Enmahez en coffres en gros murs.*
> *Escharicez, ne soiez point durs,*
> *Que le Grant Can ne vous face essorez.*
> *Songears ne soiez pour dorer,*
> *Et babignez tousjours aux ys,*
> *Des sires, pour les desbouser.*
> *Eschec, eschec, pour le fardis!* [5]

Is the *Grant Can* or Khan, a hidden allusion to the King of the
Coquille, or to the Provost, or merely to the sun, as he is named in
the language of the gypsies of Spain? I leave the matter there and
return to Dijon.

There follows a detailed description of the methods of operation.

*Et est vray, comme l'en dit, que les aulcuns desditz Coquillars sont
crocheteurs d'usseries, arches, & coffres. Les aultres sont tresgenteurs & des-
robent les gens en changeant or à monnoye ou monnoye à or, ou en acheptant
aulcunes marchandises. Les aultres font, portent, & vendent faulz lingoz &
faulses chainnes en façon d'or: les aultres portent & vendent ou engaigent
faulses pierreries en lieu de dyamanz rubiz & aultres pierres precieuses. Les
aultres se couchent en quelque hostellerie avec aulcun marchant & se desro-
bent eulx meismes & ledit marchant; & ont homme propre auquel ilz baillent
le larrecin, & puis se complaignent avec le marchant desrobey. Les aultres
jouent de faulx dez d'advantaige & chargiez, & y gaignent tout l'argent de
ceulx à qui ilz jouent. Les aultres sçaivent subtilitez telles au jeu de quartes
& de marelles que l'en ne pourroit guaigner contre eulx. Et, qui pis est, les*

---

[5] An attempt at elucidating some of the Jargon is made later in this book.

plusieurs sont espieurs & aggresseurs de bois & de chemins, larrons & mul-
driers, & est à presumer que ainsy soit là ou ilz mainnent telle vie dissolue.[6]

[It is also a fact, as is affirmed, that some of the said Coquillards are picklocks of coffers, chests, and treasuries. Others work with their fingers in cheating over the changing of gold to small money and back again, or in the buying of goods. Others make, carry, and sell false ingots of gold, and chains resembling gold: others carry and sell false jewels in place of diamonds, rubies, and other precious stones. Others lie at an inn with some merchant and rob themselves and him alike, passing the booty to a member of their gang; and then they lodge a complaint in company with the said merchant. Others play with loaded dice and win all the money of those who play with them. Others practise such skilful tricks at cards and *marelle* that no one can win money of them. And what is worse, most of them are footpads and bandits in the woods and on the highroads, robbers and assassins, and it is to be presumed that it is thus that they are able to lead such a dissolute life.]

It is not difficult to hear, behind the dry intoning of Master Jehan Rabustel, Procurator-Syndic and Clerk to the Tribunal of Dijon, the creaking of the rack and the yells of a score of sinister fellows as they are manipulated, none too soon, by the firm hand of Justice: and it is to be gathered that fairly full confessions were obtained. I see enigmatic forms slipping through the night in every direction from Dijon, croaking curt messages in the Jargon, warning the brotherhood that So-and-so has squealed and that the hunt is up in Burgundy and the leaders held; and vanishing into the dark again. No concerted swoop on the Coquille all over France was possible, for there was no centralised authority, and every diocese had its independent jurisdiction, but the tribunal of Dijon struck a shrewd blow and must have considerably perturbed the distant King of the Coquille amid his harem. The leaders were hanged or boiled, the rest banished. In the list of seventy-seven Coquillards of the Burgundian contingent published by the Procurator-Syndic appear many Gascons, a Spaniard, an Italian, a Savoyard, and (haud us and safe us!) a Scotsman, one Jehan d'Escosse; and also one name we know well, that of Regnier de Montigny: but Montigny was not then caught, as we have seen, and did not hang till September 1457.

[6] Another game mentioned in the Dijon evidence is the *gourd*, which was still known in Shakespeare's time, on the evidence of Pistol in *The Merry Wives:* "Let vultures gripe thy guts! for gourd and fullam holds." Fullam is cogged dice.

There is another companion in the Dijon list whose name rings familiar, one Christophe Turgis, described as a taverner, of Paris, who may conceivably have been a relative of Robin Turgis of the *Pomme de Pin*. Christophe, convicted of being a coiner, suffered the extreme sentence reserved for practitioners of that art, being boiled in oil in December 1456. The name of Colin des Cayeulx is not in the list: evidently he belonged to a different battalion of the Company—the Parisian or Ile-de-France band, no doubt. But even if he had not been officially described as a Coquillard at his trial a few years later, his name in the Jargon, "Colin de l'Escailler," set by his friend Villon in the Second Ballade, proves it.

I return to François Villon, and pause to consider a curious coincidence, discovered in a document of the Trésor des Chartes by Vitu and printed again for the first time in fifty years by Thuasne, which should not be passed over. It is a Letter of Remission for a crime of October 1455, four months after the killing of Chermoye. The accused is a certain Jehan des Loges, clerk, a native of Anjou, aged nineteen "or thereabouts" (an elastic term), calling himself a travelling packman, *mercier*, or *mercerot*. Now Villon, in a line of the *Grant Testament*, calls himself

Moy, povre mercerot de Renes.

[I, a poor packman of Rennes.]

Villon was a clerk. Villon's mother was an Angevine. One of Villon's patronymics was des Loges. Villon had given an *alias* to the barber Fouquet. Villon, in October 1455, was wandering in the provinces. The temptation to connect him with this Jehan des Loges is very strong: for travelling packmen, who had an extremely bad reputation and were affiliated very often to the Coquille, were not usually clerks. But as the clown says to Perdita, "You have of these pedlars, that have more in them than you 'ld think, sister."

The charge against Jehan des Loges was one of breaking into the house of one Guillaume des Prés in the small Angevin town of Parsé, or Parcé, sixteen leagues from Angers, and stealing goods valued at twenty-six gold crowns: also of stealing from the house of Jehan le Gay, in the same town, goods valued at two hundred gold crowns. He was caught some time later, and escaped from the prison of the Bishop of Angers, where he had been carried on his own request, and again from a chamber in the house of the Seigneur de Champagne, where he had been shoved on being recaptured; and by the hand of one of the Seigneur's servants he restored to des Prés and to le Gay part of the booty, promising to restore the rest and getting out of that country meanwhile as quickly as possible. Now a travelling packman (I echo the reasoning of M. Thuasne) who can undertake to restore, having no doubt squandered a great part of it, some 226 gold crowns, equal to about 16,000 francs in modern currency, must have respectable sureties, friends or relations, at call. Villon had an uncle, his mother's brother, a monk at Angers. Was he (if this Jehan des Loges were indeed Villon) the surety? There can be no certain answer. My own theory is that Villon did not go as far afield as Anjou at this time, whereas he certainly did in his next exile, between 1456 and 1460; therefore the line about the *mercerot de Renes* concerns his wanderings during that greater, more far-flung, and more miserable period: to which period, in the absence of any sound reason to the contrary, I assign it.

Into such frantic chasings of wild geese through bogs and fogs is the student of Villon's life led: not without pleasure.

We may take him, therefore, to be still lurking in the countryside between Sceaux and Paris, living from hand to mouth, associating at intervals with Coquillards, snapping up an occasional duck or hen from outlying farmyards, sometimes falling soft and lucky, as at Bourg-la-Reine, sometimes grubbing turnips from the fields and taking swiftly to his heels from the vengeance of an indignant farmer or from barking dogs, and always awaiting news from Paris. For evidently Master Guillaume de Villon was exerting all his influence and efforts in behalf of the prodigal: the kind, anxious man. At length, after eight months of exile, the royal Letter of Remission was granted (twice over, as we know: which argues desperate activity on some one's part), and Villon found himself able to return to his darling Paris. There were, it is true, certain formalities still to be complied with. All Letters of Remission, to be efficacious, had to be confirmed by a Court of Inquiry, which examined the written documents and tested the veracity of every ſtatement made by the accused. If they were found true, the judge confirmed the Letter and the accused was a free man. If any flaws were discovered, the Letter was cancelled and the accused became automatically eligible for fresh trouble. For mark you that at this time there was (notwithſtanding the laxity of the age) a belief that a lie told on oath carried with it not only temporal punishment but what was then considered a much worse one. We have since altered all that, happily.

And laſtly, the law was that the accused had to present himself in person before the Court of *entérinement* or ratification, carrying his Letter of Remission: he could not employ a solicitor or a procurator. But it is safe to assume that in Villon's case this formality might, given Maſter Guillaume's honourable reputation and intimate acquaintance among the notables of the Law and of the Parliament, have been tacitly waived. Certainly there is no evidence of François Villon's having appeared personally in this inſtance.[7]

He secured his pardon, then, and had it confirmed for him, and returned wing-footed to Paris. His ſtay was to be not long, but profitable.

§ 5

Fiddle, or fence, or mace, or mack,
  Or moskeneer, or flash the drag;
Dead-lurk a crib, or do a crack,
  Pad with a slang, or chuck a fag;
  Bonnet, or tout, or mump and gag,
Rattle the tats or mark the spot:
  You cannot bag a single ſtag,
Booze and the blowens cop the lot.

W. E. HENLEY.

Si videbas furem, currebas cum eo; et cum adulteris portionem tuam ponebas. —Ps. xlix.

HE came home to Paris.

For the next ten months there is no news of him, beyond an echo in the *Petit Teſtament* of a ravaging and unrequited love, and

[7] See Appendix C: *The Double Remission.*

also what might appear, on the face of it, to be a hint at one piece of honeſt work, the tutoring of

> *trois petis enfans tous nus,*
> *Nommez en ce present traiƈtié,*
> *Povres orphelins impourveus,*

[Three little naked shivering children, named in this present document, poor defenceless orphans.]

whose names are

> *Colin Laurens,*
> *Girart Gossouyn & Jehan Marceau,*
> *Despouveus de biens, de parens,*
> *Qui n'ont vaillant l'ance d'ung seau.*

[Colin Laurens, Girart Gossouyn, and Jehan Marceau; all without goods or parents, and not worth the handle of a bucket.]

This indeed was for a long time assumed, until it was discovered that these three poor children, Laurens, Gossouyn, and Marceau, to whom Villon recurs again in the Great Teſtament with such rare and oſtensible affeƈtion, are actually three rich and aged Parisian financiers, usurers, and speculators in salt, a byword for griping and sharp praƈtice: in which light Villon's apparent tenderness resolves into biting irony and hate.[1] He might, perhaps, have done a little desultory tutoring at this time; there is no reason for or against believing it: but it may be gathered from the *Petit Teſtament* that he began before many weeks to console his aching heart with the old company of the taverns and the ſtews, the girls and the roaring companions, Maſter Rash, and Maſter Caper, and young Dizy, and young Maſter Deep-vow, and Maſter Starve-lackey the rapier and dagger man, and young Drop-heir that killed luſty Pudding, and Maſter Forthlight the tilter, and wild Half-can, that ſtabbed Pots. From time to time, no doubt, as the need for money became pressing, he did a little light copying for scriveners, or worked among the notaries with references to whom his verse is so ſtuffed. Marcel Schwob thinks he may have been a clerk for a time to Pierre St. Amant of the Treasury, to whom he leaves a jocular bequeſt early

---

[1] Marceau's huge speculations, in particular, ruined many of the nobility. He was imprisoned under Charles VII. and Louis XI.

in the *Petit Testament*, and to whom he may have been introduced by the family of his friend Regnier de Montigny. His "simple-tonsure" benefice, which he leaves to one Chappelain, I have already mentioned. It is obviously nothing but a jest.

He may have tried honest living and failed. Towards the end of the year (1456), in any case, his position had become desperate: his heart and his purse were both wounded to death. For this reason, more especially, as he himself says, to escape from the toils of one

Qui m'a esté felonne et dure,

[Who has been so faithless and harsh to me.]

he made up his mind to leave Paris and travel to Angers, where his mother had a brother, a religious of that town.

The enigmatic figure of this love of Villon's, his life's torment, his rigorous mistress, his obsession, must here be considered.

It would appear from the evidence of the Testaments that her name was Katherine de Vausselles. He mentions her once by name, in the Double Ballade; again, as *ma damoyselle au nez tortu,* my lady of the twisted nose; again, as *ma chiere rose;* and many times indirectly. Her estate, as is to be deduced from the title *damoyselle,* was of the bourgeoisie. She may even have been a married woman. Research has brought to light the existence of a Pierre de Vaucel, or du Vaucel, one of the Canons of St. Benoît-le-Bientourné, a colleague of Guillaume de Villon, and Master of the Collège de Navarre during the years 1450 and 1456. I identify him confidently with one "Petru de Vaucello," whose neat, firm signature, underlined, with an ornament following and underneath, I have encountered at regular intervals, in examining the Registers of the Faculty of Theology, in juxtaposition with those of other members of the Faculty deputed to sign accounts and witness receipts. It might be, vaguely, that Katherine was a relative of Pierre de Vaucel; a niece, possibly.[2] Villon's acquaintance with her in this case would be long, since her putative uncle lived in the cloister of St. Benoît. If her

---

[2] P. Champion rejects the hypothesis. The name Vausselles, he finds, was not uncommon in Paris at this time, and there was a Vausselles family living in the St. Benoît quarter. Katherine may have belonged to this. On the other hand . . .

conduct does not seem, by Barchester standards, that becoming a
Canon's niece, it must be remembered that she lived in (as Mrs.
Barlow so well puts it in her *Utilitarian History of Europe for the
Young*) a less enlightened age: though to be sure a rake in a modern
English comedy has observed that given charm of manner a great
deal of amusement may be obtained in an English cathedral town.

Villon's passion for Katherine de Vausselles is undoubtedly the
nearest thing to a pure and steadfast love, free from commercial
preoccupations, that he ever experienced. Gathering together the
threads of his complaints all through the Testament, it is clear that
Katherine treated him with a high hand. She was *felonne et dure*.
She led him on with dissimulation and sugared lies:

> *Et ainsi m'aloit amusant,*
> *Et me souffroit tout raconter,*
> *Mais ce n-estoit qu'en m'abusant.*
>
> *Abusé m'a et fait entendre*
> *Tousjours d'ung que ce fust ung aultre. . . .*

> [Thus she went fooling me for her amusement, and let me open
> my heart to her, but only to make mock of me. . . . She fooled
> me, making me believe always one thing to be another.]

So his complaint continues, grotesque and lamentable. She could
make him believe anything, such was her power over him, poor
ninny: he would take a brazen warming-pan to be Heaven and the
clouds thereof to be made of calfskin; morning to be evening, small
beer new wine, a sow a windmill, a stout priest a pursuivant.

> *Du ciel une paelle d'arain,*
> *Des nues une peau de veau,*
> *Du matin qu'estoit le serain,*
> *D'ung trognon de chou ung naveau,*
> *D'orde cervoise vin nouveau,*
> *D'une truie ung molin a vent,*
> *Et d'une hart ung escheveau,*
> *D'ung gros abbé ung poursuyvant.*

He revolted, and came cringing back. She at last tired of the
game, and ordered him away, and took another lover—from the

context one Noé or Noël Joliz, who, as is seen in the Double Ballade, in due course thrashed the poet, presumably in the presence of the mistress.[3]

> *J'en fus batu comme a ru toiles,*
> *Tout mu, ja ne le quiers celer.*
> *Qui me feist maschier ces groselles*
> *Fors Katherine de Vausselles?*
> *Noel le tiers est, qui fut la.*

[I was thrashed like linen in a stream, stark naked; I have no wish to conceal it. Who made me swallow such humiliations but Katherine de Vausselles? Noel was the third person present.]

There had thus fallen to him the double indignity promised to Panurge on his marriage: he had been *cocu et battu*. Noël, M. Longnon conjectures, was the brother of Marguerite Joliz, who married Robin Turgis, of the *Pomme de Pin*. The thrashing, the humiliation, did not kill Villon's passion. It runs and recurs a *leit-motif* through both Testaments. He is sore, he is longing, he is desperate, he is vicious, he is furious, he is insulting, but he cannot get the image of Katherine out of his heart, and the troop of Jehannetons and Margots and Guillemettes and Macées and Blanches and Perrettes and Ysabeaus who flit through his verse are only temporary lenitives. He realises this, with a shrug of resignation.

> *Ainsi m'ont amours abusé*
> *Et pourmené de l'uys au pesle.*
> *Je croy qu'omme n'est si rusé,*
> *Fust fin comme argent de coepelle,*
> *Qui n'y laissast linge, drappelle;*
> *Mais qu'il fust ainsi manyé*
> *Comme moy, qui partout m'appelle*
> *L'amant remys et regnyé.*

[Thus has Love made a gull of me, bandying me from pillar to post. I swear there is no man, however cunning, were he as fine as assayed silver, who would not be stripped by Love of every shred and handled even as I, who am everywhere called "The lover flouted and cast off."]

[3] There is an alternative hypothesis. Villon may have put his love into a public ballad and, on her complaint, have been whipped by Justice, as was customary in such cases. But the other seems more likely.

From this it is plain that his fate was well known, and the common tavern talk of his circle. He is the melancholy Don of the old comedies, a furnace of sighs; and though he mitigates his suffering with the kisses of other women, he will carry Love's wounds to his grave and die a martyr, among those (as he says in his Epitaph)

Qu'Amours occist de son raillon.

[Whom Love slew with his bolt.]

I pause here to consider a problem which must not be ignored, glided over without comment, or not perceived at all. This is the plain existence, in the Ballade called *Ballade de Villon à s'Amye*, of the name "Marthe" in acrostic, with his own:

Faulse beaulté qui tant me couste chier,
Rude en effect, ypocrite doulceur,
Amour dure plus que fer a maschier,
Nommer que puis, de ma desfaçon seur,
Cherme felon, la mort d'ung povre cuer,
Orgueil mussié qui gens met au mourir,
Yeulx sans pitié, ne veult droit de rigueur,
Sans empirer, ung povre secourir?

Mieulx m'eust valu avoir este serchier
Ailleurs secours: c'eust esté mon onneur;
Riens ne m'eust sceu lors de ce fait hachier.
Trotter m'en fault, en fuyte et deshonneur.
Haro, haro, le grant et le mineur!
Et qu'est ce cy? Mourray sans coup ferir? . . .

[False lovely one, that hath cost me so dear; ruthless one, false sweeting, love harder in the mouth than steel, harder than I can say, to my destruction kin; O traitorous charms, death of my poor heart! O scornful pride, driving men to their doom! O pitiless eyes, will rigour not allow her, ere worse betide, to succour one forlorn?

Better were it for me to have sought help elsewhere, better for my own pride: nothing would then have wrung this pain from me. But I must fly, in shame and dishonour! Haro! haro! both great and small! But what is this? Shall I, then, die, without a blow? Or will pity move her, ere worse betide, to succour one forlorn?]

This Ballade, Catullus-like in its dragging pain, is preceded by a verse of plain direction. Villon sends it, by the hand of Pernet

de la Barre, to his *damoyselle au nez tortu;* and in the last line of
the huitain his pain bursts forth into a sudden spitting fury.

> *Ceste ballade luy envoye*
> *Qui se termine tout par R.*
> *Qui luy portera? Que je voye:*
> *Ce sera Pernet de la Barre,*
> *Pourveu, s'il rencontre en son erre,*
> *Ma damoyselle au nez tortu,*
> *Il luy dira sans plus enquerre:*
> *"Orde paillarde, dont viens tu?"*

[This Ballade, all ending in R, I send her. By whose hand?
Let me see. . . . It shall be by Pernet de la Barre: provided that
if on his way he meets my lady of the twisted nose he shall say to
her, without further ceremony: "Dirty trull, where have you
been?"]

Now if this woman who has so tortured him, this girl with the
twisted nose, the cause of all his griefs, is Katherine de Vausselles,
whom he has mentioned by name just before, why does he thus
couple his name, in a Ballade ostensibly addressed to her, with the
name of a mysterious Marthe, who is nowhere mentioned by him
before or afterwards? Immediately half a dozen hypotheses, all
equally plausible, or seemingly, will occur. One need not make a
Star Chamber matter of them. My own theory, which seems supported alike by the meagre evidence, by probability, and our poor
frailty, is that Villon, retreating from the scornful one, desperately
offered the remains of his heart to the shadowy Marthe. Whether
Marthe was one of the procession of light-of-loves or a more serious
rival to Katherine I cannot judge. She consoled him, possibly, for
the time, playing Eliante to his Alceste.

ELIANTE

Moy, vous venger! comment?

ALCESTE

En recevant mon cœur.
Acceptez-le, Madame, au lieu de l'infidelle,
C'est par là que je puis prendre vengeance d'elle.

ELIANTE.

[I avenge you? How?

131

ALCESTE.
By accepting my heart.
Take it, Madam, instead of the unfaithful one;
It is by this that I can revenge myself on her.]

It is, as I see it, an air from the noble comical tragedy and most tragical comedy of the *Misanthrope*, played in a coarser key and on a thinner pipe. The poet strives to suffocate in another's woman's embraces the passion that is tearing at his bowels; and fails, as such poor devils do. He writes Katherine his Ballade, setting down with voluptuous misery all his pain; and since he is himself writhing he must needs try to get in a swift stab at the creature's pride by blazoning abroad his new mistress. This he does, and sets Marthe ostentatiously in his second stanza for all the world to see: so far as he is concerned, for one pair of eyes to see only.

So much for this problem, which it was necessary to examine here. And so much for Katherine de Vausselles also. She was plainly nothing more than a cold-hearted *enjôleuse*, attracted for a time by the moping poet, amused and flattered by his salt wit and his skill at stringing verses. It is evident that Villon, with his scarecrow figure and dark hangdog face, had no more hope of the creature's love than the Cyclops had of Galatea; and even as the Sicilian sang, preluding the idyll of that pathetic monster ("*Against Love there is no remedy, Nikias . . .* "), so Villon found no antidote, unguent, philtre, nor potion, except in the commerce of the Pierides. Katherine used him, grew tired, and threw him away. Her only love, if we can believe her lover, was money, for which (on the thin evidence of a Ballade only vaguely attributed to Villon) she in the end sold her body to a rich, old, dirty, and horrible buyer. She is a perennial type. As I write her name I see her clearly, with her twisted nose and her red lips and her hard dark eyes. Some sort of perverse beauty she must have had. I see the fur-edged gown closely sheathing her slim body, the heart-shaped velvet headdress, the finicking airs. I see also a narrow street in the dusk, and hear a slammed door and a light laugh from the open casement above, and see again a poor fool stumbling blindly along the cobbles, drunk with pain and rage. We need not mention Katherine de Vausselles again until we come to the Testaments, but she is there, perpetual, pervasive, the background of Villon's life and his enduring sickness.

The time was nearing Christmas,

Sur le Noel, morte saison,
Que les loups se vivent de vent,
Et qu'on se tient en sa maison,
Pour le frimas, pres du tison.

[At this time, as I have said, near Christmas, in the dead of the year, when the wolves feed on wind and men stay indoors, hugging the hearth, on account of the cold, there came to me a desire to break my prison, where Love has held my heart in such duress.]

Villon's decision to leave Paris was made; and from it sprang the idea of making a burlesque will on his departure which blossomed into the *Lais,* otherwise the *Petit Testament.* Gaston Paris thinks it impossible that Villon can have read the "Farewells" of the three poets of Arras his predecessors, Jehan Bodel, Baulde Fastoul, and above all Adam de la Halle, each of whom on quitting Arras had bidden adieu to his fellow-citizens in satiric verses, Jehan and Baulde retiring to a lazar-house and Adam travelling to Paris: but Villon may easily have come upon these verses in a library, or have heard them quoted. The *Petit Testament* was written, then: rapidly, I should say, for there is no body in it, and a poet of any metal at all could reel off half the verses between drinks. But it is clear that the end of it was composed in Master Guillaume's house in the cloister of St. Benoît, where the ringing of the nine o'clock Angelus from Sorbonne, just above, would most loudly be heard.

The date of the departure for Angers is fixed by the *Petit Testament.* It was on the edge of Christmas 1456. Villon, it may be presumed, had everything arranged, his farewells said, his final pot drunk, his last leave taken of the cruel one whose eyes were so false and killing—

Ces doulx regars et beaulx semblans
De tres decevante saveur,
Me trespersant jusques aux flans . . .

133

[If I succumbed to her dear looks and lovely deceits, of such sweet treachery that they pierce my very heart, they have now left me well in the lurch, forlorn in my greatest need. I am fain to carry my plaint elsewhere and to strike out afresh.]

He says good-bye to her, and to his mother, no doubt, and to Master Guillaume, accepting from both a little journey-money. And then, it may have been on Christmas Eve, Villon abruptly changes his plans.

The *Mule* tavern stood in the Rue St. Jacques, facing the Hospice of the Mathurins, or Religious of the Sacred Trinity: that is to say, on the opposite side of the road from the Sorbonne and St. Benoît, lower down, nearer the river, facing what is now the Rue du Sommerard.[4] Here, on the night when Villon changed his mind, which we will take to have been Christmas Eve, 1456—in the Interrogatory of 1458 the phrase is *circa festum Nativitatis Domini,* which may mean any night in the week preceding Christmas—five men met for supper. I give their names and descriptions as they appear in the examination of Master Guy Tabarie before the Officiality of Paris, on July 22, 1458. One of them was Master François Villon; the second, Colin des Cayeulx, whom we have already met; the third, Guy Tabarie, clerk, Master of Arts, the *homs veritable* who copied out the Romance of the *Pet-au-Deable;* the fourth, a lapsed Picard monk called Dom Nicolas, *quidam monachus nuncupatus dompnus Nicolaus, de partibus Picardie;* the fifth, one Petit-Jehan, a stumpy personage with a black beard, wearing a short cloak, of whom it is written:

. . . *dictus des Cahyeus est fortis operator crochetorum, sed dictus Petit-Jehan, ejus socius, est forcius operator.*

[The said des Cayeulx is a powerful operator of picklocks, but the said Petit-Jehan, his companion, still more skilful.]

He was cleverer at picking locks even than his associate Colin des Cayeulx: the tribute is official.

These five supped at the *Mule:* after which (I quote from Guy Tabarie's evidence before the Officiality) the said Master François

[4] The Order of the Mathurins was founded in the twelfth century for the ransom of captives. The hostel in the Rue St. Jacques was early thirteenth century.

Villon, the said Colin des Cayeulx, and the said Dom Nicolas took Master Tabarie aside and made him swear to reveal nothing of what he was about to see and hear. This done, and the account for wine settled, or otherwise, the five issued from the *Mule* and proceeded in the direction of the College of Navarre.[5] The *Mule* has vanished, but the site off the College of Navarre is still permanent. It is to-day the Ecole Polytechnique, which was built over the cloister and the College in 1738. I have walked from the approximate site of the *Mule* to the site of the College easily in ten minutes. In 1456, when a rabbit-warren of short cuts made going easier, it probably took half that time. The five companions, then, had but a brief journey. Their plans had been completed earlier. Guy Tabarie knew nothing of them. He was obviously a simple fool, and the right man for his part in the night's work.

They came, slinking cautiously through narrow byways, to the College of Navarre, dark and silent at this late hour—it was just on ten o'clock—and on the eve of the Feast. The exact account of the night's operations is contained in the report of the examination of Tabarie on July 5, 1458, when he was persuaded by irresistible arguments, a month after being caught, to reveal what he knew.[6] I will continue with the smooth colloquial Latin of the clerk to the Official or Diocesan Judge of the Most Reverend Father in God Guillelmus, by Divine grace Bishop of Paris, by whom Tabarie was claimed and dealt with. The document begins, after the preliminary formal salutations to all those to whom these presents shall come:

Magister Guido Tabary, clericus, adductus de Castelleto Parisiensi, anno Domini millesimo quadringentesimo quinquagesimo octavo, die xxvi Iunii ultimate lapsa, ubi detinebatur propter hoc quod sibi imponitur quod ipse & sui complices furati fuerunt & male ceperunt in Collegio & vestiario Collegii Navarre Parisiensis, quingenta scuta auri eidem Facultati spectancia.

[Master Guy Tabarie, clerk, brought hither from the Châtelet of Paris, in the year of our Lord 1458, in which prison he has been detained since the twenty-sixth day of June on a charge that he and his accomplices did burglariously break and enter the College and the sacristy of the College of Navarre,

---

[5] The Collège de Navarre was Armagnac and loyalist, whereas the rest of University was Burgundian and pro-English. It had been pillaged in 1418, and its fine library wrecked.

[6] University of Paris. Arch. nat., M 180, no. 9 (Fonds du Collège de Navarre).

of Paris, and take therefrom 500 gold crowns belonging to the said Faculty [of Theology].

And proceeds:

Die vero Mercurii quinta mensis Iulii, dictus clericus super hoc iuratus, tactis per eum sacris ewangeliis, dicere & confiteri veritatem sponte confessus fuit, & recognovit quod verum est: quod fuit unus annus circa festum Nativitatis Domini ultimate lapsum, quod quadam die ipse obviavit magistro Francisco Villon, Colino des Cahyeux quem nunquam viderat ut dicit, nisi semel quod ipsum viderat cum dicto magistro Francisco, qui ipsum loquentem onaverit de emendo preparatum ad cenandum pro ipsis in taberna ad intersignum Mule ante Sanctum Mathurinum, quod & fecit ipse loquens. Et simul ibidem cenaverunt & cum ipsis quidam monachus nuncupatus dompnus Nicolaus, de partibus Picardie, & quidem nuncupatus Petit Iehan, quem ipse loquens non novit. Et dicit quod, post cenam, prenominati magister Franciscus, Colinus des Cahyeux, dompnus Nicolaus ipsum loquentem adiuraverunt nichil dicere de his que videret & audiret, & quod ipse cum eis iret, sine aliud tunc sibi declarando. Et, hoc facto, ipsi simul iverunt in domo in qua morari solebat magister Robertus de Saint Symon, in qua ipsi omnes unus post alium intraverunt per supra unum parvum murum &, ipsis in eadem existentibus, prenominati se spoliaverunt in suis gipponibus, & iverunt versus dictum Collegium Navarre in quo ipsi intraverunt per supra unum magnum murum respondentem in curte dicti Collegii cum adiutorio cuiusdam ratelarii quem ipsi, in dicta domo in qua se spoliaverunt, ceperant. Ipse vero loquens non intravit dictum Collegium, sed stetit & mansit in eadem domo usque ad eorum regressum.

Et dicit quod quando ipsi dictum Collegium intraverunt erat decima hora de nocte vel eocirca & quando redierunt erat quasi duodecima, & ipsi loquenti dixerunt quod ipsi lucrati fuerunt centum scuta auri & sibi monstraverunt unum parvum sacum de grossa tela in quo erat aurum, sed nescit quantum, sibi dicendo quod si ipse aliquid diceret quod ipsi eum occiderent; & ut hoc secretius teneret sibi dederunt decem scuta auri que ipse loquens cepit & retinuit. Residuum vero inter se butinaverunt & ipsum loquentem recedere fecerunt, ipsumque conduxerunt & sibi dixerunt quod erant duo scuta bona que essent pro prandendo in crastinum. Dixit tamen quos postmodum audivit quod maiorem summam inter se butinaverunt. Et dicit quod, quadam die sequenti, ipse prenominatus dixit quod ipsi maiorem summam habuerant quam sibi declaraverunt; qui responderunt quod ipse verum dicebat, & quod quilibet eorum habuerat centum scuta.

O the lovely Latin! A vivid, flexible, easy, dressing-gown-and-slippers tongue, fit for pedants to gnash their gums over! Let us see what the wretched Tabarie, on his own showing a notorious geck and gull and the butt of the party, had to reveal on this Wednesday the fifth of July 1458, being first sworn on the Holy Gospels.

He deposed that on a day immediately before Christmas 1456 he met Master François Villon in company with Colin des Cayeulx, whom (*i.e.* des Cayeulx) he had never seen before but once, in Master Villon's society. He deposed that he was charged by these two to provide supper for them at the *Mule* tavern that night, which he did. He said that there were present at supper Master Villon, Colin des Cayeulx, himself, a monk of Picardy called Dom Nicolas, and a person named Petit-Jehan, whom he did not know; that after supper the said Master François, Colin des Cayeulx, and Dom Nicolas took him aside and made him swear to hold his tongue over what he was about to see and hear, at the same time omitting to specify what that might be; that all five then issued from the *Mule* and came to a house formerly occupied by Master Robert de Saint-Simon, into which they all, one after the other, entered by climbing a low wall; that the above-mentioned four (excluding Tabarie) there divested themselves of their cloaks, climbed a high wall giving on to the court of the College of Navarre with the help of a ladder which they found in Master de Saint-Simon's house, and broke into the College; but that he, the said Tabarie, speaking, did not accompany them over the wall, but stayed to guard the cloaks until they reappeared. He deposed further that when his companions broke into the College of Navarre the time was about ten o'clock, and when they returned it was nearly midnight; that they told him that they had secured a hundred crowns, showing him a small bag of coarse stuff containing booty, but he did not know how much; that they warned him that if he breathed a word they would murder him, and that they then gave him, to keep his mouth shut, the sum of ten crowns, which he took and retained. That they divided the remainder between them, first ordering the said Tabarie to step aside; that they then approached him, saying that there were two good crowns to spend on the morrow's dinner. He deposed further that afterwards he heard that the sum they had divided was much larger than they had said, and that the next day he charged them with it, and that they admitted it, saying that each of them had received for his share a hundred crowns.

137

Here the major part of Master Guy Tabarie's evidence ends. Is anything easier than to summon up from this statement, yanked out of Master Tabarie by the sweating fear of what lay before him, a living picture of the scene? The night must have been for the most part silent, for the bells (if it was Christmas Eve, as we may not too violently decide, for lack of any evidence to the contrary) would not begin clashing for the Midnight Mass of Christmas until after eleven. Was there snow on the ground? It is highly possible. Was the night sky overcast, or was there a moon, greeted with oaths by Master François, Colin, the dissolute Picard monk Dom Nicolas, and furtive Petit-Jehan, with his beard and his short cloak and his clever fingers, itching to be at the work? They dropped easily over the low wall into Master Robert's garden: he was away, and the house was empty. The ladder they found so easily had, no doubt, been placed beforehand in readiness for the getting over the high wall into the College courtyard, and the outer College door of oak gave little difficulty—unless indeed they forced a window, which was much easier. Observe that the Staff work was perfect and the position of the coffer exactly known. There was no fumbling. It may be assumed that, once inside, the work was apportioned as follows: Petit-Jehan, the principal expert, to the coffer, assisted by Colin des Cayeulx, and Villon and Dom Nicolas posted to give the alarm if need arose; had need arisen there would most probably have been a murder added to the burglary. The sacristy of course opened into the College chapel, where there would be a *veilleuse*, a hanging lamp, before the altar: from this, no doubt, a shaded lantern was lighted and placed on the floor by the coffer for the experts to work by. O admirable medieval locksmiths! Single-minded craftsmen! It took Petit-Jehan, a notable artificer, and his assistant nearly two whole hours to get at the money. The coffer, indeed, was no child's-play. It is described exactly in the report of the preliminary Châtelet inquiry, and consisted of a strong outer shell, quadruple-locked and bound with iron, having inside, securely fastened and joined, a smaller coffer with three locks, equally iron-bound.[7] I see the sweat pouring off Petit-Jehan, the stumpy, excellent fellow, as he toils, grunting and calling on his Maker in a

---

[7] It cost the Faculty, as we shall see later, sixteen deniers Parisis for repairs.

hoarse whisper. I see the four start suddenly as a bell gives tongue somewhere near, the echoes booming and reverberating under the arches. I hear the stifled yelp of relief and exultation as Petit-Jehan and des Cayeulx finally wrench open the inner coffer-lid, prise up or smash any interior fastening, and dive deep among the money-bags. What were the Faculty of Theology about, to leave their gold unguarded, with never a watchman going his rounds?

The four thieves, having tried other doors and an aumbry without success, slip out again into the night, clutching their loot, shin over the high wall into Master Robert's garden, snap up their cloaks from Tabarie and scramble helter-skelter over the low wall into the safety of the street. We may continue now with the inquest:

Interrogatus ubi dictas peccunias ceperunt, dicit quod nescit nisi in dicto Collegio, sed in quo loco dixit quod nescit, nec etiam scire dicere.

Super hoc interrogatus, si seras levaverunt aut cum crochetis aperuerunt, nec ab eis aliquid audivit, nec eis vidit aliquos crochetos, dicit tamen quod ipse audivit quod dictus des Cahyeus est fortis operator crochetorum, sed dictus Petit Iehan, eius socius, est forcius operator, quamvis, ut dicit, ipse nunquam scivit quod ipsi aliquod aliud furtum commisserint quam supradictum.

[Questioned as to where they took the said money, he answers that he does not know, unless it was in the said College; but he does not know in what place there, even by hearsay.

Questioned as to whether they removed the locks or opened them with picklocks, whether he heard anything, or saw any picklocks, he deposes that he has heard that the said des Cayeulx is a powerful operator of picklocks, but Petit-Jehan, his companion, more so; although, he says, he has never known them to commit any burglary other than the aforesaid.]

The miserable Tabarie is quite evidently torn between two terrors: the terror of the Official's rack and the terror of what awaits him if his comrades, whom he is giving away, get hold of him. And here his tormentors switch off suddenly and question him concerning another robbery in which this same band has been concerned, but of which nothing is known except from this inquiry.

Item, interrogatus super furto per ipsum & suos complices perpetrato in monasterio Augustiniensium Parisiensium, in camera alicuius religiosorum eiusdem, dicit quod nichil scit nec fuit in dicto furto. Ymo dicit quod, tempore dicti furti commissi, ipse prisionarius detentus erat mancipatus in carceribus nostris, propter hoc quod ipse & Casinus Cholet [8] sese verberaverant.

[*Item,* questioned concerning the burglary committed by him and his accomplices in the monastery of the Augustinians at Paris, in the chamber of a religious of that house, he says that he knows nothing and was not concerned in the said burglary. He says, indeed, that at the time of the said burglary he was a prisoner in our dungeons, on account of his quarrel with Casin Cholet and their thrashing of each other.]

If Tabarie spoke the truth, the burglary at the Augustinians must have taken place (the Official is careless of exact dates) some little time before the affair of the College of Navarre. The remaining questions of this, the first day of Tabarie's examination, I will summarise briefly.

Asked if he ever spoke to a certain Master Pierre Marchant about the burglary at the College of Navarre, he replied *No.*

Asked if he had ever told the said Master Pierre that certain moneys stolen from Friar Guillaume Coiffier [the Augustinian, the victim in the minor charge] had got him out of prison, he replied *No.*

Asked if he had ever heard it said by his companions, or had ever said himself, that they had tried to break into the church of St. Mathurin but had been driven away by the barking of dogs, he replied *No.*

Asked if he had ever said that Master François Villon was about to set out for Angers, to visit a certain churchman who was comfortably well off, and that the companions were to set out there later in order to rob him, he replied *No.*

Asked how long he had known his accomplices, he replied that he had known Master François Villon a long time, but had never before seen the said Petit-Jehan; and that he knew des Cayeulx only a little through seeing him with the said Master Villon.

Propter quod, says the report, *fuit remissus in carcerem nostrum:* following which he was placed once more in our prison; the officials present being Master Guillaume Sohyer, Master Jehan Rebours, Master Denys Commitis, Master François de Vaccarie, Master Jehan Laurens, Master Jehan le Fourbeur, and me, the notary subscribed.

An important character now arrives on the scene, the Master Pierre Marchant of whom a passing mention has been made. Since

[8] Casin Cholet is the expert duck-thief of the two *Testaments.*

this shrewd personage was responsible for the ultimate capture of Tabarie and the bringing to light of the whole story of the burglary, we will take his evidence next, leaving Tabarie, very glum and apprehensive, sitting for the moment in his cell. The evidence of Master Pierre Marchant, set down not in Latin but in French, opens a wide window on the Alsatia of old Paris and its citizens.

On the eve of the Sunday called (from its Introit) Quasimodo, or Low Sunday, 1457, there arrived in Paris from the diocese of Chartres the *venerable & discrete personne* (I quote from the Official's report) *messire Pierre Marchant, prestre, prieur curé de Paraiz.*

[The venerable and discreet person Master Pierre Marchant, priest, Prior and Curé of Paray.]

His age was about forty, his reputation irreproachable. He put up at the sign of the *Three Chandeliers* in the Rue de la Huchette. The street still stands, with the same name: it runs off the Rue St. Jacques, close to and parallel with the quays. The venerable and discreet Prior of Paray,[9] having washed off the dust of his journey, slept, and duly said his Mass on Sunday morning, issued from the *Three Chandeliers* towards noon (or it may have been the following day—he will not swear to it) and walked over to the tavern called the *Chayere*, or Pulpit, which stood on the Petit-Pont: and here, having ordered breakfast, he found himself in casual conversation with a certain Master Guy, whose surname he did not know, and one calling himself (pretty doubtfully) a priest, whose name the Prior did not catch at all. Master Guy seems to have been garrulous drunk. He began, after salutations, by asking the Prior "What news?" and immediately, without apparently awaiting for any reply, continued

à compter de ces adventures & à dire audit deposant qu'il avoit esté long temps prisonnier es prisons de monseigneur l'evesque de Paris, & que on luy avoit imposé & mis sus qu'il estoit crocheteur.

[9] Paray-le-Moniau, near Chartres: not to be confused with the famous shrine of Paray-le-Monial, near Mâcon.

141

[. . . to tell tales of his adventures, and to inform the said witness [Master Pierre] that he had been a long time held in the prisons of my Lord the Bishop of Paris, on the charge of being a picker of locks.]

He is in an expansive mood. I see the Prior gravely beginning his breakfast, while the idiot Tabarie sprawls over a table near by, flushed and pot-valiant, seeing in his hearer, no doubt, a simple bumpkin, and being not averse to displaying himself, the Parisian Tabarie, a devil of a fellow. And I see the Prior suddenly prick up his ears at the word *crocheteur*, picklock.

Et adonc ledit deposant, oyant ce que dit est, saichant que puis nagaires on avoit desrobé v ou vi° escus d'or en la chambre de frere Guillaume Coiffier, religieux des Augustins à Paris, à ceste cause print à interroguer ledit maistre Guy sur le fait desditz crochetz & de la maniere d'en ouvrer, pour sentir s'il porroit aucune chose sçavoir de la larrecin faicte en la chambre dudit Coiffier. Et à ceste cause ledit deposant se print à faindre qu'il vouloit bien estre de ces complices pour avoir de l'argent.

[At which the said witness, hearing this and knowing that a little time before there had been 500 or 600 gold crowns stolen from the chamber of Friar Guillaume Coiffier, of the Augustinians of Paris, for this reason began to interrogate the said Master Guy concerning the said picklocks and their use, in order to see if he could discover anything touching the burglary in the chamber of the said Coiffier. And for this reason the said witness set himself to pretend that he would like to join this band and make some money.]

The venerable and discreet person instantly felt within him, it is clear, all the glow of the amateur detective who has stumbled by pure chance on a hot clue. Tabarie, gesticulating and reckless, was completely disarmed by his frankness and simplicity, and at once patronisingly offered to procure and show Master Pierre one day soon some good picklocks used by himself and his companions. "A little time ago" (Tabarie speaking) "he had had some in his possession, but had thrown them into the Seine for fear of their being found on him." He added that a certain Thibault of his acquaintance, a goldsmith by trade, was a fine fashioner of picklocks of all shapes and sizes, and a good man to know when you had gold or silver plate to melt down, a friend to the band. All this the Prior of Paray received with well-simulated envy and admiration, and departed, promising to meet Master Guy next day.

The next day the Prior met Maſter Guy and took him to the famous *Pomme de Pin*, in the Rue de la Juiverie, where he treated him handsomely to wine, at the same time repeating his wish to become a member of the gang. Later the same day, Maſter Guy being no doubt reeling ripe, but the Prior abſtemious and keenly perceptive, Maſter Guy took his new friend and aspirant to Notre-Dame, where he showed him, in the Precinct, four or five companions lounging there, being lately escaped from the prisons of the Bishop of Paris; [10] and among them one especially of whom the Prior made a careful note, so that this companion rises before our eyes a full-length sketch:

ung qui eſtoit petit homme & jeune de xxvi ans ou environ, lequel avoit longs cheveux par derriere, & luy diſt que c'eſtoit le plus soutil de toute la compaignie & le plus habille à crocheter, & que riens ne luy eſtoit impossible en tel cas.

[One who was a small young man, of about twenty-six years old or thereabouts, with long hair behind; and [Maſter Guy] told him [the witness] that this was the moſt skilful of all the company, and the clevereſt at picking locks, and that nothing was ever impossible to him.]

Maſter Guy approached several of the companions, informing them of the arrival of his new friend, who so greatly desired to be of their society. They received the Prior with fair words, *bonne chiere & beau langaige*, but ſtudiously forebore in his presence to say anything of their plans, paſt, present, or future: and so after a short space Maſter Guy and the Prior left them and went out of the Cathedral. They walked together thence very amicably, and Maſter Guy was moved to a fresh outburſt of confidences. He told the Prior of several schemes ripe for execution as soon as the companions could safely get clear of the freedom of Notre-Dame; and particularly he outlined with loving pride a coming burglary at the house of a certain Maſter Robert de la Porte, for which Thibault had all the tools ready, and for which a cousin of Thibault's had promised to lend them monaſtic disguises. In passing, Maſter Guy (I assume that more and more wine had filled his skin) mentioned that he himself had only recently got out of the Bishop's prison,

[10] They had taken sanctuary in the Cloiſters, within the freedom of the Metropolitan: and no doubt were watching for the favourable moment to get away.

and that some of the money ſtolen from Friar Guillaume Coiffier of the Auguſtinians had been responsible for getting him out.

The Prior at this (I see him doing it) reſtrained a whoop of satisfaction, and refilled Maſter Guy's cup. He was, as children say, getting warm. He began to queſtion Maſter Guy guardedly about this business of the burglary at the Auguſtinian house. Observe that this amateur police work might at any moment, had Tabarie's suspicions been aroused, have led the Prior of Paray into an underground den, and thence swiftly, with a cut throat, into the river: but it was written that Juſtice should be served. Tabarie opened out like an oyſter:

Lequel maiſtre Guy luy diſt que puis nagaires ledit Coiffier avoit eſté desbourcé de v ou vi° escus & qu'il en avoit eu pour sa part environ viii escus, lesquelz ledit Thibault luy avoit apportez es prisons de la court de l'evesque de Paris pour paier le geaulier en disant, oultre, par ledit maiſtre Guy, que c'eſtoit peu de chose & que luy & ces compaignons avoient entencion d'en avoir mieulx.

[The said Maſter Guy told him [the Prior] that a little time ago the said Coiffier had been relieved of 500 or 600 crowns and that he [Tabarie] had had for his share about 8 crowns, which the said Thibault had brought into the court of the prisons of the Bishop of Paris to bribe the gaoler with; at the same time saying, according to the said Maſter Guy, that this was nothing, and that he and his companions could do better than that.]

This was good, but better was to follow immediately.

Et, encore, ledit maiſtre diſt audit deposant que, puis de tempts en ça, luy et ces complices avoient eſté au colliege de Navarre à ung coffre ouquel ilz avoient prins v ou vi° escus, & que l'ung d'eulx les avoit deſtournez & empeschez de crocheter unes aulmoires qui eſtoient audit lieu de Navarre pres dudit coffre, lesquelles aulmoires avoient bien plus grant chevance comme iiii ou vᵐ escus, & disoit ledit maiſtre Guy que les autres compaignons maudisoient leur compaignon qui les avoit deſtournez de crocheter lesdiĉtes aulmoires.

[And, continuing, the said Maſter Guy told the witness that a short time ago he and his companions had been at the College of Navarre after a cheſt there, from which they had taken 500 or 600 crowns, and that one of them had hindered and prevented the others from picking certain aumbries which were in that place, which held much greater treasure, to the probable amount of 4000 or 5000 crowns; and the said Maſter Guy added that the companions cursed the one who so prevented them from picking the said aumbries.]

Master Tabarie, babbling artlessly on, drunk equally with vain-glory and wine, has by now run his head well into the noose. But he has by no means finished yet. He rambles on with a story of how he and his companions had tried to break into the Mathurins' church in the Rue St. Jacques, but were driven away by the bark-ing of watchdogs; how, on the morning of the burglary at the Augustinians, one of the band had called on Friar Guillaume Coiffier, their victim, and requested the friar to say a Mass for his intention in St. Mathurin, and how, while the friar was duly saying his Mass, the other companions had broken into his chamber and carried off a small coffer containing 500 or 600 crowns, and also some silver plate. Master Pierre Marchant noted all this, and took his leave. One day following Tabarie brought with him one of the companions, aged between twenty-eight and thirty, a little man called Master Jehan, very clever, with a black beard and a short cloak. It was arranged to meet together at St. Germain-des-Prés the following Monday, where they would be joined by Thibault with a selection of picklocks. But the Prior evaded the meeting, and Tabarie, calling later that day at the *Three Chandeliers* in the Rue de la Huchette to inquire, was fobbed off with the explanation that he had had urgent business elsewhere. The Prior nevertheless carried Tabarie to dine and extracted from him the information that the projected burglary at the house of Master Robert de la Porte, for which this meeting had been called to discuss final ways and means, was postponed for a little time because certain persons had got wind of it. There is one more piece of illumination for the Prior, and for us, and then his evidence is finished.

Oultre, ledit maistre Guy dist audit deposant que ilz avoient ung aultre complice nommé maistre François Villon, lequel estoit allé à Angiers en une abbaye en laquelle il avoit ung sien oncle qui estoit religieulx en ladite abbaye, & qu'il y estoit alé pour sçavoir l'estat d'ung ancien religieulx dudit lieu, lequel estoit renommé d'estre riche de v ou vi° escus, & que, luy retourné, selon ce qu'il rapporteroit par de çà aux autres compaignons, ilz yroient tous par delà pour le desbourcer, & que, à quelque matin, ilz auroient tout le sien nettement.

[Moreover, the said Master Guy told the witness that they had another accomplice named Master François Villon, who had gone to Angers, to an

145

abbey where he had an uncle, a religious in the said abbey; that he had gone there to discover the circumstances of an aged monk of the said place, reputed to possess some 500 or 600 crowns; and that on his return and according to his report to the companions they would all make their way there to rob this monk, and that one fine day they would clean him out.]

Et plus n'en scet. The Prior's testimony ends here, abruptly. He had squeezed Tabarie dry, and now held in his hands enough evidence to hang him and the principals of the band twice over. Early one morning soon after his last talk with Tabarie—or rather, after listening patiently to Tabarie's last monologue—the Prior issued discreetly from the *Three Chandeliers* and made his way to the Provost's house in the Rue de Jouy, bearing with him notes of all his conversations with that blabber and windbag.

He was too late. The alarm had been given, the birds had flown. Tabarie, no doubt, awaking sober a morning or two before and remembering with a start of apprehension some scraps of the things he had been pouring so continuously into the sympathetic stranger's ear, suddenly sniffed danger. When the Provost's men came searching for him and his friends they had vanished. It was thirteen months before the police laid hands on Tabarie. The slowness of the Faculty of Theology in this matter seems rather extraordinary. The burglary was not discovered for three months; it was by pure luck that Master Jehan Mautaint, Examiner at the Châtelet, and Master Jehan du Four, who were in charge of the inquiry then set up, were furnished on May 17, 1457, with the names of the thieves by the Prior of Paray; it was not till June 25 in the next year that Tabarie was arrested; and as we shall see later, it was apparently not till some time between February and March 1459 that the Faculty collaborated with the King's Procurator in pursuing the inquiry.

We may finish with Tabarie, this thickhead, for the time being. He was the *poire*, in modern slang, of the band: the booby and hanger-on, who did the rough work and got ten crowns for his night's work where the booty ran into hundreds. We left him awaiting his second day's examination, with the Prior's evidence still to come. Having heard this, and admitted it to be true, broadly speaking, he proved slightly stubborn under cross-examination. They therefore applied to him the Question Ordinary.[11] Greatly disliking it, as anybody would, for under the pressure of water the heart and bowels felt like to burst, Tabarie was in the grip of a greater fear, and uttered no intelligible word. The ministers of Justice therefore removed him into another chamber for the application of the Question Extraordinary; and having been bound on the rack, *applicato magno tretello*, he was further treated, and after a brief but painful interval broke down and promised to confess the whole truth. This he did, and was removed once more to his dungeon, the officials present being the venerable Masters Estienne de Montigny, Robert Tuleu, Doctor in Canon Law, Simon Chappitault, Denys Commitis, François Ferrebouc, and François de Vaccarie.

This is the end, so far as we are concerned, of Master Guy Tabarie, *homs veritable* (observe the irony), a man of parts, but buffle-headed and unable to carry his drink. M. Longnon assumes that his confessions in this business led him direct from his cell in the Bishop's prison to the gibbet; but, as will appear later, he was eventually released (on the civil charge) on a bond by which he undertook to pay back to the Faculty fifty gold crowns. It is more than likely that he ended soon or late on the gibbet. Nothing more is heard of him. As for the Prior, the quite legitimate satisfaction of that venerable and discreet personage probably lasted till death.

We return to the Christmas of 1456. The day after the burglary, as we gather from Tabarie's examination, there was a dinner to

[11] The Question Ordinary, or Question by Water, was applied as part of the routine procedure of Justice to recalcitrant or to taciturn prisoners. The stubborn one was bound, hand and foot, to staples in such a manner as to stretch his body as far as possible: a rack or trestle two feet high was placed under him, supporting his middle. The Questioner, with his assistant, then proceeded, the one to hold the prisoner's nose and thus compel him to swallow, the other to place over his mouth a horn funnel. Into this water was poured, generally four *coquemars* or pipkins-full, about nine litres altogether, by degrees, sometimes through a linen cloth. The patient was then unbound and allowed to recuperate before the treatment was (if adjudged necessary) repeated. See Evelyn's *Diary*, March 11, 1651.

The Question Extraordinary employed a higher rack. The punishment of the Boot, the favourite pastime of James I. of England and Scotland, was occasionally substituted. There is no evidence of the existence at this period of the torture of disembowelling the hanged alive, which flourished in the spacious days of Great Elizabeth and accounted for so many aged priests. Coiners at this time were boiled in oil; thieves for a first offence had an ear cut off; blasphemers had a lip slit, and if hardened might have their tongues removed. And so forth.

celebrate the affair: a feast, as one may imagine, of roaring spirits and congratulation, with lashings of the good wine of Arbois, scented of raspberries, and Aunis flowing, and the table loaded with roast goose and tarts, and the girls in fine feather, and red gold clinking in the purse, and laughter, and song, and kisses, and toasts. Whether Villon pursued his journey to Angers immediately is very doubtful. More likely he gorged himself for a space on the pleasures of the town, never so richly at his command as now: the luscious food, *savoureux morceaulx et frians*, of which his verse is mindful, over which he so often, in writing it down, smacked his hungry lips. Flawns, and larded capons, and fowl: golden-crusted pasties; the roasting partridges and plover which filled with their fragrance the *rostisserie* of Mother Machecoue at the sign of the *Golden Lion*, by the Châtelet; crackling pork, on which he had battened so joyously a year before at the barber's at Bourg-la-Reine; *grasses souppes jacoppines*, rich with eggs, sugar, and milk,

> *Saulces, brouetz, et gros poissons,*
> *Tartes, flaons, œfs fritz et pochez,*

[Sauces, broths, plump fish, tarts, flawns, eggs fried and poached.]

cheese-tarts, *goyers*; the cream, and frumenty, and rice which he remembered in gazing on the piled human bones in the Innocents charnel: all washed down with fine wines, Hypocras, spiced with cinnamon and ginger, and Beaune,

> *Vinum Belnense super omnia vina recense*

[The wine of Beaune, excelling all others.]

(so a devout and lettered Pantagruelist saluted this noble vintage a century before him), and Morillon, pressed from the black grapes of Auvergne.[12] And for dessert, women, with their red laughing lips and enigmatic eyes. "*Tenez*," says the shameless Nephew of Rameau three hundred years later, "*vive la philosophie, vive la sagesse de Salomon: boire de bon vin, se gorger de mets délicats, se rouler sur de jolies femmes, se reposer dans des lits bien mollets! excepté cela,*

---

[12] Some think Morillon was a black Burgundy.

148

le reste n'est que vanité." * In the cravings of one strong side of his nature Villon is own blood-brother to the Nephew, that *reductio ad absurdum* (as somebody or other has well said) of the whole Sensualist philosophy of the eighteenth century.

There were plenty of sharp noses to sniff gold in the air, and plenty of joyous companions to drink his health. The girls naturally got their share of the windfall. Obviously Villon is thinking directly of his hundred-odd gold crowns from the College of Navarre when, years later, he composes the rueful Ballade of Good Counsel to those of Naughty Life:

> *Car ou soies porteur de bulles,*
> *Pipeur ou hasardeur de dez,*
> *Tailleur de faulx coings, tu te brusles,*
> *Comme ceulx qui sont eschaudez,*
> *Traistres parjurs, de foy vuydez;*
> *Soies larron, ravis ou pilles:*
> *Ou en va l'acquest, que cuidez?*
> *Tout aux tavernes et aux filles.*

At length, awaking one morning, I gather, to the fact that his purse was rapidly bleeding to death, and spurred by some disquieting hint dropped in a tavern, he packed his bundle and prudently got clear of Paris and on the road to Angers. Whether Tabarie's allegation concerning Villon's designs on the old religious, his uncle's friend, was true or a bit of gasconade with which to dazzle the Prior of Paray, is not patent. He had to begin with, at any rate, a comfortable feeling that when the money of the Faculty was finally dissipated another source lay at hand when he reached his journey's end, and would be well worth looking into. For the time being it was healthier to get out of Paris, where any day now the police might be on his track: actually we know that it was in May of this year, 1457, that the fateful meeting of Tabarie with Master Pierre Marchant at the sign of the *Pulpit* took place, two months after Jehan Mautaint, Examiner of the Châtelet, assisted by Jehan du Four, took up the case. Villon was by then well out of

---

*[Come, three cheers for the philosophy and wisdom of Solomon: to drink good wine, to gorge yourself on delicate meats; to lie and toy with pretty women, and to sleep in good soft beds—except for this, all is but vanity!]

danger. The other companions, once the alarm was given, had scattered to the four winds. Colin des Cayeulx, as we have seen, fled to Normandy, and was later captured. The hiding-place of Dom Nicolas the Picard monk, of Petit-Jehan, and of Tabarie himself is not known, nor have the *dossiers* of the monk and the expert picklock been discovered, nor any trace of their being caught and dealt with for their share in the adventure: as they doubtless were in due course.

We see Villon, therefore, making his way into Anjou in the rain and cold of early spring, in the sunshine, sniffing the clean air and (though he had no lust for the country) observing with a poet's eye the little white clouds bowling overhead before a shouting April wind, the primroses and violets in the hedges, the ruffling brooks, the spreading fields: taking the road by day, putting up at night in hedge-taverns and barns, or in deserted shepherd's huts on the outskirts of villages, and at intervals exchanging the sign of the Coquille with some dubious slouching figure at a cross-road, who could inform him if it were safe to enter the town away on the horizon.

It would reasonably appear from a line of the *Grant Testament* to which I have already referred, in which he calls himself

Moy, povre mercerot de Renes,

that he had taken the precaution of getting himself a pedlar's pack, partly to avoid awkward questionings on his journey, and partly to eke out his failing stock of money: a pack stuffed with the things Charles d'Orléans recites in a laughing verse—writing-tablets, lute-strings, glass rosary-beads, pocket-knives, amber signets; and also, undoubtedly, coloured ribands, laces, tags, lengths of silk and stuff, "pins and poking-sticks of steel," imitation jewellery, and other women's gauds, with perhaps a sheaf of manuscript ballads and a few crudely coloured pictures of popular saints—St. Louis the King, St. Christopher protector against sudden death, St. Laurence patron of cookshop-keepers, St. Julian patron of innkeepers, St. Victor protector against epilepsy, St. Eloy protector against throat-complaints; and with these, possibly, some representing the Maid of Orleans, and St. Denis, and the Four Sons of Aymon, and the Last Judgment. In a *Dictz du Mercier* I have seen there is set forth, with a breath of *The Winter's Tale*, a long list of the gauds the medieval mercer sold:

> *J'ay les mignotes ceinturetes,*
> *J'ay beax ganz a damoyseletes,*
> *J'ay ganz forrez, doubles & sangles,*
> *J'ay de bonnes boucles a cengles,*
> *J'ay chainetes de fer beles,*
> *J'ay bonnes cordes a vieles,*
> *J'ay les guimples ensafranees,*
> *J'ay ayguilles encharnelees,*
> *J'ay escrins a mettre joiax,*
> *J'ai borses de cuir a noiax,*

—belts, gloves, buckles, chains, needles, jewel-cases, leather purses, strings for viols, and a hundred toys. Villon, who was not in the trade for the trade's sake but for his health's, would have made no very careful selection, I imagine, but would have taken indifferently what the mercer supplying him suggested. I am now assuming boldly that he did for a time carry a travelling pedlar's pack, for it seems on consideration more and more likely.

I find the theory all the more tenable because the *mercerots*, itinerant hawkers and pedlars, were more often than not affiliated with the Gueux and the Coquillards, spoke a jargon, carried about the cards for playing *glic* (which our fathers called Gleek), and sets of loaded dice, used their profession to cloak more secret and dubious traffic, and had generally the worst possible reputation. Vitu alleges that the Gild of the Mercers, one of the six Great Companies of Paris, winked at the doings of the *mercerots* and very equably collected dues from them, but I find no support for this. There was honour in the land.

Why Villon mentions Rennes, otherwise than for the sake of a rhyme, is not clear, except that it was a headquarters for *mercerots,* according to Le Duchat. He may have attached himself to this provincial branch. Certainly the life, till he grew tired of it, would be congenial. "Ha, ha! what a fool Honesty is! and Trust, his sworn brother, a very simple gentleman! I have sold all my trumpery . . . 'twas nothing to geld the codpiece of a purse; I would have filed keys off that hung in chains. . . . So that in this time of lethargy I picked and cut most of their festival purses, and had not the old man come in with a whoobub against his daughter and the king's son and scared my choughs from the chaff, I had not left a purse alive in the whole army." This tramping pedlar, with his sharp eyes, glib tongue, quick fingers, and salted and outrageous Parisian wit, could have stood in any village market-square for the picture of Autolycus. Re-reading *The Winter's Tale* I see and hear him in every line of his successor's patter. No doubt the round-eyed inhabitants of Fouilly-les-Oies, and Ste. Chouette-en-Bobigny, and Buzançay-le-Fangeux, and St. Nigaud-sur-Marais, and a dozen more villages (and especially the girls in them) remembered his passing years afterwards.

As the highroad runs direct from Paris he would find in his way only two towns, Chartres and Le Mans. Whether he made a sweep to avoid them, for fear of embarrassing encounters, or whether he plunged into them by night and went to ground at some selected tavern or house of entertainment made known to him through the Coquille, one may pleasantly conjecture. I fancy such a town-bird would have had his bellyful of the open road long before the incomparable great shrine of Chartres rose before him, like a tall ship riding at anchor, from the plain of the Beauce. Entering the cathedral city discreetly he would be given a sign by a brother of the Coquille, and would know where to direct his steps. Once there, snug and cosy, with a pot of wine before him and a girl or two at hand, he could very comfortably get rid of one or two more pieces from his fast-thinning supply of crowns. It was his misfortune, recollect, not to be able to live without women. Next day, or the next, or a week later, in a mood of weariness, or disgust, or apprehension, he would rise and take the road for Anjou again.

There is no evidence that he ever reached chiming Angers, with its clustered steeples, a University town of which it says in the ancient abusive jingle,

> *Angers, basse ville & haults clochers,*
> *Riches putains, povres escholiers,*

[Angers, low town and high steeples, rich whores and poor scholars.]

152

though it is permissible to believe that he at least paid a call on his uncle for the purpose of spying out the land for future operations. I cannot think that the apparition of a dusty vagabond from Paris, bearing in his face and figure the traces of recent debauch and in his glancing eye a sinister promise, awoke any vehement pleasure in the breast of his host. Possibly, also, the little hoard of the old monk his uncle's colleague was too obviously closely guarded to permit of a flying shot. I think Villon sighed, and after a brief stay (but not at the monastery) shook off the Angers dust and took the road again. The year is now a little riper, and the days more pleasant. As he trudges out of the town of Angers and a blackbird pipes above his head I see him involuntarily brighten, as scraps of poetry bud and flower in his mind. Perhaps he bursts into a verse of a bawdy song, frightening the birds and scattering the sheep in the meadow: for with a face and figure like his the accompanying voice, *sauf vostre grace,* must needs have been as melodious as a corncrake or an ungreased cart-wheel.

He came at length—we can trace him now—into Poitou, and lingered for a time in the village of St. Généroux, near Parthenay, on the Vendée border, where there were two girls,

> *tres belles et gentes,*
> *Demourans a Saint-Generou,*
> *Pres Saint-Julien de Voventes,*
> *Marche de Bretaigne ou Poictou.*
> *Mais i ne di proprement ou*
> *Ycelles passent tous les jours,*
> *M'arme! i ne seu mie si fou!*
> *Car i vueil celer mes amours.*

[Very beautiful and charming, dwelling at St. Généroux, near St. Julien de Voventes by the Marches of Brittany in Poitou. But I woänt rightly zaäy whurr they paass their taïme. Gorm me! I'm not such a vule! I laïke to haïde my gooings-on.]

He liked his two Arcadians, and they liked him, and he must have spent some time in their village. They taught him a little of the dialect of Poitou, which he mimics in the verse above, and also in introducing it:

153

Se i parle ung peu poictevin,
Yce m'ont deux dames appris.

[If I do speäk a liddle furrin, 'tes two purty girls larnt me.]

The character of these ladies seems not to difficult to judge:
gay, I should call them, laughing, hospitable country creatures,
easy, eupeptic, apple-cheeked, exchanging smacks and repartee with
this queer dark, dry, sharp-tongued scarecrow from Paris, so different from the ruck of country louts. To Villon, who took his fun
where he found it, this interlude was an extremely pleasant one,
and stored long in his memory. It is a trifle surprising to find Gaston Paris taking this pastoral adventure *au sérieux* and weaving out
of it a little sentimental romance, sweet and idyllic. "*Villon avait
pu rencontrer à Saint-Généroux un accueil gracieux qui lui avait
laissé un honnête et plaisant souvenir.*" Lacroix, going to the other
extreme, reads "Saint-Genou" for "Saint-Généroux," deliberately
evoking a rude popular jest, quoted by Rabelais, which makes a lady
from "St. Genou" nothing better than a common strumpet.[13] I
fancy the girls Villon met were not so loose as all that. Rustic manners are ever free.

Malo me Galatea petit, lasciva puella,
Et fugit salices, et se cupit ante videri.

[My Phyllis me with pelted Apples plies,
    Then tripping to the Woods the Wanton hies,
    And wishes to be seen before she flies.]
                        (*Dryden,* Vergil, Bucolic III.)

How long he loitered with Galatea and Delia in the meadows
of Poitou I do not know.[14] The next trace of him, towards the end
of 1457, is discovered leagues away in the country of the Loire.
Here, under a ducal roof, there lived for a brief time the two greatest European poets of their age.

---

[13] The joke is "from Brisepaille, near St. Genou"; referring to the straw of the lady's
mattress and the knees of her gallants.

[14] Not far from St. Généroux (Deux-Sèvres) is St. Maixent, where, according to the
legend preserved in the Fourth Book of *Pantagruel,* Villon retired in his old age and produced a *Passion* in the Poitevin language. It may be that he went on there now, before
leaving the country altogether.

Enguirlandés de fleurs les printemps passeront,
Puis les étés ardents, puis les automnes graves:
Mais, sans charmer mon âme, ils se succéderont.

Abandonné, lié de toutes parts d'entraves,
Sur le rivage mort où je suis exilé,
Je n'apercevrai plus, partout, que mes épaves.
—Louis le Cardonnel, *L'Attente Mystique.*

There mark what ills the Scholar's life assail:
Toil, envy, want, the Patron, and the Jail.
—Dr Samuel Johnson, *The Vanity of Human Wishes.*

He said good-bye to the *filles tres belles et gentes,* reluctantly, and perhaps with relief, and came wandering out of Poitou, through the vineyards of Touraine, by Châtellerault, probably by little Chinon clustered under its amber cliff overhanging the sleepy Vienne, by Tours, stately with spires, along the Loire, the noble Loire, smooth-sliding among her golden sands and tufted islands, on the road to Blois.

There met his moody eyes as he wandered none of the palaces which now evoke such cries of delight and admiration from pilgrims of the New World as they are whirled swiftly past in powerful machines; for the Renaissance was still under the horizon, and of those sonnets in stone and glass which are now strung along the Loire country, Amboise, Blois, and Chenonceau, Chambord, Ussé, Valençay, Montrésor, Luynes, St. Aignan, Cheverny, little Azay-le-Rideau on the Indre, the greater number were still feudal; but the thick piles of Villandry, or Coulombiers, Loches, and Langeais, and Chaumont were even now, I think, beginning their interior transition, although it was nearly forty years later that Charles viii.'s army, storming over the Alps and getting their first glimpse of the Paradise beyond the snows, returned with wonder in their eyes. In the pile of Chaumont is still mingled the last of the Middle Ages and the first of the new glories breaking on Europe. The stout triple mass of Chinon Castle, with its memories of St. Louis and his mother, and Richard Lion-Heart, and St. Joan, Villon must have seen, for it commands the valley of the Vienne and the road to Tours. I should like to think that he loitered in this tiny beautiful town, and perhaps drank in the Painted Cellar there, where the Father of Laughter was to drink years afterwards, *maints verres de vin frais.*[1]

He was now suffering bitterly from what the medieval facetious called Saint Francis' Diſtemper, referring to Holy Poverty; but aggravated, malignant, and amounting to sheer beggary. The laſt of the gold pieces of the Faculty of Theology had doubtless long since gone spinning down the wind. "And where are they?" asks Epiſtemon, liſtening to Panurge's ſtory of the Turkish Bashaw and his gift of a *braguette*-full of seraphs, and diamonds, and moſt excellent rubies. "By Saint John," returns Panurge, "they are a good Way hence, if they always keep going. But where is the laſt yeare's Snow? This was the greateſt Care that Villon the Parisian Poet took." The business of finding something *mettre sous la dent* was now imperative. He reached Blois at length, and made direƈtly for the Caſtle, a little later to become, with its rich carven woods and windows, its tall lantern, its splendid court, its massy fireplaces, wide delicate ſtaircases, shining floors, its air and light and space and proportion, the perfeƈt Renaissance type of the House Royal and the mirror of that superb age. In Villon's time it was still a fortress. Here, in this year 1457, Charles Duke of Orleans, the King's cousin, held his retired ſtate.

The Duke had returned to Blois on a November day seventeen years before from his long exile, where the disaſter of Agincourt had sent him at the age of twenty-four, having been taken in that gallant smash by Richard Waller of Groomsbridge in Kent. Under our skies he had lived the beſt of his manhood, a high prisoner, and in twenty-five dragging years had written much verse full of longing and melancholy. A frigid train of personages out of the *Roman de la Rose* parades through much of it, a faded tapeſtry of Amours and Venus, with Beaulté their miniſter, Bonne-Foy their secretary, Courtoisie, Bel-Accueil, and Plaisance the intendants of

---

[1] "I know, return'd Pantagruel, where Chinon lies, and the Painted Cellar also, having my self drunk there many a Glass of cool Wine."—Bk. v., xxxv.

the palace, Bonne-Nouvelle and Loyal-Rapport their messengers; their subjects Desir, Comfort, Bon-Conseil, Dangier, Trahison, Desespoir, Destresse, and Soussy; in their demesne the Ermitage de Pensée, the Bois de Merencolie, and the Forest de Tristesse. But with all these dusty conceits the Valois could mingle lovely, quick, fresh lyrics, poised and perfect. I have lingered a moment over one or two of them elsewhere in this book.

When Villon came to the castle of Blois the Duke Charles, now in his sixty-fourth year, grey, long-necked, hard of hearing, but patient, courteous, and kind, wearing perpetually a long furred gown of black velvet, held open house for men of letters, in that magnificent fashion in which great men once behaved, and especially in Italy—and the Duke's mother was a princess of Milan. Poets of all degrees especially were welcome in his household, and received a stipend from their patron; and in his library the scribes toiled at engrossing anthologies of his and their verse. The preservation of a volume of this kind containing two pieces composed by Villon has helped to fix the time of his arriving. It was in the winter of 1457.[2] Soon or late after his arrival Villon found a tourney of the antique kind in progress, perhaps in the thirteenth-century Salle des Etats; one of those competitions, the sport of lettered men, in which the academy of assembled poets embroidered from their fancy a given theme. Charles, whose melancholy had been soothed by years of repose in the *patrios longo post tempore fines,* though gathering age and the King's enmity weighed permanently on him, had amused himself by setting the first line. It was

Je meurs de soif auprès de la fontaine.

[I die of thirst by the fountain's edge.]

The shabby Parisian, considering the assembly, felt within him the awaking of his wits. The Ballade he composed on this theme, called later *Ballade du Concours de Blois,* is not one of his third-best even, and yet it is stamped with his unmistakable personality,

[2] De Maulde, in his History of Louis XII., fixes the date of this volume at 1456: if this is so, then Villon took no part in the tourney, but contributed his Ballade on arrival, and had it accepted by the Duke and bound up with chosen pieces of the previous year. I can find no support for de Maulde. The volume, the Orleans MS., is Fr. 1104 in the Bibliothèque nationale.

narguant le destin, sharp with his mingled gaiety and despair. The first stanza gives the quality of it.

> *Je meurs de seuf auprès de la fontaine,*
> *Chault comme feu, et tremble dent a dent;*
> *En mon païs suis en terre loingtaine;*
> *Lez ung brasier frissonne tout ardent;*
> *Nu comme ung ver, vestu en president,*
> *Je ris en pleurs et attens sans espoir;*
> *Confort reprens en triste desespoir;*
> *Je m'esjouÿs et n'ay plaisir aucun;*
> *Puissant je suis sans force et sans povoir,*
> *Bien recueully, debouté de chascun.*

[I die of thirst by the fountain's edge; I am hot as fire, and my teeth are a-chatter; in my own country I am afar off; by a brazier I shiver, all aflame; naked as a worm, yet clothed richly; I laugh, in tears, and hope without a hope; I take comfort in harsh despair, I rejoice, and have no pleasure; I am strong, without strength or power; eagerly welcomed, and rebuffed by all.]

See how the laboured conceit is informed by something vital. The Envoi descends jerkily to a begging appeal.

> *Prince clement, or vous plaise sçavoir*
> *Que j'entens moult et n'ay sens ne sçavoir:*
> *Parcial suis, a toutes loys commun.*
> *Que sais je plus? Quoy? Les gaiges ravoir,*
> *Bien recueully, debouté de chascun.*

[My clement Prince, may it please you to know that I understand much, yet have neither sense nor knowledge. I have preferences, yet am subject to every law. What more can I want? What? To receive a wage once more; eagerly welcomed, and rebuffed by all.]

The rhyme is the image of his own life, and, it has been often observed, contains his life's device:

> *Je ris en pleurs.*

Charles of Orleans welcomed and subsidised this tramping poet of such different genius from his own, and Villon stayed on at Blois for a time: how long it is not possible to say, but at any rate, I should think, over the period of feasts and rejoicings which welcomed the birth, on December 19, of a daughter to Charles of Orleans and his wife Marie of Cleves, the child Princess Marie, who was a little later to save Villon's life. One may imagine that fairly soon afterwards the vagabond in his blood began to ſtir. The ordered, spacious life of the household at Blois, and especially the cluſter of smug poetaſters and criticaſters there, their petty intriguing—this is moſt certain, as any one may decide who has ever mixed, by Heaven, with the children of the Muse—their jealousies, their backbiting, their flattery of their patron, irked this *frondeur* of Paris. I see his glittering, contemptuous eye taking them in. Moſt of all, I think, he would hate the conventions of a ducal house, the obligatory attention to behaviour and dress and clean linen, the ceremonial entrances and exits, the ritual of food and drink (in his own world, recollect, you brought your own food to the tavern and gobbled it on a sloppy table, amid oaths and brawling), the necessity for polite conversation, the watchful, disapproving eyes of seneschals, majordomos, and all the cynical flunkeys of the great. Beyond this there is undoubted evidence in the Ballade de Blois, if it is examined again with attention, of a coolness between Villon and his hoſt: the whole Envoi becomes a humble and apologetic plea for pardon for some offence, and in the line

Que sais je plus? Quoy? Les gaiges ravoir,

there is a cryſtal-clear showing that Villon had had his wage ſtopped for some solecism or misdemeanour. Had he broken out suddenly at table with an oath or a too ripe ſtory from the *Trou Perrette*? Had he burſt at length into the mincing, exclusive circle of little literary men and blackened a poetic eye? Had he had trouble with the seneschals, or created a scandal in the servants' hall, or attempted gallantry with my Lady's maids? He had offended the Duke, it is obvious, and the Duke had cut off his stipend. But whether or not Charles relented and gave him more money, the growing longing for the pothouse and the riffraff became ſtronger, and the regrets for the old unbuttoned freedom for which a Duke's hospitality, with its obligations, could not make up: and fairly soon, certainly within the beginning of the year 1458, and leaving his noble hoſt not heartbroken, he is off again, turning his

159

back on the tall lighted windows of Blois and plugging joyfully down the long road into the rain and the darkness.

From now the thread of his wandering becomes tangled, and not even his direction in starting from Blois is certain. From the faint echoes in his verse of these weary years it is nevertheless possible to construct an approximate plan of this next phase of vagabondage. From Blois, I think, he followed the Loire by easy stages to Orleans, where he certainly rested, and had trouble with a girl. The evidence I take from the *Grant Testament,* verse cxii.:

> *Mais qu'a la petite Macee*
> *D'Orleans, qui ot ma sainture,*
> *L'amende soit bien hault taxee:*
> *Elle est une mauvaise ordure.*[3]

[But in the matter of little Macée of Orleans, who had my belt [*i.e.* purse], let her fine be made pretty heavy: she is a dirty trull.]

This points obviously to a row in a brothel. Prostitutes of Macée's class who were found wearing a belt of any value were fined under the sumptuary laws, and their belt confiscated.[4] She had presumably snatched Villon's, to which his purse was attached. The sequel to the incident remains unknown. It is permissible to believe that the poet clipped her over the ear in the morning on discovering his loss, that there was screaming and a fight, and trouble with the brothel-keeper, and that the poet, unanxious to have explanations with the Orleans watch, slunk away spitting insults.

He quitted Orleans, and loitering southwards along the wide bend of the Loire halted at length at the village of Sancerre, where in the churchyard he came upon an epitaph that tickled his raffish humour. I see him lounging moodily among the tombs, meditating the next step; and then bursting into a hoot of laughter as his eyes rest on the stone of one Michault, whose physical virtues were (or so Villon seems to suggest, and I should not be surprised) set forth above his mortal clay. Villon made a note of Michault, and reproduced him in the *Grant Testament.*

---

[3] L. Thuasne, alone among commentators, claims that this is a stroke at Master Macé d'Orléans, lieutenant to the Bailli of Berry.

[4] In Paris they were also confined to certain quarters, and ordered off the streets at 6 p.m.

Michault,
Qui fut nommé le Bon Fouterre.
Priez pour luy, faictes ung sault:
A Saint-Satur gist, soubz Sancerre.[5]

[Michault, surnamed the Good ——. Pray for him, with a leap! He lies at Saint-Satur, under Sancerre.]

Saint-Satur (*Sanctus Satyrus*) is the same place as Sancerre, in the Cher. The late Michault—I doubt, on reconsideration, whether even the frank and unembarrassed Middle Ages, so entirely free from prudery, would celebrate his prowess on his tombstone: Villon probably, inspired by the name of the village, attached the legend to the tombstone of some other Michault, a less distinguished forefather of the hamlet, while taking a swig in the village tavern—lightened the poet's gloom, I think, for many a day.

From Sancerre he wandered south-west a few miles to the cathedral city of Bourges: and here again Fate was to deal him a whack. A furious verse (cxxx.) of the *Grant Testament* makes this clear.

Item, a sire Jehan Perdrier,
Riens, n'a Françoys, son secont frere.
Cilz m'ont tousjours voulu aider,
Et de leurs biens faire confrere;
Combien que Françoys, mon compere,
Langues cuisans, flambans et rouges,
My commandement my priere
Me recommanda fort a Bourges.

[*Item,* to the sire Jehan Perdrier, nothing; and to his second brother François the same. They have always wanted to help me and place their goods at my disposal, like good comrades: instead of which my gossip François, setting red and flaming tongues a-frying without command or prayer, gave me a good recommendation at Bourges!]

The precise nature of the trouble remains a mystery, and Villon is extremely guarded over it, veiling his language and aiming it at only the eyes and ears it is meant for. From the significant *recommanda* it has been deduced that sacrilege or heresy was in the air;

[5] The amorous feats of this personage are celebrated in the poem of *Renart le Contrefait* of the fourteenth century.

161

that Villon, either drunk and blaspheming in a tavern or caught rifling an almsbox or prowling inexplicably in some church, was brought before the Archbishop of Bourges, Jehan Cœur; that he discovered his old *compere* François Perdrier and possibly his brother Jehan), and hailed François confidently, counting on his assistance; and that the snake François turned round and denounced him. This verse and one following serve in the *Grant Testament* to introduce the raving Ballade invoking thirty-five different kinds of damnation on envious tongues. It is clear that the mess was, while it lasted, a fairly serious one: but it would seem (in the absence of any document concerning it) that Villon was able to satisfy his questioners after more or less taste of the Archbishop's prison, and was allowed to get away from Bourges. This he would do with the greater alacrity because in May 1458, as the registers of the Chapter of the Sainte-Chapelle of Bourges reveal, a severe epidemic was sweeping the city. It is also noteworthy that the Coquillards had been in the district, and at their favourite occupation—I mean the thieving branch of the Company—of stealing chalices. It is by no means improbable, therefore, that Villon's trouble was in some way connected with the Coquille. M. Louis Thuasne quotes the case, in this year, of a miserable goldsmith of Bourges, who, having buried three children of the plague and being near starvation, succumbed to temptation and received from two companions strongly suspected to be Coquillards a couple of golden chalices, stolen by them from St. Jean de Bourges, to melt down. In consideration of his desperate condition the goldsmith received a letter of remission. There can be no harm in conjecturing, with M. Thuasne, that there might have been some connection between this business and Villon's *recommendation* and presumable appearance before the Archbishop.

This escapade seems to have sickened him of the unfriendly country into which he had wandered. He remembered the Bourbonnais, his father's country, and the little village of Montcorbier,[6] and the poverty-stricken *métairie* of des Loges. Some ties undoubtedly bound him to the Bourbons and their lands. On leaving

---

[6] The hamlet of Rue-Neuve now occupies the place of the village of Montcorbier. It has still within its bounds a meadow called the *Pré Corbier*, a relic of the ancient fief.

Bourges, therefore, he turned south, following the Loire once more, and then the Allier, passing the town of Nevers on his right and coming at length to Moulins in the Bourbonnais,

Combien qu'au plus fort de mes maulx,
En cheminant sans croix ni pille,
Dieu, qui les pelerins d'Esmaus
Conforta, ce dit l'Evangille,
Me monstra une bonne ville
Et paurveut du don d'esperance,

[Yet at the worst of my trials, and trudging the roads without a brass farthing in my poke, God, who comforted the pilgrims of Emmaus, as the Gospel says, showed me a fine town and gave me the gift of hope.]

entered the town penniless, footsore, and dusty, and, limping into the great Bourbon house there, found Jean ii., Duke of Bourbon, in residence. To the Duke, his *seigneur,* whose motto "Esperance" he quotes in this verse, he may have been known; or at least Charles d'Orléans, in whose nature there was nothing but a fine generosity and courtliness, may have given his raffish and turbulent guest, on parting, a letter to him. Jean ii. was a young man, only three years older than Villon, and a dabbler in poetry. He was moreover a friend and a frequent guest of Charles d'Orléans, and would be in every way disposed to treat Villon kindly. One may presume that Villon soon found among the servants of the ducal house a friendly soul who introduced him into the presence. From the Ballade called *La Requeste que Villon bailla à Mgr. de Bourbon* we know that he approached the Duke, borrowed six crowns of him, and coolly asked for more; which he probably got as well, for his dunning Ballade is a charming, graceful thing, sparkling and humble, gay and mock-desperate, from its opening lines:

Le mien Seigneur et Prince redoubté
Fleuron de Lys, royalle geniture,
Françoys Villon, que Travail a dompté
A coups orbes, par force de bature,
Vous supplie par ceste humble escripture
Que lui faciez quelque gracieux prest . . .

[See page 323 for translation.]
163

(in which, observe, he subtly strikes the tribal note, as of one calling to his chieftain), down to the skipping postscript to his Envoi,

Allez, lettres, faictes ung sault!

I have reproduced most of this Ballade in another place. It is most evident that it gave pleasure to Jean ii., a dilettante, and could not help giving it: and without doubt it had its effect.

Here is Villon once more under the roof of a great seigneur, his feudal lord, enjoying high protection but also subject once more to the irksome discipline of ducal houses which so galled his kibe at Blois. Did he stay long after making his second loan of the Duke? Did he repeat the experiment too often, and weary his host, and was he eventually shown the door? Or perhaps, as has been surmised, did the proximity of the Sire Girard de Montcorbier, his hereditary overlord, a frequent guest, no doubt, at the Bourbon house, make him uneasy? To bear a great man's name and have no blood-right to it, to have a reputation as an all-round blackguard, and to be brought into contact with him, to see displeasure and fury dawning in the severe eyes, cannot be pleasant. I fancy Villon slipped away from Moulins at the first convenient moment, when there seemed finally to be no more money coming from the Duke, and resumed the road,

Remote, unfriended, melancholy, slow,

but a free agent nevertheless and at no man's beck.

The next echo of him is very faint, and from a long distance away, though still on Bourbon land: the village of Roussillon [7] nearly fifty leagues to the south-east in Dauphiny, below Lyons and Vienne, on the left bank of the yellow, turbulent Rhône. Villon came to Roussillon possibly by degrees across country by Roanne, striking the Rhône above Lyons; or perhaps he came at it by Charolles and Mâcon, going thence up the river. Or (finally) he may never have reached Roussillon at all, and may simply have stuck it into his sad *Ballade pour servir de conclusion* for the sake of the rhyme.

[7] Roussillon (Isère). Not to be confused with other Roussillons in France, and above all with the Pyrenean province of the Roussillon, then held by the King of Aragon.

Car chassié fut comme ung souillon
De ses amours hayneusement,
Tant que, d'icy a Roussillon,
Brosse n'y a ne brossillon,
Qui n'eust, ce dit il sans mentir,
Ung lambeau de son cotillon.

[For he was driven from his love with humiliation, like a scullion; so that from here to Roussillon there is not a bush or shrub on which there does not hang some tatter of his shirt: this is no lie.]

"From here to Roussillon" may be merely a vague poetic sweep, like "from here to Babylon" in another Ballade of his. But one may equally assume that the lank, dark, enigmatic figure in its ſtained and ragged hose was seen spitting misanthropically into the Rhône at Roussillon on a fine summer evening. How long he ſtayed there, whether six hours, six days, or six months, where he wandered from Roussillon and in what direction, what villages and towns he passed through or avoided in his dreary, lackadaisical mouching, tattered and homeless and penniless, I cannot tell, nor any one else either. The next news of him is out of one of his own poems, and fixes him at a place diſtant from Roussillon, ſtraight across country as the crow limps, to the north-weſt, about a hundred leagues: in English miles, about two hundred and fifty. Of all his five years' wandering this muſt be the wearieſt ſtretch; and the long road, so loathsome by now to this child of the Town, ends in a dungeon of Orleans Prison, under the shadow of the gibbet.[8]

Let us look back.

He had wandered about half France for four whole years, lying at night now under a Duke's roof and now in a filthy doss-house, now under a hedge, now in a wench's chamber, now in prison, awaiting the morning's queſtioning, now again in a Duke's house. His chance companions had been thieves, trulls, poets, drunken men-at-arms without pay turned off from the English wars, Coquillards, tramping minſtrels, quacks, an unfrocked monk or two, gypsies, ſtudents going to the Medicine Schools at Montpellier or the Law Schools at Orleans, beggars true and false, ſtrolling mumpers, *siflant six à six,* farm labourers, idle fellows, fortune-tellers, dice-

[8] See Appendix D: *The Road to Orleans.*

165

coggers, coiners, criminals hiding from justice, pardoned and penitent criminals tramping to St. James's Tomb at Compostela,[9] the *bateleurs traynant marmotes,* bear-leaders, dancing-ape trainers, jugglers, and miscellaneous showmen and mountebanks of whom he sarcastically cries pardon in the last Ballade but one of the Great Testament. He had seen the life of the Road and (what interested him not at all) the life of the fields, waking in five hundred weary dawns to damn the birds and their infernal clatter. Pah! Not a word of it shall ever get into his verse, except in hatred. He had trudged white with dust, burned by summer suns, drenched with rain, chattering and blue in the nip of winter mornings, sludging through mushy seas of leaves in autumn woods and coppices, through icy mud, fording streams, lying idle through endless afternoons of June, on his back in wheatfields, staring at the sky; he had hidden in leafy glades while mounted Archers trotted by, searching the roads for him, or, if not for him, for some of his tribe; he had held his frozen hands to the fire in country alehouses, listening dully to the broad singing country speech, pricking up his ears suddenly at a name and sidling out of the door to take swiftly to his heels. He had lain, sullen and bored and heart-sick, in bed in the purlieus of obscure towns, cursing the streaming sunlight, deaf to the prattle or the scolding of his partner of the night. *Omne animal triste.* . . . He had exchanged rude jokes with swarthy farm-girls wielding pitchforks in the hay, and had dismally yawned away the night in hedge taverns among boozy clowns, thinking of Paris and Katherine and the *Pomme de Pin.* He had whipped out his knife in a fight more than once, probably, and had more than once run for his life with an enemy pounding behind, spitting oaths and swearing to cut his liver out. He had slunk into brothels in dreary provincial towns and unloosed his bitter tongue among the women, screaming and blowsy there: and had again waked in the morning with a leaden heart, an aching head, and an overwhelming disgust at his fate, his body, his driving passions; feeling in his soul the apathy and despair which a later Parisian poet was to express so terribly:

[9] Thus working off their sentence. They carried a candle and were bound to recite prayers for the King.

Dans ton île, ô Vénus, je n'ai trouvé debout
Qu'un gibet symbolique où pendoit mon image.

He had ſtolen on either hand everything he could lay his fingers on to satisfy his craving belly: roots from the fields, apples in orchards, ſtray rolls from bakers' windows, eggs from hen-rooſts, and, if lucky, the hens themselves. He had begged in towns and been prodded off the ſtreet by Archers. He had picked occasional pockets, snapped up a purse or two in taverns, odd coppers from the ſtockings of proſtitutes, taper-scraps out of churches, farthings, possibly, from the very dishes of blind beggars. And the spring, and the summer, and the autumn, and the winter had found him moving on, reſtless and dogged and predatory, trudging with head up or down, whiſtling, or cursing, or even singing a defiant ſtave in his harsh voice, always knowing himself a hunted man, always dodging the police, always on the alert for the moment to dash for cover. He had long fallen, by the circumſtances of his fate (as he said later, blaming Saturn), by his own folly, *in profundum malorum,* as the King's Procurator observed of his friend Regnier de Montigny: and there was no way out save one. Now he has come to the end of his road, in this early summer of 1460, and lies shackled in the prison of Orleans, awaiting death.

What brought him there, why the final sentence and the shadow of the rope, the common jeſt of his circle over their wine, had come upon him, there is nothing to show. Only the year, and the circumſtance that he was condemned to die but was released in time by what in France in the Middle Ages was called a *joyeulx advenement,* the providential passage of a royal or semi-royal personage ceremonially through a countryside, whether after coronation or making a firſt entry into a domain, freeing prisoners and captives after a cuſtom once common to Chriſtendom and even now, I think, lingering here and there—only these two things we know. The personage whose progress through Orleans delivered Villon was the Princess Marie d'Orléans, daughter of Charles the Duke, the child at whose birth in December 1457 Villon had moſt likely got rolling drunk in the servants' hall at Blois. The Princess, now nearly three years old, was making her first entry on the seventeenth of July 1460 into the capital of her father's duchy; and the prisons were flung open, disgorging their contents half-blinded into the sunlit ſtreets, amid the ſtrewn flowers, the tapeſtries and flags, the clashing of all the bells of Orleans, the populace crying *"Noël!"*, the prancing of gaily-caparisoned troops, and the ſtately procession, like a flower-bed for bright colours, of the Princess and her father, their suite, the town dignitaries, the Bishop and Chapter, the religious communities, the notable burgesses, gay in their feſtal habits.

Villon, peering half-dazed behind the press of the mob, saw the little Princess go by, and her father, his late hoſt and patron: and full of gratitude (which he never lacked) at his deliverance, found a lodging and in haſte wrote the long dithyrambic *Epiſtre a Marie d'Orleans*,[10] ſtuffed with quotations from the Psalmiſt and Cato and the Fourth Bucolic, crammed with joy and incoherence. "O blessed birth!" he burſts out, harking back to the December day in Blois when he drank the new-born Princess's health:

> O louee Concepcion!
> Envoiee ça jus des cieulx,
> Du noble Lis digne Syon,
> Don de Jhesus tres precieulx,
> MARIE, nom tres gracieulx,
> Fons de pitié, source de grace,
> La joye, confort de mes yeulx,
> Qui noſtre paix batiſt et brasse!

[O blessed birth, sent hither from the skies! O worthy Scion of the noble Lily, most precious gift of Jesus, Marie, of the moſt gracious name, fount of pity, source of forgiveness, joy and comfort of my eyes, who doſt build and confirm our peace!]

And so continues, half-religiously, praising God and swearing fealty to the little Princess, celebrating her grace and pity, soaring into an ecſtasy of gratitude, glorifying the child in the Vergilian ſtrain.

> Nova progenies celo,
> Car c'eſt du poëte le dit,
> Jamjam demittitur alto.
> Saige Cassandre, belle Echo

[10] Wrongly adjudged by G. Paris a poem simply celebrating the Princess's birth. Internal evidence for the later event is sufficiently ſtrong.

Digne Judith, caste Lucresse,
Je vous congnois, noble Dido,
A ma seule dame et maistresse.

[Now (as the Poet has said) "a golden progeny from Heaven descends." O, wise as Cassandra, lovely as Echo, worthy as Judith, chaste as Lucretia, I salute thee, noble Dido, as my only Lady and Mistress!]

It is but middling poetry, but it holds as in a shell all the shouting and colour and exultation of that day of July in Orleans. Bells and the *Te Deum* clamour in it, and censers swing, and the steeples rock.

Du Psalmiste je prens les dis:
Delectasti me, Domine,
In factura tua, si dis:
Noble enfant, de bonne heure né,
A toute doulceur destiné,
Manne du Ciel, celeste don. . . .

[I take the Psalmist's words: "Thou hast given me delight, Lord, in thy way." O noble child, born in a happy hour, destined to all sweetness, manna from Heaven, celestial gift. . . .]

So his eager pen rushes on.

Nom recourvré, joye de peuple,
Confort des bons, de maulx retraicte,
Du doulx seigneur premiere et seule
Fille, de son cler sang extraicte,
Du dextre costé Clovis traicte,
Glorieuse ymage en tous fais. . . .

[O recovered Name, joy of thy people, comfort of the good, shielded from evil, first and only daughter of thy sweet Lord, sprung from his clear blood, and from the right side of Clovis, glorious image in every feature.]

The salute to Charles of Orleans, *doulx seigneur,* is just and courteous, and brushed away, I should think, the last lingering shred of displeasure against the ruffian poet held in that gentle heart. And Villon proceeds, saluting the child a lovely work of God, endowed with all gifts and all virtues, more precious than a balas ruby,

Plus que rubis noble ou balais,

169

and ending finally in a prayer at her baby feet, in which he begs
God to preserve her and to allow him to serve her always:

> J'espoir de vous servir ainçoys,
> Certes, se Dieu plaiſt, que devie
> Voſtre povre escolier Françoys.

Of the hundred and thirty-two of this dithyramb there are
eight precious lines which give the reason for his outburſt of thank-
fulness:

> Cy, devant Dieu, fais congnoissance
> Que creature feusse morte,
> Ne feuſt voſtre doulce naissance
> En charité puissant et forte,
> Qui ressuscite et reconforte
> Ce que Mort avoit prins pour sien;
> Voſtre presence me conforte:
> On doit dire du bien le bien.

[For here, before God, I acknowledge that I was a creature as
good as dead, were it not for Your sweet birth, Your ſtrong and
compassionate charity, raising up and comforting one whom Death
had already marked his own. Your presence revives me. One should
return praise for good.]

This is as plain as it could be. The poet, lying under his dreadful sentence, awaiting the end, already (he says) the property of
Death, is raised to life and comfort again by the Heaven-sent passage of the Princess Marie. No other interpretation seems possible,
coupling this poem with the hiſtorical faċt of the entry into Orleans,
with the general release of prisoners, and the date. Whether Villon
caused his panegyric to be conveyed at this time to the little Princess
and her father I do not know. I think some lingering feeling of
decency would keep him away from those ſtreets in which the
Duke's processions were likely to pass, and in which he might have
met his hoſt face to face.

He is now, in July 1460, delivered miraculously from the gibbet
and free to go where he will. It is not known where he spent his
time for the next nine or ten months. It seems evident that he hung
about the Orléanais, living from hand to mouth in his now accustomed manner. The countryside was one of the areas operated by

the Coquille, and not improbably Villon existed in their company for some time, thieving here and there and living among the woods. There is a complete blank in his history for nearly a year; and then, in the beginning of the summer of 1461, we find him again, still in this neighbourhood.

The Most Reverend Father and Lord, Monseigneur Thibault d'Aussigny, Bishop of Orleans, had worn the amethyst ring nine years when there was brought before him, one morning in the early summer of 1461, a criminal clerk, a bird with a gallows look and a gashed lip. There is no authentic portrait extant of the Bishop or his prisoner, yet we may pause here very profitably and presume to make one of each. For myself, I see the face and figure of François Villon as clearly as if he stood before me, for he has described himself almost entire in his works.[11] He is of medium height, dark, haggard, dried-up, famished,

Triste, failly, plus noir que meure,

meagre as a hunted cat, prematurely bald, sharp-featured, pinshanked, with a long predatory nose and the loose mouth of the sensual; his eyes close-set and roving, his upper lip deeply scarred from the slash of Chermoye's dagger five years before. His academic gown has long been worn to rags and flung over a hedge. A short cloak no doubt replaces it, stained, patched, and faded. His hose are dusty, particoloured with mud and sun, and in holes, here and there partially darned by some kind-hearted drab for the price of a drink; his shoes bulge and flap, and gape to Heaven. At his belt hangs a shabby purse of leather, full of cobwebs, like Catullus's, and a knife in its sheath. His air is hangdog, yet dashed with a kind of jauntiness. Huysmans' vision of him would fit this moment: *"Je me figure, ô vieux maître, ton visage exsangue, coiffé d'un galeux bicoquet; je me figure ton ventre vague, tes longs bras osseux, tes*

[11] There is only one ancient drawing of Villon, a conventional one adorning the edition of 1489 and an early edition of the *Repues Franches;* in one case holding a scroll inscribed "F. Villon." But since this was a stock figure used also by printers for Martial d'Auvergne and Vergil, it is unlikely to be a true limning of the Parisian. There is a fake of 1830, said to be from an edition of Marot, but untraceable: it is by Rulemann, and makes the haggard poet a fat and jovial fellow.

jambes héronnières enroulées de bas d'un rose louche, étoilés de déchirures, papelonnés d'écailles de bouè." *[12]

The portrait of Monseigneur Thibault d'Aussigny is more difficult to reconstruct, though his character may be clearly reviewed, and in common justice requires so to be. The rancorous and undying hatred vowed him by Villon, and bursting out so frequently in the *Grant Testament,* gives a completely false view. Thibault d'Aussigny was, apart from a notorious avarice and a devouring passion for lawsuits, rather an admirable personality than otherwise; admirable, but not lovable. He had been a Canon of Orleans Cathedral and Archdeacon of the Sologne, and in May 1452 was raised to the See of Orleans by Nicolas v. Before his enthronement there had been considerable difficulties, for the other candidate for the see, Pierre Bureau, a relative of the Grand Master of Artillery, had the determined backing of Charles vii. In this delicate position, with heavy odds against him, Thibault d'Aussigny had behaved, as is amply shown in the records of his election, in a manner at once firm, dignified, and based equally on right and good sense, and after election his modesty and entire correctness of bearing alike as a subject towards his King and a priest towards his Pope stamp him a man of considerable quality. As a Bishop he proved himself a strong administrator, a reformer, a founder, an honest diplomat yet not unskilful, and an exemplary father of the faithful.[13] For Villon's flaming picture of the purple tyrant and monster whose delight was to grind the face of downtrodden poets it is necessary, therefore, to substitute that of a severe, single-minded prelate, a just man, fixed in purpose and accustomed to pursue a moral obligation to the end, having in his nature no sentimentality, carrying himself in the eye of God and man with an inclement and profound devotion to duty: a type called in England (and God alone knows why) the Puritan type. The Bishop's reputation,

*[I see before me, O venerable master, your bloodless visage, crowned with its mangy *bicoquet;* I see your hollow stomach, your long bony arms, your heron-like legs, encased in hose of a dirty pink, starred with rents, covered, as with scales, by mud-splashes.]

[12] *Le Drageoir aux Epices.*
[13] *Gallia Christiana,* 1744: qu. Thusnae. F. de Villaret, *Mémoires de l'Orléanais.* Lottain, *Recherches historiques sur la Ville d'Orléans.*

avarice apart—*si iniquitates observaveris, Domine, Domine, quis sustinebit?*—must be acknowledged entirely honourable, and he plainly has other claims to fame than that of having shoved into prison the greatest poet of his age. He died in September 1473, having governed the diocese of Orleans well for twenty years, and was buried in the Franciscan church at Meun-sur-Loire, which he had founded. He appears to me a portly, imposing figure, clean-shaven, with a heavy jowl, a compressed firm mouth, and severe eyes under twin pent-houses of bushy brow, the whole completed by the episcopal purple. As he enters his Court chamber this sunny morning and curtly acknowledges the reverences of his officers, a perceptible chill comes into the atmosphere; and with reason.

The charge against François Villon, clerk, Master of Arts, is not known, but it has been supplied. There was a vague tradition in the Orléanais, founded on some document now lost, that Villon was arrested by the local Archers for the theft of a votive lamp from the church at Baccon-sur-Loire, a village close to Meun.[14] The severity of his punishment, indeed, points to at least attempted sacrilege. It is evident, if we agree to accept this fairly legitimate assumption, that his fortunes were now at a feverishly low ebb; for what could be sneaked from a village church save an ornament of no great value and the poor contents of an almsbox or two? I perceive the lean figure skulking in the dusk, slipping into the church of Baccon, slinking apologetically past Our Lady's altar (cherishing a vague certitude meanwhile that She in her clemency will not be too hard on a poor devil driven to extremity), and finally, after a quick glance round, beginning his operations. He slid out again, was gathered in by the police, declared himself a clerk, and was taken to Orleans and brought before Thibault d'Aussigny; and after a preliminary examination by the Bishop and his official was conducted to the prison of Meun, which belonged to the See of Orleans, and thrust into a *fosse*, one of the lower dungeons, dark, airless, dripping with water (since it was on or under moat-level), rat-ridden, and infested with toads. Here, chained by the ankles to a staple—all this Villon chews over again and remembers in his verse, spitting hatred—he was left to his meditations.

[14] The story is hinted at by Prosper Marchand in his *Dictionnaire historique*, 1758.

It is only equitable to pause for a moment and consider the position of Thibault d'Aussigny in this matter: of Villon's point of view, God knows, we have enough and to spare. The Bishop of Orleans found before him a ruffian clerk of the worst character, whom he had probably had before him on a serious charge not a year before, whom he knew to have been held in Orleans Prison under sentence of death and released only by the general amnesty. If by any chance the Bishop had not seen Villon at Orleans, if his official had dealt with the case in his absence, then at any rate it is certain that there lay on the Bishop's table the full *dossier* concerning Villon's activities at Orleans, and probably much more. His clear duty, then, was to punish this relapsed clerk with severity. I have seen it suggested that the Bishop's known devotion to Saint Francis should have inclined him a little to indulgence towards a criminal bearing his patron's name: but this reasoning is, I think, bad psychology. The coincidence, if it affected the Bishop's judgment at all (which is doubtful), would make him the more determined to chastise this backslider memorably. Villon's treatment at Meun bears out this view.

He had plenty on which to meditate in his dungeon under the moat, for his position was in general extremely discomfortable. The Paris police were still on the lookout for him in the eternal matter of the College of Navarre, and he could not be certain that the Orleans authorities were unaware of it. Add to this his present charge, most probably of sacrilege, with the affair of Orleans (and possibly the mysterious trouble at Bourges also) swelling his *dossier*, and his black record generally, and it may be judged that his lean body stood once more in some peril, if not of the gibbet, at any rate of prolonged imprisonment. Montpipeau, where Colin des Cayeulx, now dangling from a Paris gibbet, had presumably partaken of his last frolic, was only two and a half leagues away to the north of Meun. It seems not possible that Villon can yet have heard this depressing news, since he was in the Bishop's power earlier in the summer, and Colin was hanged in September; but he had undoubtedly heard of Montigny's end by this time from one or other of the Companions, and it was an untimely thing to remember. The future was dark indeed, and sitting in his damp

174

straw, distastefully nibbling at hard bread and sipping from his water-pitcher—he who loved rich food so—he brooded over his position from every angle, as the Ballade called the Debate between the Heart and Body of Villon shows.

His days and nights in the dungeon of Meun were not all devoted to reflection. Presumably the Bishop was not satisfied with his prisoner's answers, and desired more information: and so there came a day when Villon, looking up at the grating of a flung-open door, was summoned and taken up to where the examiners awaited him with the apparatus of the Question Ordinary. He says, remembering it ruefully in his lovely, graceful *Epistre en forme de Ballade, à ses Amys*:

> *Après pain sec, non pas après gasteaux,*
> *En ses boyaulx verse eaue a gros bouillon.*

[After dry bread, and no cake, he washes down his guts with lashings of water.]

These "lashings of water" were not his ordinary prison diet, but water forcibly absorbed through the funnel, which ceremony was part of the normal judicial procedure when a prisoner was reluctant to supply information, the equivalent of what is now called in America and England the Third Degree. Villon suffered it at Meun, I think, more than once, as I gather from the growls and snarls of rage with which he remembers the hospitality of his Lordship of Orleans:

> *Non obstant maintes peines eues*
> *Lesquelles j'ay toutes receues*
> *Soubz la main Thibault d'Aussigny . . .*[15]

[Notwithstanding my many miseries, which I have all received at the hands of Thibault d'Aussigny.]

And again:

> *Peu m'a d'une petite miche*
> *Et de froide eaue tout ung esté*

[A summer long he nourished me
Upon cold water and dry bread.]
(Payne)

[15] See Part III: *The Works.*

(though this may be the prison diet); and again,

> Et s'esté m'a dur et cruel
> Trop plus que cy ne le raconte;

[And was harsher and crueller to me than I can tell here.]

and again,

> Or est vray qu'après plainz et pleurs
> Et angoisseux gemissemens,

[True it is that after so many plaints and tears, and groans of anguish. . . .]

—groans, tears, cries, and griefs on the rack, obviously: whether the lesser rack of the Question Ordinary or the more painful rack of the Question Extraordinary. And again, much later in the *Grant Testament*,

> Dieu mercy et Tacque Thibault,
> Qui tant d'eaue froide m'a fait boire,
> Mis en bas lieu, non pas en hault,
> Mengier d'angoisse mainte poire. . . .[16]

[Thank God—and Tacque Thibault, who made me swallow so much cold water, who shoved me into a low place, not a high one, and made me chew so many fruits of pain. . . .]

The *poire d'angoisse* was in one of its meanings the gag used during the process of the Question. And finally, a significant and bitter piece of sarcasm in the next following verse:

> Toutesfois, je n'y pense mal
> Pour luy, ne pour son lieutenant,
> Aussi pour son official,
> Qui est plaisant et advenant;
> Que faire n'ay du remenant,
> Mais du petit maistre Robert.
> Je les ayme, tout d'ung tenant,
> Ainsi que fait Dieu le Lombart.

[Nevertheless, I think no evil of him, nor of his Lieutenant, nor even for his Official, who is so pleasant and engaging. With the rest I have nothing to do, save with little Master Robert. Lord! I love them, all of them, as much as God loves a Lombard!]

---

[16] *Tacque Thibault*: the hated creature of a fourteenth-century Duke of Berry. Villon is insulting the Bishop. *Poire d'angoisse*: a double jest. The pears of Angoisse, in the Dordogne, were celebrated since the twelfth century.

The iron hand of the Bishop of Orleans, descending heavily and smiting this ruffian with the rods of the righteous, is here manifeſt. "Little Maſter Robert," whom Villon couples with the Bishop, is the hangman of Orleans, whose horny fiſts were without doubt a memory for the shuddering poet.

This cheerless exiſtence dragged on, as Villon shows, *tout ung eſté*, all the long summer of 1461, and might possibly at laſt have left him drying in the sun, with René and Colin his friends, had not Heaven seen fit that Charles vii., St. Joan's Dauphin, should pass from this life on July 22, 1461, thirty years after the martyrdom of the saint who had secured him his throne, and that his successor, Louis xi., after coronation at Reims and a solemn entry into Paris on Auguſt 31, should make a progress through France down to Bordeaux, passing through Touraine and the Orléanais and freeing prisoners (according to the merciful cuſtom) at all the ſtations of his journey. The King made his *joyeulse entrée* into the town of Orleans on the nineteenth of Oċtober, and leaving next day, came to Meun within a few hours. The anguish and suspense of Villon in his darkness on hearing (as he would hear) from his gaoler of the old King's death, then of the new King's progress, the near proximity of Louis, the thought of freedom almoſt within his grasp, muſt have been unendurable. It is permissible to believe that Maſter Guillaume and his other friends in Paris, who may or may not have received the Ballade crying to them for help,[17] had certainly received by devious means other message from him, describing his condition and its urgency, and that they had laid his case at once before powerful influences—possibly before Louis himself, praying his Majeſty to make a ſtation at Meun. And with success: for this King, if he was hard, cunning, and ruthless (when fortune favoured him) towards the rich, was easy for the poor, the intelligent, and the Bohemian, and had, beyond his skill in kingship, a taſte for letters.[18] There is a half-consecrated legend that he observed, whether on this occasion or not I do not know, that he could not

---

[17] Did he aċtually write this lovely thing in prison? It was a general regulation that prisoners could not have pen and ink without special permission—"*Item, que nul prisonnier ne fase faire ne escripre lettres closes ne autres en la geole, se ce n'est par congié*" (*Ordinances royaulx du Chastellet*, 1425). But his gaoler may have been good-natured, or at leaſt open to bribes; and Villon certainly had friends.
[18] He is the titular author of the *Cent Nouvelles nouvelles*.

afford to hang this fellow, because although his kingdom held a hundred thousand other rascals of equal rascality it held only one poet, François Villon, so excelling in *gentilz dictz & ingenieux sçavoir*. The story is no doubt apocryphal; and yet one should not forget, in considering it, that in that age a Prince and a poet might have met in a tavern or held talk together in a public street.

It is unlikely, I think, that Charles d'Orléans could, as some have suggested, have had any part in helping Villon now: for Charles was no more in the favour of Louis xi. than in that of his predecessor. The papers concerning all this matter are presumably lost for ever, and we shall never know the exact crime for which Villon was held by the Bishop, nor review those missing links in his past which would have been included in the *dossier*.

Louis xi., wearing his old shabby hat with the row of blessed leaden images round its greasy brim, fingering a medal of the True Cross of Saint Lô, to which he had a notable devotion, blinking with his sardonic eyes, signed Villon's remission. The date of the pardon—the second issued to this poet, up to date, *a cause d'un joyeulx advenement*: high Heaven was certainly moving its royal pawns on his behalf—is October 20, as is fixed by the date of other papers signed by Louis at Meun. The King passed on, leaving the poet, as we perceive from his verse, incoherent with joy and patriotism and dancing a grotesque fandango in his straw. The letter of remission was received. Monseigneur Thibault d'Aussigny's severe mouth drooped in a pout, and his observations to his secretary were brief, dry, and cold: but he was a just man, and had no malignity nor pettiness in his nature. He might easily, at the first rumour of the forthcoming passage of the King through that country, have had his captive whisked away to some prison well out of the Royal path and the showers of clemency watering it. This had been done before in the history of Europe, and might easily have been done again: the King might possibly have asked after the poet, or again, he might have completely forgotten him. But the Bishop behaved in his own manner, which was that of a Christian and a bleak, but not malicious, and whole-hearted pastor of souls. He would willingly, no doubt, have brought his prisoner to a state of wholesome penitence by scourging his wicked flesh a trifle more, by admonishing him and by purging him with the bread and water of affliction: as was his duty. But the King had come, and signed, and gone. Monseigneur relinquished his prey, and Villon, winking owlishly at the unaccustomed sky, was conducted to the gates of the episcopal prison, under the glowering mass of the Tower of Manassès, and booted into freedom.

§ 7

I that in heill was and gladness
Am trublit now with great sickness
And feblit with infirmitie:—
Timor Mortis conturbat me.
Dunbar, *Lament for the Makars.*

But though he had succeeded in pulling a long snook at the gallows once more, and had the King's pardon behind him, Villon could not at once return openly to the Paris for which his soul craved. His mind was now big with his greatest work, which bears in its opening the date of this year 1461,

Escript l'ay l'an soixante et ung,
Que le bon roy me delivra
De la dure prison de Mehun,

[Written by me in the year '61, when the good King delivered me from the harsh prison of Meung.]

and he was itching, no doubt, to begin it, but it was prudent to avoid for a time the streets of Paris in broad day. He may or may not have suppressed, in his desperation at Meun, something vital— possibly, even, the affair of the College of Navarre. In any case his letter of remission was not yet confirmed. He may also have had more recent reasons for not desiring to attract the attention of the Provost's men. Though (as we may believe) repentant, sobered, and wishful to make a fresh start, he can have had no immediate lust for further arrests and inquiries.

Three extracts from the *Grant Testament* show that even if, entering one of the southern gates of Paris cautiously from the Orleans road, he paid by night a swift call on Master Guillaume and his mother, he did not linger, but slipped out of the town again to some safe place which remains unknown. The first of these clues is the fact that he did not know that Robert d'Estouteville, his protector, had ceased, at the new King's order, to be Provost of Paris on the first of September, being replaced by the Seigneur Jacques Villiers de l'Isle-Adam.[1] In the *Grant Testament* Villon assumes that d'Estouteville is still in office: *ergo*, Villon neither wrote his work in Paris nor stayed in Paris, if he visited it, long enough to learn what everybody knew.

The second clue is contained in verse xcii. of the *Grant Testament*:

> Item, quant est de Merebeuf
> Et de Nicolas de Louviers,
> Vache ne leur donne ne beuf,
> Car vachiers ne sont, ne bouviers,
> Mais gens a porter esperviers,
> Ne cuidez pas que je me joue,
> Et pour prendre perdis, plouviers,
> Sans faillir, sur la Machecoue.

[*Item*, in the matter of Merebeuf and Nicolas de Louviers, I give them neither cow nor bull, for they are neither cowkeepers nor cattlemen, but persons skilled in falconry (don't think I am fooling), permission to bag partridges and plovers, without fail, at Mother Machecoue's.]

These two highly fatted burgesses—Pierre Merebeuf was a wealthy draper and Nicolas de Louviers an alderman of Paris—to whom Villon jocularly gives leave to bag partridges and plovers in the shop of Mother Machecoue, would have been unable to do so in 1461: the widow of Arnoul Machecoue, who still kept a renowned cookshop, the *Golden Lion*, near the Châtelet, when Villon left Paris early in 1457, was now dead, and her *rostisserie* to let.

The third clue is contained in verse cxvii., where Villon turns hatefully to speak of his three "orphans."

[1] Robert d'Estouteville resumed office in 1465; too late to help Villon any more, it seems.

> *Item, j'ay sceu, en ce voyage,*
> *Que mes trois povres orphelins*
> *Sont creuz et deviennent en aage.*

[*Item,* I have heard, during this journey, that my three poor
orphans are grown up and nearly of age.]

This *voyage* may be his journey back from Meun, or it may,
of course, mean any part of his travels during the four years of exile;
or more likely, a brief and inconspicuous irruption into Paris and
out again some time after his arrival from Meun. The clue is in any
case weak, but worthy of mention. I find a much stronger one in
verse ciii.: a passing gibe at Robin Turgis of the *Pomme de Pin,*
Villon's creditor and standing butt.

> *Item, viengne Robin Turgis*
> *A moy, je luy paieray son vin;*
> *Combien, s'il treuve mon logis,*
> *Plus fort sera que devin.*

This seems daylight-clear. "If Robin Turgis comes to me I'll
pay him for his wine; but if he finds out my lodging he'll be
something cleverer than a wizard." *Ergo,* the poet is in hiding, and
in a haunt where no client of the *Pomme de Pin* is likely to discover him and betray him to the foaming landlord. *Ergo,* he is
outside Paris altogether, somewhere in the suburbs, and laughing
up his sleeve. It is here, in retreat, then, that the greater part of the
Grant Testament is compiled.

Most probably this hiding-place was one of his old haunts of
1456 in the quiet neighbourhood between Sceaux and Paris, the
country where he had so richly fooled the barber of Bourg-la-Reine.
He was wiser now, and melancholy, and more philosophical, and
prematurely ageing, and haggard with miseries and vice, yet
possessing at this time, as Longnon justly observes, *"quatre sentiments dont sans doute le Juge Eternel lui aura tenu compte: la foi
religieuse, le patriotisme, l'amour filial, et la reconnaissance."* His
faith he pours out in the Ballade to Our Lady and elsewhere; his
patriotism shines in his salute, as with a sword, to St. Joan, *la bonne
Lorraine,* in the Ballade of Dead Ladies, and in the minor but lusty
Ballade roaring for judgment on the enemies of France; his filial
love appears in his tender thought for his aged mother, expressed

just before he writes his Ballade for her to the Mother of God; and his gratitude to Master Guillaume de Villon, "my more than father," and to the King for rescuing him at Meun, appears very early in the Testament.

These four things must be placed to his credit—or, as we should say to-day, to his debit. He is now to be regarded, in Boswell's phrase, as tugging at his oar for some little time in this secret place, secure from surprises and alarms. It is hardly possible that he composed the whole of the *Grant Testament* at once and in this place. Much of it must have been singing in his mind for years, as he wandered and loafed away his exile. Probably he had some of the Ballades finished already, and it was necessary only to polish them and decide their place in the plan of the Testament. As I have shown in another place, the arrangement of the *Grant Testament* betrays no haphazard planning. Such a piece of high song as the Dead Ladies may have been meditated and re-meditated, and set down on paper, and again meditated and completed after the first lovely gush of his inspiration; and often, I imagine, he would at this period dismay his chance companion of the suburban tavern by suddenly falling into a fit of abstraction, seizing his tablets, scribbling on them, on the corner of a sloppy wooden table (or elsewhere, beside a trull's untidy bed-head in the small hours, to the accompaniment of shrill curses), a memorandum for the next day.

He is therefore steadily at work on what he must know to be a masterpiece: but his mind is perturbed and hag-ridden for the most part, and apprehension hangs over him. Of the bubbles of this unease which rise here and there in the Testament one of the more obvious is the Rondeau (or more strictly Chanson, or Bergeronnette) which chimes the sad deepening note announcing the end:

> *Au retour de dure prison,*
> *Ou j'ai laissié presque la vie,*
> *Se Fortune a sur moy envie,*
> *Jugiez s'elle fait mesprison!*
> *Il me semble que, par raison,*
> *Elle deust bien estre assouvie*
> *Au retour.*

182

Cecy plain eſt de desraison
Qui vueille que du tout devie,
Plaise a Dieu que l'ame ravie
En soit, lassus, en sa maison,
Au retour!

[If Fortune, on my return from the harsh prison where I almoſt left behind my life, has still designs on me, judge whether she be not vindictive! It would reasonably seem to me that she should have had her fill of me, on my return.

Altogether unjuſt it is that she should require my deſtruction: please God, my soul at leaſt, released from this flesh, may find reſt above . . . on its return.]

His anxiety is plain in this bitter, weary complaint againſt persecuting Fortune. So, too, his bequeſt to Guillaume de Villon refers directly to present fears.

Item, et a mon plus que pere
Maiſtre Guillaume de Villon,
Qui m'eſté a plus doulx que mere
A enfant levé de maillon:
Degeté m'a de maint bouillon,
Et de cestuy pas ne s'esjoye,
Si luy requier a genouillon
Qu'il m'en laisse toute sa joye.

[*Item*, to Guillaume de Villon,—
My more than father, who indeed
To me more tenderness hath shown
Than mothers to the babes they feed,
Who me from many a scrape hath freed
And now of me hath scant liesse—
I do entreat him, bended-kneed,
He leave me to my present ſtress.]

(*Payne.*)

Ceſtuy is his present overhanging trouble, the non-confirmation of his letter of remission from Meun, his being forced ſtill to hide; and I read into it also a certain quite natural despondency on the part of the chaplain of St. Benoît, whom his criminal ward begs desperately on his knees, since this present trouble after so many others can give the kind man less than joy, to leave him to his fate.

183

In this state of disquietude and dejection, relieved no doubt by careless and roaring moods, for he was moody, Villon composed at any rate a great part of the *Grant Testament*, which had been simmering in his brain for so many years. How long his work took him, how soon he was able to leave his hole and enter Paris openly again, is not known, but it must have been in the early part of 1462. It is not too much to assume that Guillaume de Villon, coming out of his abstraction with a long sigh, had set himself very soon to get the letter of remission confirmed, and either with or without his friends' support had issued once more from the Red Door and (sighing deeply again) resolutely bearded the powers and wrung from them the needful signatures. The application, by whomsoever made, was successful, and the letter *entériné* by the competent authority. Before the summer of 1462 François Villon had once more taken up his quarters in Master Guillaume's house, the Red Door in St. Bennet's cloister. Be sure that Master Guillaume welcomed him back with all his old kindness, and summoned his mother to dinner, and opened a precious bottle of Beaune, and had a fatted goose stuffed and roasted, and later that night saw the repentant sinner mount the stairs to his old room with a huge sigh of relief. I see Master Jehan Flastrier the barber-surgeon shrugging and turning up his eyes to Heaven on his next visit, when the news was told him. He thought Master Guillaume an old fool, and already in his dotage.

The next few months pass in comparative placidity. There are many worse things, after one has endured so many years of foot-slogging, hunger, prison, and stripes, than a roof, a warm bed, and the certainty of a dinner. Moreover, one returns exhausted and more wary, and less inclined to seek out trouble. Therefore, I think, for some time Villon's old room in the Porte Rouge was regularly occupied, and the chaplain, beaming with pleasure, was able to assure his friends that François had made up his mind to begin a fresh life. . . . I see the dark emaciated figure, hard-bitten, enigmatic, ill and worn with privations and debaucheries, sitting silent by the fire, brooding for hours on end.

His literary work in this year, 1462, consisted, highly probably, in the final arrangement and polishing of the *Grant Testament*; and also, almost certainly, in the composing of the seven Ballades of the Jargon. It is permissible to assume this last because Colin des Cayeulx, whose end is so genially touched in the first verse of the second Ballade, was (as we have seen) hanged in 1461. It is hence equally permissible to assume that the penitent, within a few weeks, had begun to feel his nature and the old life tugging at him once more, and had unostentatiously renewed acquaintance with some of his old comrades of the Coquille. Guillaume de Villon, seeing the nightly candle burning in the wanderer's chamber, little guessed what kind of work was being turned out there, with such gust.

I use the word gust. It is evident in every graceless line of the Ballades of the Jargon, though they are for the great part obscure as if they were written in Etruscan or the language of the Cocqci-grues. The words whose meaning has since been painfully deciphered give their keynote: truculent gaiety, the chuckling of thugs and assassins toasting the gallows where they will presently hang. The swing of these Ballades is irresistible, and the vigour of the Jargon superb. I have elsewhere transcribed the whole of the Third.[2] Here is the opening verse of the First.

> *A Parouart, la grant Mathe Gaudie,*
> *Ou accollez sont duppes & noirciz,*
> *Et par angelz suivans la paillardie,*
>   *Sont graffiz & prins cinq ou six.*
> *Là sont beffleurs, au plus hault bout assiz*
> *Pour le hevaige, & bien hault mis au vent.*
> *Eschequez moy tost ces coffres massiz,*
> *Car vendengeurs des ances circoncis*
>   *S'en brouent du tout a neant.*
>   *Eschec, eschec, pour le fardis!*

Parouart is Paris. The *grant Mathe Gaudie* is either Paris or the gibbet. *Angelz* are Archers of the Watch. *Eschequez* and *eschec* have affinity with "check" in the game of chess—"Look out!" *Fardis* is the rope by which *duppes* (fools, dupes) are *accollez*, or hanged by the neck.

[2] For this, and a general survey of the Jargon, see p. 368: *A Ballade from the Jargon.*

185

The Ballade continues:

> Brouez moy sur gours passans,
> Advisez moy bien toſt le blanc,
> Et pietonnez au large sus les champs.
> Qu'au mariage ne soiez sur le banc
> Plus qu'un sac n'eſt de plaſtre blanc;
> Si gruppez eſtes des carieux,
> Rebignez toſt ces enterveux
> Et leur montrez des trois le bris
> Qu'enclavez ne soiez deux a deux.
> Eschec, eschec, pour le fardis!
>
> Plantez aux hurmes voz picons,
> De paour des bisans si tres durs,
> Et aussi s'eſtre sur les joncz
> Enmahez en coffres en gros murs
> Escharicez, ne soiez point durs,
> Que le Grant Can ne vous face essorez,
> Songears ne soiez pour dorer,
> Et babignez toùsjours aux ys
> Des sires, pour les desbouser.
> Eschec, eschec, pour le fardis!

ENVOY

> Prince Froart, dit des Arques Petis,
> L'un des sires si ne soit endormis,
> Levez au bec, que ne soiez greffiz,
> Et que voz empz n'en ayent du pis,
> Eschec, eschec, pour le fardis!

Mariage is hanging, a facetious word of the Paris ropemakers for the rope supplied by them to the Provoſt. The sense of the reſt is more or less plain. *Prince Froart*, Prince of Sharpers. *Arques petis*, the little dice. *Levez au bec*, "Look, pipe, caſt your optics on . . ." *Greffiz*, seized. *Empz*, bodies.

The Second Ballade also I have already quoted. There is the same ruffian laughter in the Fourth, which begins:

> Saupicquez frouans des gours arques,
> Pour desbouser beaulx sires dieux
> Allez ailleurs planter vos marques!
> Benardz, vous eſtes rouges gueux.

186

> *Berart s'en va chez les joncheux*
> *Et babigne qu'il a plongis.*
> *Mes freres, soiez embraieux*
> *Et gardez les coffres massis.*

Saupicquez are the subtle and wideawake. *Frouer des gours arques* is to manipulate cogged dice. The laſt two lines mean, "Have a care, my lads, of the yawning clink." In the second stanza the whiſtle of warning againſt the *angelz*, the Archers, is heard again, and more clearly.

> *Si gruppez eſtes desgrappez*
> *De ces angelz si graveliffes,*
> *Incontinent manteaulx chappez*
> *Pour l'emboue serez eclipses;*
> *De vos farges serez besifles,*
> *Tout debout & non pas assis;*
> *Pour ce, gardez vous d'eſtre griffes*
> *Dedens ces gros coffres massis!*

He has joſtled his rhymes, being careless, no doubt, or drunk. One sees the flying cloaks, and hears hoarse guffaws, oaths, the pounding of feet, the clink of ſteel. I will quote one more burſt of this jollity, like a grotesque jig around the gallows: the firſt verse, with the Envoi, of the Seventh Ballade, which Villon has ſtamped with his acroſtic:

> *Brouez, benardz, eschecquez a la saulve,*
> *Car escornez vous eſtes a la roue:*
> *Fourbe, joncheur, chascun de vous se saulve.*
> *Eschec, eschec, coquille si s'en broue!*
> *Cornette court nul planteur ne s'i joue,*
> *Qui eſt en plant en ce coffre joyeulx;*
> *Pour ces raisons il a, ains qu'il s'escroue,*
> *Jonc verdoiant, havre du marieux.*

"Brouez, benardz"—"Look out, fools." This, again, is a sardonic warning againſt the officers of Juſtice, *la Roue*: a possible connection with the wheel of the Place de Grève. The Envoi goes off into a yell:

> *Vive David! saint archequin la baboue!*
> *Iehan mon amy, qui les fueilles desnoue.*

Le vendengeur, beffleur comme une choue,
LOing de son plain, de ses floz curieulx,
Noe beaucop, dont il reçoit fressoue,
Jonc verdoiant, havre du marieux!

David, or King David, is a picklock, a thieves' jest for *daviet* or *davier*, the ordinary word of the period for that indispensable tool. *Saint archequin*, according to Lucien Schöne, is a continuation of the joke, meaning "he who dances before the Ark"—*arche*, a chest or coffer. *Fueilles* are coin, and *desnouer* is to bag them. A *vendengeur* is a cut-purse. *Beffleur comme une choue* is "as secret (or tricky) as a barn-owl." *Marieux* is the hangman. *Fonc verdoiant* is not explained in the Lexicons of the Jargon I have consulted; but it seems possible that it is the gibbet, the "verdant pole." Compare our fathers' name for Tyburn Tree—Deadly Nevergreen.

In such gambollings did Villon encourage his patch-eyed Muse in this year 1462, beguiling the tedium of a life outwardly, and during the daytime, respectable. Whether he did anything else with his day is problematical. Doubtless he found it difficult to get pupils again, if he ever had any before, since he was the ideal tutor ("C. of E. . . . ? Games?"—one can imagine the *tête*, as the French say, of a modern scholastic agent faced suddenly with this apparition) neither in appearance nor in reputation. Well, indeed, might he cry with Friar John of the Funnels when Gargantua offered him the Abbey of Bourgeuil: *"Comment pourrois-je gouverner autruy, qui moy-mesme gouverner ne sçaurois?"*

There was one other source of honest employment open to him. I have mentioned it before. He could become a copyist to one of the gild of scriveners, whose *escriptoires* were numerous in Paris, and especially in his own quarter, or he might work for their humbler brethren the public letter-writers.[3] The Rue des Parcheminiers, which still runs along the side of St. Sévérin, that Gothic jewel, between the Rue St. Jacques and the Rue de la Harpe, was full of the open windows of the scriveners, behind which their clerks and copyists could be seen at work. They shared the street

---

[3] They had booths in the Innocents cemetery. "Here divers Clarks get their livelyhood by inditing letters for poor mayds." (Evelyn's *Diary*, 1644).

with the parchment-merchants and binders. Across the Pont Notre-Dame, in the shadow of St. Jacques-la-Boucherie, of which the splendid south tower only remains to-day, there was another ſtreet devoted to the preparing, writing, engrossing, and illuminating of manuscripts—the Rue des Ecrivains, swept away a hundred years ago. Villon, who in the *Petit Teſtament* bequeaths to Maſter Robert Vallée, clerk of the Parlement, the proceeds of the sale of his shirt of mail

> *A acheter a ce poupart*
> *Une feneſtre emprès Saint-Jacques,*

[To buy this poor fish a window near St. Jacques.]

evidently had employment at odd times in the Rue des Ecrivains, for both Teſtaments are thickly sprinkled with allusions to writing and the law, to notaries and Procurators, clerks of the Treasury, and clerks of the Officiality. As for the Rue des Parcheminiers,[4] he was presently doomed to fall into vile trouble by supping there.

His manner of life at this period, therefore, may be taken to oscillate irresolutely between the cloiſter of St. Benoît, where he ſtill kept his room, and his old haunts, which he frequented now more cynically and more gloomily than before—he was a tired man, recollect: at the same time (I imagine) keeping a cautious eye on the door and dexterously flitting away when a brawl arose and the women began screaming for the Watch. He mingled with the comrades of the Coquille now as a non-active member, and doubtless was respected by them as their official poet. Husky laughter and approval from half a dozen ugly mouths gratified him when, warmed with wine, he recited a new Ballade in the Jargon. Gnarled hands worn with every kind of professional job clapped him on the back and refilled his cup. Hairy visages, with a black patch over one eye and old scars zigzagging across the cheek, loomed out of the shadows and split across in hideous smiles. Even those Brethren, the Plain Men, who would have spat with disguſt at the Ballade of the Dead Ladies ("I know what I like") could beat time with their knife-hafts on the table to the attractive rhythm of

---

[4] Now, for some reason, the Rue de la Parcheminerie.

Spelicans,
Qui en tous temps
Avancez dedens le pogois,
Gourde piarde,
Et sur la tarde
Desbousez les povres nyois . . .

In the first week of November he is lying in the Châtelet on a small charge of theft. A thick fog hangs around this circumstance, and nothing can be gleaned of its nature. This minor affliction, nevertheless, is important for its consequences. Villon is in the Châtelet, possibly in the chamber called the *Troys Lis* he had so joked about in the Little Testament. The unimportant charge against him is not fully proved, and he is just about to be released when his Fortune steps in once more and claps her iron fist on the poor devil's shoulder. The Faculty of Theology, which has been licking its wounds for nearly six years, is to get a little vengeance of him at last.

Let us return and review the situation. The burglary at the College of Navarre took place on a night between ten and midnight, on the threshold of Christmas, 1456. The sacristy of the College was broken into by Villon and three companions: Petit Jehan, the expert picklock; Colin des Cayeulx, now hanged and rotting, his capable assistant; and the lapsed monk of Picardy called Dom Nicolas, with Guy Tabarie keeping watch and guarding the cloaks outside. A treasure-chest had been forced and five hundred gold crowns abstracted, of which Tabarie received ten as hush-money and the principals the rest, equally divided. In March 1457 the burglary had been discovered. In May the fool Tabarie blabbed away the whole story to the Prior of Paray-le-Moniau and the names of all concerned were given by the Prior to the police, thus enriching the information at the disposal of the court of inquiry set up in the previous March under Jehan Mautaint, Examiner at the Châtelet, and Jehan du Four his colleague. Tabarie, arrested in June 1458, and put to the Question in July, made a full confession, strongly involving his friend Villon. Between February 15 and March 15, 1459, finally, there is an entry in the Register of the

Faculty of Theology recording the payment of a fee of five sols Parisis for *"deux commissions scellées ou Chastelet adressant a tous juges & sergens royaulx afin de prendre les malfaiteurs du larcin fait dans le coffre de la Faculté . . . a la requeste du procureur du Roy"*: which shows that the Faculty was still on the lookout for Tabarie's accomplices. But there seems to have been no great result. The *dossier* of Colin des Cayeulx does not appear to have contained any sentence relative to the affair of the Collège de Navarre, though he was certainly implicated in it on his arrest. He is, at any rate, well out of it by this year 1462, high and dry and twirling. We can now proceed.

The Faculty of Theology had been put to great trouble and expense. Their treasure had been stolen, and they had spent money in trying to trace it; and in addition it had cost them sixteen good deniers Parisis to make good the results of Petit Jehan's handiwork, as appears from an entry in their Register, signed by their Grand Beadle Master Laurent Poutrel, priest and notary:

> *Item, pro reparando seraturam et clavem Facultatis in archa Universitatis*   .   .   .   .   *xvj d.p.*[5]

[*Item,* to repairing the lock and key of the Faculty's coffer . . . xvi deniers Parisis.]

Mark well the *grant bedeau* Laurent Poutrel. It is he who is to have the handling of Master François Villon shortly. He had already, on the Faculty's behalf, sharing the map with other commissaries, made journeys as far afield as Caen, Montlhéry, and Lyons in an endeavour to trace some of the money, *in prosecucione recuperacionis pecuniarum Facultatis.* From the inquiry of Mautaint and du Four in 1457 it appears that of the five hundred crowns stolen three hundred and forty belonged to the Faculty, a hundred to one of their members, Master Roger de Gaillon, since dead, and sixty to the Grand Beadle Poutrel. It does not seem that the detective work of Poutrel and his fellow-commissaries had much effect beyond increasing the Faculty's expenses; but the Faculty at any rate held Guy Tabarie firmly in their grasp in July 1458, and he was made to disgorge. Tabarie's mother, poor woman, went

[5] Univ. Archiv. Lat. 5657 C, fol. 35 v°.

surety for him, and an agreement was drawn up with the Faculty by which he was to pay back fifty gold crowns in two annual instalments. This is duly set forth in the Faculty's Register in a sturdy, angular, beautiful hand, written with a broad quill, on stout paper, still almost white, in ink which remains black after four hundred years. The greater part of the Register, which is a record of Masses said for deceased members and others as well as a receipt-book for moneys paid and received on behalf of the Faculty, is written in this hand. The entry concerning Tabarie follows an entry of a Mass offering, and reads:

Alia recepta extraordinaria:
Item a matre magistri Guidonis Tabary cum qua Facultas fecit compositionem ad sommam L^ta scutorum auri solvendorum duobus terminis pro actione incarceracionis dicti Tabary, sui filii, alterius depredatorum pecuniarum predictarum Facultatis. Recepit dominus Poutrelli medietatem dicte somme ascendentem ad xxv scuta, de quibus xxv scutis ordinavit dicta Facultas quod executores deffuncti mag. Rogeri de Gaillon et dominus Poutrelli haberent decem scuta in recompensam suarum pecuniarum perditarum. Et sic dominus Poutrelli facit receptam de xv scutis vallentibus xvj l. x s.p.

[*Other Extraordinary Receipts:*
Item, received of the mother of Master Guy Tabarie, with whom the Faculty made a composition for the sum of fifty gold crowns to be restored in two instalments, in consideration of the release of the said Tabarie her son, another person concerned in the theft of the said Faculty's treasure.— Master Poutrel received half the said sum, amounting to twenty-five crowns, of which sum the said Faculty ordered ten to be awarded between the executors of the late Master Roger de Gaillon and Master Poutrel, on account of their stolen money. And thus Master Poutrel gives a receipt [on the Faculty's behalf] for fifteen crowns, valued at sixteen livres and ten sols Parisis.] (MS. Lat. 5657 c, fol. 46 v°.)

Thus the imbecile Tabarie, having made ten crowns out of the affair, is forced to pay back fivefold. How his mother was able to raise this money is not known. The Faculty, observe, was merciful, and did not press the criminal charge, and Tabarie was released on this bond. There is another receipt in the Register for money received on Tabarie's account by the Grand Beadle: and then, after an interval of a score of pages recording Masses and accounts, we come upon our own friend, who appears suddenly in an entry made by Master Poutrel in November 1462, recording a payment to the criminal *greffier* at the Châtelet.[6]

Item, tradidit dictus Poutrelli graffario criminali Curie Castelleti pro registrando opposicionem factam per Johannem Collet procuratorem Facultatis expedicioni magistri Francisci Villon alterius depredatorum pecuniarum Facultatis in carceribus dicti Castelleti auctoritate justicie tunc detenti pro certo latrocinio quod tunc sibi imponebatur . . . . xvi d.

[*Item,* the said Poutrel paid to the criminal *greffier* of the Court of the Châtelet for registering the opposition made by Jehan Collet, Procurator of the Faculty, to the release of Master François Villon, another person concerned in the theft of the Faculty's treasure, then lying in the said Châtelet and detained there by the order of justice on account of a certain theft laid to his charge . . . xvi deniers.] (MS. Lat. 5657 c, fol. 79 v°.)

What happened is plain. Master Jehan Collet, Procurator of the Faculty, having just relaxed his grip on Tabarie, learned of the providential presence of one of the master-thieves, François Villon, in the Châtelet and of his imminent discharge, and at once (I can hear his grunt of surprise and pleasure) applied to the Court of the Châtelet for a writ of *Ne exeat.* The application was, of course, granted immediately, and Villon, as appears from Poutrel's next entry, was brought before the Court again, examined—whether with or without the Question is not stated: without, I conclude— and made a full confession. For the copy of this confession,

. . . pro dupplo confessionis facte per dictum magistrum Franciscum Villon . . .

the Grand Beadle paid the *greffier* another eleven sols Parisis. Well might Magister Franciscus feel (*"Domine, quid multiplicati sunt . . . !"*) that his enemies were round about him, digging a pit for his bones. Master Laurent Poutrel knew the Faculty's prisoner well, his record, his haunts, his friends, his relatives, and more especially his resources. Master Poutrel was a Canon of St. Benoît-le-Bientourné and lived round the corner from the Rue St. Jacques, in the

[6] He is the Pierre Basenier, notary, to whom Villon facetiously bequeaths, in the *Petit Testament,* the good will of the Provost, and again, in the *Grand Testament,* a basketful of cloves; this last concealing some private gibe.

Rue des Noyers,[7] at the sign of the Magdalen: his nephew Henry Alexandre, like himself a priest, an ecclesiastical lawyer, and an official of the Faculty of Theology, was also attached to St. Benoît.[8] The honourable name of his colleague Guillaume de Villon, therefore, rang instantly and very pleasantly in the ears of Master Laurent Poutrel. Behold, accordingly, the Grand Beadle setting forth from the Faculty a day or so after Villon's confession and appearing at the Porte Rouge in the cloister of St. Benoît, requesting an interview with Master Guillaume. He got his interview, and a melancholy one for the chaplain it must have been. The Grand Beadle, issuing from the Porte Rouge, leaving behind him no doubt a weary, unhappy old man rolling dazed eyes around him and appealing mutely to Heaven, was able to return to the Faculty and announce that he could come to an agreement with certain sureties in the matter of the prisoner Villon. The Faculty accepted, and stated their conditions. The prisoner would undertake to repay to the Faculty the sum of one hundred and twenty gold crowns in yearly instalments, forty crowns a year for three years, and on that undertaking could be released. The penalty for breaking the agreement was to be immediate re-imprisonment in the Châtelet.

The bond was drawn up, and the Grand Beadle noted it in his register.

Item pro littera condempnacionis passate per dictum Villon de somma sexviginti scutorum auri quam promisit solvere Facultati et execucioni defuncti magistri Rogeri de Gaillon ac dicto Poutrelli infra tres annos proxime venturos usque ad quod tempus elargitus est a dictis carceribus . . v s.p.

[*Item,* for the letter binding the said Villon in the sum of one hundred and twenty gold crowns, which he has bound himself to repay to the Faculty, the executor of the late Master Roger de Gaillon, and the said Poutrel within the next three years to come from the time of his release from the said prison . . . v sols Parisis.] (MS. Lat. 5657 c, fol. 79.)

The date is between the third and seventh of November 1462, when Villon, on signing the bond, was at once released. The bargain was not a severe one, considering the extent of the burglary;

[7] Now incorporated in the eastern portion of the Boulevard St. Germain.
[8] They were both buried in St. Benoît, Poutrel in 1470, his nephew in 1496. The stone covering their bodies, with its inscription *Priez Dieu pour l'ame d'eux,* existed until the church was demolished in 1854.

and the Faculty, as in Tabarie's case, waived the criminal charge. It is true that as far as Villon was concerned the Royal letter of remission at Meun was plenary, covering all anterior criminal offences, and that technically he could not, therefore, be proceeded against criminally in the matter: but it is also probable that the Faculty could, if they had cared to take the trouble, fairly soon have discovered a gaping loophole in the very rickety status of their prisoner. They did not, however; probably, I should imagine, to spare Master Guillaume de Villon more pain; contenting themselves with the civil proceedings, which letters of remission did not cover.[9]

The homing of the prodigal this time cannot have been so cordially celebrated, and the atmosphere must have been strained, until very soon, no doubt, the tears and self-reproaches of François once more melted the old man's resentment. Master Guillaume's face must have become, since his interview with the Grand Beadle, a little grave. To find a hundred and twenty gold crowns, eight thousand five hundred modern French francs at par, equal normally to three hundred and forty English pounds, one does not go and pick them up in the kennel in the Rue St. Jacques. It is curious to observe that the available Register of the Faculty, which continues till March 1465, three years afterwards, contains no evidence of any repayment whatsoever by Villon or his sureties: one must therefore assume that the entries pertaining were made in some other register now lost,[10] for though Villon himself could not (as we shall soon see) be clapped back into the Châtelet in the following year for non-payment, the chaplain of St. Benoît was accountable, and would have been summoned at once before the courts. But I think there can be no doubt that the Grand Beadle Poutrel got the money back. Guillaume de Villon was a man of integrity. It is possible that the little vine enclosure in the Clos Bourgeois at Vaugirard had to go, and with it one, or even two, of the houses from which the chaplain derived most of his private

---

[9] Villon's letters of remission of 1456, after the Chermoye affair, contained this clause: *"Item, que le prince ne donne jamais drois d'autruy, ne pardonne le cas, si non satisfaccion faicte a partie civilement."* This may or may not have been repeated in the letter of Meun, but the principle was axiomatic.

[10] It must be remembered that this was, by God's mercy, before the age of Efficiency.

income; and for the next few months, I imagine, the days of abstinence from flesh-meat observed in the Porte Rouge were in excess of those ordered by the Church. Were there recriminations? Did the archangelic patience of Master Guillaume break down at last under this heavy trial? Did bitter words pass between him and the reprobate he loved, and did François fling out, cursing, to return and fall, crying and imploring, at his benefactor's feet? At any rate the old man's affection very quickly resumed its accustomed place, and François Villon once more took up his old quarters in the Porte Rouge.

It is the month of November 1462, the first or second week. Before the end of the month he is in trouble again, and one of the sorest troubles of his turbulent life. It is part of his character that a little after his repentances he drifted back automatically to his old companions; for he was weak, and sinful, and in every way dissimilar from a *Quarterly Reviewer;* and like Falstaff, leaving the fear of God on the left hand and hiding honour in necessity, was fain to shuffle, to hedge, and to lurch. His resolutions were good, and he had a conscience, and struggled intermittently to obey it.

Laisser les folz!—Bien j'y adviseray . . .

But that was the resolution of a year ago, in the prison of Meun. *Deteriora sequor*—the tag is eternal. His apologies, his reparation, his prayers, his promises to Master Guillaume were still being poured out, his eyes were hardly dry, when he met three jovial *folz* and spent an evening with them, eating and drinking, and so was drawn into a stupid brawl which was to leave him for the second time (at least) lying under sentence of death, condemned to be hanged and strangled, and at the last—for his luck, what was left of it, still held—banished from Paris and from history.

8

The flesh is bruckle, the Feynd is slee:—
Timor Mortis conturbat me.
—DUNBAR.

OF this, the last and one of the most big with disaster of Villon's known adventures, there is a solid account in a letter of remission accorded by Louis XI. to one Robin Dogis, dated November 1463.[11] The Rue des Parcheminiers, where the affair began, runs still, as I have said, from the Rue St. Jacques to the Rue de la Harpe, along the south side of St. Sévérin, and is full of ghosts.

The letter states that Robin Dogis,

estant en sa maison où pend pour enseigne le Chariot, située & assise en nostre ville de Paris en la rue des Parcheminiers, vint vers lui maistre François Villon & lui demanda si lui donneroit à souper, lequel suppliant lui respondit que ouy, & avec eulx vindrent souper Rogier Pichart & Hutin du Moustier.

[Being in his house at the sign of the *Chariot,* situate in Our town of Paris in the Rue des Parcheminiers, there came to him Master François Villon asking if he would give him supper: to which the said petitioner [Dogis] replied in the affirmative. And with them there came to supper Roger Pichart and Hutin du Moustier.]

Of this supper-party three at least were rank bad hats. Robin Dogis' profession is not known, nor his record. Hutin du Moustier, a *sergent à verge* of the Châtelet—some of the Sergeants, observes Gaston Paris, were scarcely better than the criminals they arrested— is believed to have been hanged later. Roger Pichart, the instigator of the affray of this night, is known to have ended on the gibbet in February 1465. The third we know.

They went to supper at the *Chariot,* Robin's lodgings, and the wine, it is evident from the subsequent happenings, flowed freely.

Après lequel souper, environ sept ou huit heures, ledit suppliant & les autres dessusdits partirent ensemble de ladite maison d'icelluy suppliant pour aler en la chambre dudit maistre François Villon.

[11] Archives of Parliament (X²ᵃ 30, fol. 294 r°).

[After which supper, towards seven or eight o'clock, the said petitioner with the others foresaid left the said house together to go to the room of the said Master François Villon.]

The four, flushed and ripe for a row, issue unsteadily from the sign of the *Chariot* and turn into the Rue St. Jacques on their way to the cloister of St. Benoît. No doubt Master Guillaume de Villon, much enduring, had long become accustomed to passing gallows faces on the stairs in his own house and to hearing oaths and staves of raucous song and the clink of bottles from the room above. He must have loved François Villon a great deal. . . . But to-night there was to be no assembly of jovial companions in François' room.

En passant pour y aler par la rue St. Jacques de nostre dite ville de Paris, ledit Rogier Pichart s'arresta à la fenestre de l'escriptoire de maistre François Ferrebourg, raillant les clercs d'icelluy maistre François Ferrebourg & crachant dedans ladite escriptoire, pourquoy incontinent les clercs dudit maistre François Ferrebourg saillirent d'icelle escriptoire avec la chandelle allumée, disans par telz mots: "Quels paillars sont ce là?" Auxquelz ledit Rogier Pichart respondit s'ilz vouloient aceter des flustes, &, en ce disant, les volut fraper. Pour laquelle cause se meut noyse tant que ledit Hutin du Moustier fut pris des clercs dudit maistre François Ferrebourg & mis en l'ostel d'icelluy Ferrebourg, en criant par telz mots ou semblables: "Au meutre! On me tue! Je suis mort!"

[On the way there, by way of the Rue St. Jacques in Our said town of Paris, the said Roger Pichart halted by the window of the *escriptoire* of Master François Ferrebourg, taunting the clerks of the said Master François Ferrebourg and spitting into the window: on account of which the clerks of the said Master François Ferrebourg issued from the said *escriptoire* with the lighted candle, saying: "What ruffians are these?" To whom the said Roger Pichart answered, demanding if they wished to buy any flutes [*i.e.* if they wanted a fight]; and with these words tried to strike them. On account of which there arose a brawl, in the course of which the said Hutin du Moustier was captured by the clerks of the said Master François Ferrebourg and taken into the house of the said Ferrebourg, crying "Murder! They are killing me! I am dead!"]

Master François Ferrebourg, or Ferrebouc, is a grave personage of some importance, a priest, Bachelor of Arts, Licenciate in Canon Law, Pontifical Notary, and Writer to the Officiality of the Bishop of Paris: he was one of the notaries concerned in the *procès de réhabilitation* of St. Joan in 1458, and one of the examining magistrates at Tabarie's trial. The exact position of his *escriptoire* is given in a rent-roll of the *grant rue Saint-Jacques* of 1452: he occupied a house at the sign of the *Barillet,* or Keg, next door to the *Mule* tavern and facing the convent, church, and enclosure of the Order of the Sacred Trinity, or Mathurins; with whose General, Robert Gaguin, the humanist and traveller, he was on terms of intimate friendship. Thus the four companions, having turned to the right out of the Rue des Parcheminiers, had crossed the road and proceeded only a matter of forty or fifty yards when they stopped to jeer in at the lighted window of Master Ferrebourg's *escriptoire.*[12]

The scene is illuminated for us as in a camera-obscura. The black street, with its high overhanging eaves and gables: the broad splash of light poured across the cobbles from Master François Ferrebourg's open window, where his clerks sit toiling into the night over some urgent piece of law-writing: the loud voices, growing nearer, and caterwauling of four half-tipsy ruffians stumbling along the kennel; the thick voice of Roger Pichart as they halt by the window, taunting the clerks; the spitting through the window; the quick uprising of the outraged clerks and the dashing into the street; the blows; the scuffling; the oaths; the capture of Hutin du Moustier, who is hustled indoors, bawling murder.

The uproar brought from his inner room, where he sat poring over a roll of parchments, Master François Ferrebourg himself. Master Ferrebourg was a man of action, and wasted no time in asking questions.

Auquel cry sailly incontinent ledit maistre François Ferrebourg hors de sondit hostel & bouta si rudement ledit suppliant qu'il le fir cheoir à terre.

[At which cry there issued incontinent from his aforesaid house Master François Ferrebourg, and gave the aforesaid petitioner such a strong shove that he made him fall to the ground.]

The vigorous shove sent Robin Dogis sprawling. He picked himself up, whipped out his dagger, aimed a flying stab at Master Ferrebourg, wounding that personage, and took to his heels, re-

---

[12] He was by his office exempt from the ordinary curfew of Paris, which was rung from Notre-Dame at eight p.m. for the Right Bank, and from Sorbonne at nine, the hour of Angelus.

joining Roger Pichart by St. Benoît-le-Bientourné. Here he addressed Pichart (or so he is reported in his letter of remission) severely, saying *qu'il eſtoit ung très mauvais paillart*, and forthwith retired to his own house, the *Chariot* in the Rue des Parcheminiers, to bed. But notwithstanding his virtuous chiding of Pichart, Dogis was presently hoicked out of bed by the police and caſt into the Châtelet, *en grant dangier de sa personne,* and being presumably a Savoyard, since the letter mentions expressly

en faveur & contemplacion de la nouvelle venue & entrée en noſtre dite ville de Paris de noſtre tres cher & tres amé pere le duc de Savoye, & de la priere & requeſte qui de par luy a eſté sur ce faiɛte, etc.,

[Viewing and contemplating the recent arrival and entry into Our said Town of Paris of Our moſt dear and moſt beloved father, the Duke of Savoy, and the prayer and requeſt made on his behalf in this matter,] etc.

eventually got a pardon, after nearly a year of prison. Meanwhile Roger Pichart, whom we left outside St. Benoît, had taken to his heels again, and dodging skilfully among the turnings weſt of the Rue St. Jacques had reached the Cordeliers' cloiſters and church and claimed sanɛtuary: and an hour or two later was traced there and dislodged by a couple of Sergeants, and sent to join his friend Robin Dogis in the Châtelet. The Friars Minor, whose right of sanɛtuary had thus been defied, *conspué,* and set at naught, brought an aɛtion againſt the Provoſt on this account, and judgment was given in the following year, as appears from an entry in the Criminal Regiſter of the Court of Parliament, dated May 16, 1464.

Entre les gardien & couvent des Freres mineurs a Paris demandeurs & requerant l'immunité de leur eglise eſtre reintegree &, en ce faisant, leur remettre ung nommé Pichart, a present prisonnier en la Conciergerie, en ladiɛte eglise dont il a eſté extraiɛt, d'une part. Et le procureur general opposant, d'autre. Sur le plaidoyé desdites parties du viie jour de ce present moys dit a eſté que ladite eglise sera reintegree & reſtituee & joyra ledit Pichart de ladite immunité. Et en ce faisant sera remis en ladite eglise en l'eſtat qu'il eſtoit a l'eure qu'il pris par le prevoſt de Paris.[13]

[Between the superior and convent of the Friars Minor of Paris, complainants, demanding the reſtoration of the immunity of their church, and

---

[13] MS. Dupuy 250, fol. 65; fr. 5908, fol. 116.

The Friars, then, successfully asserted their rights and got Pichart their prisoner back after eighteen months in the Conciergerie, whither he had been removed, with the others, from the Châtelet; a significant move, and an ominous. Since the said Pichart was anyhow hanged a year or two later, his reclaimed sanctuary was not so advantageous to him as it might have been.

We have accounted for Dogis and Pichart. The third of the supper-party, Hutin du Moustier, was held by Master Ferrebourg's clerks, handed over to the Watch, and by them clapped into the Châtelet also. The fourth member of the party was François Villon. Now it is noteworthy that the name of Villon is nowhere mentioned in Robin Dogis' letter of remission after the actual setting forth from the sign of the *Chariot* after supper; hence Villon's part in the evening's turmoil is clear. He is last seen halting a little unsteadily in front of Master Ferrebourg's window, as Roger Pichart lifts up his voice and begins to taunt the clerks and spit among them: and at the moment when the rather attractive frolic shows the first symptom of developing into trouble Master Villon, as an unbiassed spectator, judges it advisable to slip away, as swiftly as Gilles and the girl Ysabeau had vanished that June evening under the clock of St. Benoît so many years ago. *Erupit, evasit*; slinking like a cat by short cuts home to the safety of the Red Door. He had seen enough of trouble, or so he no doubt told himself: but his ironic Dæmon had arranged otherwise. Master François Ferrebourg, having sent Robin Dogis with such a vigorous shove into the kennel, had caught sight of Villon's ugly face at the moment he turned tail to fly. Master Ferrebourg had a keen eye, and he was not only a Pontifical Notary, but had also—alas! unlucky poet—powerful friends at the Châtelet. He doubtless had known Villon by sight and reputation for years. Master Ferrebourg therefore, having instantly recognised this notorious criminal, gave his name to the police when they came up at the double to collect Hutin du Moustier and to draw up the *procès-verbal*. Later the same night Villon, having retired prudently to bed in his chamber, heard the tramp of Archers coming up the cloister of St. Benoît, heard them halt, with a clatter of arms, outside the Porte Rouge; heard himself summoned; and ruefully descended. He was taken away and thrust into the Châtelet with the others, and within the twenty-four hours the charge had been formally drawn up against all four by the Criminal Lieutenant, Pierre de la Dehors.

Villon's position in this affair demands, in common justice, a little sympathy. He had had no share whatsoever in the night's brawl—for if he had, be sure his friend Robin Dogis would not have lost the chance of shifting a little of the responsibility on to such celebrated shoulders. Villon therefore lay in the Châtelet once more under a not very grave charge, and nothing serious could be proved against him. But he had to reckon with the new Criminal Lieutenant and his master the Provost; no longer, alas! Robert d'Estouteville, but Jacques Villiers de l'Isle-Adam, a man of wrath.

Pierre de la Dehors, finding by the grace of God this incorrigible gaol-bird once more in the hands of Justice, had decided to finish with him, charge or no charge. He possessed, as I perceive, at least four excellent reasons for detesting Villon and grinding his teeth with satisfaction at the thought of holding him: *primo*, Villon was a clerk of University, and therefore, automatically and his record apart, the enemy; *secundo*, the Criminal Lieutenant was Master of the Grande Boucherie of Paris, and had probably not forgotten the affray with the butchers and the theft of hooks during the *Pet-au-Deable* celebrations all those years ago; *tertio*, he held in the hollow of his hand one of the most troublesome blackguards within the liberties of Paris, a rioter, a burglar, an assassin, a robber of churches, hand-in-glove with some of the most desperate characters of the underworld; and *quarto*, the fellow was a poet, God help us all! To intelligences of the police and military kind the word "poet" has ever been as the red cloak to the black bull of

Andalusia. Poet! *Poet*, is he? Well, we shall hear him squeak a pretty song before very long! The Criminal Lieutenant emits a short, unpleasing laugh, echoed by his satellites, and turns to direct his labour of love, the assembling of the voluminous *dossier* of this poet, letters of remission and all, since the year 1455. This time the fellow is not going to slip through our fingers, *beau sire Dieux*!

The Criminal Lieutenant, with the hearty approval of Messire de l'Isle-Adam, opened the proceedings with a little light torture, as we know from a Ballade I shall presently quote. *Ledict* François Villon, sitting pensive in his straw once more, conjecturing what was about to befall him this time, was summoned, taken to his dismay into the chamber of the Question, and forced again to the agonising water-treatment, all the more hideous this time for his still acute memories of the prison at Meun. But with his pain now was mixed an intolerable sense of the injustice of his punishment; his gasps and shrieks were the more bitter, and with his sobbing and half-incoherent appeals there mingled a half-mad fury and despair. The Criminal Lieutenant at length nodded to his assistants. Villon, half dead with pain, his lean scarred body shaking as with the ague, a drooping wreck, was helped down the steps again and thrust swooning upon his straw. The turn of his friends had come.

It is not difficult to share the sequence of thoughts pouring confusedly into Villon's mind as he awoke, shivering, from his faint and became capable of reasoning. I see him brooding in the darkness, head on knees, hands tightly clenched, reviewing in a dull desperation the past, the present, the immediate future. What was all this? Did they mean to do for him this time? He had observed in the eyes of Pierre de la Dehors an ominous glitter. They had captured him on a charge which would not bear looking into for one moment. He had had no part in the insulting of Master Ferrebourg's clerks, or in the row which followed, or in the stabbing of Master Ferrebourg. He had run for it the moment the trouble began. By God, they couldn't hang a man for that, could they? But he remembers again the expression in the Criminal Lieutenant's eyes, and of a sudden shivers violently.

Whether he was given the Question again, whether he felt the ghastly linen placed on his mouth, the hellish gurgle of the water, the steady pouring, whether he felt his heart flooded and his belly about to burst, every fibre of his agonised body distended and starting apart, is not clear. Pierre de la Dehors would no doubt have welcomed additional information wrenched from this fellow, to be compared with the statements of his companions. Nevertheless this was not the main business. He wanted the fellow out of the way once and for all.[14] And so very soon Master Pierre de la Dehors, issuing from a conference with the Provost, ordered his secretaries to prepare at once the documents required for a condemnation, followed by the extreme sentence. The documents were drawn up. The accused Villon heard the rasp and grate of his dungeon door being flung open, and once more the dreaded summons. He staggers out, sick with preliminary terror, and is taken by two Archers not to the Question chamber, but up the stairs to the Court hall, where he had appeared only a short time before, when the Faculty of Theology discovered him. The Provost Villiers de l'Isle-Adam sits in his chair on the dais, an assessor on either side of him, the Criminal Lieutenant in attendance. The prisoner Villon, supported by his two Archers, confronts him. A *greffier* begins to read over in a rapid voice, conversationally, a number of papers, of which Villon, dazed and weak, can only catch the flying ends of sentences. *"Veu que . . . mmm . . . et veu . . . ceste Court . . . mmm . . . ledict Villon . . . mauvaise vie . . . mmm . . . en villain cas . . . mmm . . . Chrm . . . mm . . ."* The rigmarole comes to an end. The Provost's cold voice is heard, his cold eyes do not rest on the prisoner. Then suddenly an Archer is nudging Villon in the ribs, and it is over. What was it? What did he say? *Pend——?*

The Archer jerks a thumb. The Court rises. The Provost passes out, chatting with an assessor and fingering the jewel at his neck. The two Archers turn to their prisoner, drooping and bewildered there, licking his dry lips. Right about turn! They march him down to his cell and leave him.

Pend——?

The door has clanged, the footsteps recede along the stone corridor. Yes. He has got it this time all right. This is the end.

---

[14] It would seem that the Bishop had washed his hands of Villon, as of Regnier de Montigny and Colin des Cayeulx, and left him to the temporal arm.

Saturn has played him his last trick. He is to be hanged by the neck, *pendu et estranglé*. By God, it has come at last! Well.

He stares into the darkness, hugging his knees, seeing Death, as once before, beckoning and grinning before him, feeling in the thick musty air of the chamber that creeping graveyard chill, that faint smell of damp mould he has felt and smelt before—once before—twice before. This time it is final. The King is not likely to die again to oblige him, nor is there any little Princess on the horizon, about to make a timely entry into Paris. His turn has arrived. The others have all gone before him. Colin? Colin is a rattling bag of bones, if he still swings—or perhaps they have pulled him down by now and bundled him into his hole, without priest, without sprinkling, without a prayer for his sinful soul. . . . He closes his eyes and sees Colin still hanging, with the last strips and tatters of flesh fluttering on him, like the pictures of Death in the Innocents gallery. He holds out his thin arm and feels it, curiously, picturing it in a year's time on Montfaucon. He feels the jerk of the cart pulling from underneath, hears the thick choke he has heard more than once on an execution day, sees the convulsions and the twitching. He counterfeits in the darkness the final grimace, *la moe,* out of which he made a few good jokes in a Ballade of the Jargon a year or so ago.

> *Prince, qui n'a bauderie*
> *Pour eschever de la soe,*
> *Danger de grup en arderie*
> *Fait aux sires faire la moe!*

Brrr! He will soon know all about the *halle-grup* himself now. God! What an end, after all! He gets as little pleasure out of thinking of it as Christy Mahon out of the forecast of Pegeen Mike. "It's queer joys they have, and who knows the thing they'd do, if it'd make the green stones cry itself to think of you swaying and swiggling at the butt of a rope, and you with a fine stout neck, God bless you! the way you'd be half an hour, in great anguish, getting your death." And then to dangle there and rot. Rain to wash your bones, and sun to dry and blacken you, and the birds to peck out your eyes, and all the toughs of Paris bringing their mopsies out to

205

laugh at you! He hears the dry creak of the rope chafing in the pulley-block again, and the rattle of Colin as a breeze takes him and dances him round and round. . . . And Montigny has gone too, the same way. And the fat traitor Tabarie too, no doubt, dribbling and blabbing his friends' lives away—*homs veritable!* Well for Tabarie—Villon's eyes narrow and a speck of sombre light glows in them—if the *amboureux* has got him first. A few nice gentlemen, all old friends, were waiting round the corner to welcome that wind-bag when the *angelz* let him loose. Pah!

And Christophe Turgis? He is dead years ago, screaming in a bath of hot oil. And the Wolf? God knows. Cholet? God knows. All his friends are gone. And the girls? Kissing and whispering on some other fool's knee, the drabs of hell. And Katherine? A spasm of pain shakes his body. Katherine! If it were not for her cruelty would he be lying here now, waiting for the birds to stab his eyes out? He covers his face with his hands, and his soul passes down into the nether darkness.

So a few days dragged on, and black misery alternated with a fatalist shrugging. It was his fate. *"J'en seray dehors quant je tres-passeray!"* In this mood, with a momentary return of his old swagger, he composed the Tetrastic or Quatrain summing up his position in a cynical jest.

> *Je suis François, dont ce me poise,*
> *Né de Paris empres Pontoise,*
> *Et d'une corde d'une toise,*
> *Sçaura mon col que mon cul poise.*

[François am I,—woe worth it me!
 At Paris born, near Pontoise citie,
 Whose neck, in the bight of a rope of three,
 Must prove how heavy my buttocks be.]
 (Payne.)

He recited this, I think, to his gaoler, and it provoked a mutual snigger. But one evening, with his hunk of hard bread and his water-pitcher, came the friar to prepare him for death; and his blackguard doggedness vanished, leaving him humble, a sinner trembling on the brink of Eternity. It was then, with the returning

206

hold of his religion warming and comforting him, that his thoughts on his end shaped themselves into that great music which is the Ballade of the Hanged, beginning with that cry to his fellow-men, on behalf of himself and his doomed companions:

> Freres humains qui après nous vivez,
> N'ayez les cuers contre nous endurcis,
> Car, se pitié de nous povres avez,
> Dieu en aura plus tost de vous mercis . . .

Then comes the swelling note, like a rising wind, and in his vision he sees the black shadow of Montfaucon with its rotting, swinging shapes, his own body, the bodies of those who hang with him.

> Vous nous voiez cy attachez cinq, six,
> Quant de la char, que trop avons nourrie,
> Elle est pieça devoree et pourrie,
> Et nous, les os, devenons cendre et pouldre.
> De nostre mal personne ne s'en rie;
> Mais priez Dieu que tous nous vueille absouldre!

And he cries again to his brother-men to hush their mockery and heave up their hands for him and his companions:

> Envers le Fils de la Vierge Marie,
> Que sa grace ne soit pour nous tarie,
> Nous preservant de l'infernale fouldre . . .

Then the profundity of genius shakes him, and he makes that picture of the gallows and its fruit which is like a painting of Zurburan or El Greco in its sombre splendour, its vision of mortality:

> La pluye nous a buez et lavez,
> Et le soleil dessechiez et noircis;
> Pies, corbeaulx, nous ont les yeulx cavez,
> Et arrachié la barbe et les sourcis:
> Jamais nul temps nous ne sommes assis;
> Puis ça, puis la, comme le vent varie,
> A son plaisir sans cesser nous charie,
> Plus becquetez d'oiseaulx que dez a couldre . . .

And so to the final passionate prayer:

> Prince Jhesus, qui sur tous seigneurie,
> Garde qu'Enfer n'ait de nous la maistrie;

A luy n'ayons que faire ne que souldre.
Hommes, icy n'a point de mocquerie;
Mais priez Dieu que tous nous vueille absouldre!

Such a poem has never been written before him, nor since.

Sentence being delivered, in due course Villon and his companions Dogis, Pichart, and du Moustier were removed from the Châtelet to the "condemn'd hold" of the Conciergerie in the Palais, for the poet the first stage of the journey to Montfaucon. It does not appear that any sentence had been passed on any of the other three, but, as we know, the turn of Pichart at least was more or less at hand. With the transference to a fresh prison, and the knowledge of its significance, there awoke in Villon once more the instinct to fight for life. He had no illusions. Nothing could save him this time unless he bestirred himself at once; and so, waking from his stupor and fascinated gaze on Death, he was visited by a spurt of energy. After all, his sentence was patently absurd. The Provost (he knew) was rushing him out of the way on a flimsy pretext that no law could justify for a moment, counting on a swift execution. But although the Provost held the power, there was still justice left somewhere, was there not? They could not hang a man for running away from a street row, whatever his past, could they? At once his spirits began to revive, his mood to change, a new light to come into his eyes. He realised that his time for making an appeal was short, and might even be smothered unless he exerted every fibre: and before many hours of his occupation of the Conciergerie dungeon, I imagine, a messenger was speeding once more to the cloister of St. Benoit with a message, scrawled with the gaoler's connivance, pleading instant action for the love of God. At the same time Villon applied for leave to appeal to the Parliament, and was granted leave. It is evident that the conscience of Villiers de l'Isle-Adam was not entirely at rest in this matter.

Villon had a strong case, and the Provost had overstepped the mark most patently: and Guillaume de Villon, who had so often saved the situation before, was not the man to turn a deaf ear to this desperate cry. He acted, I presume, at once, even if he had not already done so on learning of the disaster. Treading once more the

208

well-worn path to the houses of those men of power whose esteem he had constantly enjoyed, the old priest must have set in motion every influence he could come at, every legal and parliamentary influence which might buttress François' already respectable case. The result is seen in an order of the Court of Parliament, the last of the judicial documents concerning François Villon's life, under the date of January 5, 1462 (Old Style); that is, January 3, 1463 (New Style):

> *v⁰ janvier lxxii (v. st.).—Veu par la Court le proces fait par le prevost de Paris ou son lieutenant a l'encontre de maistre François Villon appellant d'estre pendu et estranglé.*
>
> Finaliter *ladicte appellacio net ce dont a esté appellé mis au neant, et eu regard a la mauvaise vie dudict Villon, le bannist jusques a dix ans de la ville, prevosté, & viconté de Paris.*[15]

[January 5, 1462 (Old Style).—The Court having considered the case brought by the Provost of Paris and his Lieutenant against Master François Villon, and the latter having appealed from the sentence of hanging and strangling: It is finally ordered that the said appeal, and the sentence preceding, be annulled, and having regard to the bad character of the said Villon, that he be banished for ten years from the Town, Provosty, and Viscounty of Paris.]

This precious document, this final entry of such extreme value to the biographer, I have myself struggled painfully to decipher, letter by letter. It appears at the very bottom of the fifty-ninth page of a register of *Arrests,* or Orders of the Court, compiled by the *greffiers* of the Tournelle; a Newgate Calendar in summary, embracing the periods April 1433—November 1400 and December 1440—July 1485.[16] It is written in thin faded ink in vile crabbed characters, devilishly cramped and run together, as much like colloquial Urdu as French; in the left-hand margin a laconic sign-post, the one word *Villon.* It is probable that in no way did the *greffier* who made the entry distinguish the prisoner Villon from any other prisoner whose sentence it was his duty to record. Staring at it, fingering the paper, I have seen in a vision this official running his

¹⁵ MS. Dupuy 250, fol. 59.
¹⁶ The register includes also, very curiously, one or two historical records, particularly a bald note of the wounding of St. Joan before Compiègne (. . . *Jehanne la Pucelle blecée devant Compiengne*), and her martyrdom.

finger down his list of names, ticking them off one by one, entering the reprieve of the prisoner Villon, sanding his wet ink, stolidly turning over the page and continuing with the next item. So three hundred years later in Paris another block-headed minister of Justice will be writing down the sentence of one Chénier, André, of the next morning's batch for the guillotine. The one poet escaped, the other died. It is all one.

The entry, then, is made. Messire Villiers de l'Isle-Adam has lost the game. The excessive injustice of his award has cried to Parliament. The said Villon has escaped the gallows again, at the eleventh hour, and is a free and happy man—for what is ten years' banishment when the neck is safe? All the joy of the said Villon bursts out into one terrific whoop in the Ballade addressed, on learning of the quashing of his sentence, to Estienne Garnier, Clerk of the Guichet to the Châtelet.[17]

> Que vous semble de mon appel,
> Garnier? Feis je sens ou folie?

I have dealt with it more fully in another place. We may glance in passing at the second stanza, which remembers with indignation, mixed with triumph, the Question and the agony of the water.

> Se feusse des hoirs Hue Cappel,
> Qui fut extrait de boucherie,
> On ne m'eust, parmy ce drappel,
> Fait boire en ceste escorcherie!
> Vous entendez bien joncherie?
> Mais quant ceste paine arbitraire
> On me juga par tricherie,
> Estoit il lors temps de moy taire?

The dancing in the straw, the mad waving of arms and legs, the cracked voice bellowing joyously to the roof, the frantic hugging of the gaoler, the frenzy of relief, are patent in every line of this loud song. What was banishment when he had just by a nail's breadth escaped the doleful jig of Montfaucon? As for the sentence of banishment, it will appear on examination not so harsh as it

[17] The Clerk of the Guichet at the Châtelet kept the register of prisoners, their incoming and outgoing, their descriptions and identity. He could be punished for extracting money from prisoners under any pretext whatsoever.

sounds. In the *Grant Cou&tumier de France* [18] there appears a defini-
tion of the meaning of the phrase "banishment from the Town,
Provo&ty, and Viscounty of Paris," and the area to which it applies.
I will summarise.

The Town of Paris includes the *banlieue,* all that area within a
circular line drawn round Paris from the centre (on the Parvis of
Notre-Dame), a league in diameter.

The *Prévôté* of Paris is all that area controlled by the Provo&t
in common law from the Châtelet.

The *Vicomté* of Paris includes certain outlying &trong-points for
which the Provo&t is *bailli* under the King, as the ca&tles of
Montlhéry, Gonnesse, Corbueil, and Poissy, and the di&trict from
Poissy on the north-we&t to La Ferté-Alais on the south-ea&t.

The sentence of banishment carried with it confiscation of all
property and all rights at common law: a rider which left our Villon
cold enough, since he had never had the one and could well do
without the other for a time, as he had done before. The ceremony
of publishing the sentence had a certain spacious air, as had so
many vanished things of this age. The Clerk of the Prévôté despatched to one of his official criers a copy of the sentence, and the
crier, proceeding therewith to every cross-roads within the liberties
of Paris, cried in a loud voice that François de Montcorbier, *dit*
Villon, was banished for ten years from the Town, Provo&ty, and
Viscounty: at the same time warning all lieges that they mu&t not
receive, comfort, nor aid in any way the said Montcorbier, *dit*
Villon, on pain of forfeiting body and goods to the King our Lord:
and that on the contrary, whoever should perceive the said Montcorbier, *dit* Villon, in any place within the proscribed area—excluding a holy place—was at once bound to take him *"a assemblee de
gens & cry a haro! a son de cloches, & par toutes manieres que l'en
pourra."* This done, the said Montcorbier, *dit* Villon, was to be
haled before Justice to receive his punishment.[19]

It is plain that a sentence of banishment took effect within a
few hours of its promulgation, for Villon had one more prayer to
make to Parliament, and made it as a poet should, in a Ballade. This

[18] Fr. 10816, fol. 183 v 184; fr. n. acq. 3555, fol. 78. Q. Thuasne.
[19] *Grant Cou&tumier,* fr. 23637, fol. 110.

is the very clamorous Ballade in which he calls on all his five senses, eyes, ears, and mouth,

Le nez, et vous, le sensitif aussy,

to cry aloud his gratitude to the Sovereign Court, Mother of the Good, Sister of the Blessed Angels; to his heart to pierce itself, as with a spit, and dissolve in tears of praise; and to his teeth, his lungs and liver, and his vile body,

Et vous, mes dens, chascune si s'esloche;
Saillez avant, rendez toutes mercy,
Plus haultement qu'orgue, trompe, ne cloche,
Et de maschier n'ayez ores soulcy,
Considerez que je feusse transy;
Foye, polmon et rate, qui respire,
Et vous, mon corps, qui vil estes et pire,
Qu'ours ne pourceau qui fait son nyt es fanges,
Louez la Court, avant qu'il vous empire,
Mere des bons et seur des benois anges!

[And you, my teeth, if each one of you can clatter, leap forward, and render thanks more loudly than organ, or trump, or bell, and take no thought of chewing food now; for consider that I was paralysed with fear. And you, my liver, my lungs, my spleen, since you are still alive, and you, my body, who art so vile, fouler than any bear or swine who rolls himself in filth, give praises to the Court, lest worse arrive—to the Mother of the good, and sister of the blessed angels!]

The reason for all this noise and rodomontade appears in the Envoi.

Prince, trois jours ne vueillez m'escondire,
Pour moy pourveoir et aux miens adieu dire;
Sans eulx argent n'ay, icy n'aux changes.
Court triumphant, fiat, sans me desdire,
·Mere des bons et seur des benois anges!

[Prince, deny me not three days' grace, to provide for my journey and bid my folk adieu. Without them I have no money, here or at the changers'. Triumphant Court, give this your *fiat*, and reject me not, Mother of the good, and sister of the blessed angels.]

212

Thus he begs humbly of Parliament three days' grace to prepare for his long journey, to bid his folk farewell, and to supply himself with money from that fount of benevolence which had never failed him, the thin purse of Guillaume de Villon. The three days' grace was granted. He sought out his mother in her poor room and said good-bye to her, and left her, with what tears and blessings of hers it is easy to imagine. She probably never saw her son again on this earth.

The laſt hour with Maſter Guillaume de Villon may be well imagined also: the overhanging cloud of sorrow; the forced cheerfulness of the old man; the visage of the poet, darker and more haggard than ever; the old prieſt and his servant striving to keep their grief in check by fussing over the boy's bundle, his change of hose, the half-paſty, the bottle of Beaune saved for him, 'the laſt of the good year; and at length the final embrace, the purse thruſt into his hand, the laſt benediction muttered over his head by an old man blinded with tears; the ſtooping figure in its black gown ſtanding in the open doorway of the Porte Rouge, blessing and comforting the wanderer for the laſt time with the Cross; and the slouching figure of the poet going heavily down the cloiſter, paſt the flagſtone where Chermoye had fallen, paſt the house of Maſter Pierre de Vaucel (ah! Katherine!), paſt the ſtone bench under the clock, where he had sat that night of Corpus Chriſti and risen to kill his man, out to the right into the Rue St. Jacques and up the long hill, paſt Sorbonne, paſt the old house of Jehan de Meung, paſt the Dominicans to the Porte St. Jacques, thick and frowning under the grey January sky, looking out to the Orleans road.

We, too, shall never see him again.

9

Et je m'en vais
Au vent mauvais
  Qui m'emporte
Deçà, delà,
Pareil à la
  Feuille morte.
    —PAUL VERLAINE.

HE disappears into the void, and there is no more news of him; only two very faint far-off echoes, nearly a hundred years after, in Rabelais, who loved him. Both are almoſt without doubt pure fantasy.

The firſt of them has been shown to be an echo itself of a ſtory attributed to a half-mythical personage, Primate d'Orléans, a predecessor of Villon as the laureate of vagabond clerks and *goliards*.[1] It is a patriotic but not a polite ſtory. Rabelais places the scene of Villon's retirement, after being banished, in England, at the court of Edward v.

Maiſtre François Villon banny de France s'eſtoit vers luy retiré: il l'avoit en si grande privauté receu, que rien ne luy celoit des menuës negoces de sa maison.

[Maſter Francis Villon being banish'd France, fled to him [Edward v.], and got so far into his Favour as to be privy to all his Household Affairs.— *Pantagruel,* Bk. iv, lxvii.[2]]

One day the King of England, having made Maſter Villon thus free of his household, showed him the Royal Arms of France hung in a retired part of the palace, at the same time calling Maſter Villon mockingly to witness in what reverence he, the King of England, held the Arms of France, in that he had them hung there. Upon which Villon, firing, explained to the King of England the real reason why his Majeſty had had the Arms of France hung in that place, namely, to make a practical use of the terror they inspired in his Majeſty, as in all the English.

[1] Also to Hugues le Noir, at the court of King John.
[2] Le Motteux, trans., 1694.

Sacre-Dieu, respondit Villon, tant vous estes saige, prudent, entendu, &
curieux de vostre santé, & tant bien estes servy de vostre docte medecin
Thomas Linacre!

["Od's Life," answer'd Villon, "how wise, Prudent, and careful of your
Health your Highness is, and how carefully your learned Doctor Thomas
Linacre looks after you!"]

The repartee (there is more of it than that) is in character with
the patriotic temper of the singer of *la bonne Lorraine* and the
composer of the bellowing Ballade against the Enemies of France,
and Rabelais, who bore us no love,[3] could not have fathered his gibe
better. There is no evidence of Villon's ever having been in England.
This joke may certainly be set down as having been borrowed by
Rabelais from an earlier source, probably the thirteenth-century
farceur I have mentioned. It is full also of Rabelais' characteristic
treatment of history; for Villon was not banished France, but only
part of France; Edward v. died in the year of his accession, 1483,
being thirteen years old; and Linacre was physician to Henry vII.
and Henry vIII., as Rabelais, a doctor himself, should have known.
It is clear that he needed only a lay-figure to drape a joke on, and
used Villon as the most decorative.

The second anecdote, also from the Fourth Book of *Pantagruel,*
has more likelihood of being true, in foundation if not in development. The scene is Poitou, where, as we know, Villon had wandered during his exile of 1456-1460. I proceed with the story entire
in Peter le Motteux' translation.

Master Francis Villon, in his old Age, retir'd to St. Maixent in Poitou,
under the Patronage of a good honest Abbot of that place.[4] There to make
sport for the Mob he undertook to get the *Passion* acted after the Way and
in the Dialect of the Country. The Parts being distributed, the Play having
been rehears'd, and the Stage prepar'd, he told the Mayor and Aldermen,
that the Mystery might be ready after *Niort* Fair, and that there only wanted

[3] Compare, for example, the clownish figure of Thaumaste, *grand Clerc d'Angleterre,*
who in Bk. II. xviii-xix is vanquished with such contumely by Panurge. In my Lyons
edition of 1588 a contemporary hand has written against the name of Thaumaste: *Thomas
Morus.* Blessed Thomas More, who loved a jest, may have laughed over this caricature.
Pantagruel came out in 1532. He went to the scaffold in 1535. Rabelais owed something
to the *Utopia.*

[4] The Abbot of St. Maixent, 1461-1475, was Jacques Chevalier. Nothing is known of
any connection between him and Villon.

Properties and Necessaries, but chiefly Clothes fit for the Parts; so the Mayor and his Brethren took care to get them.

Villon, to dress an old Father Grey-Beard, who was to represent God the Father, begg'd for Fryar Stephen Tickletoby, sacriſtan to the Franciscan Fryars of the Place, to lend him a Cope and a Stole. Tickletoby refus'd him, alledging that by their Provincial Statutes, it was rigorously forbidden to give or lend any thing to Players.[5] Villon reply'd, That the Statute reached no farther than Farces, Drolls, Anticks, loose and dissolute Games, and that he ask'd no more than what he had seen allow'd at Brussels and other Places. Tickletoby, notwithſtanding, peremptorily bid him provide himself elsewhere if he would, and not to hope for any thing out of his Monaſtical Wardrobe.

The Parisian, the hero of so many town-exploits and the official poet of the Coquillards, was not likely, even in his repentant old age, to ſtand such treatment from a bumpkin lay-brother. The reference to Brussels is an embellishment.

Villon gave an account of this to the Players, as of a moſt abominable Action; adding, that God would shortly revenge himself, and make an Example of Tickletoby.

The Saturday following he had notice given them, that Tickletoby upon the Filly of the Convent was gone a-mumping to St. Ligarius, and would be back about two in the Afternoon. Knowing this, he made a Cavalcade of his Devils of the *Passion* through the Town. They were all rigg'd with Wolves, Calves, and Rams Skins, lac'd and trimm'd with Sheeps Heads, Bulls Feathers, and large Kitchen Tenter-Hooks, girt with broad Leathern Girdles, whereat hang'd dangling huge Cow-Bells and Horse-Bells, which made a horrid Din. Some held in their Claws black Sticks full of Squibs and Crackers; others had long lighted pieces of Wood, upon which at the corner of every Street they flung whole Handfuls of Rosin-dust, that made a terrible Fire and Smoak: having thus led them about, to the great Diversion of the Mob, and the dreadful fear of little Children, he finally carry'd them to an Entertainment at a Summer-House without the Gate that leads to St. Ligarius.

As they came near the Place, he spy'd Tickletoby afar off, coming home from Mumping, and told them in Macaronick Verse,

> Hic eſt Mumpator natus de gente Cucowli,
> Qui solet antiquo scrappas portare bisacco.[6]

[5] The lay-brother Tickletoby—in the original, Frère Eſtienne Tappecoue—was ſtrictly within his rights, religious and civil.

[6] In the original:
> Hic de patria, natus de gente beliſtra,
> Qui solet antiquo bribas portare bissaco.

Why le Motteux improved on Rabelais I cannot tell.

A Plague on his Fryarship (said the Devils then) the lowsie Beggar would not lend a poor Cope to the Fatherly Father, let us fright him. Well said, cry'd Villon; but let us hide our selves till he comes by, and then charge home briskly with your Squibs and burning Sticks. Tickletoby being come to the Place, they all rush'd on a sudden into the Road to meet him, and in a frightful Manner threw Fire from all sides upon him and his Filly Foal, ringing and tingling their Bells, and howling like so many real Devils, hho, hhho, hhho, hhho, brrou, rrou, rrourrs, rrrourrs, hoo, hou, hou, hho, hho, hhoi, Fryar Stephen, don't we play the Devils rarely? The Filly was soon scar'd out of her seven Senses, and began to ſtart, to funk it, to trot it, to bound it, to gallop it, to kick it, to spurn it, to calcitrate it, to winse it, to frisk it, to leap it, to curvet it, with double Jirks, and bum-motions; in so much that she threw down Tickletoby, tho' he held faſt by the Tree of the Pack-Saddle with might and main: now his Traps and Stirrups were of Cord, and on the right side, his Sandal was so entangled and twiſted, that he could not for the Hearts Blood of him get out his Foot. Thus he was dragg'd about by the Filly through the Road, scratching his bare Breech all the way, she still multiplying her Kicks againſt him and ſtraying for fear, over Hedge and Ditch; in so much that she trepann'd his thick Skull so, that his Cockle Brains were dash'd out near the *Osanna,* or High Cross. Then his Arms fell to pieces, one this way and t'other that way, and even so were his Legs serv'd at the same time: then she made a bloody Havock with his Puddings, and being got to the Convent, brought back only his right Foot and twiſted Sandal, leaving them to guess what was become of the Reſt.

Villon seeing that things had succeeded as he intended, said to his Devils, you will act rarely, Gentlemen Devils, you will act rarely; I dare engage you'll top your Parts. I defie the Devils of Saumur, Douay, Montmorillon, Langez, St. Espain, Angers; nay, *voire par Dieu,* even those of Poiƈtiers, for all their bragging and vapouring, to match you.

It is impossible not to recognise in the development of this ſtory the ferocious gaiety, the enormous guſto of the author of the Battle of the Abbey Close and the Battle of the Chitterlings. Rabelais no doubt heard the legend on a journey into Poitou, or from some wandering Poitevin, over a cup of Chinon wine, on a summer evening by the silver, sleepy Vienne, and so wove out of an ordinary ridiculous mishap this truculent farce ending in slaughter. But here again there are echoes. The *diablerie* of the Repue Franche of Montfaucon, which I have quoted early in this book, will occur as resembling this ſtory; and it has been noted also that in one of the Colloquies of Erasmus, *Exorcismus, sive Speƈtrum,* there is a ſtory

217

of a very similar nature attached to a country house near London in the year 1498, long after Villon's death at the most liberal computation. Rabelais' general way with history, we all know, is the smashing way of Friar John with the invaders of the vineyards, and the reference in his story to a visit of Villon to Brussels at once removes, or seems to remove, any pretence to actuality.

Beyond these two stories, then, both very doubtful, both attached to Villon's name so long after, there is nothing.

It is certain that he could not have lived long. When he wrote his greater work, in 1461, he was already, as we have seen, worn out, bald, and prematurely aged at thirty. There is an indication, indeed, that he may have been in the first stages of consumption; the verse lxii. of the *Grant Testament*:

> *Je congnois approcher ma seuf;*
> *Je crache, blanc comme coton,*
> *Jaccopins gros comme ung esteuf.*

This points directly to lung-disease—a result, probably, of the months spent in the *fosse* at Meun: both the recurring thirst and the "spitting white." The verse continues, pathetically underlining his haggard superannuation:

> *Qu'est ce a dire? que Jehanneton*
> *Plus ne me tient pour valeton,*
> *Mais pour ung viel usé roquart . . .*
> *De viel porte voix et le ton,*
> *Et ne suys qu'ung jeune coquart.*

[I feel my thirst approaching; I spit gobbets of phlegm as big as tennis-balls. . . . What is there to be said? Only that Jehanneton no more takes me for her gallant, but a worn-out old hack. I have the voice and bearing of age, and yet I am still but a cockerel.]

One more fragment of his own evidence completes the diagnosis. It is the last huitain of the *Grant Testament,* immediately before the Ballade crying Pardon to One and All, completing his funeral arrangements.

> *Quant au regart du luminaire,*
> *Guillaume du Ru j'y commetz.*

Pour porter les coings du suaire,
Aux executeurs le remetz.
Trop plus mal me font qu'oncques mais
Barbe, cheveulx, penil, sourcis.
Mal me presse; eſt temps desormais
Que crie a toutes gens mercis.

[In the matter of wax-lights, I leave them to Guillaume du Ru; and as to who shall bear the pall, I entruſt my executors with it. Now more than ever my body gives me pain—groin, hair, beard, and eyebrows. I am harassed with ills: it is time for me to cry pardon of all and sundry.]

He is seen here a sick man; and to the lung trouble shadowed forth in the earlier verse we may now certainly add, unless he is exaggerating, that disability called (by the French) the *mal de Naples,* which has been shown to have exiſted epidemically almoſt as long as the world, though Charles VIII.'s army has been blamed for bringing it from Calabria, towards 1492. To a man thus harassed the road of exile could hardly fail to lead, and before very long, to the grave.

Did Villon wander into Anjou, where his maternal uncle, the religious of Angers, might have helped him to prepare his latter days? Did he return by painful ſtages to Poitou, to the girls there, or did he trudge in the end back to Paris? "Maybe," thinks Mr. Belloc, "he only ceased to write; took to teaching soberly in the University, and lived in a decent inheritance to see new splendours growing upon Europe." If it were so! But if it were, would not such a miracle, the conversion of such a famous blackguard, have been blazed about? Would not the University Rolls have noted it? Above all (for rolls may be loſt and burned), would there not have been a living tradition in Paris of his return and enrollment among decent men? And again, had Villon come back to live peaceably in Paris, could he have helped writing more verse? Could a poet of his ſtature, knowing the things he had already written, feeling his maſtery and seeing his end approaching before his pen had gleaned his teeming brain, have been able to ſtifle the voice within him? The *Grant Teſtament* had brought him fame, his verses were in every Parisian mouth already. Would he not have been compelled by his genius, ftronger than sickness of body or mind, to make more songs?

There is no answer. The will of Mafter Guillaume de Villon, which undoubtedly contained some entry concerning the beloved rascal, whether a thankful *Nunc Dimittis* or (more likely) a laft commendation to the mercy of God and the prayers of God's Mother, has never been found. And there is one laft consideration. Had Villon returned and slipped back once more into the old life with the old companions, he would have ended, this time, more or less swiftly, either in the Hôtel-Dieu, in the Châtelet, or on Mont-faucon; and there would be, once more, in the absence of documents recording it, some legend, some ballad, some tradition about his laft days in Paris. For the Parisians loved him, and he was their own poet.

But there is no single legend about him. . . . He passes wearily, with his ftaff and bundle, cloaked, his hood pulled well over his eyes, under the arch of the St. Jacques Gate, the massive sweating arch of ftone with its portcullis, flanked by its two ftout round towers, the guard pacing above, the hollow echo repeating the exile's footfteps. He crosses the bridge over the moat, going heavily and slouching, clogged with melancholy, sickness, and weariness of body and spirit. He trudges off along the southern road once more, and the gathering January darkness receives him.

We ftrain our eyes into the dark, but he has vanished utterly, and no sound comes back. He wrote not a single known word of poetry after the *Grant Teftament*. Twenty-six years after his disappearance the firft printed edition of the Works was issued in Paris by Pierre Levet, a Gothic quarto.[7]

Le grant teftament villon/et le petit. Son codicille. Le iargon ⁊ fes balades

FACSIMILE OF THE TITLE OF THE FIRST PRINTED EDITION.

This, it seems clear, Villon never saw. He was dead, then, by 1489 at the lateft. *"Quant à moy,"* says Guillaume Colletet, his brief

[7] Bibl. nat. Rés., Ye. 245.

biographer about 1650, *"je conjecture qu'il abandonna cette vie sur la fin de celluy du roy Louis XI., c'est-à-dire environ l'an 1482."* La Monnoye agrees. Prosper Marchand supposes he died not in exile, but in Paris; on what grounds I know not. It seems most likely of all, since there was the faint legend of him years after in Poitou, that he found his way there in the end and later died; whether among the Franciscans of St. Maixent, shriven and houselled by his protector, the good honest Abbot of that place, whether in a village tavern-brawl, whether alone, in some obscure hovel far from friends, whether in the arms of a wench, whether hanged from a country gibbet, will never be known until the Day.

> I see that makaris amang the lave
> Playis here their padyanis, syne gois to grave;
> Sparit is nocht their facultie:—
> *Timor Mortis conturbat me.*

He was a very great sinner, and a poet to whose fame there will eternally stand the *monumentum aere perennius* which the Roman so superbly ordered. During his hunted life he had twice, possibly three times, lain under sentence of death, had been half a dozen times punished by the Question, twice banished voluntarily, once by the State. He had committed homicide at twenty-four and burglary and sacrilege at twenty-five, and his unrecorded thefts, stabbings, cheats, and brawlings are probably innumerable. He was poor and stung by strong passions, and his miserable life alternated between the tavern, the brothel, and the prison. He was a very bad character indeed, and would never have had a chance against (let us say) Lord Tennyson for the Laureateship of the British Nation, had he been of our race and lived in our time: apart from his being an adherent of the Romish Church, whose tenets are so reflected in his writings. In his nature the fine and the gross were inextricably mingled. He was as weak as water, as variable as a weathercock, mercurial, impulsive, idle, mocking, childlike, egoistic, warmhearted, sensual, careless, driven before every gust of desire; a rake and a spendthrift worshipping beauty; a common criminal firm in faith and affection; a companion of thieves and whores and vagabonds, producing from the dregs of his life an exquisite flower of

221

Cy comence le grant codicille ⁊ te
stamēt maistre francois Villon

Ey lan de mon trentiesme aage
Que toutes mes hontes ieuz beues
Ne du tout fol encor ñe saige
Nonobstant maintes peines eues
Lesquelles iay toutes receues
Soubz la main thibault danssigny
Seuesque il est seignant les rues
Quil soit le mien ie le regny

FACSIMILE OF THE FIRST PAGE OF THE FIRST PRINTED EDITION.

222

pure poetry; a temper as flecked with dark and light as an April day. Above all, melancholy possessed him soon, whether his mood was gaiety, or defiance, or recollection.

His soul is displayed naked in his works, and there is a minor Ballade in which he sums up compactly, in his half-shrugging, half-remorseful way, his nature; and ours.

Je congnois pourpoint au colet,
Je congnois le moyne a la gonne,
Je congnois le maistre au varlet,
Je congnois au voille la nonne,
Je congnois quant pipeur jargonne,
Je congnois folz nourris de cresmes,
Je congnois le vir a la tonne,
Je congnois tout, fors que moy mesmes.

The Envoi:

Prince, je congnois tout en somme,
Je congnois coulourez et blesmes,
Je congnois Mort qui tout consomme,
Je congnois tout, fors que moy mesmes.

[I know the doublet by its collar; I know the monk by his habit; I know the master by his servant; I know the nun by her veil; I know the sharper by the Jargon; I know fools fed on creams; I know wine by its barrel; I know all, except myself.

Prince, I know all things; I know the coloured from the plain; I know Death, which devours all; I know all, except myself.] (*B. des Menus Propos.*)

There were moments in his soiled and guilty life when his spirit revolted from the stews,

troubled the gold gateways of the stars,
Smiting for shelter on their clangèd bars;
Fretted to dulcet jars
And silvern chatter the pale ports o' the moon.

And moments when he saw himself clearly and shivered, and called on God: but this mood passed. He had nearly every human weakness except insincerity.

But whether he died swiftly, by the knife or the rope, and was thrust carelessly into his unknown grave; or whether he died calmly in his bed, fortified for his longest journey with the Viaticum; or whether he lingered miserable and alone and saw Death beckoning hollow-eyed, *terribili squalore,* from a muddy ditch, I should like to think that the last thing that came to him, as his eyes closed for ever on this false world, was not the memory of Katherine's red mouth, nor the laughing of Tabarie in a tavern, nor the twang of a lute, nor the gasp of the angry priest he struck down that June evening, nor the clatter of Archers running along the street, nor a harlot's giggle, nor the drone of his master commenting Aristotle in the Schools, nor the coughing and spectacles of kind Master Guillaume de Villon, nor the blood-freezing rattle of pulleys in the Question-Chamber of the Châtelet, nor the rushing of Seine in spring flood under the bridges, nor the cry of ravens turning and wheeling round the black gibbet of Montfaucon: but, infinitely warm and comforting, the vision of a high Gothic window, its ruby and turquoise fading into the winter dark, and underneath, by a tall pillar, in the last glow of tapers wasting before Our Lady's image, a bent, huddled old woman stretching out worn hands and stammering his name.

> *Repos eternel donne a cil,*
> *Sire, & clarté perpetuelle.*

III

THE WORKS

Allons, madones d'amour qu'il a chantées, hahay! Margot, Rose, Jehanne la
Saulcissière, hahay! Guillemette, Marion la Peautarde, hahay! la petite Macée,
hahay! toute la folle quenaille des ribaudes, des truandes, des grivoises, des
raillardes, des villotières! . . .

Oh! tu es seul et bien seul! Meurs donc, larron; crève donc dans ta fosse,
souteneur de gouges; tu n'en seras pas moins immortel, poète glorieusement
fangeux, ciseleur inimitable du vers, joaillier non pareil de la Ballade!

J. K. HUYSMANS.

[Come, ladies of love whom he has sung, hahay! Margot, Rose, Jehane
the Sausage-Maker, hahay! Guillemette, Marion la Peautarde, hahay! Little
Macée, hahay! All the mad rout of trollops, truands, mopsies, laughing
baggages, and minxes of the town! . . .

But you are alone, deserted! Die, then, thief; die in your ditch, pimp for
street-sluts! You shall be none the less immortal, poet of glory and the gutter,
inimitable sculptor of verse, incomparable craftsman of the Ballade!]

J. K. Huysmans.

❀ ❀ ❀ ❀ ❀ ❀ ❀ ❀ ❀ ❀ ❀ ❀ ❀ ❀

I

THE LITTLE TESTAMENT, 1456

(LES LAIS)

§ 1

Le meilleur poëte parisien qui se trouve.
—CLÉMENT MAROT OF CAHORS.

IN the April morning of the Renaissance, François I., surnamed the Father of Letters, being on the throne of France and the Roman and Venetian and Florentine and Milanese presses pouring scholarship a silver torrent into Europe,[1] the poet Clément Marot undertook to make, at the Royal command, the first critical edition of the poems of François Villon. This, the twenty-first printed edition at that day, appeared in 1533, and is remarkable, I think, for two things: firstly, that a poet of the Renaissance should lavish such admiration on the last poet of a dead world, and secondly, that Marot was (at least for a time) a Calvinist; though the Dear knows he must have been as severe a disappointment, with his sunny Pantagruelism, to the sadist of Geneva as Rabelais was.[2] Nevertheless he escaped the dreadful town and the fires which burned for Servetus.

---

[1] The Aldines of Venice and the Giuntas of Florence particularly.
[2] Contemplate the foaming of Calvin in the treatise *De Scandalis*, in which he rends Rabelais with full tusks as one who, at first following the light (by which Calvin means insulting certain aspects of the Catholic Church), was later blinded, and profaned with sacrilegious laughter the eternal verities (by which Calvin means Calvinism).

Marot's edition, a small octavo, with its Genevan distich, appears in the Catalogue of the Bibliothèque nationale in Paris, where it is preserved, thus:

Les Œuvres de||Françoys Villon||de Paris, reveues et remises en||leur entier par Clement Ma-||rot valet de chambre||du Roy.|| Distique du dict Marot||Peu de Villons en bon savoir||Trop de Villons pour deceuoir||On les vend a Paris en la grant salle du Palais, en la bouticque de||Galiot du Pre.— *Fin des œuvres de Françoys Villon de*||*Paris, reveues et remises en leur entier par*||*Clemêt Marot, valet de chambre du Roys*||*et furent paracheuees de imprimer le der-*||*nier iour de Septembre, Lan mil cinq*||*cens trente et troys.*[3]

His homage flowers in his Preface. The dead poet is the best of all Parisian singers. His genius, apart from the low and obscure buffoonery scattered through the Testaments, is *vrayment belle & heroïque.* Marot has undertaken his difficult task *pour l'amour de son gentil entendement & en recompense de ce que je puys avoir aprins de luy en lisant ses œuvres.* The best poetry of Villon is of such excellence,

tant plain de bonne doctrine, & tellement painct de mille belle couleurs, que le Temps, qui tout efface, jusques icy ne l'a sceu effacer, & moins encor l'effacera, ores & d'icy en avant, que les bonnes escriptures françoyses sont & seront myeulx congneues & receuillies que jamais.

[so full of good doctrine, so glowing with a thousand lovely colours, that Time, which effaces all, has till now been powerless to touch it; and will henceforth be still more powerless, as the fine literature of France is and will be more known and cherished than ever before.]

Had this poet, adds Marot, but had the advantage of getting a little polish in the courts of princes (and thank God he did not, we may cry), he would have carried off the laurels from every poet of his time. It is evident that Marot admired him enough to take pains to present the best edition possible. He confesses himself at the outset astonished that *les imprimeurs de Paris & les enfans de la ville* had not taken better care of Villon's text. He ransacked and collated previous editions, manuscript and printed, all full of repeated errors, obscurities, and lacunæ. He tells how he collected versions from the lips of *bons vieillards,* old men who could repeat large tracts of

[8] Bibl. nat. Rés., Ye. 1297.

Villon's poetry by heart, without having seen a text. Finally he used his own judgment, *partie par deviner avecques jugement naturel,* in restoring dubious passages; not with good results. One sees, considering the mass of editions before him, that Marot's task was not light. The first printed book of Villon's verse bearing a date is Levet's of 1489, seventeen years after the first public press in Paris was set up in the Rue St. Jacques.[4] Of the manuscript editions before 1489 some few were in libraries—in Charles d'Orléans', for example, and in the Bourbon's, and certainly in the King's library, for François I. had a powerful love for Villon's verse—and a large number circulating among the poet's admirers from hand to hand: these last, grimy and dog's-eared with continual thumbing, stained brown with wine, and possibly a trifle of blood, smeared with the droppings of tallow candles, grease, and tavern slops, preciously conserved and recopied, with all their transmitted errors. Marot's evidence shows, too, that Villon's verse was repeated all over the town by many mouths, and remembered lovingly like Euripides' by the folk of Abdera; recited with most applause, I well imagine, by the fireside in those haunts where the poet's lank figure seemed still to lurk in the shadow cast by guttering torches. And this was no posthumous fame. When Villon calls himself already in the Little Testament *le bien renommé Villon* it can have been no fanfaronnade. He had a reputation in the University quarter before 1456, and got many a drink on the strength of it, no doubt, and not a few kisses for nothing also: for women worship a successful poet, as Tennyson knew, and Alfred de Musset, and Martin Tupper, and Browning, and a score beside.

His fame has waned, and waxed, and waned, and waxed again through the centuries. A dozen years after Marot edited him the young bright gods of the Pléiade descended in a burst of glory, Ronsard and du Bellay and Jodelle and their company, bringing high Spring and recovered learning like a lovely storm into French poetry; and Villon slipped into the shadows. A poet who, like Ronsard, would lock himself into his chamber for three days to

[4] The first press in France had been established in Sorbonne by two professors, Jehan Heynlin and Guillaume Fichet, in 1469. Both presses were by Ulrich Gering, Michel Friburger, and Martin Kranz.

read the *Iliad* through,[5] had no point of contact with the *escholier* and his slapdash scholarship. Villon had no Greek, and the whole Pléiade was drunk on Greek. Villon's Latin learning was sketchy, the scraps of an outworn curriculum, often negligently gathered between a debauch and a riot. To the humanists of the Renaissance, Latin, the golden Latin of the Augustans, was a second mother-tongue. Yet their joyous salute to the new scholarship was not so final and sharp as that of the Abbé Coignard ("What is a woman by the side of an Alexandrine papyrus?"), for they were great lovers of beautiful women, as also of stringed music, and finely printed books, and well-engraved sword-hilts, and softly-cut coins, and clear paintings, and wine, and trees, and clouds, and every gracious toy under Heaven. Placed between a Greek manuscript and a laughing girl, I think, they would certainly have turned instinctively to pay homage to beauty incarnate; but with the manuscript firmly tucked under one arm.

The seventeenth century, ruled by Malherbe, at whose order the nervous Muse, like a fifteen-year-old miss at Bath under the frown of Nash, preserved decorum, ignored Villon completely. In the eighteenth a small number of wits and poets favoured, rather freakishly, the medieval barbarian, among them Voltaire, La Fontaine, and the Jesuit Father du Cerceau, who re-edited him in 1723, remarking on the ease of his writing and the richness of his rhymes. The great Boileau, in a patronising couplet which is often quoted,

> Villon sut le premier, dans ces siècles grossiers,
> Débrouiller l'art confus de nos vieux romanciers,

[Villon, in that barbarous age, was the first to unravel the confused handiwork of our old romance-writers.]

expressed the opinion that Villon was the first of the old French authors who was readable: not (as Gaston Paris observes) that Boileau had ever read Villon. He was no fingerer of antique books. M. Paris thinks Boileau took his opinion from Patru, called the

[5] *Je veux lire en trois jours l'Iliade d'Homere,*
Et pour ce, Corydon, ferme bien l'huis sur moy.
—From the *Sonnets.*

Quintilian of his age, who had quite surprisingly in that classic period commended Villon's style and lordship of language.

The nineteenth century brought in the Romantics, with the cravat tied *à l'infidèle, à la mélancolique,* and *à la turque*; and with these came the re-discovery proper. To the fine poet Théophile Gautier, above all, Villon came as a precious gift. The mixed misery and gaiety! The self-searching! The devil-may-care and the debauchery! The virility! Laughter and tears! The buffoon mingled with the tragedian! A true Romantic! The acid Sainte-Beuve threw a little necessary cold water on these raptures, but the curve was steadily rising. Henceforth the fame of Villon is to be set and secure. By the end of the century Scots and Dutchmen have heard of him, and are athrob with enthusiasm: and (what is worse) the Rossetti School in England hear of him a little later as well and adopt him, among the lilies and flames and ladies with long awkward necks, among the refined perversities, the decorative but muzzy mysticism, the hand-woven æsthetics and what not of their academy. By what chance Mr. Beerbohm, in his series of caricatures of the Rossetti period, refrained from celebrating the advent of Villon into this select company I cannot tell. I can only think that Piety, indignant, rose, and Licence, wild-eyed, retired.

At this moment Villon (in the modern literary phrase) is briskly quoted. In France fresh editions of the Testaments and the Ballades appear regularly, critical and uncritical, decorated and undecorated. In England, I believe, though there is not much movement, the stock is firm. A fresh translation of the Testaments was quite recently issued for the Casanova Society. *C'est vertueusement opéré,* as the great Rabelais says in his Prologue to the Fourth Book; but speaking of a sovran remedy against thirst.

2

IT was a quaint device of the Schoolmen to pretend that clear thinking is an exact science, with laws and definitions. Among their axioms was this, that created things are of two kinds, those sub-sisting of themselves and those subsisting in a subject.[1] The first kind they called Substance: as an angel, a man, a horse. The second kind they called Accident: as colour, movement, emotion. The Substance could exist without Accident, but the Accident had need of the Substance and could not exist without it: except (as the School-men said in their queer manner) in one case only, and that (if I may be forgiven for saying so) the Mystery of the Altar. If I have stumbled for the moment into elementary Scholastic Logic it is purely for the purpose of beginning the task of discussing the poetry of François Villon in a clear and ordered manner. I propose divid-ing it, in the manner of the Schools, into two distinct parts—the form of his verse (corresponding roughly to the Substance) and the colour, emotion, and spirit of the words which compose it (corre-sponding to the Accident). The form we shall discuss soberly and with precision; but what will happen when we come to the other (and especially the *Grant Testament*) I cannot say, for there is a deal of beauty in it.

> *Tale tuum carmen nobis, divine poëta,*
> *Quale sopor fessis in gramine, quale per æstum*
> *Dulcis aquæ saliente sitim restinguere rivo.*

> [O heavenly Poet! such thy Verse appears,
> So sweet, so charming to my ravish'd Ears,
> As to the weary Swain, with Cares opprest,
> Beneath the sylvan Shade, refreshing Rest;
> As to the fev'rish Traveller, when first
> He finds a Crystal Stream to quench his Thirst.]
> (*Dryden,* Vergil, Bucolic V.)

The known works of François Villon are the *Petit Testament* (1456), consisting of forty verses, or *huitains,* each verse an octave, each line octosyllabic: and the *Grant Testament* (1461), consisting of one hundred and seventy-two verses of precisely the same kind, broken at intervals by sixteen Ballades, three Rondels, the Lament

[1] Mrs. Bossom disagrees.

of the Belle Heaulmière (which is a triple Ballade), and one other separate piece, the *Belle Leçon,* of the same texture as the mass of the Testaments. In addition to this, the main body of the Works, there is what a number of Villon's editors call the Codicil, which contains the glorious Ballade of the Hanged, the Debate (in the form of a Ballade) between the Heart and Body of Villon, the wry Quatrain written after his condemnation, and three other Ballades of minor importance. Beyond this, again, there is a loose handful of mediocre Ballades, a dithyramb in the Testament metre celebrating the infant Princess Marie de Bourgogne, and lastly the Jargon, in thieves'-Latin, on which I touch later in this book.

This is all that can be definitely said to be from Villon's hand.

A number of other Ballades and Rondels, the comic Monologue of the Free Archer of Baignollet, and the long comic dialogue between the Messieurs de Mallepaye and de Baillevent, may be grouped together under the label "School of——": for though attributed to Villon they are rejected by every conscientious editor. With these may certainly go the *Repues Franches,* which are believed to be the work of Friar Baulde de la Mare, one of Villon's joyous companions and a bad bargain of the Carmelite Order.

I will begin by dissecting briefly and describing the form which is of chief importance in Villon's poetry, and in which he achieved his loveliest flight.

THE BALLADE

From all the moulds into which poets have poured their thoughts the Ballade stands apart: for it is fixed, yet flexible; stiff in form, yet capable of reflecting a thousand moods; antique, yet vigorous and ever young. I would willingly compare it also to such a piece of embroidery as one sees painted in the *Très Riches Heures du Duc de Berry* at Chantilly: a stiff flowered fabric, on which are worked the massiest gold, rich flowers, glowing jewels, a superb range (within its limits) of colour and fantasy.

In its correct and ritual form the Ballade is constructed of three stanzas, each of eight octosyllabic lines, finished by an *Envoi* of four.[2] (I do not speak of the Chant-Royal, which is but a swollen

---

[2] You may have two extra feet in the line and two extra lines in each stanza. Villon's Double Ballade (page 316) has six stanzas and no Envoi.

Ballade and a cumbrous, pompous beaſt.) The rhymes of the Ballade—I speak of the ſtandard form—run irrevocable *a b a b b c b c*
in each ſtanza, and in the Envoi *b c b c*. I display the pattern in a
ſtanza from Dunbar's Ballade in Honour of the City of London,
which carries the two extra feet allowed by the rubric:

> London, thou art of townes *A per se*:
>   Soveraign of cities, seemlieſt in sight,
> Of high renoun, riches and royaltie,
>   Of lordis, barons, and many a goodly knyght;
>   Of most deleƈtable luſty ladies bright;
> Of famous prelatis, in habitis clericall;
>   Of merchauntis full of subſtaunce and of myght:
> London, thou art the Flour of Cities all.[3]

Again, in a slightly different mood, oƈtosyllabic and modern:

> Saint Michael of the Flaming Sword,
> Provoſt of Paradise, dear Knight,
> High Seneschal of Heaven, Lord
> Of legions massing for the Fight—
> Monseigneur! on its way laſt night,
> Aspersing terror like a dew,
> There passed in ſtrong decisive flight
> The soul of Lady Barbecue.

The Envoi perhaps requires a note to itself. It begins moſt
usually with the vocative "Prince!": an echo of the old days when
poets rhyming in competition at academic tourneys addressed their
Ballades to the Prince or seigneur who presided. But it is often
addressed, according to the mood of its Ballade, to a miſtress, or
a poet, or to Venus, or to Fortune, or to Almighty God—as in the
Ballade of Charles d'Orléans, very tender and plaining, on the death
of his young wife:

> *Dieu, sur tout souverain Seigneur,*
> *Ordonnez par grace et doulceur*
> *De l'ame d'elle, tellement*
> *Qu'elle ne soit pas longuement*
> *En paine, soussi, et doleur.*

---

[3] I would have quoted Chaucer's lovely "Hyd, Absolon, thy giltë tresses clere," but
it has, alas, only seven lines to the ſtanza. The older English poets took liberties, almoſt
without exception.

[O God, high Sovereign over all, by Thy grace and kindness so order her soul that she may not long remain in pain, care, and sorrow.]

And again:

> Prince, I can hear the trumpet of Germinal,
> The tumbrils toiling up the terrible way;
> Even to-day your royal head may fall—
> I think I will not hang myself to-day.[4]

It will be readily perceived that some of the beauty of the Ballade form lies directly in its apparent difficulty, its unyielding frame, the strict economy of its three rhymes. In medieval French and English, and particularly among the predecessors of Villon (after whom it went out of fashion for four hundred years, to be revived as bric-à-brac first by Banville and Richepin and others in France, by Andrew Lang and Austin Dobson and others in England), it has every possible change rung on it: it is used for religion, for love, for war, for politics, for despair; it is devout, courteous, sardonic, languishing, minatory, moral, triumphant, what you will. Chiefly among Villon's predecessors it is used for love-complaints and rhapsodies, of which a charming example is that fragrant Herrick-like little thing of Eustace Deschamps about a lover coming upon his mistress plucking roses in a May garden, which begins:

> Le droit jour d'une Penthecouste
> En ce gracieux moys de May
> Celle ou j'ay m'esperance toute
> En un jolis vergier trouvay
> Cueillant roses, puis luy priay:
> Baisiez moy. Se dit: Voulentiers.
> Aise fu; adonc la baisay
> Par amours, entre les rosiers.

[Right on a day of Pentecost, in the sweet month of May, I found her in all whom my hopes are centred in a pretty orchard, plucking roses. Then, "Kiss me," I prayed her. And she answered "Right willingly," with joy. Thereupon I kissed her for love, among the rose-trees.]

[4] G. K. Chesterton, Ballade of Suicide.

235

So much for love. In the matter of war, there is Deschamps'
watery Ballade or Lament for the death of the great Bertrand du
Guesclin:

> O Bretaingne, ploure ton esperance,
> Normandie, fay son entierement,
> Guyenne aussy, et Auvergne or t'avence,
> Et Languedoc, quier luy son mouvement;
> Picardye, Champaigne, et Occident
>   Doivent pour plourer acquerre
> Tragediens, Arethusa requerre
> Qui en eaue fut par plour convertie,
> Afin qu'a touz de sa mort les cuers serre:
> Plourez, plourez flour de chevalerie.

[O Brittany, weep thy hope. Normandy, make his obsequies,
and Guienne also, and you, Auvergne, be not backward; and you,
Languedoc, follow his passing. Let Picardy, Champagne, and the
West find them tragedians to lament; Arethusa herself, dissolved
into water by weeping, requires it, in order that every heart might
be wrung by his death. Weep, O weep, flower of chivalry.]

And, for courtesy, Deschamps' salute to Geoffrey Chaucer:

> O Socrates plains de philosophie,
> Seneque en meurs et Anglux en pratique,
> Ovides grans en ta poeterie,
> Bries en parler, saiges en rethorique,
> Aigles treshautz, qui par ta theorique
> Enlumines le regne d'Eneas,
> L'Isle aux Geans, ceuls de Bruth, et qui'as
> Semé les fleurs et planté le rosier,
> Aux ignorans de la langue pandras,
> Grant translateur, noble Geffroy Chaucier!

[O very Socrates, filled with philosophy! O Seneca in morals,
Englishman in deeds! O great as Ovid in thy poetry, sober in
speech, sage in rhetoric! High-soaring Eagle, who by thy Muse
illuminest the reign of Aeneas, the Isle of Giants and the race of
Brutus, who hast sowed such flowers and planted such roses! O
succour of those ignorant of the [French] tongue, great translator,
noble Geoffrey Chaucer!]

I will not quote anything of Guillaume de Machault or Eus-
tache Morel or Alain Chartier, since their Ballades are in the great

part amorous and didactic and often, if classic in form, excessively tedious; Alain Chartier's especially, although he is a master of this medium, and dominated the first half of the fifteenth century. Froissart's are not much better, and he is often irregular, falling into the heresy of the nine-line stanza with no Envoi. I cannot omit mention of Christine de Pisan, that daughter of Charles v.'s astrologer, in whose white hands the Ballade assumes a delicacy apart. Greater than these, and a living master in Villon's time, is Charles d'Orléans, whom some have compared with Petrarch and some with Heine. The poetry of Charles d'Orléans exhales a high melancholy, an aristocratic lettered grace, a sure poise, a fine irony, but no vigour: exile and weariness are often in it, but no profundity of experience or bitterness. But he could produce sudden lovely things like the First Rondeau of Spring, full of the plash of water, the green, the song of birds.

> Le temps a laissié son manteau
> De vent, de froidure et de pluye,
> Et s'est vestu de brouderie,
> De soleil luysant, cler et beau;
>   Il n'y a beste ne oyseau
> Qu'en son jargon ne chant ou crie:
> Le temps a laissié son manteau
> De vent, de froidure et de pluye.
>   Riviere, fontaine et ruisseau
> Portent, en livrée jolie,
> Gouttes d'argent et d'orfaverie,
> Chascun s'abille de nouveau.
>   Le temps a laissié son manteau.

[The Year has flung off his mantle of wind, of cold, and rain, and has vested himself in broidery, in sparkling sunshine, clear and splendid; there is no bird nor animal which does not sing or cry aloud in his jargon. The Year has flung off his mantle of wind, and cold, and rain. Each river, fountain, and stream wears its lovely livery of jewelled and silver drops; the whole world is clothed anew. The Year has flung off his mantle.]

Of one aspect of him (though a Valois and a soldier) it might be said, as it says of another in the sonnet:

> Your life is like a little flute complaining
> A long way off, beyond the willow trees;
> A long way off, and nothing left remaining
> But memory of a music on the breeze.[5]

He is a poet nevertheless, and must be read: some of his songs are perfect pieces of fresh beauty. When Villon stayed at the Castle of Blois that brief space during his wanderings he no doubt devoured in the well-warmed, well-furnished, candle-lit library there more than one manuscript containing poems of the Duke's and the best earlier poets. The manuscript now in the Bibliothèque nationale (Fr. 1104) his eyes may well have contemplated: it is an anthology by the Duke and his circle of lesser poets, containing as well the two Ballades Villon himself composed at Blois and Orleans. But what he learned at Blois and what he gathered from the poetry of his predecessors the Parisian vagabond infused with vigour and made his own, excelling those from whom he had (or had not) learned his trade.

THE RONDEAU

This is the other, and lesser, fixed form in medieval French poetry. It has two principal variants, the Virelay and the Bergeronnette.

The Rondeau (like the Ballade) had been nearly done to death by Villon's time. It would be idle to pretend that Villon's Rondeaux, with one exception, are any better or any worse than a hundred others turned out by poets and poetasters since the decay of the Trouvères. Charles d'Orléans, even, made only half a dozen fine Rondeaux: chiefly the two on the advent of Spring, the gush of pure ecstasy which begins *Dieu, qu'il la fait bon regarder!,* and that final ironic thing, *Saluez moy toute la compaignie,* which is so full of resignation and farewell. Villon's one great Rondeau is his Epitaph; also a leave-taking.

The form is elastic, but it has a constant: the recurrence of the opening line, as in a fugue. The Rondeau may be seven lines long, like one of Christine de Pisan's, or thirteen, like some of Charles

---

[5] H. Belloc, *Sonnets and Verse.*

d'Orléans'. At its average it is nothing more than a vehicle for mannered conceits. I quote the second-best of Villon, on a dead mistress,
made for Master Ythier Marchant; it is saved from mediocrity by
one vivid line.

LAY

> Mort, j'appelle de ta rigueur,
> Qui m'as ma maistresse ravie,
> Et n' es pas encore assouvie
> Se tu ne me tiens en langueur:
> Onc puis n'eus force ne vigueur;
> Mais que te nuysoit elle en vie,
> > Mort?
>
> Deux estions et n'avions qu'ung cuer;
> S'il est mort, force est que devie,
> Voire, ou que je vive sans vie
> Comme les images, par cuer,
> > Mort!

Rossetti has put this into English song:

> Death, of thee do I make my moan,
> > Who hadst my lady away from me,
> > Nor wilt assuage thine enmity
> Till with her life thou hast mine own;
> For since that hour my strength has flown.
> > Lo! what wrong was her life to thee,
> > > Death?
>
> Two we were, and the heart was one;
> > Which now being dead, dead I must be,
> > Or seem alive as lifelessly
> As in the choir the painted stone,
> > > Death!

The line that is alive is the eighth, the rest is a poetic exercise.
It is not, moreover, a true Rondeau according to the statutes. Marot
calls it *Lay, ou plustost Rondeau*. But as it is the best Villon has
done in this way, short of the Epitaph, which is high poetry and
appears elsewhere in this book, we will let it stand, and so jog
on.

3

L'an quatre cens cinquante six,
Je, Françoys Villon, escollier . . .

STUDYING for the five hundredth time the *Petit Testament* (which
Villon calls the *Lais,* or Bequests) I muse once more on what five
years of vagabondage, with a taste of prison and the Question, can
do for a man. In 1456 he is devising hobbledehoy jokes with tavern
signs and stuffing a mock will full of bequests which when hot and
fresh were comprehensible only to a contemporary of Paris. In 1461
he is writing the Ballade of Dead Ladies, and becomes straightway
one of the master poets of Christendom.

The *Petit Testament,* except for its pictures of Parisian life, is
green fruit. Of its forty verses about half a dozen, perhaps, are poetry
as Villon can write it. The personal quips which (as in the *Grant
Testament*) aroused the loud laughter of Villon's friends of the
University and the town, were unintelligible much less than a
hundred years after him. "Sufficiently to understand the point of
them," explains Marot, "it is necessary to have been a Parisian of his
own time, and to have known all the places, men, and things of
which he speaks: as the memory of them passes away, so in less and
less degree will the significance of his allusions be comprehended."
Now Marot, writing in 1533, was as near to Villon as we are to
Matthew Arnold and Browning. For us the true savour of these
gibes is completely lost; and yet they are bright with a splendid
vigour.

The *Petit Testament* begins in a manner characteristic of Villon's careless mood, rare as it is. The first verse has no master-verb
and ends in the air.

L'an quatre cens cinquante six,
Je, Françoys Villon, escollier,
Considerant, de sens rassis,
Le frain aux dens, franc au collier,
Qu'on doit ses oeuvres conseillier,
Comme Vegece le raconte,
Sage Rommain, grant conseillier,
Ou autrement on se mesconte . . .

[In the year 1456, I, François Villon, clerk, with my senses clear, bit between the teeth, collar-free, considering that a man muſt look to his own works (as Vegetius, the wise Roman and venerable counsellor, has declared), or otherwise he reckons amiss. . . .]

But in the second verse he is a craftsman again. This little glowing miniature, as in a Book of Hours, of Old Paris in the grip of winter I count, in its economy of words, a thing of maſtery.

En ce temps que j'ay dit devant,
Sur le Noel, morte saison,
Que les loups se vivent de vent
Et qu'on se tient en sa maison,
Pour le frimas, pres du tison,
Me vint ung vouloir de brisier
La tres amoureuse prison
Qui souloit mon cuer debrisier.

[At this time, as I have said, near Chriſtmas, in the dead of the year, when the wolves feed on wind and men ſtay indoors, hugging the hearth, on account of the cold, there came to me a desire to break my prison, where Love has held my heart in such duress.]

Here is a clear piƈture: the gabled ſtreets, dumb, muffled in snow, under an iron sky; the wolves baying and sharpening their teeth outside the walls, driven ravenous from the woods of Montmartre and Rouvray; behind barred doors, the blazing log fire and the family cluſtered around, sipping hot wine, roaſting cheſtnuts, and telling ſtories of the Loup-Garou and the Moine Bourru.[1] Rabelais, I think, remembered this verse when he saw in a vision the good Grandgousier toaſting his legs before *"un beau clair & grand feu, & attendans griller des chaſtaignes escrit au foyer avec un baſton bruslé d'un bout, dont on escarbote le feu, faisant à sa femme & famille de beaux contes du temps jadis."* *

*[A good, clear, great Fire, and, waiting upon the broyling of some Cheſtnuts, is very serious in drawing Scratches on the Hearth, with a Stick burnt at the one end, wherewith they did ſtirre up the Fire, telling to his Wife and reſt of the Family pleasant old Stories and Tales of Former Times.]   (*Urquhart's trans.*)

[1] The Moine Bourru, an incarnation of the Devil, the ſtock bogey and night-demon of Old Paris. Late at night, and especially during Advent, he glided through the ſtreets, shrouded in a gown of coarse ſtuff, attempting to ſtrangle all who crossed his path. He was to Paris what the Loup-Garou is to Brittany.

But something more than the cold is tormenting the poet. The cruel mistress, *felonne et dure,* has given him his *congé.*

> *Et se j'ay prins en ma faveur*
> *Ces doulx regars et beaux semblans*
> *De tres decevante saveur*
> *Me trespersans jusques aux flans,*
> *Bien ilz ont vers moy les piez blans*
> *Et me faillent au grant besoing.*
> *Planter me fault autres complans*
> *Et frapper en ung autre coing.*

[If I succumbed to her dear looks and lovely deceits, of such sweet treachery that they pierce my very heart, they have now left me well in the lurch, forlorn in my greatest need. I am fain to carry my plaint elsewhere and to strike out afresh.]

He broods over it, and it inspires him (as so often happens—O Queen! *Mater sæva Cupidinum!*) to a little deathly mediocre rhyming. He cries haro to the heavens on the false one, wearying with his clamour Death and the little gods, for a score of lines or more: and then in a breath, abruptly, announces his departure from Paris.

> *Adieu! Je m'en vois a Angiers:*
> *Puis qu'el ne me veult impartir*
> *Sa grace, il me convient partir.*

[Good-bye. I am off to Angers. Since she will not yield me her grace it is better to get away.]

It is at this moment, on the eve of leaving the town (which, as we know, he omits to do for a little time, the affair of the College of Navarre intervening), that the dying lover is visited with the rich thought of a burlesque will and testament; some vague memories floating in his mind, possibly, of Adam de la Halle or Jean Regnier of Auxerre, of whose testaments he may have heard, and having almost certainly a distinct remembrance of those facetious lines of Eustace Deschamps which he must have known by heart, and which obviously helped to inspire the form of the Testaments:

> *Item, je laisse a l'ordre grise*
> *Ma viez braie & ma viez chemise,*
> *Et s'ay laissé pareillement*
> *Au Roy, le Louvre & le Palays*
> *Et la Tour de Bois: c'est beau lays.*

242

[*Item,* I leave to the Greyfriars my old drawers and my old shirt, and similarly to the King I leave the Louvre, the Palais, and the Tour de Bois: this is a good bequest.]

The ninth verse of the *Petit Testament* is the preface to this will: a deliberate use of the customary invocation of the Sacred Trinity and the Mother of God; yet no ignoble use, for it is mixed with faith and true affection. "Firstly, in the name of the Father, and of the Son, and of the Holy Ghost, and of the glorious Mother by whose mediation none is lost, I leave, in God's name, my fame to Master Guillaume Villon. . . ."

> Premierement, ou nom du Pere,
> Du Filz et du Saint Esperit,
> Et de sa glorieuse Mere
> Par qui grace riens ne perit,
> Je laisse, de par Dieu, mon bruit
> A maistre Guillaume Villon,
> Qui en l'onneur de son nom bruit,
> Mes tentes et mon pavillon.

There follows one despairing verse bequeathing his poor stabbed heart to the cruel one, and after that he forgets her, plunging with growing absorption and joy into the comic possibilities of his plan. We are at the eleventh *huitain.* The list of bequests carries us to the thirty-fourth. We may consider in full only the more vigorous.

> Item, a maistre Ythier Marchant,
> Auquel je me sens tres tenu,
> Laisse mon branc d'assier tranchant,
> Ou a maistre Jehan le Cornu,
> Qui est en gaige detenu
> Pour ung escot huit solz montant;
> Si vueil, selon le contenu,
> Qu'on leur livre, en le rachetant.

[*Item,* to Master Ythier Marchant, to whom I am greatly beholden, I leave my *branc* [short sword] of sharp steel, which is held in pawn for a scot of eight sols; or else to Master Jehan le Cornu. Let it be delivered to them, according to this demand, on defrayment of the costs.]

Master Ythier Marchant was a sombre, wealthy, and considerable personage in contemporary Parisian politics; a Burgundian, and later an implacable enemy of Louis XI. In 1473 he was concerned, with the Duke of Burgundy, in a plot to poison the King, and died mysteriously in prison the following year. Whether Villon knew him (and with him many more of the wealthy and powerful who appear in the two Testaments) it is not always possible to tell. The society of that age was easy enough, and University acquaintance no doubt opened many doors. Master Guillaume had friends in high places also. But probably the poet knew a large number of these personages by repute only, leaving aside the police and Châtelet officials, and put them into his verse to amuse his sniggering audiences of the *Pomme de Pin* and the *Espée de Bois*. He knew something of the affairs of Ythier Marchant, nevertheless, and bequeaths him in the *Grant Testament* a Rondeau for his dead loves. Master Jehan le Cornu was Criminal Clerk to the Châtelet, and had helped Villon, who mentions him again in the *Grant Testament*:

> *Item, a maistre Jehan Cornu*
> *Autre nouveau lais luy vueil faire,*
> *Car il m'a tous jours secouru*
> *A mon grant besoing et affaire.*

[*Item*, I wish to make a new bequest to Master Jehan le Cornu, who has always befriended me in the days of my greatest need.]

But the intention may here be sarcasm, as in so many of the bequests.

> *Item, je laisse a Saint Amant*
> Le Cheval Blanc, *avec* la Mulle
> (*Et a Blarru mon dyamant*)
> *Et l'Asne Royé qui reculle.*
> *Et le decret qui articulle*
> Omnis utriusque sexus,
> *Contre la Carmeliste bulle*
> *Laisse aux curez, pour mettre sus.*

[*Item*, I leave to Saint-Amant the *White Horse*, with the *Mule* and to Blarru my diamond) and the jibbing *Striped Ass*. The decree *Omnis utriusque sexus*, against the Carmelite Bull, I leave to the seculars, to hearten them.]

Pierre de Saint-Amant was Clerk to the Treasury, and from the context a great rider before the Lord. Villon may, thinks Marcel

244

Schwob, have been for a brief period in St. Amant's employ as a writer, since his friend Regnier de Montigny's family was connected with the St. Amants. Blarru is identified by Longnon with Jehan de Blarru, a goldsmith of the Pont au Change. Prompsault thinks he is another person, a loose character. The *White Horse,* the *Mule,* and the *Striped Ass* (or Zebra) are tavern signs. The Lateran Decree *Omnis utriusque sexus,* which Villon bequeaths to the priests of the diocese of Paris, had in 1215 given the seculars the exclusive right of confessing their own parishioners of either sex, once a year at least. The Mendicant Friars in 1449 obtained a Bull, *la Carmeliste bulle,* from Nicolas v. empowering them to share this right. At about the time when Villon was composing the *Petit Testament,* or soon afterwards, delegates of the seculars returned triumphant from Rome, having with the support of University and the French bishops succeeded in obtaining a Bull of Calixtus iii. revoking his predecessor's award. Villon bequeaths the zealous seculars of Paris their old Decree to hearten them.

To Master Robert Vallée, *povre clerjot en Parlement* (he belonged to a wealthy family of financiers), Villon leaves his breeks, now detained at the Trumelières tavern, by the Halles, to make a better headdress for his mistress Jehanne de Millières; also, since he is a blockhead, the *Ars Memorandi,* that pedagogic manual; finally directing that out of the sale of the testator's mail-shirt Master Vallée, this poor fish, *ce poupart,* is to be bought a scrivener's stall by St. Jacques-la-Boucherie. To Jacques Cardon, rich burgess and merchant draper, the poet leaves the acorn from a willow plantation; which must conceal a gibe of the best; also, for his refection every day, a plump goose, a capon rich in fat, and ten hogsheads of white wine: but also (lest the said Cardon should grow too corpulent) a couple of lawsuits.

> *Item, je laisse a ce noble homme*
> *Regnier de Montigny, trois chiens.*

[*Item,* I leave to that noble man Regnier de Montigny three dogs.]

The *dossier* of Regnier de Montigny we have already seen. To the Seigneur de Grigny the poet leaves six dogs more than to Montigny; also the ward of Nijon and the castle and donjon of Bicestre; both haunts of ruffians. The Seigneur was a notable litigant and violent character, perpetually in the Courts. To a certain Mouton are left three lashes with a stirrup-leather and a lodging in prison.

Et a maistre Jaques Raguier
Laisse l'Abruvouër Popin,
Pesches, poires, sucre, figuier,
Tousjours le chois d'ung bon loppin,
Le trou de la Pomme de Pin,
Clos et couvert, au feu la plante,
Emmailloté en jacoppin:
Et qui voudra planter, si plante.

[And to Master Jacques Raguier I leave the Abreuvoir Popin, together with peaches, pears, sugar, and a fig-tree [Longnon says the *Fig-Tree* was a tavern]; a good mouthful at all times, and the tavern of the *Pomme de Pin,* roof and cover: where he may sit feet to the fire, wrapped in his mantle; and let the world wag as it may.] (*Planter* is an unseemly verb of the Jargon.)

Eight lines as closely packed with medieval life, when they are examined closely, as you could wish. Master Jacques Raguier, who is for ever installed in front of the fire at the *Pomme de Pin,* wrapped in his mantle, is in himself an epitome of one aspect of the Middle Ages: for having been in his youth a notable boozer and one of Villon's circle, drinking from dawn to dawn and immersed in rapscallionism, he repented and cast off his dirty life and was assoiled, and took Orders, and died at a great age Bishop of Troyes in 1518, being also titular Abbot of Montiéramey and of St. Jean-de-Provins, in that diocese. So at least M. Longnon discovers: and I should be sorry to think he had mistaken his man. As for the great water-trough called the Abreuvoir Popin, a good gift (save for its contents) for such a *rude beuveur,* it stood at the bridge-head near the Châtelet, and was a lounging-place and rendezvous for all the loose fellows, gipsies, night-birds, and brazen doxies of the quarter. There was an inn of disreputable fame near, bearing its name. The *Pomme de Pin* in the Rue de la Juiverie, in the Cité, is familiar.

The next *huitain* holds the first of Villon's two respectful oblique references to the great Robert d'Estouteville, his patron.

246

Item, a maistre Jehan Mautaint
Et maistre Pierre Basennier,
Le gré du seigneur qui attaint
Troubles, forfaiz, sans espargnier;
Et a mon procureur Fournier,
Bonnetz cours, chausses semelees,
Taillees sur mon cordouannier,
Pour porter durant ces gelees.

[*Item*, to Master Jehan Mautaint and to Master Pierre Basennier, the good-will of the seigneur who strictly punishes all turbulence and transgression; and to my procurator Fournier, bonnets without earflaps and well-soled shoes at my cordwainer's, to wear during these present frosts.]

The "seigneur" is the Provost. Master Jehan Mautaint, Examiner at the Châtelet, as we know, will about three months hence be opening an official inquiry into the burglary at the College of Navarre. Master Pierre Basennier, notary, was *greffier criminel* at the Châtelet. The procurator Pierre Fournier, *procureur, de Saint-Benôit* at the Châtelet, had from the context done Villon some service one way or the other: he is not, says Longnon, the Pierre Fournier whose daughter married the poet Martial d'Auvergne, but an elder Fournier, later a counsellor of Parliament.

Item, a Jehan Trouvé, bouchier,
Laisse le Mouton franc et tendre,
Et ung tacon pour esmouchier
Le Beuf Couronné qu'on veult vendre,
Et la Vache:

[*Item*, to Jehan Trouvé, butcher, I leave the fresh and tender Sheep, and a whisk to keep flies off the Crowned Ox, which is for sale; also the Cow.]

Jehan Trouvé, master-butcher of Paris, was no doubt one of the butchers of the University whose hooks were stolen during the *Pet-au-Deable* riots. The *Sheep*, the *Crowned Ox*, and the *Cow* are taverns.

Item, au Chevalier du Guet,
Le Hëaulme luy establis;
Et aux pietons qui vont d'aguet
Tastonnant par ces establis,

247

Je leur laisse deux beaux riblis,
La Lanterne a la Pierre au Let.
Voire, mais j'auray les Troys Lis,
S'ilz me mainent en Chastellet.

[*Item,* to the Captain of the Watch I leave the *Helmet;* and to his foot-Sergeants who go the rounds, groping among the stalls, I leave two good street brawls and the *Lantern* of the Pierre au Let [the Rue des Ecrivains, by St. Jacques-la-Boucherie]. But faith, I must have the chamber called the Three Beds if they hale me to the Châtelet.]

The grinning poet heard this gibe at the police, the natural enemies of his companions, greeted, I think, with a shout of applause which rattled the windows.

To Perrenet Marchant, called the Bastard de la Barre (it is by his hands that the Ballade to *ma damoyselle au nez tortu* is to be delivered, in the *Grant Testament*), are bequeathed three sheaves of straw for him to lay on the ground, and so pursue the *amoureux mestier,* the only trade he knows.

In the twenty-fourth verse Villon remembers the duck-stealing nights around the moats of Paris.

Item, au Loup et a Cholet
Je laisse a la fois ung canart
Prins sur les murs, comme on souloit,
Envers les fossez, sur le tart,
Et a chascun ung grant tabart
De cordelier jusques aux piez,
Busche, charbon et poix au lart,
Et mes houseaulx sans avantpiez.

[*Item,* to the Wolf and to Cholet I leave each a duck taken by the walls, as we used, along the moats towards dark: and to each a long tabard like a Franciscan's, reaching to the feet; also firewood, coal, and peas and bacon, and my thick boots without uppers.]

One sees the three heroes skulking round the ramparts, one hears the muffled squawk of a strangled duck, and a stifled laugh, and hoarse whispers, and one sees three shadowy forms withdrawing stealthily, hugging the walls, gliding in the shadow for fear of the Watch.

Here the Testament takes a sudden turn, ostensibly tender and warm-hearted, but actually bitter and mocking, as will appear.

De rechief, je laisse, en pitié,
A trois petis enfans tous nus
Nommez en ce present traictié,
Povres orphelins impourveus,
Tous deschaussiez, tous desvestus,
Et desnuez comme le ver;
J'ordonne qu'ilz soient pourveus
Au moins pour passer cest yver:

Premierement, Colin Laurens,
Girart Gossouyn et Jehan Marceau,
Despourveus de biens, de parents,
Qui n'ont vaillant l'ance d'ung seau,
Chascun de mes biens ung fesseau,
Ou quatre blans, s'ilz l'ayment mieulx.
Ilz mengeront maint bon morceau,
Les enfans, quant je seray vieulx.

[*Item,* I leave of my charity to thee little shivering children, named in this present document, poor orphans, uncared for, unshod, and naked to the winds [the following]. I direct that they be provided for, at least till this winter is past:

Firstly, to Colin Laurens, Girard Gossouyn, and Jehan Marceau, having neither kindred nor substance, and worth not the handle of a bucket, I leave each a share of my estate: or, if they prefer it, four *blancs* [say, fourpence]. They will fare well, dear children, when I am old.]

"Three poor orphans of University," says Longnon. "Three rich and griping old usurers of Paris, notorious speculators in salt," discover later commentators. The mockery obviously has it, even if there were no documentary evidence for this identification; for Villon proceeds:

Item, ma nominacion,[2]
Que j'ay de l'Université,
Laisse par resignacion
Pour seclurre d'aversité
Povres clers de ceste cité. . . . .

[2] [The Letter of Nomination, sealed by University, showed a graduate's eligibility to be presented for a benefice.]

249

[*Item*, my Letter of Nomination, which I hold of University, I resign and bequeath to rescue from adversity certain poor clerks of this city.]

The "poor clerks" are

> *maiſtre Guillaume Cotin*
> *Et maiſtre Thibault de Viĉtry,*
> *Deux povres clers, parlans Latin,*
> *Paisibles enfans, sans eſtry,*
> *Humbles, chantans bien au leĉtry.*

[Maſter Guillaume Cotin and Maſter Thibault de Viĉtry, two poor prieſts learned in Latin, peaceful fellows, of quiet diſpositions; humble, and sweet chanters at the leĉtern.]

Maſter Cotin and Maſter de Viĉtry were two aged and extremely rich Counsellors of Parliament and Canons of Notre-Dame. Villon leaves them a rent-charge on the house of one Gueldry, butcher; a house in the Rue St. Jacques, whose tenant, having a ſtrong aversion to paying any rent at all, was sued in this year 1456 by the Chapter of St. Benoît, to whom the house belonged.

He leaves to "those taken in the trap," by which he means the prisoners of the Châtelet, his mirror, and the good graces of the gaoler's wife; to the hospitals, his window-curtains, spun from spiders' webs; to the *gueux* and vagabonds lying and freezing at night beneath the ſtalls, a punch in the eye; to his barber, the clippings of his hair; to his cobbler, his old shoes; to his *fripier*, his worn-out duds, all for less than they coſt when new.

> *Item, je laisse aux Mendians,*
> *Aux Filles Dieu et aux Beguines,*
> *Savoureux morceaulx et frians,*
> *Flaons, chappons, et grasses gelines,*
> *Et puis preschier les Quinze Signes.*

[*Item*, I leave to the Mendicants, the *Filles-Dieu* and the *Béguines*, luscious and dainty morsels, flawns, capons, and plump fowls; and then to preach the Fifteen Signs.]

His hungry lips are smacking, his mouth watering. The Mendicants are the four Mendicant Orders: the Dominicans (in France,

Jacobins), the Franciscans (or Cordeliers), the Carmelites, and the Augustinians. The Filles-Dieu are the good sisters by the Porte St. Denis, who comforted with a cup of wine and a roll of bread all condemned gallows-birds on their way in procession to Montfaucon. The Béguines are the pious widows of St. Avoye, in the Rue du Temple. The Fifteen Signs are the fifteen signs which shall precede the Last Judgment, a topic for so many preachers, poets, and artists of the Middle Ages. There was in Villon's time a facetious piece in verse by Jehan d'Abundance called *Les Quinze grans & merveilleux Signes nouvellement descendus du ciel au pays d'Angleterre:* and in some ancient versions of the Dance of Death a review of the Fifteen Signs follows the Dance.

To Jehan de la Garde, a rich grocer of Paris, Villon leaves the sign of the *Golden Mortar,* and also a votive crutch from the abbey of St. Maur-les-Fossés, to the south-east of Paris, to make him a mustard-pestle. There follows an inexplicable burst of rage:

> *A celluy qui fist l'avant garde*
> *Pour faire sur moy griefz exploiz,*
> *De par moy saint Anthoine l'arde!*
> *Je ne luy feray autre laiz.*

[To him who went with the advance-guard [? of the watch] to do me such grievous mischief, for my part may St. Anthony scorch him! I make no other bequest.]

It concerns, no doubt, a street affray in which the poet's heels were not quite quick enough. St. Anthony's Fire was a kind of erysipelas, epidemic and common to this period, called also the *mal des ardens.*[3] It had its name from the religious of St. Antoine in Dauphiny, who were instituted to nurse the afflicted. The oath is a favourite one with Rabelais.

> *Item, je laisse a Merebeuf,*
> *Et a Nicolas de Louvieux,*
> *A chascun l'escaille d'ung œuf,*
> *Plaine de frans et d'escus vieulx.*

[*Item,* I leave to Merebeuf and to Nicolas de Louvieux each an eggshell full of francs and old crowns.]

[3] It has also been identified with the slow consumption called *l'ergotisme gangréneux,* due to lack of food and hygiene.

251

The jest behind this bequest, again, remains enigma. Pierre Merebeuf and Nicolas de Louvieux were two wealthy and powerful bourgeois, the one a draper of the Rue des Lombards, the other an alderman of Paris, a councillor of the Chambre des Comptes, finally ennobled. From such personages the bequest of an eggshell full of francs and old crowns—the *escu* being worth about three francs—must have produced dignified snorts of contempt: if indeed they ever knew about it. They are Villon's butts again in the *Grant Testament*.

And so we come to that passage with which I have begun this book, in which the sound of Angelus from Sorbonne, booming on the shivering night, is caught and fixed for ever in a verse; and with it (I am sorry to have to mention this again, but there it is) a sudden upspringing flame of devotion and recollection. And afterwards, the night being still again and the prayers despatched, the poet's fancy goes off, "zigzag and woodcock fashion," harum-scarum at a tangent, into a parody of the language of the Schools, *"le fatras,"* says P. Champion, *"du commentaire aristotélique."* He feels (so he says) Dame Memory at work, locking into her aumbry, atop of Collateral Species, False Opinative and other toys of the intellect:

> Et mesmement l'Estimative,
> Par quoy prospective nous vient,
> Similative, formative . . .

[Also the Estimative [faculty of judging], by which enters the Perspective [or judgment], the Simulative [or faculty of imitation], the Formative [or faculty of giving form to the Idea] . . . [or words to that effect].]

In the gradually silting-up bed of that Aristotelian flood, so silver, so spacious, and so majestic in St. Thomas's time, many pedants had gambolled during the two hundred years before Villon, till now it wandered feebly through arid acres of glose and commentary a mere trickle of clarity. It had become more and more like Algebra, but without the low cunning against which the aged Classic (God bless the aged Classic!) so gallantly protested; and it was simple to make chaff of the dry chopped formulæ trampled and tossed about in the Schools. Nor was Villon the last to have a fling. Rabelais followed him with the derisive and Lewis-Carrolish *Cresme Philosophale des Questions Encyclopédiques de Pantagruel, lesquelles furent disputées Sorbonificabilitudissinement és Escoles de Decret prez Sainct Denis de la Chartre à Paris:* "*Utrum,* une Idée Platonique voltigeant dextrement sur l'orifice du Chaos pourroit chasser les esquadrons des atomes Democritiques. *Utrum,* les Ratepenades volans par la transtudicité de la porte cornée, pourroient espionnitiquement découvrir les visions Morifiques, devidant gironniquement le fil du Crespemerveilleux enveloppant les attiles des Cerveaux mal calfretez," etc. And as late as the eighteenth century a Spanish Jesuit composed the satire called *The History of the famous Preacher, Fray Gerundo de Campazas,* in whose convent the Lector in Philosophy was such a raging Aristotelian that if he were asked merely how he did, he would answer: "*Materialiter,* well; *formaliter, subdistinguo, reduplicative ut homo,* nothing ails me: *reduplicative ut religiosus,* I am not without my troubles." [4]

Villon devotes three verses to pulling a long snook at the Schools, firmly alleging that by concentration on such operations of the mind a man becomes

> *Fol et lunatique par mois:*
> *Je l'ay leu, se bien m'en souvient,*
> *En Aristote aucunes foiz.*

[Mad and lunatic for months: I have read it so (if I remember rightly) in Aristotle, many a time.]

But I think he is lying. He was no such fanatical Aristotelian.

He perceives at this that his ink is freezing and his candle going out, that his fire is dead, and that he can get no more: and so, sketching a brief self-portrait (and remembering his fame, already stirring) he ends abruptly.

> *Fait au tempts de ladite date*
> *Par le bien renommé Villon,*
> *Qui ne menjue figue ne date.*
> *Sec et noir comme escouvillon,*

---

[4] Prior Bracey, O.P., *Eighteenth-Century Studies.*

Il n'a tente ne pavillon
Qu'il n'ait laissié a ses amis,
Et n'a mais qu'ung peu de billon
Qui sera tantost a fin mis.

[Made at the aforesaid date [Christmas 1456] by the celebrated Villon, who eats neither fig nor date. Dried-up and black as a maulkin, he has no tent nor pavilion that he has not bequeathed to his friends. Only a few coppers remain; and there will soon be an end of them.]

There is written under this in some manuscripts, *Cy fine le Testament Villon,* here ends the Testament of Villon. In one, the Arsenal MS., there stands before this formula a schoolboy whoop: *"Et ho!"* I think it should always stand there. It is the *Petit Testament* (saving about four verses) in two words.

ET HO.

II

THE GREAT TESTAMENT, 1461
(*LE TESTAMENT*)

WITH THE CODICIL AND THE LESSER POEMS

---

§ 1

Dure chose eft a souftenir
Quant cuer pleure et la bouche chante.

CHRISTINE DE PISAN.

[Hard it is to bear, when the heart weeps but the mouth sings.]

A BALLADE in dialogue called the Debate between the Heart and Body of Villon ftrikes like a shaft of sunlight through the darkness of the Bishop of Orleans' prison at Meun-sur-Loire and reveals the kind of man who in the summer of 1461 sat very dolefully in his ftraw in one of the lower dungeons, his feet shackled to a ftaple: that haggard, worn, dark, meagre, hunted creature we have already seen, prematurely bald, a kind of scarecrow, very near the gibbet; but in his sunken eyes a gleam, the enduring *narquois* spirit of this Parisian.

Of the two Ballades which bear every mark of having been composed in this prison, the Debate is the more significant. It is metaphysical, the work of a grown man, no more a royfter about University; and a man trying gropingly to probe his soul and account for the obscure treachery of his fate, but for which he

255

had not now been Sorrow's heritor,
Or stood a lackey in the House of Pain.

Yet ſtill (as with the philosopher in Boswell) cheerfulness keeps breaking in—or at leaſt that salt sardonic humour of his. His heart begins the Debate by attacking Villon bitterly for his *folle plaisance,* which has brought his body, see! to this ſtate, like a poor whipped cur trembling in the corner.

Le Debat du Cuer et du Corps de Villon

[*La com-
plainte
Villon a
son cuer.*]

Qu'eſt ce que j'oy?—Ce suis je!—Qui?—Ton cuer,
Qui ne tient mais qu'a ung petit filet
Force n'ay plus, subſtance ne liqueur,
Quant je te voy retraiĉt ainsi seulet,
Com povre chien tapy en reculet.—
Pour quoy eſt ce?—Pour ta folle plaisance.—
Que t'en chault il?—J'en ay la desplaisance.—
Laisse m'en paix!—Pour quoy?—J'y penseray.—
Quant sera ce?—Quant seray hors d'enfance.—
Plus ne t'en dis.—Et je m'en passeray.

[Who is this I hear?—Lo, this is I, thine heart,
　　That holds on merely now by a slender ſtring.
Strength fails me, shape and sense are rent apart,
　　The blood in me is turned to a bitter thing,
　　Seeing thee skulk here like a dog shivering.—
Yea, and for what?—For that thy sense found sweet.—
What irks it thee?—I feel the ſting of it.—
　　Leave me at peace!—Why?—Nay now, leave me at peace;
I will repent when I grow ripe in wit.—
　　I say no more.—I care not though thou cease.]

(*Swinburne.*)

The poet defends himself, parrying the thruſts firſt with impudence, then with defiance. "Come!" replies his heart, "face your pretty position! You are thirty years old. You are no infant. If you were a half-wit you'd have some excuse for playing the fool like this!"

J'en ay le dueil; toy, le mal et douleur.
Se feusses ung povre ydiot et folet,
Encore eusses de t'excuser couleur:

256

Si n'as tu soing, tout t'eſt ung, bel ou let.
Ou la teſte as plus dure qu'ung jalet,
Ou mieulx te plaiſt qu'onneur ceſte meschance!
Que respondras a ceſte consequence?

[I have the sorrow of it, and thou the smart.
   Wert thou a poor mad fool or weak of wit,
Then might'ſt thou plead this pretext with thine heart;
   But if thou know not good from evil a whit,
   Either thy head is hard as ſtone to hit,
Or shame, not honour, gives thee moſt content.
What canſt thou answer to this argument?]

                          (Swinburne.)

    "I'll be out of it all when I'm dead," answers Villon recklessly. "My God!" says his heart, "what a consolation!" "And what wisdom! what eloquence!" sneers the poet.

J'en seray hors quante je trespasseray.—
Dieu, quel confort—Quelle sage eloquence!—
Plus ne t'en dis.—Et je m'en passeray.

[When I am dead I shall be well at ease.—
God! what good luck!—Thou art over eloquent!—
I say no more.—I care not though thou cease.]

                          (Swinburne.)

    And then, turning on his tormentor, Villon lays the blame for everything on Saturn, the siniſter planet under which he was born. (His heart speaks firſt.)

Dont vient ce mal?—Il vient de mon maleur.
Quant Saturne me feist mon fardelet,
Ces maulx y meist, je le croy.

["Whence, then, this misery?" "It's my bad fortune. When Saturn piled on my load he added all this, I think."]

    "Rubbish!" scoffs his heart. "Is not the wise man maſter of such things?"

Voy que Salmon escript en son rolet:
"Homme sage, ce dit il, a puissance
Sur planetes et sur leur influence."

["See, Solomon writes in his scroll: 'The wise man has power (he says) over planets and their influences.' "]¹

The poet replies heavily:

Je n'en croy riens; tel qu'ilz m'ont fait seray.

["I believe nothing of that. What I made I shall remain."]

And the dialogue proceeds.

Que dis tu?—Dea! certes, c'est, c'est ma creance—
Plus ne t'en dis—Et je m'en passeray.

["What do you say?" "I' faith, I believe it!" "I say no more." "And I can do without."]

The Envoi holds final promises of reformation.

Veulx tu vivre?Dieu m'en doint la puissance!—
Il te fault . . . —Quoy?—Remors de conscience,
Lire sans fin.—En quoy?—Lire en science,
Laisser les folz!—Bien j'y adviseray.—
Or le retien!—J'en ay bien souvenance.—
N'atens pas tant que tourne a desplaisance.
Plus ne t'en dis.—Et je m'en passeray.

["You want to live?" "God give me strength to do it!" "You must have, then——" "What?" "Penitence. You must read diligently." "What?" "Books of value." "And you must give up your loose companions." "Very well. I'll see to it." "You won't forget?" "I have made a note of it." "Don't exepect too much, or you'll be disappointed. I say no more." "And I can do without."]

O rueful, hopeful, weathercock heart of man!—I mean, of course, medieval man: penitence throbs in every line of this, and a longing to ſtruggle clear of the morass and get both feet on the firm road, among the virtuous and the well-found: but life is too ſtrong, and there are too many women. And, I fancy, the earneſt mood changes within the octave. It is difficult to say. The other Ballade composed (at leaſt in his mind) in the dungeon at Meun, whether earlier or later, is a different thing altogether, and a delicious thing,

¹ The allusion is to the Book of Wisdom, vii. 19: *Ipse enim dedit mihi horum, quæ sunt, scientiam veram: ut sciam dispositionem orbis terrarum, et virtutes elementorum . . . anni cursus et ſtellarum dispositiones.*

half-smiling, half-desperate, gay, even; informed with a sort of affectionate pleading confidence in his friends, the unbuttoned band of rhymers and wits and joyous companions far away in Paris, who (it is obvious) love the unlucky rogue. He begins:

[Epistre.]   EPISTRE EN FORME DE BALLADE, A SES AMYS

> Aiez pitié, aiez pitié de moy,
> A tout le moins, si vous plaist, mes amis!
> En fosse gis, non pas soubz houx ne may,
> En cest exil ouquel je suis transmis
> Par Fortune, comme Dieu l'a permis.
>
> Filles, amans, jeunes gens et nouveaulx,
> Danceurs, saulteurs, faisans les piez de veaux,
> Vifz comme dars, agus comme aguillon,
> Gousiers tintans cler comme cascaveaux,
> Le lesserez la, le povre Villon?

[Have pity, have pity on me, my friends—at least, if it please you! Here I lie in the ditch, not under the holly nor yet under the May, in exile, into which fortune has brought me, by God's will. Girls! Lovers, old, young, or new! Dancers, and you, leapers, who dance the Calf's Feet [a comic acrobatic dance], swift as darts, sharp as a spur! O melodious gullets, clear as mule-bells, will you leave him here—your poor Villon?][2]

and so continues, running over in his mind the ranks of his old companions and mixing regret and nostalgia for the bright jostle of the streets with his cry:

> Chantres chantans a plaisance, sans loy,
> Galans, rians, plaisans en fais et dis,
> Courens, alans, francs de faulx or, d'aloy,
> Gens d'esperit, ung petit estourdis.
> Trop demourez, car il meurt entandis.
> Faiseurs de laiz, de motetz et rondeaux
> Quant mort sera, vous lui ferez chaudeaux!
> Ou gist, il n'entre escler ne tourbillon:
> De murs espoix on lui a fait bandeaux.
> Le lesserez la, le povre Villon?

[2] The opening line is a plain echo of the Book of Job, xix. 21: *Miseremini mei, miseremini mei, saltem vos amici mei, quia manus Domini tetigit me.*

[O singers, singing sweetly at your pleasure, without commandment; laughing gallants, so excellent in word and deed; rovers and ramblers of quality, free of your counterfeit gold; O wits, madcaps you delay too long, and he perishes meanwhile. Makers of lays, and motets, and roundels! when he's dead you'll make him hot possets! [Or, if the reading *chandeaux* is preferred, 'When he's dead you'll burn candles for him.'] Where he lies there enters neither light nor breeze; thick ramparts are a bandage for his eyes. Will you leave him here, your poor Villon?]

In his third stanza he describes for them, not without a twisted smile, his present condition, how he fasts every Sunday and Tuesday—which means the week round, since Wednesday, Friday, and Saturday were days of abstinence, and even fasts for the devout; how he eats only dry bread, and how his drink is water . . . and here he is certainly thinking of the Question with its horrid draughts of cold water. "Come," he says:

> *Venez le veoir en ce piteux arroy*
> *Nobles hommes, francs de quart et de dix,*
> *Qui ne tenez d'empereur ne de roy,*
> *Mais seulement de Dieu de Paradis:*
> *Jeuner lui fault dimenches et merdis*
> *Dont les dens a plus longues que ratteaux;*
> *Après pain sec, non pas après gasteaux,*
> *En ses boyaulx verse eaue a gros bouillon;*
> *Bas en terre, table n'a ne tresteaulx.*
> *Le lesserez la, le povre Villon?*

[Come, see him in his piteous array, my noble friends, living tax-free and obeying no man's ban, Emperor's or King's, but only God's in Heaven. See, he is constrained to fast on Sundays and Tuesdays, and his teeth are longer than a rake's! His meat is dry bread and no cake, and he washes his guts after it with lashings of water! See how low he lies, lacking table and trestles! Will you leave him here, your poor Villon?]

Envoi

> *Princes nommez, anciens, jouvenceaux,*
> *Impetrez moy graces et royaulx seaux,*
> *Et me montez en quelque corbillon.*
> *Ainsi le font, l'un a l'autre, pourceaux,*
> *Car, ou l'un brait, ils fuyent a monceaux.*
> *Le lesserez la, le povre Villon?*

[O Princes aforesaid, young and old, obtain for me the Royal grace and seal, and draw me up from here in some basket! Why, even swine, when one of their fellows squeaks for help, fly to his aid in a heap! Will you leave him here, your poor Villon?]

There is one more Ballade, *Problème ou Ballade de la Fortune*, supposed to have been made about this time, in which Fortune holds a conversation with the poet, very soberly and heavily, showing him how many great kings and warriors have been led into dole by her, Priam, and Hannibal, and Scipio of Africa, Julius Cæsar and Pompey also, and Jason, Arphaxad, King of the Medes, Alexander, Holofernes, and Absolon; advising him to take his thwackings quietly. The Monk's Tale enumerates similar "old ensamples" and has much the same moral:

> I wol biwaille, in manere of tragédie,
> The harm of hem that ſtoode in heigh degree,
> And fillen so that ther nas no remédie
> To brynge hem out of hir adverſitee;
> For certein, whan that Fortune liſt to flee,
> Ther may no man the cours of hir with-holde.

It is a dull Ballade of no merit, and I shall not ſtay to quote it. The passage through Meun of Louis xi. changed Villon's moralisings and groans alike into whoops of joy. Paris received him eventually to her arms again, and in 1461-2, as we have seen, the *Grant Teſtament* was composed, which we are now broaching.

THE GRANT TESTAMENT

He begins in a sullen rage, remembering his wrongs, but collectedly:

> *En l'an de mon trentiesme aage,*
> *Que toutes mes hontes j'eus beus*
> *Ne du tout fol, ne du tout sage,*
> *Non obſtant maintes peines eues,*
> *Lesquelles j'ay toutes receues*
> *Soubz la main Thibault d'Aussigny . . .*
> *S'evesque il eſt, seignant les rues,*
> *Qu'il soit le mien je le regny.*

[In the thirtieth year of my age, having supped my fill of shame, being neither altogether foolish nor altogether wise, and

261

notwithstanding the many punishments I have suffered at the hand of Thibault d'Aussigny—is he a bishop, blessing people in the street? No bishop of mine, by God!]

He chews his anger and resentment over and over, rumbling and grumbling. He is not Thibault's serf and chattel, is he? No, faith. A good summer on bread and water! May God reward Thibault for it! Holy Church tells us to pray for our enemies, does she? Very well. He'll say him a Picard's prayer.[2] But wait! There is a verse in the Psalter which will do for his lordship of Orleans very well:

> Le verselet escript septiesme
> De psëaulme Deus laudem.

[The verse which is written the seventh of the Psalm *Deus laudem.*]

The poet's face (I see it from here) has a wide grin of pleasure as he writes this down. The seventh verse of Psalm cviii., *Deus laudem,* recited on Saturdays at None, is this: *Fiant dies ejus pauci: et episcopatum ejus accipiat alter.*—"May his days be few, and may another take his bishopric." Good! Justice is satisfied. The poet turns to praise God at the full of his lungs for his deliverance, and Our Lady also, and *"Loys, le bon roy de France."* May the King be endowed (he roars) with the fortune of Jacob, the honour and glory of Solomon, and the years of Methusaleh! May twelve goodly children, all sons, issue from his royal loins,[3] each as brave as Charlemagne and as virtuous as St. Martial, and may he get Paradise at the end! And so, to end these transports:

> Escript l'ay l'an soixante et ung,
> Que le bon roy me delivra
> De la dure prison de Mehun,
> Et que vie me recouvra,
> Dont suis, tant que mon cuer vivra,
> Tenu vers luy m'humilier,

---

[2] The Picards were a curious fifteenth-century sub-sect of heretics in Hungary, preaching common property in women: they were exterminated by Zisca, chief of the Hussites, and their name became attached to other obscure heretics in the Low Countries. The proverb *Prière de Picard,* quoted by Villon, concerns their habit of saying no prayers at all for their dead.

[3] Actually Louis xi. had four sons, of whom two died in infancy: also two daughters. I do not count his natural children.

Ce que feray tant qu'il mourra:
Bienfait ne se doit oublier.

[Written in the year '61, when the good King delivered me from the harsh prison of Meun and I thereby recovered life: on which account I hold myself humbly beholden to him as long as my heart beats, and will do so till death; for such a benefit must not be forgot.]

There now is displayed by Marot the rubric

ICY COMMENCE VILLON À ENTRER EN MATIERE PLAINE
D'ERUDITION ET DE BON SÇAVOIR,

[Here begins Villon to enter into matter full of erudition and good learning.]

under which the poet begins very deliberately an Apology, or Confession, of his whole life, his turbulent youth, and his sins; finding his soul, he says, after so many plaints and tears, groans of anguish, miseries, dolours, and chastisements, ground by these griefs and sharpened like a needle, pricking him more than all the Commentaries of Averroës on Aristotle. He brands himself a great sinner, yet a hanger-on to the infinite mercy of God, humbly hoping, like our own old poet, for "a gobbet of His grace"; and explaining and excusing his wildness he tells the ancient story from the *Policraticus* of John of Salisbury, heard in the Schools, and held in the poet's wayward mind no doubt for years, of the sea-pirate Diomedes, who was brought before Alexander, condemned to death. On the Emperor asking this man why he was a bandit he answered shortly that had he had an emperor's fortune he might have been Alexander, but poverty knows no law: for which defence Alexander released and favoured this *raisonneur.* Alas! says Villon. If Almighty God had seen fit to give me, too, such a patron, I should have had a different tale to tell!

Necessité faict gens mesprendre,
Et faim saillir le loup du boys.

[Necessity drives men astray, and hunger goads wolves snarling from the wood.]

This was also the defence of the blackguard Nephew of Rameau. "*La voix de la conscience et de l'honneur est bien faible,*

263

lorsque les boyaux crient." Such immorality has always been most bitterly condemned by those of the righteous with a well-lined belly.

Follows a quick gush of regret for the wasted years, for youth soiled and thrown away, and shame for dishonourable old age now tapping at the door. The cry is loud and sincere:

> *Je plaings le temps de ma jeunesse,*
> *(Ouquel j'ay plus qu'autre gallé*
> *Jusques a l'entree de viellesse),*
> *Qui son partement m'a celé.*
> *Il ne s'en est a pié allé*
> *N'a cheval: helas! comment don?*
> *Soudainement s'en est vollé*
> *Et ne m'a laissié quelque don.*
>
> *Allé s'en est, et je demeure,*
> *Povre de sens et de savoir,*
> *Triste, failly, plus noir que meure . . .*

[I regret the days of my youth when I sported more than most, right up to the brink of age—for youth's departure escaped me: he vanished neither afoot nor on horseback. Alas! how then? He flew away suddenly, leaving me naught.]

Aië! he laments. The flying golden years are past, leaving me here sad, weary, poor, burdened with miseries, blacker than a mulberry. See what idleness and the love of women can do for a man! Women! Why, even now—

> *Bien est verté que j'ay amé*
> *Et ameroie voulentiers;*
> *Mais triste cuer, ventre affamé*
> *Qui n'est rassasié au tiers,*
> *M'oste des amoureux sentiers.*

[I have loved, faith! and I would love again gladly; but my sad heart and empty belly, not a third satisfied, drag me from the byways of dalliance.]

This is the unembarrassed self-revelation which echoes in so much of the world's great literature, in St. Augustine, and Byron, and Baudelaire, and Verlaine, and Heine. Observe, though, that Villon, this human sinner, pretends no singleness of moral and spiritual aspiration. He is thinking of his soul, certainly; but of the fleshpots also, the soft sheltered life which might have been his had he not burned his youth away in chambering and wantonness.

> *Hé! Dieu, se j'eusse estudié*
> *Ou temps de ma jeunesse folle*
> *Et a bonnes meurs dedié,*
> *J'eusse maison et couche molle.*
> *Mais quoi? je fuyoie l'escolle,*
> *Comme fait le mauvais enfant.*
> *En escripvant cesle parolle,*
> *A peu que le cuer ne me fent.*

[Dear God! had I but heeded my books in the days of my flaming youth, and given some thought to good conduct, I might have had my own house, and a soft bed to lie in! But Lord! I fled the Schoole like a naughty child. . . . As I write this my heart is like to break.][3]

He broods on this for a time, remembering from Holy Writ the Sage Ecclesiastes and the Patriarch Job on the brevity of life and the fleeing vanity of all the joys of youth. "My days," he groans, "are consumed like flaming tow."

> *Mes jours s'en sont allez errant*
> *Comme, dit Job, d'une touaille*
> *Font les filetz, quant tisserant*
> *En son poing tient ardent paille.*

[My days have run and vanished away like threads of tow (as Job says) when the weaver lays a burning straw to them.]

Dies mei velocius transierunt, quam a texente tela succiditur, et consumpti sunt absque ulla spe. It is the sixth of the seventh of the Book of Job. So in *The Hound of Heaven* a later Francis echoes the cry:

> I stand amid the dust o' the mounded years—
> My mangled youth lies dead beneath the heap.
> My days have crackled and gone up in smoke,
> Have puffed and burst as sun-starts on a stream.
> Yea, faileth now even dream
> The dreamer, and the lute the lutanist.

Compare, in this mood, Verlaine, whose agitated life so resembled Villon's:

> *Qu'as-tu fait, ô toi que voilà*
> *Pleurant sans cesse,*
> *Dis, qu'as-tu fait, toi que voilà,*
> *De ta jeunesse?*

And Villon passes to that lovely lament for his bright companions,

> *Ou sont les gracieux gallans*
> *Que je suivoye ou temps jadis,*
> *Si bien chantans, si bien parlans,*
> *Si plaisans en faiz et en dis? . . .*

which I have placed in full elsewhere: that lament in which he reviews their present state, how some of the ruffling lads he sang and rioted with are now great seigneurs, but others naked beggars in the gutter, and others dead and rotted, and others retired in the cloister. The fit takes him then to remember his poverty and his extraction.

> *Povre je suis de ma jeunesse,*
> *De povre et de petite extrace;*
> *Mon pere n'ot oncq grant richesse,*
> *Ne son ayeul, nommé Orace;*
> *Povreté tous nous suit et trace.*
> *Sur les tombeaulx de mes ancestres,*
> *Les ames desquelz Dieu embrasse!*
> *On n'y voit couronnes ne ceptres.*

[Poor I am, from my childhood, poor, and of humble stock. My father had little wealth, nor his grandfather Horace either. Poverty has dogged and tracked us all; and on the tombs of my sires (may God receive their souls!) there are neither crowns nor sceptres.]

His father is long dead, God rest him, and his mother has not very long to live now; and her son will follow her. . . . Reaching out largely and gazing, as it were, on Mortality face to face, he falls into that musing and obsession which was so familiar to the medieval mind, but which is in our own day bad form, and worse: a musing on and acknowledgment of Death, its inevitability, its embracing swoop.

> *Je congois que povres et riches,*
> *Sages, et folz, prestres et laiz,*
> *Nobles, villains, larges et chiches,*
> *Petiz et grans, et beaulx et laiz,*

Dames a rebrassez colletz,
De quelconque condicion,
Portans atours et bourreletz,
Mort saisit sans excepcion.

[Well, I know that poor and rich, wise and fools, priests and laity, nobles, churls, spenders and screws, great and small, beautiful and ugly, ladies in fur-necked gowns, ladies of quality, wearing rich ornaments and high headdresses—all, all, without exception, are seized by Death.]

It is simply a summary of all the quatrains written under the Dance of Death in the Innocents cemetery, where the poet had no doubt lately been, pondering the paintings and ogling the women.

But now across his verses here, as one reads, over the chill scent of tombs, there comes an almost imperceptible soft Ausonian air, like the *candidi Favonii* which greet the traveller over the Alps as he approaches the gates of Italy: for Villon is reaching the goal of his meditations and his loveliest song: yet his dread continues through two more verses.

Et meure Paris ou Helaine,
Quiconques meurt, meurt a douleur
Telle qu'il pert vent et alaine;
Son fiel se creve sur son cuer!
Puis sue, Dieu scet quelle sueur!
Et n'est qui de ses maux l'alege:
Car enfant n'a, frere ne seur,
Qui lors voulsist estre son plege:

[So Paris dies, and so Helen; and whoever dies, dies with pain: his breath fails, his gall bursts over his heart, he sweats— God! what sweat! And there is no one who relieves him of his agony, no child, or brother, or sister, who would take his place.]

He is in a sort of trance, gazing fascinated on the pain and horror of dissolution, the failing breath, the death-sweat: and his love of women's bodies, so soft and precious, completes his engulfment in dismay at their fate.

La mort le fait fremir, pallir,
Le nez courber, les vaines tendre,
Le col enfler, la chair mollir,
Joinctes et nerfs croistre et estendre.

267

Corps femenin, qui tant es tendre,
Poly, souef si precieux,
Te fauldra il ces maux attendre?
Oy, ou tout vif aller es cieulx.

[Death makes him shiver and go white, makes the nose a hook, the veins tight-strung, the neck swell, the flesh turn flabby, the nerves and joints stretch and dilate. . . . O body of woman, so tender, so smooth, and soft, and precious, does this doom wait for you, too? Assuredly: or else one needs must go to Heaven alive.]

And then, then comes the miracle, the strain of music to becalm his fever.

> Charm me asleep, and melt me soe
> With thy delicious Numbers
> That, being ravish'd, hence I goe
> Away in easy Slumbers.
> Ease my sick Head,
> And make my Bed,
> Thou Power that canst sever
> Me from this Ill,
> And quickly still,
> Though thou not kill
> My Fever.

This music is the Ballade of the Dead Ladies, which I have printed in its place with the notes proper to it, later in this book. It is one of the towering poems of the world, both for its melody, its sadness, the dreamy, shimmering fabric of which it is composed, the beauty of its separate evocations, its rhythm, its sequence of words, and its crescendo and culmination. It was possibly composed in a thieves' cellar, or in a riverside stews.

The poet, intoxicated by the thing he had wrought (and who would not be?), endeavours to repeat it immediately in the Ballade of the Dead Lords; a piece of verse comparatively inferior, and although not despicable, and far above the run of its type (it is of a common pattern, the Methodical Enumerative, unfired by ecstasy), not of the glorious stuff of the Dead Ladies. It deals, moreover, with great lords lately dead, and does not range the ages of history and faëry like its predecessor. I give two stanzas and the Envoi.

268

DES SEIGNEURS DU TEMPS JADIS

*[Autre
ballade.]*

Qui plus, ou est le tiers Calixte,
Dernier decedé de ce nom,
Qui quatre ans tint le papaliste?
Alphonce le roy d'Arragon,
Le gracieux duc de Bourbon,
Et Artus le duc de Bretaigne,
Et Charles septiesme le bon?
Mais ou est le preux Charlemaigne?

Semblablement, le roy Scotiste
Qui demy face ot, ce dit on,
Vermeille comme une amatiste
Depuis le front jusqu'au menton?
Le roy de Chippre de renon,
Helas et le bon roy d'Espaigne
Duquel je ne sçay pas le nom?
Mais ou est le preux Charlemaigne?

BALLADE

OF THE LORDS OF OLD TIME

[What more? Where is the third Calixt,
   Last of that name, now dead and gone,
Who held four years the Papalist?
   Alfonso King of Aragon,
   The gracious lord, Duke of Bourbon,
And Arthur, Duke of old Britaine?
   And Charles the Seventh, that worthy one?—
Even with the good knight Charlemain.

The Scot too, king of mount and mist.
   With half his face vermilion,
Men tell us, like an amethyst,
   From brow to chin that blazed and shone;
   The Cypriote King of old renown,
Alas! and that good King of Spain,
   Whose name I cannot think upon?
Even with the good knight Charlemain.]

(*Swinburne.*)

There is, after all, a sort of processional music in it. One hears
silver trumpets shrilling and sees the Kings passing, in robes stiff

with embroidered flower-work and jewels. A poet's delight in transcribing stately names for their own sake, which Villon shares with Milton (*que diable!*), [4] and a not ignoble worship of heroic or merely splendid or decorative personality—these inform the Ballade also. As for the names contained in it, Calixtus III. held the Papal throne for only three years and eight months, from April 1455; Alphonse V., called the Magnanimous, King of Aragon, Naples, and Sicily, reigned 1416-1458; Jean, Duke of Bourbon, an uncle of Charles VI. and one of the most lettered and art-loving men of his age, died 1453; Artus III., Duke of Brittany, Constable of France, surnamed the Dispenser of Justice, died 1458: Clément Marot confuses him with Arthur the King, the great half-legendary Arthur of the Celts, who is quite obviously out of place in this gallery; Charles VII. of France, called the Good, died at Meun in July 1461. In the second stanza the personages are less important or more vague. The Scottish King with the amethyst birthmark down his face is James II., son of the royal poet. *"1436 wes the coronacioun,"* says the Winton MS., *"of K. James the secund with the Red Scheik callit James with the fyr in the face, he beand bot sax yer ald and ane half, in the abbay of Halyrudhous, quhar now his banys lyis."* In August 1460, at the siege of Roxburgh Castle, James *"unhappely was slane with ane gun, the quhilk brak in the fyring."* The King of Cyprus of renown may be one of three, but is probably the last of his line, Jean de Lusignan, thirteenth of the name, who died in 1458 without issue-male; the good King of Spain, whose name Villon pretends not to know—whether for a joke or to get another rhyme in "om" or "on"—is most likely Juan II., King of Castile and Leon, who died in 1454. As for the Envoi,

> *Ou est Claquin le bon Breton?*
> *Ou le conte Daulphin d'Auvergne*
> *Et le bon feu duc d'Alençon?*
> *Mais ou est le preux Charlemaigne?,*

[4] Compare, from *Paradise Lost*, I.:

> And all who since, baptized or infidel,
> Jousted in Aspramont or Montalban,
> Damascus, or Morocco, or Trebizond,
> Or whom Bizerta sent from Africk shore
> When Charlemagne with all his peerage fell
> By Fontarabia.

it is soon resolved. Claquin is the great Du Guesclin of Brittany, hero of a whole epic. The Dauphin of Auvergne is Béraud III., last of his hereditary branch, who died in 1428. The "late good" Duke of Alençon is another joke, since he was not dead at all, but had been sentenced in 1456 to perpetual imprisonment for high treason. Louis XI. pardoned him in 1460. Of Charlemagne, *Charles li reis, nostre emperedre maignes,* the refrain of this Ballade, I need explain little, I hope. The Song of Roland is at the bed-head of every man who loves high poetry, and inevitably before his eyes as they light on the word "Charlemagne" there rises at once a vision of the Emperor of the Western World as he appears in Dürer's picture, with his terrible eyes and his great white flowing beard; vested in dalmatic and crowned with his tall crown surmounted by the Cross; grasping in his right hand the sword Joyeuse, with the relic of the Holy Lance in its pommel, and in his left hand the orb. And with this vision there is heard in the mind (I speak not of the genteel, but of men of good report) a loud fanfare and a galloping of hoofs, as when the Emperor on his *destrier* Tencendor went clanging and pounding, hot with anger, through the awful passes of the Pyrenees (as it says in the Song) to succour Roland.

> *Par grant iror chevalchet Charlemaignes,*
> *Desor sa broigne li gist sa barbe blanche.*

[Blazing with anger rides Charlemagne; his white beard flying shrouds his breast of mail.]

Observe that all the personages in the Ballade of Dead Lords are roughly contemporary with Villon, and that he was not ignorant of European affairs.

Immediately on the heels of this follows another *Ballade à ce propos, en vieil langage françoys* (Marot) in the same key, but a failure—an attempt, it seems, at a pastiche of thirteenth-century

271

French. It is enumerative, like the others, but bald, dry, and of little value. Nevertheless it has one line glittering like a Byzantine ikon.

> *Voire, ou soit de Constantinobles*
> *L'emperieres au poing dorez,*
> *Ou de France ly roy tres nobles*
> *Sur tous autres roys decorez,*
> *Qui pour ly grans Dieux aourez*
> *Bastist eglises et couvens,*
> *S'en son temps il fut honnorez,*
> *Autant en emporte ly vens.*

[Why, where is that Emperor of Constantinople with the golden fists? Where is that most noble King of France, glorious above all other Kings, who for the love of God built such churches and convents? If he was honoured in his time, the wind has blown as much away.]

"The Emperor with golden fists" gives you at once the Orient: the minarets; the coloured domes; the Liturgy of Chrysostom; the *ikonostasis* and its array of strange framed oval-faced saints with heads and vestments of solid gold and silver, studded with gems; the flowery Greek rites. Where had a shabby Parisian poet seen a picture like this, unless in the hall of some great seigneur, the Valois or the Bourbon?

As a master of the organ who has pushed back his great stops after the final thunder of some fugue still lingers abstracted at the keyboard, repeating and embroidering his theme on a slenderer reed, so Villon now runs on with the Death theme in *huitains*; but his thoughts are shaping themselves definitely and concentrating on one aspect, an absorbing one to him perpetually: the decay of women's beauty, and the tragedy of it. There flower in due course the ten verses of the Lament of the Belle Heaulmière, the old woman keening over her dying fire, remembering her youth, her vanished beauty, and the hot sweet sins which remain to her (as a poet has said) like the perfume of wine lingering in an empty jar. A hundred years before her the Wife of Bath had raised the same loud complaint:

But Lord Crist! whan that it remembreth me
Upon my yowthe, and on my jolitee,
It tikleth me aboute myn hertë roote!
Unto this day it dooth myn hertë boote
That I have had my world, as in my tyme.
But Age, allas! that al wole envenyme,
Hath me biraft my beautee and my pith,—
Lat go, fare wel, the devel go therwith!
The flour is goon, ther is namoore to telle,
The bren, as I best kan, now moste I selle.

Of the Belle Heaulmière's very frank and fierce lament for physical beauty the invention was actually not Villon's, but Jean de Meung's, who had incorporated a plaint of the kind into his continuation of the immense *Roman de la Rose* a century before.[5] The old woman (called the Belle Heaulmière presumably from the *heaulme,* the distinctive headdress, like the *mitra* of the Roman strumpets, or possibly from her having been the bride of an armourer) passes in review, relentlessly, her dried and skinny members, evoking the time of their soft whiteness and their ravishing spring, bewailing and reviling old age, which has spoiled her of all her treasures.

LES REGRETS DE LA BELLE HEAULMIÈRE *

[*La vieille
en regre-
tant le
temps de sa
jeunesse.*]

*Advis m'est que j'oy regreter
La belle qui fut hëaulmiere,
Soy jeune fille soushaitter
Et parler en telle maniere:
"Ha! viellesse felonne et fiere,
Pourquoi m'as si tost abatue?
Qui me tient, qui, que ne me fiere,
Et qu'a ce coup je ne me tue?"*

[Methought I heard the complaint of the fair who was formerly the Heaulmière, crying for her youth and lamenting in this wise: "Ha! Age, brutal, relentless Age! why hast vanquished me so soon? What hinders me from slaying myself, and so ending all at one blow?"]

She remembers the loveliness of her body, which once no man could resist, but which is now scorned even by *truandailles,* the very beg-

---

[5] From verse 13,526 on: but I have not read it.

* Swinburne's translation of "The Lament" will be found on page 386.

gars, dregs, and riffraff. She remembers also the graceless darling lover of her youth, to whom she gave so freely what others were glad to purchase, getting in exchange merely blows and betrayal, but forgetting all these in his infrequent kiss.

> "Or est il mort, passé trente ans,
> Et je remains vielle, chenue.
> Quant je pense, lasse! au bon temps,
> Quelle fus, quelle devenue;
> Quant me regarde toute nue,
> Et je me voy si tres changiee,
> Povre, seiche, megre, menue,
> Je suis presque toute enragiee.
>
> "Qu'est devenu ce front poly,
> Cheveulz blons, ces sourcils voultiz
> Grant entroeil, ce regart joly,
> Dont prenoie les plus soubtilz;
> Ce beau nez droit, grant ne petiz,
> Ces petites joinctes oreilles,
> Menton fourchu, cler vis traictiz,
> Et ces belles levres vermeilles?

["Well, he is dead these thirty years and more, and here am I left a grey old woman. Aïe! when I think of the good days, what I was then, what I am now, when I look at myself naked and see myself so changed, poor, dried-up, skinny, shrivelled, I could be beside myself with rage almost.

"Where is my smooth forehead, my golden hair, my well-arched eyebrows, the broad space between my eyes, and my lovely look, which fired the cleverest of them? Where is my fine straight nose, neither too big nor too little, my pretty small ears, my dimpled chin, my clear features, and my beautiful red lips?"]

It is not accounted refined to follow the catalogue of charms further, nor yet to transcribe the old women's bitter outcry of contempt at their present ruin: for she is through, and spares no inch of herself.[6]

> "Ces gentes espaules menues,
> Ces bras longs et ces mains traictisses,
> Petiz tetins, hanches charnues,
> Eslevees, propres, faictisses

[6] See Appendix E: *The Blazon of Beauty.*

A tenir amoureuses lises;
Ces larges rains, ce sadinet
Assis sur grosses fermes cuisses;
Dedens son joly jardinet?

"Le front ridé, les cheveux gris,
Les sourcilz cheus, les yeuls estains,
Qui faisoient regars et ris
Dont mains marchans furent attains;
Nez courbes de beaulté loingtains,
Oreilles pendantes, mousues,
Le vis pally, mort et destains,
Menton froncé levres peaussues:

"C'est d'umaine beaulté l'issue!
Les bras cours et les mains contraites,
Des espaules toute bossue;
Mamelles, quoy? toutes retraites;
Telles les hanches que les tettes;
Du sadinet, fy! Quant de cuisses,
Cuises ne sont plus, mais cuissettes
Grivelees comme saulcisses."

I

[Those sweet slim shoulders, those long arms and pretty hands, those little breasts and fine plump hips, so high, so fair, so excellent for Love's tourneys; those broad loins, and that jewel, enshrined within its charming garden, set upon such plump firm thighs?

II

[The forehead is wrinkled, the hair grey, the eyebrows have fallen, the eyes are dead—those eyes which flung such looks and smiles, whereby so many passers-by were wounded. The nose is hooked, and its beauty is fled, the ears hang down, shrunken; the whole face is waxen, dead, and extinguished, the chin puckered, the lips grown coarse.]

III

[Such is the end of human loveliness! My arms are shrivelled, my hands withered, my shoulders humped, my breasts—Aïe! all shrunken, hips and paps alike. And that jewel—fie! fie! And as for my thighs, thighs they are no more, but skin and bone, speckled like sausages!]

She comes at laſt to silence, and a final brooding.

> *"Ainsi le bon temps regretons*
> *Entre nous, povres vielles sotes*
> *Assises bas, a crouppetons,*
> *Tout en ung tas comme pelotes,*
> *A petit feu de chenevotes*
> *Toſt allumees, toſt eſtaintes;*
> *Et jadis fusmes si mignotes! . . .*
> *Ainsi en prent a mains et maintes."*

["So do we regret our good time, we poor silly old fools, crouching on our hunkers in a heap, like a bundle of old clothes, over a little fire of hemp-stalks, soon alight and soon out . . . we that once were so tasty. Thus it happens to one and all."]

I cannot refrain from quoting from J. M. Synge's free and lovely prose-paraphrase of this Lament.

The man I had a great love for—a great rascal would kick me in the gutter—is dead thirty years and over it, and it is I am left behind, grey and aged. When I do be minding the good days I had, minding what I was one time, and what it is I'm come to, and when I do look on my own self, poor and dry, and pinched together, it wouldn't be much would set me raging in the ſtreets.

Where is the round forehead I had, the fine hair, and the two eyebrows, and the eyes with a big gay look out of them would bring folly from a great scholar? Where is my straight shapely nose, and two ears, and my chin with a valley in it, and my lips were red and open? . . .

It's the way I am this day—my forehead is gone away into furrows, the hair of my head is grey and whitish, my eyebrows are tumbled from me, and my two eyes have died out within my head—those eyes that would be laughing to the men: my nose has a hook on it, and my ears are hanging down; and my lips are sharp and skinny.

That's what's left over from the beauty of a right woman—a bag of bones, and legs the like of two shrivelled sausages going beneath it.

It's of the like of that we old hags do be thinking, of the good times are gone away from us, and we crouching on our hunkers by a little fire of twigs, soon kindled and soon spent, we that were the pick of many.

We are nearing the beginning of the Teſtament proper; but there is some very pretty moralising before we reach it. The Ballade of the Belle Heaulmière to the Daughters of Joy follows after her Lament, and is a piece of advice which some have deemed cynical. The firſt ſtanza gives the doctrine of it.

"Or y pensez, belle Gantiere
Qui m'escoliere souliez eſtre,
Et vous, Blanche la Savetiere,
Or eſt il temps de vous congnoistre.
Prenez a deſtre et a senestre;
N'espargnez homme, je vous prie:
Car vielles n'ont ne cours ne eſtre,
Ne que monnoye qu'on descrie."

["Now, my sweet Glover, once my pupil, consider this well. You, too, Blanche the Cobbler. Now is the time to consolidate. Take them right and left, I beg you, and spare no man; for aged trulls have neither currency nor place, any more than a worn-out coinage."]

It is addressed to six ladies of Paris, not harlots exclusively by profession, but demi-mondaines of the lower bourgeoisie, mingling Cyprian exercises with their daily occupation: the firſt being the Belle Gantière, who sells gloves in her spare time; the second Blanche la Savetière, whose husband (an easy man) cobbles shoes; the third the Gente Saulcissière, goddess of the sausage-shop; the fourth Guillemette la Tapiſſière, who works in tapeſtry; the fifth Jehanneton la Chaperonnière, skilled alike in making hoods and horns; and the sixth Katherine l'Esperonnière, who has a husband (a wittol, I fear) in the spur-making gild. To all these the Belle Heaulmière's warning is brief and praᴄtical: "Gather ye roses while ye may." Now is the time! Take them where you can and spare none, for in a short time, sweethearts, you won't get the chance! No coyness, I beg! You'll wish one day, my dears, you'd had more Business Method.

Such is the giſt of the old lady's homily: a model of clear, brisk, conſtructive commercial theory.

The Ballade to the Daughters of Joy (it is not a very good one) sets Villon meditating on the nature and quiddity of lights-o'-love, and their beginnings; and thence on the nature of women generally and their inclination to toying; and his very reasonable conclusion is that, taken by and large, the love of women is the devil. *Pour ung plaisir mille doulours.* He burſts ſtraight into the sardonic Double Ballade, which is printed later in this book: but having finished, his old wound begins to ache again. I think it is as clear as it can be that the lady must be the same who stabbed his poor heart in 1456. *Ma chiere rose,* on whom a little later in the Testament he turns with a sudden snarl, hurling a well-conceived insult, is obviously a lover's conceit for Katherine de Vausselles. It is plain, as we have seen, that Villon cherished for one woman what is his nearest approach to pure love. His pain on her account is genuine, and his complaint, though dressed in the jargon of the old school of interminable martyrs to Love, obviously nourished on a burning sickness. "If she whom I formerly served," he begins lamentably,

> *Se celle que jadis servoie*
> *De si bon cuer et loyaument,*
> *Dont tant de maulx et griefz j'avoie*
> *Et souffroie tant de torment,*
> *Se dit m'eust, au commencement,*
> *Sa voulenté (mais nennil! las),*
> *J'eusse mis paine aucunement*
> *De moy retraire de ses las.*

[If she whom I formerly served with such faith and so loyally, she for whom I have suffered so many griefs, miseries, and tortures—if she had only told me her will at the beginning (but alas! she did not), I might have done something to free myself from her toils.]

This does not sound like a chagrin for a passing trull. The evidence (as I have said before, but it may be repeated) that Katherine de Vausselles is Villon's enduring torment is very strong. She was socially above the ruck of the poet's loves. She had had him whipped, as he makes plain in the fifth verse of the Double Ballade.

> *De moy, povre, je vueil parler:*
> *J'en fus batu comme a ru toiles,*
> *Tout nu, ja ne le quiers celer.*
> *Qui me feist machier ces groselles,*
> *Fors Katherine de Vausselles?*
> *Noel le tiers est, qui fut la.*
> *Mitaines e ces nopces telles . . .*
> *Bien est eureux qui riens n'y a!*

[I would speak too of myself—poor fool! I was thrashed (on this account) like linen washed in a stream, stark naked—why

278

should I seek to conceal it now? And who made me chew such bitter humiliation but Katherine de Vausselles? Noel was the third person present. Of the thwackings received at such festivities— happy is he who knows them not!]

He had indeed endured at her fair hands (as we have noted) the double indignity promised Panurge on his marriage. If this is indeed the suffering he means, he broods over it for five verses, bitterly remembering his bondage, and how she had led him by the nose with a thousand fooleries; and then with a sudden harsh laugh sends the whole business to the devil.

> *Je regnie Amours et despite*
> *Et deffie a feu et a sang.*
> *Mort par elles me precipite,*
> *Et ne leur en chault pas d'ung blanc.*
> *Ma vïelle ay mys soubz le banc;*
> *Amans je ne suyvray jamais:*
> *Se jadis je fus de leur ranc,*
> *Je desclare que n'en suis mais.*

[I renounce and curse all loves, and defy them, with blood and fire! They send a man to the brink of death, and care not a brass farthing! I've shoved my hurdygurdy under the seat [a minstrel's locution signifying the end of an occupation]; and if I ever walked with lovers or counted myself among them, I hereby swear it will happen no more.]

"I've flung my plume into the wind," he says, swaggering defiantly. "I'm henceforth free to blaspheme love as I please! If any fool wants to know why I do it, let him be content with this: A dying man may speak his mind." For some whimsical reason— perhaps because he is in a black, tearing rage and looking round for something to satisfy it—the Bishop of Orleans comes immediately into his mind, and at once he is off again. The Question Ordinaire presents itself to his memory once more: I can hear him grinding his teeth and snarling.

> *. . . Quant j'en ay memoire,*
> *Je pry pour luy et reliqua,*
> *Que Dieu luy doint, et voire, voire!*
> *Ce que je pense . . . et cetera.*

279

[When I remember these things, I pray for him . . . and the rest of it. May God give him (indeed, by God!) all I think his due . . . et cetera.]

"Not that I wish him ill," he adds, grinning with fury. "Oh, no! Nor his lieutenant either! Nor his Official, who is such a charming helpful character! (Grrrr-rr!) And as for little Master Robert . . . !¹ Lord, I love them all, the whole bunch; as much as God loves a Lombard!" And thinking of the bloodsucking usurers of the Rue des Lombards he emits a harsh chuckle; and is at once off again zigzag on a fresh tack. A thought has just come to him. He will make a new edition of the mocking Testament which he wrote in 1456, and which was such a popular success.

> Si me souvient bien, Dieu mercis,
> Que je feis a mon partement
> Certains laiz, l'an cinquante six,
> Qu'aucuns, sans mon consentement,
> Voulurent nommer Testament;
> Leur plaisir fut et non le mien.
> Mais quoy? on dit communement
> Qu'ung chascun n'est maistre du sien.

[I remember very well (God be praised!) that I composed certain Bequests in the year '56, on going away. Some people have been determined to call this a *Testament,* but without my consent. It was their wish, not mine. But what of that? They say nobody is completely master of his own.]

As we observe, *Testament* is not the title of his own choosing: he had called it *Les Lais.* But the artist bows gracefully to popular clamour. They want to call it a Testament? Very well, then. As they like. If (he adds) there is any one who did not receive the bequest reserved for him in that previous will, let him apply after Villon's death to his heirs, namely Moreau, Provins, and Robin Turgis. Robin Turgis, a large creditor of the poet's, kept the *Pomme de Pin,* as we know. Moreau has been identified with a master-cook, Provins with a master-confectioner both of Paris.² And now, since the drawing up of a more elaborate will and Testament is

¹ Hangman of Orleans.
² There is here, thinks P. Champion, an echo of an unpublished *repue Franche.*

280

necessary, Villon summons his clerk Frémin, who does not exist; and ordering him to take his seat by the bedside, with pens, ink, and paper, takes a deep breath and begins.

It is my intention to pluck from the *Grant Testament* proper, now beginning at verse lxx., under Marot's rubric

Icy commence Villon à tester,

[Here begins Villon to make his Testament.]

what St. François de Sales (but referring to a work of greater piety) calls a posy to sniff at all day long. Of the hundred verses which compose it, leaving aside the Ballades and Rondels with which it is studded, a few are dull and a few obscure and a few trifling. But it contains also verses of tenderness, irony, merriment, anger, and beauty.

He begins, as in the lesser Testament, with the customary invocation of the Blessed Trinity; wandering off thence very curiously for the space of three verses into a disquisition on the state of the souls of the Patriarchs and Prophets in Limbo. "Never," he meditates, "did Hell's flames lick their thighs." And then apologetically:

> *Qui me diroit: "Qui vous fait metre*
> *Si tres avant ceste parolle,*
> *Qui n'estes en theologie maistre?*
> *A vous est presumpcion folle!"*

[Some, no doubt, will say to me: "What is all this? Who made *you* a Doctor in Theology? What is this ridiculous presumption of yours!"]

To this he retorts that Christ Himself has revealed it, in the parable of Dives and Lazarus: and in recalling the condition of Dives his thirsty sympathy is awakened. Lord! The hot place! A bad look-out for bottle-whackers! God's mercy save us from it! He pulls himself up with a jerk, just as he is about to develop this fascinating theme; and with a swift glance at his own condition at present—*plus megre que chimere,* more haggard than a chimera—returns to his subject and resolutely begins the Testament with a second devout preface, commending his soul and writings to God and Our Lady.

281

Ou nom de Dieu, comme j'ay dit,
Et de sa glorieuse Mere,
Sans pechié soit parfait ce dit
Par moy, plus megre que chimere;
Se je n'ey eu fievre enfumere,
Ce m'a fait divine clemence;
Mais d'autre dueil et perte amere
Je me tais, et ainsi commence.

Premier, je donne ma povre ame
A la benoiste Trinité.
Et la commande a Nostre Dame,
Chambre de la divinité,
Priant toute la charité
Des dignes neuf Ordres des cieulx
Que par eulx soit ce don porté
Devant le Trosne precieux.

[In the Name of God, as I have said, and of His glorious Mother, may this be without sin that is written by me, who am more haggard than chimera. If I have not had the diurnal fever [or ague] it is by the Divine clemency. . . . But I will say no more of my other miseries and bitter loss, but keep silence, and so begin:

Firstly, I bequeath my poor soul to the Blessed Trinity and commend it to Our Lady, Chamber of Divinity; praying all the Nine Orders of the sky that of their charity they will convey this gift before the precious Throne.]

There succeeds to this preface immediately a verse full of a sad humour.

Item, mon corps j'ordonne et laisse
A nostre grant mere la terre.
Les vers n'y trouveront grant gresse:
Trop luy a faict faim dure guerre.
Or luy soit delivré grant erre:
De terre vint, en terre tourne.
Toute chose, se par trop n'erre,
Voulentiers en son lieu retourne.

[*Item,* I give and bequeath my body to the Earth, our common Mother. The worms will not find much meat on it, for hunger has bitten it too near the bone already. Let it be delivered as soon as may be: of earth it was made, to earth it returns. Everything, unless I err, goes willingly back to the place whence it came.]

Then follows that verse of sudden affection and remorse dedicated to his guardian, "more than father, more tender than a mother," the good prieſt Guillaume de Villon, chaplain of St. Benoît. And then comes a flash of autobiography. He leaves to Maſter Guillaume de Villon

> ma librairie,
> Et le Rommant du Pet-au-Deable,
> Lequel maiſtre Guy Tabarie
> Grossa, qui eſt homs veritable,
> Par cayers eſt soubz une table;
> Combien qu'il soit rudement fait,
> La matiere eſt si tres notable
> Qu'elle amende tout le mesfait.

[My library, and the Romance of the *Pet-au-Deable*, copied out by Master Guy Tabarie, a man of truth; the manuscript-books lie under the table. Though inelegant, its matter is so notable that it makes up for all defects.]

This Romance recounted in burlesque heroics, doubtless parodying the *Chansons de Geſte*, the great adventure which, as we have seen, so metagrabolised and incornifuſtibulated the University quarter. As for Maſter Tabarie, his skill with the pen did not save him from being sorely beset and bedevilled. The Romance, Villon's firſt known poem, is gone for ever, like the loſt works of Livy, the Sibylline Books, and Panurge's great volume on Braguettes.

Very abruptly then there ſtirs in the poet's mind the thought of his aged mother; and with this comes a rush of remorse again, and tenderness, and a sudden surge of love and devotion to Her, his laſt refuge and his mother's, his Caſtle and Fortress,

> Help of the half-defeated, House of Gold,
> Shrine of the Sword, and Tower of Ivory . . .

And to his mother, as if he were once more kneeling hand-in-hand with her before the compassionate Mother of God, he makes his bequeſt.

> Item, donne a ma povre mere
> Pour saluer Noſtre Maiſtresse
> (Qui pour moy ot douleur amere,
> Dieu le scet, et mainte triſtesse),

Autre chastel n'ay, ne fortresse,
Ou me retraye corps et ame,
Quant sur moy court malle destresse,
Ne ma mere, la povre femme!

[*Item,* I leave to my poor mother—and God knows she has
suffered bitter sorrow through me, and many a grief—[this]—for a
salute to Our Lady: for beyond Her I have no castle nor fortress
where I may hide me body and soul when stark Despair marches
against me . . . nor my mother either, poor soul!]

The verse is left without an objective, and leads directly without pause to the greatest work of this poet, the Ballade made by
Villon, at his mother's request, for a prayer to Our Lady. I have
later in this book transcribed and noted this Ballade,* a cry of fer-
vent religion mixed with filial love. It is as four-square and imperishable as the Faith whence it is drawn.

Almost before the last echoes of the Envoi, like plainsong rolling in the arches of Solesmes, have died away, the love of women
has gripped this poor devil again, and he is stung and smarting
and bitter in his insults: so compact of earth and fire, of aspirations
and lusts, of lovely and gross, is mortal man.[9] "Item," he begins,

Item, m'amour, ma chiere rose—

There is an ugly look on his face. He bequeaths her the thing
she loves more than his heart or liver—a large silk purse full of
crowns, though she has plenty already: let him be hanged who
leaves her any more! And spitting out a bitter *"Orde paillarde!"* he
pours his suffering and humiliation into a Ballade which has been
deemed inferior, but in which I detect the unmistakable genuine
fury of love scorned and raging. I have already considered its mysterious "Marthe" acrostic.

BALLADE

DE VILLON À S'AMYE

Faulse beaulté qui tant me couste chier,
Rude en effect, ypocrite doulceur,
Amour dure plus que fer a maschier,
Nommer que puis, de ma desfaçon seur,

Cherme felon, la mort d'ung povre cuer,
Orgueil mussié qui gens met au mourir,
Yeulx sans pitié, ne veult droit de rigueur,
Sans empirer, ung povre secourir?

Mieulx m'eust value avoir esté serchier
Ailleurs secours: c'eust esté mon onneur;
Riens ne m'eust sceu lors de ce fait hachier.
Trotter m'en fault en fuyte et deshonneur.
Haro, haro, le grant et le mineur!
Et qu'est ce cy? Mourray sans coup ferir?
Ou Pitié veult, selon ceste teneur,
Sans empirer, ung povre secourir?

I

[False, lovely one, that hath cost me so dear; ruthless one, false sweeting, love harder in the mouth than steel, harder than I can say, to my destruction kin; O traitorous charms, death of my poor heart! O scornful pride, driving men to their doom! O pitiless eyes, will rigour not allow her, ere worse betide, to succour one forlorn?

II

Better were it for me to have sought help elsewhere, better for my own pride: nothing would then have wrung this pain from me. But I must fly, in shame and dishonour! Haro! haro! both great and small! But what is this? Shall I, then, die, without a blow? Or will pity move her, ere worse betide, to succour one forlorn?]

It is the slow, grinding, intolerable pain of Catullus in his complaint of Lesbia's treachery.

Caeli, Lesbia nostra, Lesbia illa,
Illa Lesbia, quam Catullus unam
Plus quam se atque suos amavit omnes . . .

A taunt of the third stanza holds a breath of the Renaissance, that contemplation of fresh beauty withering like the flower which moved Ronsard and his companions so strongly.

Vng temps viendra qui fera dessechier,
Jaunir, flestrir vostre espanye fleur;
Je m'en risse, se tant peusse maschier
Lors; mais nennil, ce seroit donc foleur:
Las! viel seray; vous, laide, sans couleur;

285

[A time will come when your flower will be dried-up, yellow, faded: I should laugh then, if I could bear as much—but no, alas! That would be folly. I shall be old, and you too, ugly and colourless.]

And with a desperate attempt at mockery he advises her to drink deep and drown her cruelty.

> Or beuvez fort, tant que ru peut courir;
> Ne donnez pas a tous ceste douleur,
> Sans empirer, ung povre secourir.

[Therefore, drink deep, before the stream runs dry; inflict not this pain on all, ere worse betide, etc.]

Debussy's music has heightened the pain of this Ballade, addressed so bitterly to *ma damoyselle au nez tortu,* my lady of the twisted nose, bought and sold, and yet (curse her) still held in his unhappy heart. It is, moreover, a Ballade of true love, and in its fashion burning and intense; and it begins, as Catullus' quatrain ends, in an insult like a whip-lash across the face.

The first common bequest of the Testament follows immediately, made to the same powerful Master Ythier Marchant to whom in his lesser Testament Villon left his short sword. He now bequeaths Master Ythier a *De Profundis* for all his dead loves, whose names he dare not tell,

> Car il me hairoit a tous jours,

[For he would hate me eternally.]

continuing with that Lay, or Rondel, on the death of a mistress I have already quoted in full. The *Grant Testament* is now fairly launched for thirty verses more. Familiar faces begin to appear. Master Jacques Raguier, the wine-cask we have met before, this time gets the Great Goblet, the famous *Grant Godet* tavern in the Place de Grève, at a strict price of four *plaques,* or coppers, even if he has to sell his breeks and go untrussed and in slippers to the *Pomme de Pin.* Jehan le Loup, the duck-stealer, colleague of Casin Cholet, gets a retriever dog and another long tabard to conceal his night's bag from the Watch. But more dignified figures than these begin to fill the poet's page—the Sire Denys Hesselin, Councillor of Paris and later Provoſt of Merchants, the equivalent of Lord Mayor; the financier, alderman, and councillor Nicolas de Louviers; Jehan Cornu, Criminal Clerk of the Châtelet; Jacques Fournier, Procurator and Member of Parliament; Pierre Basanier, Notary and Clerk of the Châtelet; Pierre de Saint-Amant, Clerk of the Treasury; Jehan Mautaint [9] and Nicolas Rosnel, examiners at the Châtelet; the Procurator Eſtienne Genevois; and a dozen more, including the Provoſt of Paris, Messire Robert d'Eſtouteville himself, for whom was composed that mediocre piece called by Marot *Ballade que Villon donna a ung Gentilhomme nouvellement marié, pour l'envoyer à son Espouse, par luy conquise à l'Espée.* I seleſt the names at random. They may show the free way in which medieval society mingled, subſtantial burgesses and legal personages and municipal officers and rapscallions alike, in the taverns which were the clubs of that age: although probably Villon, as I have said before, did not know half of them, excepting the police and Châtelet officials, personally. Nevertheless his close acquaintance with the Provoſt seems assured (as I have pointed out elsewhere), however embarrassing occasionally to both parties; since Villon, while not mentioning the Provoſt by name, dedicates his epithalamion to

Le seigneur qui sert sainſt Criſtofle.

[The seigneur who serves St. Chriſtopher.]

To know that a King's officer has a special devotion to St. Chriſtopher argues a certain familiarity of access. Much more enigma is the significance of the easy jeſt Villon permits himself in verse clxx. of the *Grant Teſtament* on a very high personage, "the Seneschal," who may be either Louis de Bourbon, Marshal and Seneschal of the Bourbonnais, or Pierre de Brézé, High Seneschal of Normandy.

Item, sera le Seneschal,
Qui une fois paya mes debtes,
En recompence, mareschal
Pour ferrer oes et canettes.

[9] He had been entruſted, with Jehan du Four, with the judicial inquiry in the matter of the burglary of the College of Navarre four years before; which argues a certain coolness in Villon here.

287

Je luy envoie ces sornettes
Pour soy desennuyer; combien,
S'il veult, face en des alumettes:
De bien chanter s'ennuye on bien.

[*Item*, the Seneschal, who once paid all my debts, shall by way of reward be a blacksmith, and shoe geese and ducks. (An international country gibe concerning the simple-minded. Cf. the Sussex jest about the men of Piddinghoe, who shoe magpies and hang ponds out to dry.) To beguile his tedium I send him these frivolities; however, if he likes, let him make spills of 'em. One gets tired of singing—even singing well.]

From the sixth line, hinting that the Seneschal was a prisoner, it might seem that the Norman personage is meant. He was held by the King in the castle of Loches in Touraine at the end of 1461. But the Bourbon, a natural brother of Jean II. of Bourbon, would be the more likely to have settled Villon's debts, since (as we have seen) the poet had some sort of bond with that family, and had lived under their protection. In either case the joke is a daring one, and even in that broad age might have cost the joker dear; for Louis de Bourbon (whom, on reflection, I judge the more likely subject of this verse—he was Seigneur of Roussillon in 1460) married a natural daughter of Louis XI., and in 1466 became Admiral of France and an extremely high personage indeed. If the verse is a careless joke, therefore, it is a dangerous one, and prisons have yawned wide for less. If (as is more likely) the reference to the payment of debts is a fact, then Villon was on such easy terms of acquaintance with the Seneschal that he could risk calling him (in black and white) a thickhead. . . .

Such are the problems one encounters.

I proceed.

To the Sire Denys Hesselin the poet leaves fourteen hogsheads of the wine of Aunis, ordered from Robin Turgis "at my risk"; from which I gather that the municipal dignitary was convivial. To the Prince of Fools, Chief and Master of Revels of the Enfans Sans-Souci, he bequeaths *ung bon sot*, one Michault du Four, a Sergeant of the Châtelet, to be his right-hand fool and mumming-lieutenant: this Michault (he says) has a pretty wit and sings a good song called *Ma doulce amour*.[10] To two of the *Unze Vingtz Sergens* of the Châtelet, his natural enemies, named Denis Richier and Jehan Vallette, *bonnes et doulces gens,* he leaves in mockery a large *cornete,* the band of velvet or silk which elegants at this period wore from their hats, tying the end beneath the chin,

> *Pour pendre a leurs chappeaulx de faultres;*
> *J'entens a ceulx a pié, hohete!*
> *Car je n'ay que faire des autres.*

[To hang from their felt hats. I mean the *foot*-Sergeants, what ho! I've nothing to do with the others.]

To Jehan Rou, a wealthy burgess and Captain of Archers, he leaves six wolves' heads, which can be nothing less than a pleasant reference to his friend Jehan surnamed the Wolf, sooner or later to be seized by the Archers and hacked or hanged: to Perrot Girart, barber at Bourg-la-Reine, two basins and a pipkin, reminding him at the same time of the good trick the poet played on him half a dozen years earlier, when he got a week's lodging and plenty of fat roast pork for nothing. To the Mendicant Friars, the Filles-Dieu, and the Béguines of St. Avoye, for whom he had some affection (since he later desired to be buried in their chapel), and also to those at Orleans, he leaves *grasses souppes jacoppines,* thick soup, according to Prompsault, made with sugar and eggs, served in the Dominican house in the Rue St. Jacques on feast-days, and flawns for their refection. To Friar Baulde, a poet and roaring companion, the reputed author of the *Repues Franches,* a back-slider from the Carmelites, he leaves a sallad, or casque without helm, and two double-edged fighting axes, or *guysarmes.*

There follow oblique references to unlucky adventures with two women: little Macée of Orleans, whom we have met, and a girl of Paris unknown, named Denise, who had summoned him before the ecclesiastical courts for cursing at her.

> *Item, a maistre Jehan Cotart,*
> *Mon procureur en court d'Eglise,*
> *Devoye environ ung patart,*
> *Car a present bien m'en advise,*

[10] Michel du Four also took part in the judicial inquiry into the burglary at the Collège de Navarre.

Quant chicaner me feist Denise,
Dìsant que l'avoye maudite:
Pour son ame, qu'es cieulx soit mise,
Ceste oroison j'ay cy escripte.

[*Item,* to Master Jehan Cotart, my Procurator in the Ecclesiastical Courts, I owe, now I remember it, about one *patart* (a Flemish and Artesian halfpenny) for his services when Denise brought her action against me, swearing I had cursed her. I have here composed this prayer for the good estate of his soul and his admission to Paradise.]

This Master Cotart, his counsel against Denise, is Bottle-Nose, the merry and aged Pantagruelist in whose honour Villon immediately proceeds to draw up the jolly Ballade and Prayer, which appears later in this book. There then returns to him that gust of mocking bitterness on the subject of the three usurers Marceau, Gossouyn, and Laurens, *mes trois povres orphelins,* and he pauses awhile to toy with them. He has heard (he says) that his three dear children are growing up nicely and becoming ripe for education, and he at once busies himself with plans for them. They shall study under Master Pierre Richier; [11] and since the *Donat,* the standard Grammar of Ælius Donatus, is too tough for their tender minds,

Ilz sauront, je l'ayme plus chier,
Ave salus, tibi decus,
Sans plus grans lettres enserchier.

[Let them get by heart (I would much prefer it) the *Ave salus, tibi decus,* and not trouble to seek more learning.]

This conceals gibes of the best, for *Donat* is a jest on *donner,* to give, and in setting them the hymn *Ave salus* to learn Villon is subtly referring to the *saluts* of the gold coinage. More mockery follows:

Cecy estudient, et ho!
Plus proceder je leur deffens.
Quant d'entendre le grant Credo,
Trop fort il est pour telz enfans.

[11] Of the Faculty of Theology, master of an important children's school. He is the only University professor mentioned by name in either Testament.

Mon long tabart en deux je fens;
Si vueil que la moitié s'en vende
Pour leur en acheter des flaons,
Car jeunesse eft ung peu friande.

[Let them study this, what ho! More I forbid them, and as for the great *Credo,* it is too difficult for such children. I tear my long tabard in half for them: let one half of it be sold to buy them flawns; for youth has a sweet tooth.]

The great *Credo,* which children learned in school, here means also long credit, which Villon sarcaftically fears is also too difficult for his three orphans. *Flaons* are both flawns or custard-tarts and also the metal disk from which coins were ftruck in the Mint.[12] He continues with that verse on deportment and good behaviour,

Chaperons auront enformez
Et les poulces sur la sainture,

[Their hoods must be worn well over the head, and their thumbs tucked into their belts,]

which I have already quoted, and which seems a genuine indication of the manners required from children of University in his time; and then passes on to gibe, as in the *Petit Teftament,* at his two *povres clerjons,* Cotin and de Victry, the rich old canons of Notre-Dame, whom he congratulates on their youthful good health and frolicsomeness, at the same time making them a further bequeft:

Les bources des Dix et Huit Clers
Auront; je m'y vueil travaillier.

[They shall have the burses of the Dix-Huit. I will see to this myself.]

The Collège des Dix-Huit, as we have seen, was the earlieft house of University, founded by the Englishman Josse de Londres on his return from the Holy Land. It was demolished in 1639, and its eighteen needy bursars were enabled to live in lodgings on the indemnity until, a century later, they were amalgamated with the

[12] Compare the word "flawn" used in much the same significance by English printers, I believe.
[For the interpretation of these two verses I am indebted to P. Champion.]

Lycée Louis-le-Grand. Villon finally drops his two canons with a "Yah yah!" line reflecting playfully on their parentage.

> Mais, foy que doy festes et veilles,
> Oncques ne vy les meres d'eulx!

[But on my honour, feasts or fasts, I never set eyes on their mothers!]

And so we come to the Ballade made for Messire Robert d'Estouteville, Provost of Paris, on his marriage to the fair Ambroise de Loré, daughter of the Baron d'Ivry. She died in the spring of 1468, carried off, it seems, by the same epidemic which took away Guillaume de Villon: *moult saige & honneste dame,* says a contemporary writer. The Ballade is a dull affair, pedantic, of no inspiration, and must have been one of Villon's earliest student experiments. The initial letters of its first two stanzas yield A-M-B-R-O-I-S-E D-E-L-O-R-E. It is followed, with an interval of two obscure growling verses, by a sudden Ballade of astonishing fire and fury directed against envious tongues; exactly as if some one had privily given the poet a great jab from behind and started him with a leap into the air. May all envious tongues, he bellows, be fried in red arsenic! in yellow arsenic! in saltpetre! in quicklime! in boiling lead! in tallow! in pitch! in aspic's blood! in venomous drugs! in the gall of wolves and foxes! and in half a dozen other tinctures even more displeasing. He continues cursing like one of Macbeth's witches:

> En cervelle de chat qui hayt peschier,
> Noir, et si viel qu'il n'ait dent en gencive,
> D'ung viel mastin, qui vault bien aussi chier
> Tout enragié, en sa bave et salive,
> En l'escume d'une mulle poussive
> Detrenchiee menu a bons ciseaulx,
> En eaue ou ratz plongent groings et museaulx,
> Raines, crappaulx et bestes dangereuses,
> Serpens, lesars et telz nobles oyseaulx,
> Soient frittes ces langues envieuses!

[In the brains of a water-shy black cat, so old that it has not a tooth in its head; in the saliva (which is just as good) of an old mastiff, foaming mad; in the frothings of a broken-winded mule cut

292

up small with good scissors; in water where rats plunge their snouts, and frogs, and toads, and dangerous reptiles, serpents, lizards, and such noble wildfowl—in all this may envious tongues be fried!]

The reason for the outburst we have detected before: it concerns one François Perdryer and a piece of treachery at Bourges. Villon repeats the form, the Enumerative-Vituperative, in two other pieces, the *Ballade Joyeuse des Taverniers* (sparingly attributed to him; but it could be by nobody else) against adulterating innkeepers, and the more scholarly and intensely patriotic Ballade against the Enemies of France. Both are much neglected; I cannot for the life of me tell why, for they are both good. I will give first the jolly Rabelaisian tirade against the Taverners.

BALLADE JOYEUSE

DES TAVERNIERS

D'ung geçt de dart, d'une lance asseree,
D'ung grant faussart, d'une grosse massue,
D'une guisarme, d'une fleche ferree,
D'ung bracquemart, d'une hache esmolue,
D'ung grand penart et d'une bisagüe,
D'ung fort espieu et d'une saqueboute;
De mau-brigands puissent trouver tel route,
Que tous leurs corps fussent mis par monceaulx,
Le cueur fendu, desciré par morceaulx,
Le col couppé d'ung bon branc achierin,
Et voisent drus aux Stygiens caveaux
Les taverniers qui brouillent noştre vin!

D'ung arc turcquois, d'une espee affilee,
Ayent les paillars la brouaille fondue,
De feu gregoys la perrucque bruslee,
Et par tempeşte la cervelle espandue,
Au grant gibet leur charongne pendue,
Et briefvement puissent mourir de goutte;
Ou je requiers et pry que l'on leur boute
Parmy leur corps force d'ardans barreaulx;
Vifs escorchez des mains de dix bourreaulx,
Et puis bouillir en huille le matin,
Desmembrez soient a quatre grans chevaulx
Les taverniers qui brouillent noştre vin!

D'un gros canon la teste escarbouillee,
Et de tonnerre acablez en la rue
Soient tous leurs corps, et leur chair despouillee,
De gros mastins bien garnye et pourvue;
De fortz esclers puissent perdre la veue;
Neige et gresil tousjours sur eux degoutte,
Avecques ce, ilz aient la pluye toute,
Sans que sur eux ayent robbes ne manteaulx;
Leurs corps trenchez de dagues et couteaulx,
Et puis traisnez jusques en l'eau du Rhin;
Desrompuz soient a quatre-vingts marteaulx
Les taverniers qui brouillent nostre vin!

ENVOY

Prince, de Dieu soient mauditz leurs boyaulx,
Et crever puissent par force de venin
Ces faulx larrons, maulditz et desloyaulx,
Les taverniers qui brouillent nostre vin!

[By the stroke of dart, by sharpened spear; by the swipe of a huge multi-bladed halbert, by a thump from an enormous club; by a battle-axe with two heads, by a steel arrow; by a double-handed sword, by a well-ground axe; by a great dagger-thrust, by a two-edged tuck; by a strong snicker, by a crook-headed lance, by howling brigands in their road, may their bodies be hacked to bits, their hearts cloven and torn to rags, their necks severed by a good steel broadsword, and they dragged to the Stygian caverns—the taverners who hocus our good wine!

May the swabs have their giblets tickled with a Turkish arrow and a sharp sword; may Greek fire scorch their thatch and a great tempest scatter their brains; may their carrion bodies hang from the high gibbet, and may they die very swiftly of the gout; I demand and pray also that they be prodded with red-hot iron bars and flayed alive by ten hangmen, boiled in oil in the morning and torn apart by four ramping great horses: the taverners who hocus our good wine!

May a great cannon-ball bash their heads, may they be struck by thunder in the street and may their flesh be gnawed by great hungry dogs; may huge flashes of lightning blind them, snow and hail beat on them perpetually, and with this pouring rain, and they without gown or cape; may their bodies be slashed with daggers and knives and dragged as far as the river of Rhine, may they be whanged to pieces by eighty great hammers—the taverners who hocus our good wine!

Prince, may God curse their bowels, may they burst asunder with the swelling of their own venom—these traitor thieves, accursed and forsworn: the taverners who hocus our good wine!]

I have given this splendid Ballade in full because it is man-verse, strong, muscled, knotty, red-blooded, roaring, and vigorous, meet to be recited in an age in which few poets have the guts to curse. The Ballade against the Enemies of France is also worth meditating.

BALLADE

CONTRE LES ENNEMIS DE LA FRANCE

[B. pour France.]

Recontré soit de bestes feu getans,
Que Jason vit, querant la toison d'or;
Ou transmué d'homme en beste sept ans,
Ainsi que fut Nabugodonosor;
Ou perte il ait et guerre aussi villaine
Que les Troyens pour la prinse d'Helaine;
Ou avallé soit avec Tantalus
Et Proserpine aux infernaulx palus; [13]
Ou plus que Job soit en griefve souffrance,
Tenant prison en la tour Dedalus,
Qui mal vouldroit au royaulme de France!

Quatre mois soit en ung vivier chantans,
La teste au fons, ainsi que le butor;
Ou au Grant Turc vendu deniers contans,
Pour estre mis au harnois comme ung tor;
Ou trente ans soit, comme la Magdalaine,
Sans drap vestir de linge ne de laine;
Ou soit noyé comme fut Narcisus,
Ou aux cheveulx, comme Absalon, pendus
Ou, comme fut Judas, par Desperance;
Ou puist perir comme Simon Magus,
Qui mal vouldroit au royaulme de France!

D'Octovien puist revenir le tems:
C'est qu'on luy coule au ventre son tresor;
Ou qu'il soit mis entre meules flotans
En ung moulin, comme fut saint Victor;

[13] Note the infernaulx palus of the Ballade to Our Lady.

Ou transglouty en la mer, sans aleine,
Pis que Jonas au corps de la baleine;
Ou soit banny de la clarté Phebus,
Des biens Juno et du soulas Venus,
Et du dieu Mars soit pugny a oultrance,
Ainsy que fut roy Sardanapalus,
Qui mal vouldroit au royaulme de France!

ENVOY

Prince, porté soit des serfs Eolus
En la forest ou domine Glaucus;
Ou privé soit de paix et d'esperance:
Car digne n'est de posseder vertus
Qui mal vouldroit au royaulme de France!

[May he encounter the monsters belching fire that Jason met when he sought the Fleece of Gold; or be changed for seven years from a man into a beast, like Nabuchodonosor; may he suffer such heavy loss and warfare as the Trojan suffered for the rape of Helen; may he be swallowed alive with Tantalus and Proserpine in the infernal marshes; may he have more dolours than Job, and be imprisoned in the Labyrinth like Dædalus, who would wish evil to the Realm of France!

May he howl for four months head downwards in a fishpond, like a bittern; may he be sold to the Grand Turk for money down and be harnessed like a steer; or may he live for thirty years, like the Magdalen, without a scrap of cloth, linen or wool, to cover him; may he drown like Narcissus, or hang, like Absolon, by his hair, or, like Judas, in despair: may he perish as did Simon Magus, who would wish evil to the Realm of France!

May the time of Octavian return, and may molten coin be poured into his belly; or may he be crushed between moving mill-stones in a mill, as was Saint Victor; or drowned deep in the sea, breathless, in worse plight than Jonas in the body of the whale; may he be driven from the light of the sun, from the treasures of Juno, and from the joys of Venus, and from the War-God receive his extreme doom (as did King Sardanapalus), who would wish evil to the Realm of France!

"Prince, may the bright-winged brood of Æolus
To sea-king Glaucus' wild wood cavernous
Bear him, bereft of peace and hope's least glance;
For worthless is he to get good of us,
Who could wish evil to the State of France!"]

—SWINBURNE.

296

The *Grant Testament* continues.

We are now directly upon a Ballade called *Les Contredictz de Franc Gontier,* a vindication of the Town against the Country, and of good living against the simple life. A popular poem called *Les Dictz de Franc Gontier* had been published a century before by Philippe de Vitry, later Bishop of Meaux: an artificial pastoral, the idyll of a Philemon and Baucis living on fair spring water, crusts, an onion or two, and the songs of birds, happy in sylvan poverty and innocence. It had already provoked a *Contredictz* by Pierre d'Ailly, Chancellor of University under Charles VI. Villon's reply is of a different sort. He calls up (licking his hungry envious lips meanwhile) the vision of a stout canon by the fireside in his well-matted chamber, with an allegorical lady by his side, Dame Sydoine, personifying Luxury.[14] The poet peeps through a crack and sees how sweetly they live:

BALLADE

DES CONTREDICTZ DE FRANC GONTIER

> *Sur mol duvet assis, ung gras chanoine,*
> *Les ung brasier, en chambre bien natee,*
> *A son costé gisant dame Sydoine,*
> *Blanche, tendre, polie, et attintee,*
> *Boire ypocras, a jour et a nuytee,*
> *Rire, jouer, mignonner, et baisier . . .*

[On a downy couch by a brasier, in a soft-matted room, I saw a fat canon seated, with Dame Sydoine at his side, so white, so soft, so sweet, so prettily decked, drinking Hypocras night and day, laughing, sporting, toying, kissing . . .]

and bursts out triumphantly with his refrain

> *Lors je cogneus que pour dueil appaisier*
> *Il n'est tresor qui de vivre a son aise!*

[Then I knew that to comfort one's sorrow there is no treasure but to live at one's ease.]

Pooh, he cries. Where are your Franc Gontier and his Helaine now, with their Arcadian nonsense, their dry crusts and water, and

---

[14] *Sydoine,* from Sidon.

their onions making their breath stink? As for the birds they keep such a stir about, why,

> *Tous les oyseaulx d'icy en Babiloine*
> *A tel escot une seule journee*
> *Ne me tendroient, non une matinee,*

—all the birds from here to Babylon could not keep me on such a diet for one day, for one single morning! "For God's sake," he says contemptuously,

> *Or s'esbate, de par Dieu, Franc Gontier,*
> *Helaine o luy, soubz le bel esglantier:*
> *Se bien leur est, cause n'ay qu'il me poise;*
> *Mais, quoy que soit du laboureux mestier,*
> *Il n'est tresor que de vivre a son aise.*

[In God's name, let Franc Gontier and his Helen get on with their idyll under the hawthorn, if it suits them. It is no affair of mine. But whatever they say about the Simple Life, there's no treasure but to live at one's ease.]

Here is the scorn of your native town-bird, and in it Villon joins hands down the ages with Johnson, and Lamb, and that honest Baronet in Boswell who preferred the smell of a flambeau at the playhouse to the fragrance of a May evening in the country.

The next Ballade following is the celebrated one of the Women of Paris, to which Debussy has put such gay cynical music. In it Villon reviews (but mostly from hearsay or imagination, for he was no traveller) the chatter-capacity of all the women of Europe. It begins:

BALLADE

DES FEMMES DE PARIS

> *Quoy qu'on tient belles langagieres*
> *Florentines, Veniciennes,*
> *Assez pour estre messagieres,*
> *Et mesmement les anciennes;*
> *Mais, soient Lombardes, Rommaines,*
> *Genevoises, a mes perilz,*
> *Pimontoises, Savoisiennes,*
> *Il n'est bon bec que de Paris.*

[Though some may esteem the women of Florence and the Venetians good talkers—enough to carry on intrigues anyway—and the ancients also, I swear at my peril, whoever they be, Lombards or Romans, Genevese, of Piedmont or of Savoy, there's no tongue like a Paris tongue!]

The second stanza runs appraisingly over the Neapolitans, Germans, Prussians (all good cacklers), Greeks, Egyptians, Hungarians, Spaniards, and Castilians; but returns to the proud refrain: There are no chatterers like the girls of Paris.

> De tres beau parler tiennent chaieres,
> Ce dit on, les Neapolitaines,
> Et sont tres bonnes caquetieres
> Allemandes et Pruciennes;
> Soient Grecques, Egipciennes,
> De Hongrie ou d'autre pays,
> Espaignolles ou Cathelennes,
> Il n'est bon bec que de Paris.

The third trips along with a chuckle:

> Brettes, Suysses, n'y sçavent guieres,
> Gasconnes, n'aussi Toulousaines:
> De Petit Pont deux harengieres
> Les concluront, et les Lorraines,
> Engloises et Calaisiennes
> (Ay je beaucoup de lieux compris?),
> Picardes de Valenciennes;
> Il n'est bon bec que de Paris.

[The Bretons and Swiss know nothing about it, nor the Gascons, nor the girls of Toulouse—why, a couple of fishwives on the Petit-Pont could shut them all up! and the Lorraines too, and the English, the women of Calais (is this enough for you?) and the Picards of Valenciennes . . . ! There's no tongue like a Paris tongue.]

And the Envoi, which Debussy ends in such a shout of laughter:

> Prince, aux dames Parisiennes
> De beau parler donne le pris;
> Quoy qu'on die d'Italiennes,
> Il n'est bon bec que de Paris.

299

[Prince, award the prize for sweet chatter to the ladies of
Paris. Whatever they may say of the Italians—there's no tongue,]
etc.

"Come, observe me the dear creatures, I pray you," goes on
Villon mischievously, "sitting by twos and threes in the churches
and whispering together so busily."

> Regarde m'en deux, trois, assises
> Sur le bas du ply de leurs robes,
> En ces mousĦiers, en ces eglises;
> Tire toy pres, et ne te hobes;
> Tu trouveras la que Macrobes
> Oncques ne fiĦ tels jugemens.
> Entens; quelque chose en desrobes:
> Ce sont tous beaulx enseignemens,

[Look at them, I beg, seated by twos and threes, on the hem
of their gowns, in minĦters and churches. Draw a little nearer, but
make no stir. You will hear such judgments as Macrobius never
delivered. LiĦten! You catch something? It is well worth learning.]

—another of those little separate glowing miniatures, evoking the
very life of his age, which Villon sets here and there so miraculously into his work. One sees the hoods wagging together under
the fretted Gothic vault and the flaming vitrails. One hears the
flying sibilants. One sees the grinning poet retreating on tiptoe,
and the offended gossips deĦtroying him with a glance. It is as vivid
as yeĦterday.

It now becomes necessary to face the Ballade of Fat Margot,
which has brought so many blushes to so many editors' virginal
cheeks, and which Swinburne has translated entire. Stevenson calls
it grimy, which is fairly descriptive. GaĦton Paris thinks Villon
wrote and preserved it out of bravado, and that its scabrous display
is purely literary. I have no theories about this. It obviously exhales a sort of despair and echoes a cry out of Hell, contradiĦting
its swagger. It is a personal and authentic document, and is pre-
luded by a mocking dedication:

300

Item, a la Grosse Margot,
Tres doulce face et pourtraicture.
Foy que doy brulare bigod,
Assez devote creature;
Je l'aime de propre nature,
Et elle moy, la doulce sade:
Qui la trouvera d'aventure,
Qu'on luy lise ceste ballade.

[*Item,* to fat Margot of the sweet phiz—and by my faith, and by God, a charming creature! I love her for nature's sake, and so does she me, the dear sweet thing. Let any one who may encounter her by chance read her the following Ballade.]

Brulare Bigod is a relic of the English occupation. *"En angloys,"* says Clément Marot, explaining it, *'par Dieu et Nostre Dame'* ": but I think he rather elaborates one of the two plain English oaths by virtue of which, in St. Joan's time, we were known all over France as the Bigods and the Goddams. However, to the Ballade, which begins defiantly:

BALLADE

DE LA GROSSE MARGOT

Se j'ayme et sers la belle de bon hait,
M'en devez vous tenir ne vil ne sot?
Elle a en soy des biens a fin souhait.
Pour son amour sains bouclier et passot;
Quant viennent gens, je cours et happe ung pot,
Au vin m'en fuis, sans demener grant bruit;
Je leur tens eaue, frommage, pain et fruit.
S'ilz paient bien, je leur dis: "Bene stat;
Retournez cy, quant vous serez en ruit,
En ce bordeau ou tenons nostre estat!"

[If I love and serve my beauty with good heart, should you thereby take me for a fool or knave? She has in herself all the charms one could desire, and for her sweet sake I gird on sword and buckler. When folk arrive, I run and get a pot and go for wine, without too much noise; I serve them water, cheese, bread, and fruit; and if they are good payers I say to them: "Excellent! Come back here when you feel like sport, to this brothel where we drive our trade."]

It is pure Hogarth. It describes, baldly and without gloss, the daily life of Villon in Fat Margot's house, his running to and fro, serving clients with wine and food, and taking the money; the quarrels and blows and oaths when the house closes and he and Fat Margot count the takings; and finally, the going heavily to bed, both drunk and one amorous—not the poet.

> Mais adoncques il y a grant deshait,
> Quant sans argent s'en vient couchier Margot;
> Veoir ne la puis, mon cuer a mort la hait,
> Sa robe prens, demy saint et surcot,
> Si luy jure qu'il tendra pour l'escot.
> Par les costés se prent cest Antecrist,
> Crie, et jure par la mort Jhesucrist
> Que non fera. Lors j'empongne ung esclat;
> Dessus son nez luy en fais ung escript,
> En ce bordeau ou tenons nostre estat.

[But then there is great unpleasantness when Margot comes to bed without the money. I cannot bear the sight of her; I hate her like death. I snatch her gown, her petticoat and surcoat, swearing I will take them to pay the scot. Then this Antichrist, arms akimbo, screams and swears by the death of Christ that she won't let me. Upon which I punch her on the nose and leave my signature there, in this brothel where we drive our trade.]

> Puis paix se fait, et me lasche ung gros pet,
> Plus enflee qu'ung vlimeux escarbot.
> Riant m'assiet son poing sur mon sommet,
> Gogo me dit, et me fiert le jambot;
> Tous deux yvres, dormons comme ung sabot.
> Et au resveil, quant le ventre luy bruit,
> Monte sur moy, que ne gaste son fruit.
> Souz elle geins, plus qu'un aiz me fait plat;
> De paillarder tout elle me destruit,
> En ce bordeau ou tenons nostre estat.

The Envoi (which bears Villon's acrostic, so that there can be no dispute over the authorship of this well-etched piece of work) sums up the position with a shrug in which are mingled shame, defiance, self-loathing, and fatalism.

302

Vente, gresle, gelle, j'ay mon pain cuit.
Ie suis paillart, la paillarde me suit.
Lequel vault mieulx? Chascun bien s'entresuit.
L'ung vault l'autre; c'est a mau rat mau chat.
Ordure amons, ordure nous assuit;
Nous deffuyons onneur, il nous deffuit,
En ce bordeau ou tenons nostre estat.

[Wind, hail, or frost, my bread is baked. I am a lecher, and my whore dogs me. Which of us is the better? We are two of a kind, and equally worth. Bad cat, bad rat. We love the dregs, and the dregs pursue us. We fly honour, and honour flies from us, in this brothel where we drive our trade.]

It is not pretty, but it is very frank. I esteem it higher of its kind than the peep-bo indecencies of the Reverend Laurence Sterne; and it is a good thing no Bowdler has ever cast it out of the editions of Villon's poems, for it is valuable and consoling to see human sinners in the round, and not posing with their best side to the footlights. The Ballade is followed by a *huitain* giving a licence (on the poet's behalf) to one Marion l'Ydolle—her name was Marion Dentu, *dite* l'Idole, and her house was in the Rue des Quatre Filz Aymon, near the Temple—and the tall Jehanne de Bretaigne to open a school for their trade, which flourishes everywhere except (perhaps) in the prison of Meun: from which it is to be conjectured that there had been words between the ladies and the poet. The next verse is personal and vindictive.

Item, et a Noel Jolis,
Autre chose je ne luy donne
Fors plain poing d'osiers frez cueillis
En mon jardin; je l'abandonne.
Chastoy est une belle aulmosne,
Ame n'en doit estre marry:
Unze vings coups luy en ordonne
Livrez par la main de Henry.

[*Item,* to Noël Jolis I leave nothing but a full handful of withies fresh plucked from my garden, and so abandon him. Correction is a good gift, and nobody should mind that! . . . I order him two hundred and twenty strokes, at the hands of Henry.] [15]

[15] P. Champion observes that Henry Cousin, appointed Executioner in 1460, was employed as a whipping Sergeant in 1457. He thinks therefore that Villon's thrashing might possibly have been judicial, and the reward for insulting Katherine de Vausselles publicly.

Henry is the Executioner of Paris, Master Henry Cousin. The severe whipping ordered by the poet for Noël Jolis at his hands brings us back again to Katherine de Vausselles, for it was probably by Noël's hands that Villon was so thrashed and despitefully used, at her orders; and it was Noël, without doubt, who supplanted him.

A hatful of minor bequests scattered up and down the Testament, and variously comic, snarling, or quaint, may be summarily dealt with all together here and dismissed. Villon leaves to the wife of Master Pierre Saint-Amant of the Treasury, the *Mare* and the *Red Ass,* to go with the *White Horse* and the *Mule* left to her husband in the *Petit Testament,* since she took him for a beggar; to his advocate Master Guillaume Charruau a sword; to Masters Merebeuf and de Louvieux a licence to hunt game in the celebrated *rostisserie* of Mother Machecoue, by the Châtelet; to Sergeant Jehan Raguier, of the Provost's bodyguard, a *tallemouse* (which is a cheese tart and also a popular locution for a bang in the eye) and, for drink, the water of the Fontaine Maubuée, which still stands off the Rue St. Martin, though they reconstructed it in 1733; to Perrenet Marchant, Bastard de la Barre, Villon's messenger to Katherine, three cogged dice for his coat-of-arms, and a pack of doctored cards; to Casin Cholet the duck-stealer a Lyons sword, in place of his cooper's mallet; to Jehan Mahé, called *l'Orfevre de Bois* (he was a Sergeant and Assistant Questioner at the Châtelet), a hundred sticks of Oriental ginger, for his own lascivious purposes; to Master Robinet Trascaille, a Royal secretary, the poet's platter, which he was afraid to borrow; to the Chancellor of the Diocese of Paris, his seal, freshly spat upon: to Master François de la Vacquerie, procurator to the Officiality,

> *Ung hault gorgerin d'Escossoys,*
> *Toutesfois sans orfaverie,*

—a Scots collaret, that is, a hemp necklace, without embroidery, to hang himself; to Master Jehan Laurens, one of Tabarie's judges, and also a procurator, the lining of the poet's bags to wipe his poor red eyes, so inflamed through his parents' devotion to the barrel:

Item, a maiſtre Jehan Laurens,
Qui a les povres yeulx si rouges
Par le pechié de ses parens
Qui burent en barilz et courges,
Je donne l'envers de mes bouges
Pour tous les matins les torchier:
S'il fuſt arcevesque de Bourges,
Du sendail euſt, mais il eſt chier

[*Item,* to Maſter Jehan Laurens, whose poor eyes are so red, through the sin of his parents in drinking from barrels and gourds, I give the linings of my bags to wipe them every morning. Had he been Archbishop of Bourges he might have had silk, but it is dear.]

—if he had been Archbishop of Bourges he might have had silk, but it coſts too much.[16]

To the Alderman Michault Cul d'Oue and to Messire Chalot Taranne, rich burgesses, a hundred sols falling like manna, and the teſtator's shoes of tawny leather, provided they salute a certain Jehanne (and another of her kind) on Villon's behalf; to the Seigneur de Grigny, who got Nijon and Biceſtre before, the Tower of Billy, another haunt of rogues; to Maſter Andry Courault of the Treasury, the *Contredictz Franc Gontier;* to Mademoiselle de Bruyères, the dowager of the *Pet-au-Deable,* and to her damsels, a licence to preach to the wantons of Paris, but not in the cemeteries —which were often, as we know, places of gallantry at night,

Item, pour ce que scet sa Bible
Ma damoyselle de Bruyeres,
Donne preschier hors l'Evangile
A elle et a ses bachelieres
Pour retraire ces villotieres
Qui ont le bec si affilé,
Mais que ce soit hors cymetieres,
Trop bien au Marchié au filé.

[*Item,* since Mademoiselle de Bruyères knows her Bible, I licence her to preach (except the Gospel), herself and her damsels, to reform these town-mopsies, who are so sharp of tongue. But let it be outside the cemeteries, and beſt of all in the String Market.]

[16] There may be here an echo of the myſterious *recommandation* at Bourges, discussed earlier in this book.

To the sick lying in the Hostel-Dieu, all the table-scraps of Paris, and the bones of the goose bequeathed already to the Mendicants; to his barber Colin Galerne, a churchwarden of St. Germainle-Vieux in the Cité, a lump of ice to be applied to his stomach; to the hill of Montmartre, with its great abbey of nuns, the Mont Valérien over against it across Paris; to the *Enfans Trouves,* the Foundling Hospital of Paris, a dependency of Notre-Dame, nothing at all; but to the *Enfans Perduz* the warning (*"Belle Leçon"*) which follows; to Master Jacquet Cardon, merchant draper, the poet's song beginning *"Au retour de dure prison,"* which (he says) may go bravely either to the popular Paris tune of *"Marionette,"* made formerly for Marion la Peautarde, or else the tune of *"Ouvrez vostre huys, Guillemette"*:

> *Item, riens a Jaquet Cardon,*
> *Car je n'ay riens pour luy d'honneste,*
> *Non pas que le gette habandon,*
> *Sinon ceste bergeronnette;*
> *S'elle eust le chant* Marionnette
> *Fait pour Marion la Peautarde,*
> *Ou d'*Ouvrez vostre huys, Guillemette,
> *Elle allast bien a la moustarde.*

[*Item,* nothing to Jaques Cardon, for I have no decent gift to give him—not that he would throw it away—save this song; if it were set to the tune of "Marionnette," made for Marion la Peautarde, or the tune of "Open your door, Guillemette," it would go excellently.]

(It is that desperate melancholy Rondeau praying for peace, which I have set in another place.)

To Master Lomer, an official of Notre-Dame, Villon leaves the power of being well loved by women without losing his head, and with this, a gift of extreme practical value in such a case. In this instance at least it is possible to understand Villon's joke, for the Capitular Registers of Notre-Dame record that Master Pierre Lomer d'Airaines was in 1456 given the necessary powers and ordered to clear women of ill repute out of the Cité. To Master Jacques James (subsequently one of Villon's appointed executors), *qui se tue d'amasser biens*—he was apparently a notorious money-grubber—is bequeathed a licence to become betrothed as often as he likes, but not to marry; and to one Chappelain the testator's simple-tonsure chapel, a tiny benefice in the gift of University, undoubtedly mythical, with the obligation of saying one dry Mass (that is, without consecration), and no cure of souls.

To these other jests there is now no satisfactory key. They have their place nevertheless in the pattern of this Parisian tapestry.

I continue the Testament at the poem of three *huitains* called by Marot *Belle Leçon de Villon aux Enfans Perduz,* Villon's Good Warning to the Good-for-Noughts. In it there rings a soberer mood. It was written obviously in a cloud of depression and foreboding. From its definite warning to the *enfans perduz* to be wary when in the vicinity of Montpipeau or Rueil, on the road to St. Germain-en-Laye—

> "Beaulx enfans, vous perdez la plus
> Belle rose de vo chappeau;
> Mes clers pres prenans comme glus,
> Se vous allez a Montpipeau
> Ou a Rueil, gardez la peau:
> Car, pour s'esbatre en ces deux lieux,
> Cuidant que vaulsist le rappeau,
> Le perdit Colin de Cayeulx.

> "Ce n'est pas ung jeu de trois mailles,
> Ou va corps, et peut estre l'ame.
> Qui pert, riens n'y sont repentailles
> Qu'on n'en meure a honte et diffame;
> Et qui gaigne n'a pas a femme
> Dido la royne de Cartage.
> L'homme est donc bien fol et infame
> Qui, pour si peu, couche tel gage.

> "Qu'ung chascun encore m'escoutel
> On dit, et il est vérité,
> Que charretee se boit toute,
> Au feu l'yver, au bois l'esté:
> S'argent avez, il n'est enté,
> Mais le despendez tost et viste.
> Qui en voyez vous herité?
> Jamais mal acquest ne prouffite"

307

["My sweet lads, you are losing the fairest rose that adorns your hats—you, my clerks, who stick to what you take like bird-lime. If you go to Montpipeau or to Rueil, look out for your skins! It was for a frolic in those parts that Colin des Cayeulx (thinking it worth the appeal) lost his.

"It is no trifling game [*maille*: a copper farthing] in which you stake body and probably soul: the loser's remorse avails him nothing, nor saves him from a shameful death. Even the winner does not receive a Dido, Queen of Carthage, for his reward. How foolish and lewd, then, is the man who risks so much to gain so little!

"Listen, all of you! They say—and it is true—that a cartload [of wine] is soon drunk out, by the fire in winter or in the woods in summer. Have you money? It does not last: you fling it away soon and swiftly. What is the advantage, then? Ill-gotten gain profits no one."]

—it may have been composed soon after the last frolic of des Cayeulx, which from the hint in the second and third stanzas I judge to have been highway robbery, alleviated with rape and a booty of wine-casks. It is without poetical merit; like most warnings.

Following the *Belle Leçon* comes the Ballade of Good Counsel to those of Naughty Life,[17] which I have transcribed elsewhere, with its shrugging refrain,

Tout aux tavernes et aux filles.

As Villon recited it in some riverside tavern, with one arm round the neck of Jehanneton and the other flourishing in the air, it must have been greeted with peals of laughter from the trulls and night-birds there assembled. But in writing it down he is in gloomy earnest. "It's to you I address this, my jovial boys, my frolicking friends," he goes on.

> *"A vous parle, compaigns de galle:*
> *Mal des ames et bien du corps,*
> *Gardez vous tous de ce mau hasle*
> *Qui noircist les gens quant sont mors;*
> *Eschevez le, c'est ung mal mors;*
> *Passez vous au mieulx que pourrez;*
> *Et, pour Dieu, soiez tous recors*
> *Qu'une fois viendra que mourrez."*

17 See p. 312.

["It is to you I speak, companions of my pleasures, with your lusty bodies and your sick souls! Beware, all of you, of that ill sun which blackens a man when he is dead! Flee from it. It's a foul death! Escape it, as well as you can: and for God's sake remember, all of you, that the time will come when you must die."]

He ends, and being recent, as is obvious, from moody loitering in the Innocents cemetery, his old obsession returns. He bequeaths, with a dark ironical look, his great spectacles to the Quinze-Vingts, the hospital for three hundred blind near the Louvre, founded by St. Louis,

> Sans les estuys, mes grans lunettes,
> Pour mettre a part, aux Innocens,[18]
> Les gens de bien des deshonnestes.

[My great spectacles, without the case; in order that they may set apart, in the Innocents, the good from the wicked.]

And in a wide sweep of the arm he embraces the vast cemetery, sleeping under a pallid moon.

> Icy n'y a ne ris ne jeu.
> Que leur valut avoir chevances,
> N'en grans lis de parement jeu,
> Engloutir vins en grosses pances,
> Mener joye, festes et dances,
> Et de ce prest estre a toute heure?
> Toutes faillent telles plaisances,
> Et la coulpe si en demeure.

[Here there is no laughter, nor any jest: what does it profit these to have enjoyed fortune, to have lain in rich beds of honour, to have drunk their fill of wine, to have revelled, and feasted, and danced, ready for pleasure at every hour? All joys like these dissolve; only the guilt remains.]

The end of the Testament is announced, as by the distant toll of a passing-bell. The ensuing broodings over the piled bones in the Innocents *charniers* I have already quoted. A verse in behalf of all Courts, Regents, and Judges follows, praying God and Saint Dom-

[18] Lacroix recalls, in connection with this reference to the Quinze-Vingts, a curious ancient tradition that they were bound by the foundation of their hostel to furnish a certain number of mourners for burial ceremonies in the Innocents.

inic to absolve them at their death: recollected melancholy is the dominant and growing note of the Testament from now to the end.

To Master Jehan de Calays, Notary to the Châtelet and a wealthy burgess, who has not seen him for thirty years (so he says), Villon leaves the whole *Grant Testament*. It would not seem to be a careless or satiric bequest. Jehan de Calays was a man of some letters, a poet,[19] and the presumed compiler of the anthology of contemporary poems called *Le Jardin de Plaisance,* in which were included nine Ballades and a Rondeau of Villon; who now awards Master Jehan a plenary faculty

> *De le gloser et commenter,*
> *De le diffinir et descripre,*
> *Diminuer ou augmenter,*
> *De le canceller et prescripre*
> *De sa main et, ne sceut escripre,*
> *Interpreter et donner sens,*
> *A son plaisir, meilleur ou pire:*
> *A tout cecy je m'y consens.*

[To gloss and to annotate, to explain and set in order, to diminish or add to it, to cancel or transcribe with his own hand, and, if he cannot write, to interpret or expand, at his own pleasure, for better or worse: to all this I give my consent.]

Observe, in the preceding verse, a faint indication—

> *Et ne scet comment je me nomme*

[And he does not know my name.]

—that the poet had assumed the name of Villon very early: if indeed this line has any significance at all.

And so we come to the winding-up, to the sad, exquisite verses beginning *Item, j'ordonne a Sainte Avoye.*[20] Like Browning's dying bishop, Villon orders his sepulchre with preoccupied care and

---

[19] He figures in Longnon's papers of the English occupation. He was implicated in a plot of 1435 to throw the English out of Paris, and saved his neck only by paying an enormous fine. Charles VII. made him an alderman. The first printed copy of the *Jardin de Plaisance* appeared towards 1501.

P. Champion thinks it doubtful if this notary, whose duty was to verify wills (and hence the bequest), can be the personage of the *Jardin.*

[20] See p. 381.

in detail. He is to be laid in the chapel of the Bonnes-Femmes or Béguines of St. Avoye, in the Rue du Temple: a community of widows living under the Augustinian Rule, serving a hospital attached to their house. The sisters' chapel, the only one in Paris of its kind, was on the first floor; and so the poet, *narquois* to the last, makes his wry jest.

> De tombel? riens: je n'en ay cure,
> Car il greveroit le planchier.

[My tomb? None at all. It doesn't matter. It would only overload the floor.]

Above the place of his interment, he directs, there is to be drawn his image or portrait in ink—if that is not too costly: and around it there is to be written his Epitaph, in reasonably large letters. This, for lack of ink, may be scratched on the wall with a piece of coal or charcoal,

> Sans en riens entamer le plastre;
> Au moins sera de moy memoire
> Telle qu'elle est d'ung bon follastre.

[Without in any way breaking the plaster. Thus there will at least remain of me a memory, as of a good crack-brained madcap.]

To this succeeds the melancholy, sardonic Epitaph, which may be read in its proper place, and the lovely Rondeau following. The poet's sad fancy runs on then for a space, appointing his executors and ordering the tolling at his funeral of the Great Bell, the Beffroi of Notre-Dame de Paris, which Jehan de Montaigu presented to the Metropolitan in 1400, and which gave tongue only at solemnities or in alarms.

> Item, je vueil qu'on sonne a bransle
> Le gros beffroy, qui n'est de voirre;
> Combien qu'il n'est cuer qui ne tremble,
> Quant de sonner est a son erre.
> Saulvé a mainte bonne terre,
> Le temps passé, chascun le scet:
> Fussent gens d'armes ou tonnerre,
> Au son de luy, tout mal cessoit.

[*Item*, I will that there be sounded at full volley the Great Bell, which is not made of glass; although there is no heart which does

311

not quiver at his tolling. He has saved many good lands in times past, as every one knows. When he gives tongue all ills cease, whether they be of men-at-arms or of thunder.]

The brazen roar of the Beffroi, rolling over the roofs of old Paris, resounds eternally in this verse. And let his ringers (says Villon) receive for their pains four or half a dozen of the usual round loaves, *miches,* their perquisite; but let these (he adds with a sudden grin) be St. Stephen's loaves—that is, the kind with which the Protomartyr was put to death. His executors, he continues, tongue placed in cheek, are to be Messire Martin Bellefaye, Criminal Lieutenant to the Provost [21] and a Counsellor of Parliament; Messire Guillaume Colombel, the immensely rich financier, Royal Counsellor, and President of the Chamber of Inquests; and Messire Michiel Jouvenel, Cup-Bearer to the King and Bailli of Troyes, sixth son of the great Parisian family of Jouvenel des Ursins, whose portrait in a kneeling group is the glory of the French Primitives in the Louvre. But if (as is faintly possible) these personages excuse themselves, he directs their office to be filled by Master Philippe Brunel, Seigneur de Grigny, a notable and violent litigant, perpetually in the Courts; Master Jacques Raguier, the celebrated tosspot, with whom we are by now familiar; and skinflint Master Jacques James, of whom nothing is known except that his father was a Master of Works of Paris.

The Probate Court is to have no pickings out of Villon's estate.

> *Des testamens qu'on dit le Maistre*
> *De mon fait n'aura* quid *ne* quod.

[The Master of Testaments shall get nothing out of me, neither *quid* nor *quod*.]

All fees are to go to a certain Thomas Tricot, a priest, a Master of Arts of Villon's year, to whose health (and at whose expense) the testator cordially expresses his readiness to drink. Master Guillaume du Ru, a wealthy wine-merchant of Paris, is charged with the provision of waxlights and tapers for the funeral Mass, and the executors with the bearing of the pall. And then, since time presses, and the testator finds himself a sick man,

[21] In 1458. The Criminal Lieutenant who nearly hanged Villon in 1462 was Pierre de la Dehors, as we have observed.

Trop plus mal me font qu'oncques mais
Barbe, cheveulx, penil, sourcis,
Mal me presse . . .,

[Now more than ever is my body—beard, hair, groin, eyebrows —sick with pain.]

he finishes, and proceeds to the Ballade crying pardon of Carthusians and Celestines, Mendicants and Filles-Dieu, of loafers and patten-clickers, servants and trollops, night-thieves and jugglers, fools, players, clowns, and tumblers.

BALLADE

PAR LAQUELLE VILLON CRYE MERCY A CHASCUN

[B. de
mercy.]

A Chartreux et a Celeſtins,
A Mendians et a Devotes,
A musars et claquepatins,
A servans et filles mignotes
Portans surcotz et juſtes cotes,
A cuidereaux d'amours transsis
Chaussans sans meshaing fauves botes,
Je crie a toutes gens mercis.

A filletes monſtrans tetins
Pour avoir plus largement d'oſtes,
A ribleurs, mouveurs de hutins,
A bateleurs traynans marmotes,
A folz, folles, a sotz et sotes,
Qui s'en vont siflant six a six,
A marmosetz et mariotes,
Je crie a toutes gens mercis.

[Carthusians and Celeſtines; Mendicant Friars and Filles-Dieu; mumpers and pattern-clickers; servants and lights o' love in surcoats and juſtaucorps; fops in love, with fawn boots falling unashamed over the inſtep—I cry you pardon, one and all.

Trollops, displaying your bosoms, thereby to have more custom; thieves and roaring boys; showmen with performing apes; fools of both sexes and farce-players, whiſtling six by six; little boys and little girls—I cry you pardon, one and all.]

But he excludes from the liſt, with a terrible scowl, the "damned traitorous dogs," *traiſtres chiens maſtins,* who fed him on hard crusts and forced the water down his gullet; meaning the Lord

Bishop of Orleans and his men. His courtesy to these is the same as Squire Western's, in argument with his lady sister; and unseemly.

> Sinon aux traistres chiens mastins,
> Qui m'ont fait rongier dures crostes
> Maschier mains soirs et mains matins,
> Qu'ores je ne crains pas trois crotes.
> Je feisse pour eulx petz et rotes;
> Je ne puis, car je suis assis.
> Au fort, pour eviter riotes,
> Je crie a toutes gens mercis.

ENVOI

> Qu'on leur froisse les quinze costes
> De gros mailletz, fors et massis,
> De plombees et telz pelotes.
> Je crie a toutes gens mercis.

[But as for those damned traitorous dogs, who made me gnaw such hard crusts, so many nights and mornings, I make them a gift of belches and f—ts; no, I can't do that, being seated. But at any rate, to avoid riots, I cry pardon of one and all.

ENVOY

[Let them have their ribs well roasted with huge mallets, strong and thick, and good clubs loaded with lead, and such trifles. I cry pardon of one and all.]

On the heels of this Ballade comes immediately, completing and closing the Testament, the *Ballade pour servir de Conclusion* (the title is Prompsault's), which is such a lamentable anticlimax. It begins sadly and soberly enough with its invitation:

BALLADE

POUR SERVIR DE CONCLUSION

> Icy se clost le testament
> Et finist du povre Villon.
> Venez a son enterrement
> Quant vous orrez le carrillon,
> Vestus rouge com vermillon,
> Car en amours mourut martir:
> Ce jura il sur son couillon,
> Quant de ce monde voult partir.

314

[Here closes and ends the Testament of poor Villon. Come ye to his burial when you hear his passing-bell, but vested in bright red; for he died a martyr to Love. Thus he swore on his virility, being about to quit this world.]

He returns, with a last groan, to his death-wound from Love and his bitter fate.

> Et je croy bien que pas n'en ment;
> Car chassié fut comme ung souillon
> De ses amours hayneusement,
> Tant que, d'icy a Roussillon,
> Brosse n'y a ne brossillon
> Qui n'eust, ce dit il sans mentir,
> Ung lambeau de son cotillon,
> Quant de ce monde voult partir.
>
> Il est ainsi et tellement,
> Quant mourut n'avoit qu'ung haillon;
> Qui plus, en mourant, mallement
> L'espoignoit d'Amours l'esguillon;
> Plus agu que le ranguillon
> D'un baudrier luy faisoit sentir
> (C'est de quoy nous esmerveillon),
> Quant de ce monde voult partir.

[And I well believe he is no liar: for he was chased out hatefully by his love, like a scullion; so that there is from here as far as Roussillon not a bush nor shrub which does not bear some shred of his shirt. This he says truthfully, being about to quit this world.

And so and thus it was that when he died he had but a rag to his back, and (what was worse) was stabbed, in dying, by the dart of Love; more piercing than the buckle-tongue of a baldric he felt it; we stood aghast at his pain, when he was about to quit this world.]

But in the Envoi the martyr to Love utters a sudden derisive yawp and executes a gambol—the one occasion, perhaps, justifying Stevenson's exclamation that Villon is always emitting tears and prayers and on a sudden running away with a whoop and his fingers to his nose. The romantic of the Velvet Jacket, I fear, had little opportunity of comprehending this poet, and so made him a grotesque.

315

Prince, gent comme esmerillon,
Saichiez qu'il fist au departir:
Ung traict but de vin morillon [22]
Quant de ce monde voult partir.

[Prince, gentle as a sparrow-hawk, hear what he did on his departure! He tossed down a ſtoup of good red wine, when about to quit this world.]

Rabelais might have fathered this roaring exit from the world in a guſt of laughter, preceded by an *horrificque traict* of red wine: but I think Villon's trick is forced, and his laugh mirthless, his noise unconvinced, and his *gambade* half-hearted. The end of the *Grant Teſtament* is the Rondeau *Repos eternel.*

§ 2

THERE now remains what is often called the Codicil, and a quantity of miscellaneous verse. Of the Codicil the Ballade of the Hanged is the captain and chief, and next to it these three—the lovely Ballade crying to his friends, the Ballade of the Debate, and the Ballade of Fortune: all three, as we have seen, having been composed, if not actually written, in the prison at Meun. The reſt of the Codicil is the Quatrain or Tetraſtic which he made on learning of his death-sentence, the Ballade to Eſtienne Garnier, full of yelps and hoots of joy, on his reprieve, and the Ballade conveying his appeal to Parliament for three days' grace before the final banishment. The Quatrain may be repeated here.

QUATRAIN
QUE FEIT VILLON QUAND IL FUT JUGÉ A MOURIR

[*Tetra-*
ſtique.]

Je suis Françoys, dont il me poise,
Né de Paris emprès Pontoise,
Et d'une corde d'une toise
Sçaura mon col que mon cul poise.

[22] *Morillon:* wine, dark-red in colour, from a black grape; assumed to be Auvergnat.

[Here am I, François—woe is me!—born at Paris by Pontoise; and by means of a six-foot rope my neck will shortly discover my breech is heavy.]

"This, Sir, was great fortitude of mind."—"No, Sir; ſtark insensibility." So the severe have echoed, judging these four lines: but I eſteem them the final grimace of that dogged shrugging resignation which on so many occasions came to the relief of this fellow. The Ballade to Garnier, Clerk of the Guichet at the Châtelet, is a very fandango and Morris-dance of a Ballade, full of shouts of triumph and wild flingings abroad of arms and legs. "What d'ye think of my appeal, Garnier, hey?" bellows the poet:

BALLADE

DE L'APPEL DE VILLON

[*Queſtion au Clerc du Guichet.*]

Que vous semble de mon appel,
Garnier? Feis je sens ou folie?
Toute beſte garde sa pel;
Qui la contraint, efforce ou lie,
S'elle peult, elle se deslie.
Quant donc par plaisir voluntaire
Chantee me fut ceſte omelie,
Eſtoit il lors temps de moy taire?

[What d'ye think of my appeal, Garnier? Was I wise or a fool? Every beaſt looks to its own skin, and when it's trapped and held it does its utmoſt to get free, if it can! When this homily [his death sentence] was sung to me, without rhyme or reason, was that the time to keep my mouth shut, hey?]

And he remembers the tortures of the Queſtion, forced on him by trickery and *joncherie.*

Se feusse des hoirs Hue Cappel,
Qui fut extrait de boucherie,[1]
On ne m'euſt, parmy ce drappel,
Fait boire en ceſte escorcherie.
Vous entendez bien joncherie?
Mais quant ceſte paine arbitraire
On me jugea par tricherie,
Eſtoit il lors temps de moy taire?

[1] The legend that Hugues Capet, "the Great," was sprung from a family of butchers has no foundation in history. Dante has perpetuated it in *Purgatorio*, xx.

[Were I of the blood of Hugues Capet (who came of butchers' stock) they would not have forced me to drink through the cloth in their devilish way. You know how it's done! But when they sentenced me by malice to this harsh punishment—was that the time to keep my mouth shut, hey?]

"Lord!" he goes on, with a wink, "d'you think I hadn't enough sense under my hood to yell out 'I appeal!' when the notary said: 'You're for the long jump?' Hey?"

> Cuidiez vous que soubz mon cappel
> N'y euſt tant de philosophie
> Comme de dire: "J'en appel"?
> Si avoit, je vous certiffie,
> Combien que point trop ne m'y fie.
> Quant on me diſt, present notaire:
> "Pendu serez!" je vous affie,
> Eſtoit il lors temps de moy taire?

And so to the hurraying conclusion:

ENVOI

> Prince, se j'eusse eu la pepie,
> Pieça je feusse ou eſt Clotaire,
> Aux champs debout comme une espie.
> Eſtoit il lors de moy taire?

[Prince, had I had the pip [i.e. been dumb, like a bird with that disease] I would long ago have been with Clotaire in the next world, my body ſtuck upright in the fields, like a blade of ſtraw. Was that the time to keep my mouth shut, hey?]

Another great bellowing follows—the Ballade to Parliament, in which the poet calls on all his five senses to praise and glorify the Sovereign Court. He begins:

La Requeste De Villon, Presentee a la Court

de Parlement, en forme de Ballade

[Louenge a la Court.]

> Tous mes cinq sens: yeulx, oreilles et bouche,
> Le nez, et vous, le sensitif aussi;
> Tous mes membres ou il y a reprouche,
> En son endroit ung chascun die ainsi:
> "Souvraine Court, par qui sommes icy,
> Vous nous avez gardé de desconfire.

Or la langue seule ne peut souffire
A vous rendre souffisantes louenges;
Si prions tous, fille du souvrain Sire,
Mere des bons et seur des benois anges!"

THE PETITION OF VILLON PRESENTED TO THE COURT,

IN THE FORM OF A BALLADE

[All my five senses, in your several place,
   Hearing and seeing, taſte and touch and smell,
Every my member branded with disgrace—
   Each on this fashion do ye speak and tell:
   "Moſt Sovereign Court, by whom we here befell,
Thou that deliveredſt us from sore dismays,
The tongue sufficeth not thy name to blaze
   Forth in such ſtrain of honour as it should:
Wherefore to thee our voices all we raise,
   Siſter of Angels, Mother of the Good!]

And continues, roaring louder than organs, trumpets, or bells, as we have already seen, and so comes at laſt to his point in the Envoy:

Prince, trois jours ne vueillez m'escondire,
Pour moy pourveoir et aux miens adieu dire . . .

This is the laſt of the Codicil.

The miscellaneous verse known to be Villon's is of indifferent value, saving the roaring Ballade of the Taverners and the Ballade againſt the Enemies of France; the firſt, as we have observed, not invariably attributed to him, the second undoubtedly his, but both having a fine flow of Billingsgate, and both ſtout poetry. The long rambling ecſtatic *Epiſtre a Marie d'Orléans,* consisting of ten *huitains* and a double Ballade, I have sufficiently considered, with its special significance, in reviewing the Life. In this group are also to be included three Ballades of the old-fashioned school of Deschamps and Chartier, a sort of formal catalogue of sententiousness, with the summing-up in the refrain—in Villon's hands sardonic and contradiĉtory. The firſt plays with the double meaning *Noël,* the cry raised by the medieval French populace in welcoming a Royal progress, and *Noël,* Chriſtmas. I give the firſt ſtanza.

319

BALLADE

DES PROVERBES

Tant grate chievre que mal giſt,
Tant va le pot a l'eaue qu'il brise,
Tant chauffe on le fer qu'il rougiſt,
Tant le maille on qu'il se debrise,
Tant vault l'homme comme on le prise,
Tant s'eslongne il qu'il n'en souvient,
Tant mauvais eſt qu'on le desprise,
Tant crie l'on Noël qu'il vient.

[So much scratch goats that they spoil their bed; so often goes the pitcher to the well that it smashes; so much is the iron heated that it turns red; so much is it hammered that it breaks; so much is a man valued as they take him; so far does he journey that he is loſt to mind; so bad is he that he is spurned; so much do folk cry *Noël* that it appears.]

The other is a better piece of work, since it concerns universal human nature and is informed with half-serious, half-mocking truth and a realisation of our mortal folly. It begins:

BALLADE

DES MENUS PROPOS

Je congnois bien mouches en let,
Je congnois a la robe l'homme,
Je congnois le beau temps du let,
Je congnois au pommier la pomme,
Je congnois l'arbre a veoir la gomme,
Je congnois quant tout eſt de mesmes,
Je congnois qui besongne ou chomme,
Je congnois tout, fors que moy mesmes.

[I know flies in the milk; I know a man by his clothes; I know fine weather from foul; I know the apple-tree by the apple; I know the tree by its sap; I know when everything's the same; I know the worker from the drone; I know everything—except myself.]

The third Ballade of this Enumerative series, having the refrain *Ne bon conseil que d'amoureux,* is quite worthless, and contains Villon's acroſtic in its Envoi: as does another Ballade of virtuous import but heavy going, called *Ballade de Bon Conseil,* dedicated (like the spelling-book published by Mr. Brown, Dr. Johnson's early schoolmaster) to the Universe. With these Longnon includes a much livelier piece, which looks innocent but is not. It has a jolly "Some-talk-of-Alexander" swing; beginning:

BALLADE

DES POVRES HOUSSEURS

> *On parle de champs labourer,*
> *De porter chaulme contre vent,*
> *Et aussy de se marier*
> *A femme qui tance souvent;*
> *De moyne de povre couvent,*
> *De gens qui vont souvent sur mer,*
> *De ceulx qui vont les bleds semer,*
> *Et de celluy qui l'asne maine;*
> *Mais, a treſtout considerer,*
> *Povres housseurs ont assez peine!*

[You may talk of ploughing, of carrying ſtubble againſt the wind, of getting married to a scold; you may talk of the hard life of a monk in a poor convent, of seafarers, of sowers in the field, and of ass-leaders: but, everything considered, poor sweeps have a devil of a life.]

Housseur means a chimney-sweep: but also, in the free and easy patois of the honeſt country folk round Amiens and Ponthieu, a quite different kind of labourer; and is so used (it appears) to this day. We may as well have the reſt of this rattling song.

> *A petits enfans gouverner,*
> *Dieu scet se c'eſt esbatement!*
> *De gens d'armes doit on parler?*
> *De faire leur commandement?*
> *De servir Malchus chauldement?*
> *De servir dames et aymer?*
> *De guerryer et bouhourder,*
> *Et de jouſter a la quintaine?*
> *Mais, a treſtout considerer,*
> *Povres housseurs ont assez peine!*
>
> *Ce n'eſt que jeu de bled soyer,*
> *Et de prez faulcher, vrayement;*

321

Ne d'orge batre, ne vanner,
Ne de plaider en Parlement;
A danger emprunter argent,
A maignans leurs poisles mener,
Et a charretiers desjeuner,
Et de jeuner la Quarantaine;
Mais, a trestout considerer,
Povres housseurs ont assez peine!

[To govern small children, God knows, is no pastime; and what of soldiery and their commands, and the fierce conduct of [Malchus] the sword? And what of serving ladies and their love? And what of battle and the jousts, and tilting at the quintain? Everything considered, poor sweeps have a devil of a life!

Sowing wheat and reaping the fields is only a game, faith! like threshing barley, and winnowing, and pleading before Parliament, and borrowing money in difficulty, and taking frying-pans to travelling tinkers, and dinner to carters, and fasting through Lent. . . . But everything considered, poor sweeps have a devil of a life!]

This Ballade has no Envoi.

Two other Ballades commonly included in this group must be lightly touched on: the first is the *Ballade du Concours de Blois*, made at Charles d'Orléans' court. This I have quoted in the Life. It is a mechanical conceit of a pattern popular a century before Villon, though stamped with his own mark; and contains the device of his whole life,

Je ris en pleurs.

The second is the Ballade asking a trifling loan of Jean II. de Bourbon. Some of it is worth repeating, since it is indeed a tactful, almost irresistible dun, and Villon got at least six more crowns out of it, I trust. See how gracefully he knows how to beg.

La Requeste

QUE VILLON BAILLA A MONSEIGNEUR DE BOURBON

[*Requeste a Mons. de Bourbon.*]

Le mien Seigneur et Prince redoubté,
Fleuron de Lys, royalle geniture,
Françoys Villon, que Travail a dompté
A coups orbes, par force de bature,
Vous supplie par ceste humble escripture
Que lui faciez quelque gracieux prest.

De s'obliger en toutes cours est prest,
Si ne doubtez que bien ne vous contente:
Sans y avoir dommaige n'interest,
Vous n'y perdrez seulement que l'attente.

[My Lord and redoubtable Prince, Flower of the Lily, offspring of Kings, François Villon, whom Fortune has stunned with heavy blows, hereby prays you, by this humble letter, to make him a gracious loan. He is ready to own the debt in any court, and doubts not that he can content you. Your Lordship will run no risk, and will lose nothing by it but the time of waiting.]

He has already received from the Duke, he says in the second stanza, six crowns, which he has laid out in food, and he promises devoutly to repay all without delay. He is so low (he says) that for two pins he would sell himself to a bloodsucking Lombard usurer. Money (he says) does not hang at everybody's belt. The only crosses he has seen for weeks, by God (he says, referring to the cross on the coinage), are wooden and stone ones.

Si je peusse vendre de ma santé
A ung Lombart, usurier par nature,
Faulte d'argent m'a si fort enchanté
Que j'en prendroie, ce cuide, l'adventure.
Argent ne pens a gippon n'a sainture;
Beau sire Dieux! je m'esbais que c'est
Que devant moy croix ne se comparoist,
Si non de bois ou pierre, que ne mente;
Mais s'une fois la vraye m'apparoist,
Vous n'y perdrez seulement que l'attente.

A sufficiently daring jest, observes Lacroix of the line concerning the crosses; for the devotion of Louis xi. to the True Cross of Saint-Lô is well known. And Villon adds a little quaint gambolling postscript to his Envoi:

SUSCRIPTION DE LADICTE REQUESTE
Allez, lettres, faites ung sault;
Combien que n'ayez pié ne langue,
Remonstrez en vostre harangue
Que faulte d'argent si m'assault.

[Go, little letters: take a leap, and (though you lack legs and a tongue) show forth in your speech that I am assailed by lack of money.]

323

This was Panurge's disease, and indeed the ill which has always dogged men of letters in all ages: I mean a flux or pernicious anæmia of the purse. *Amor ingenii neminem umquam divitem fecit,* says the rascally poet Eumolpus in the *Satiricon.* Only in this late modern day are the less delicate able to walk abroad in tall hats and mingle on practically equal terms with the rich.

§ 3

We have now reviewed the whole (leaving aside the Jargon, which is dealt with elsewhere) of the known poetical work of Villon. Of the mass of minor stuff, eleven Ballades, seventeen Rondels (mostly love-plaints), and two dramatic pieces, attributed to him on more or less plausible grounds, but rejected in all critical editions, I can myself discern only two pieces which might possibly have been from his hand; one the admirably comic Monologue of the Free Archer of Baignollet, and the other a cynical Ballade discussing the palpable truth that the rich get served first, in love as in other things. This we may consider first. The poet is very bitter in this Ballade about his mistress, a girl of business instinct, whom one is strongly tempted to connect with Katherine de Vausselles: I quote it for this reason. He loved her so desperately, he says,

> *Que nuit et jour j'en estois langoureux.*

[That I was sick of love for her both day and night.]

And for a time, while he had money, his passion was returned; until she cast her eyes on a rich, blear-eyed, dirty old man.

> *Or est ainsy que, durant ma pecune,*
> *Je fus traité comme amy precieux;*
> *Mais, tost après, sans dire chose aucune,*
> *Ceste vilaine alla jetter les yeulx*
> *Sur ung vieillard riche, mais chassieux,*
> *Laid et hideux trop plus qu'on ne propose.*
> *Ce neanmoins, il en jouit sa pose;*
> *D'ond, moy, confus, voyant un tel ouvrage,*
> *Dessus ce texte allay bouter en glose:*
> *"Riche amoureux a tousjours l'advantage."*

324

[Thus it was that while I had money I was her darling; but soon after, without a word, the hussy cast her eyes on a rich old man, foul, ugly, hideous, more than one can imagine: nevertheless he got her, and I myself, thunderstruck at this piece of work, added to it a gloss of my own: *The rich have always advantage in love.*]

"Look at the trollop!" he says, writhing in his pain and disgust. "I was so much her slave that I would have climbed the sky and torn the moon down for her, if she had asked me! But the mercenary trull must needs give her body to this old satyr!"

Or elle a tort, car noyse ny rancune
N'eut onc de moy. Tant luy fus gracieux
Que, s'elle eust dist: "Donne-moy de la lune,"
J'eusse entrepris de monter jusqu'aux cieulx,
Et, nonobstant, son corps tant vicieux
Au service de ce vieillard expose;
D'ond, ce voyant, un rondeau je compose
Que luy transmets; mais, en pou de langage,
Me respond franc: "Povreté te depose:
Riche amoureux a tousjours l'advantage!"

[Oh, she did wrong, for she had never an angry or bitter word from me. I was so much hers that if she had said "Give me the moon!" I would have undertaken to climb the skies for her. . . . And notwithstanding, she gives her vicious body to this old man! I made, on seeing this, a rondeau and sent it to her; but with no mincing of words she answered me straight back: *"Poverty counts you out. The rich have always advantage in love."*]

The Envoi sounds very like Villon, with its allusion to the *Roman de la Rose,* which he knew well, and quotes in the *Grant Testament.* "Orose" is the historian of the fourth century, whose work, composed at St. Augustine's demand, had been translated a hundred times. The poet probably puts him in simply for the rhyme.

ENVOI

Prince tout bel, trop mieulx parlant qu'Orose,
Si vous n'avez tousjours bourse desclose,
Vous abusez: car Meung, docteur tressage,
Nous a descrit que, pour cueillir la rose,
Riche amoureux a tousjours l'advantage.

[Prince, handsome as you are, and a much better *raisonneur* than Orose, if you haven't a purse perpetually open you are wasting your time. Has not Meung [Jehan de Meung], that most wise doctor, told us that in plucking the rose the rich have always the advantage in love?]

This whole Ballade, I say, might well be from Villon's hand in a careless or bitter mood, or he may have written it while drowning his pain in a cabaret. In the Manuscript of Bayeux there is a song which the poet may have known and deliberately echoed, containing the same complaint:

Hel - las, j'ai es - té des - trous - sé De la plus
Si m'a - vois el ju - ré sa foy Qu'el n'ay-me-

plai - sante à mon gré Que je vis en jor de
roit aul - tre que moy. Mais el m'a bien sa foy

ma vi - - - - - - - - - - - e.
fayl - ly - - - - - - - - - - e,

Et m'a fail - ly de co - ve -
Et s'est pour - vu d'ung aultre a -

nant; Je l'a - per - choy bien main - te - -
mant, d'ung vieil - lart gris, pel - lé de - -

nant, Ja - maiz ne la sçai - roye ay - met.
vant, Car il (l)a - voit que luy don - ner.

326

[Alas, I have been robbed of the sweeteſt one I could imagine, the sweeteſt I ever saw all my life; she swore to me that she would be faithful, that she would never love other but me. But she has betrayed her oath completely, and forsworn her vow; I now see it clearly, and never again can I love her; for she has taken another lover, a gray old man, all bald in front. For he had something to give her.

II

Par finance je perds m'amye.
Je doibs bien haïr povreté,
Jeunesse n'aura plus posseté
Or et argent à la maiſtrie.
Sachés, se je puis, j'en auray
Et puis apres je m'en yray
Vëoir la belle deguerpie;
Or, argent luy donneray,
Et puis après je chesseray,
Le vieillart à la barbe florie.

Through finance I lose my love: well ought I to hate poverty! Nevermore may Youth have at his command gold and silver; but know this, that if I can, I will find some, and afterwards I will set forth to find my fair runaway. I will give her money; and then I will rout the old fool, with his flowing beard.]

I cannot bring this survey to an end without a glance at the comic Monologue of the Free Archer of Baignollet, a theatre-piece immensely popular, whoever wrote it, right down to Rabelais' time,[1] and later. The poet's shafts are directed againſt the Militia of Free Archers eſtablished at the expense of the communes by Charles VII., and notable for braggadocio and cowardice. The body was dissolved in 1480 and replaced by mercenaries in the King's pay.

The Monologue seems to be ſtamped all over with Villon's private marks. The Free Archer swaggers on to the ſtage, pulling his mouſtaches and issuing invitations to all the world to fight. *Par le sang bieu!* The man of war is terrible, a very hippogriff, breathing smoke and flame. Will any four gentlemen ſtep up at once and

---

[1] Rabelais includes in the Catalogue of the Books which Pantagruel found in the great Library of St. Victor a tome called *Stratagemata Francarchieri de Baignolet;* and again, in Epiſtemon's account of Hell and its inhabitants (Bk. II.), brings in the Free Archer of Baignollet as the inquisitor of heresy in those regions.

oblige him with a little hand-to-hand combat? No? *Morbieu!* He took five English single-handed at the siege of Alençon: three paid him ransom, one escaped, and the laſt whanged the Free Archer over the head with a bottle, whereupon (he says) he at once begged the Englishman to be reasonable, *ventrebieu!* and have a drink, like a peaceable creature. Why, by the——

Here there is inserted in the text a ſtage-direction:

> *Cy diſt ung quidem, par derrière les gens,* COQUERICOQ.

[Here some one at the back of the audience crows thus: *Cockadoodledoo!*]

The Archer ſtarts violently; but after making a mental note of the henrooſt he continues the loud tale of his valiance: how in one engagement a cannon-ball flew through his hair, how his anger was so ferocious and his onrush in the van of battle so superb that all the great captains (he knows them all by name) hurried up to admire,

> *Le Barronet et le Marquis,*
> *Craon, Cures, l'Aigle et Bressoire,*
> *Accoururent pour veoir l'hiſtoire;*
> *La Rochefouqualt, l'Amiral,*
> *Aussy Bueil et son attirail,*
> *Pontievre, tous les capitaines,*

[The Baronet, and the Marquis, the seigneurs of Craon, Cures, l'Aigle, and Bressoire all ran up to see the sight, with La Rochefoucauld, and the Admiral, and Bueil and his ſtaff, and Penthièvre [2] and all the captains.]

taking off their ſteel gloves and being careful not to hurt him in their enthusiasm; how (but for losing his way) he and his brother Archer Guillemin would have fallen on the Bretons [3] and hewn them in pieces, but magnanimously reſtraining his fury he was prevailed on to retire. Here, observe, the Free Archer evolves a *mot* which Oscar Wilde invented, amid considerable applause, four cen-

[2] These laſt four are famous names in the wars of the fifteenth century. The Admiral is Prégent de Coetivy et de Retz, killed at Cherbourg in 1450; La Rochefoucauld is Foucauld, seigneur of La Rochefoucauld and Marsillac, one of Charles VII.'s chevaliers; Jean de Bueil, a great commander, succeeded Prégent as Admiral; and Penthièvre is a Breton captain.

[3] It ſeems to have happened during Louis XI.'s punitive expedition againſt the Dukes of Normandy and Brittany in 1466.

turies later. "I can resist anything but temptation," said Wilde. "I'm not afraid of anything but danger," remarks the Archer confidentially

> *Je ne craignoye que les dangiers,*
> *Moy; je n'avoye paour d'aultre chose.*

[I feared only danger, myself. I feared nothing else.]

The farrago of bombast, mixed with frank asides, continues. The Archer is a devil with the women, as one would expect, yet gallant, and not like the rude *canaille* of the rank and file; a dead shot at the butts, too, and in his tender youth a great performer on the flute. Well . . . The Archer, preparing to reconnoitre the henroost, becomes aware of a figure rearing behind him, dressed like a man-at-arms, an arbalest in its hand and a white (or French) cross on its breast. He stops short, staring. His terror is extreme.

> (*A part.*)
>> *Ha! le Sacrement de l'autel!*
>> *Je suis affoibly! Que'esse cy?*

[(*Aside.*) Ha! God's Body, I'm all of a tremble! What's this?]

He addresses the scarecrow.

> (*A l'espoventail.*)
>> *Ha! Monseigneur, pour Dieu, mercy!*
>> *Hault le traict, qu'aye la vie franche!*
>> *Je voy bien, à vostre croix blanche,*
>> *Que nous sommes tout d'ung party!*

[(*To the scarecrow.*) Ha! My Lord, for God's sake, mercy! Lift your arm a trifle, sir, so that I shan't be hit! I see from your white cross, sir, that we are both on the same side!]

In a moment he perceives a black Breton cross on the back of it, and breaks into a fresh sweat.

> *Par le sang bieu! c'est ung Breton,*
> *Et je dy que je suis François! . . .*
> *Il est faict de toy, ceste fois,*
> *Pernet: c'est ung parti contraire!*

['Sblood! It's a Breton! and here am I saying I'm a Frenchman! It's all up with you this time, Pernet! He's on the other side.]

329

The fun develops. The Archer grovels again, swearing by St. Denis of France and St. Yves of Brittany that he is at the gentleman's service, tripes and bowels; then resigns himself to instant death and confesses himself, calling his adversary especially to witness that he never in his life killed anything bigger than a hen. At last, after a deal of comic terror, the scarecrow falls with a crash to the ground, and the Free Archer, drawing near to it after a respectable interval, discovers what it is and breaks into a fury, rending his enemy with a torrent of oaths and huge bellowings. What! a dummy! Stuffed with ſtraw! *Par le corps bieu! Morbieu! Charbieu! Par la vertu bieu!* May the Quartan Ague nip the guts of the man who has fooled him! At any rate he will drag the thing away with him, for a gage and booty of war! And the Free Archer turns to the audience and ends his monologue.

(*Au public.*)
> *Seigneurs, je vous commande à Dieu:*
> *Et se l'on vous vient demander*
> *Qu'eſt devenu le Franc Archier,*
> *Diĉtes qu'il n'eſt pas mort encor,*
> *Et qu'il emporte dague et cor,*
> *Et reviendra par cy de brief.*
> *Adieu! Je m'en voys au relief.*

[Gentles, I commend you to God. If any ask you concerning the whereabouts of the Free Archer, say that he is not dead yet, but has gone off the field with bag and baggage, and will return presently Farewell! I go to draw my pay.]

It is a merry satire, not too subtle, on a body of militia at whom all Paris jeered, and no doubt the audience rocked with joy. In its verve, its mockery, and the arrangement of some of its phrases, it is very Villon. Guillaume Colletet, from whose Life of the poet (*circa* 1650) I have quoted elsewhere, ſtubbornly awards it to him, calling it *une satyre contre un rodomont et un pagnot de son tems.* Three of the editions before Marot include the Monologue with the Works; Marot and succeeding editors exclude it. Some think it was probably part of a repertoire of farces played by Villon and his fellows of the University at one time and another, but hesitate to declare that he wrote it. Others say that he could not possibly have

330

written it, since it did not appear till after his disappearance from history. Much more doubt enwraps the Dialogue of the Messieurs de Mallepaye et de Baillevent; a long burlesque duet of intricate rhyme from which Rabelais may have devised Panurge's dialogue with the monosyllabic Friar Fredon in the Fifth Book.[4] I give a little of it, to show the pattern. The piece is believed to have certainly formed part of the theatrical repertoire of the Enfans Sans Souci; it is a plaintive and comic avowal of poverty and covetousness bandied to and fro between M. de Mallepaye (*malle paye*) and M. de Baillevent (*bailleur de vent,* one who pays with wind, instead of money).

DIALOGUE

DE MESSIEURS DE MALLEPAYE ET DE BAILLEVENT

M. *Hée, Monsieur de Baillevent!*
>   B. *Quoy*
De neuf?
>   M. *On nous tient en aboy,*
Comme despourveuz, malheureux.
B. *Si j'avoye autant que je doy,*
Sang bieu! je seroye chez le Roy,
Un page après moy!
>   M. *Voire deux!*
B. *Nous sommes francs . . .*
>   M. *Adventureux.*
B. *Riches.*
>   M. *Bien aises.*
>   B. *Plantureux.*
M. *Voire, de souhaits.*
>   B. *C'est assez.*
M. *Gentilz hommes.*
>   B. *Hardis.*
>   M. *Et preux*
B. *Par l'huys.*
>   M. *Du joly Souffreteux*
Heritiers.[5]
>   B. *De gaiges cassez.*

[4] If Rabelais wrote the Fifth Book; which is disputed.

Another piece hardily attributed to Villon at least once is the celebrated farce of *Maistre Pierre Pathelin.* It is more probable that this might be placed among the works of Bacon.

[5] A wry grimace in the direction of the Enfans Sans Souci, that famished and predatory troop, who sometimes called themselves "heirs of the Abbé de Saintcte-Souffrette."

M. *Nous sommes, puis troys ans passez,*
Si minces.
      B. *Si mal compassez.*
M. *Si simples.*
         B. *Legiers comme vent.*
M. *Si esbaudiz.*
        B. *Si mal pansezssez.*
De donner pour Dieu dispensez,
Car nous jeusnons assez souvent.

DIALOGUE

OF MM. DE MALLEPAYE AND DE BAILLEVENT

M. Hé, Monsieur de Baillevent!
        B. What's
The news?
M. They keep us in a pretty fix,
Needy and unfortunate.
B. If I had all the money I owe,
'Sdeath, I should be at Court,
With a page attending me!
        M. Nay, two!
B. We are both honeſt. . . .
        M. Venturesome,
B. Rich.
   M. Easy
      B. Fertile . . .
M. True, of desires.
      B. That's sufficient.
M. Men of worth . . .
     B. Intrepid.
        M. And doughty.
B. Behind the door.
      M. Heirs of the Abbot
Of Starveling.
      B. Cashiered.
M. We have been for three years paſt
So slender.
     B. So badly ſtarched!
M. So simple.
     B. Light as a wind!
M. So jolly.
     B. So ill-equipped
To beſtow gifts for God,
For we faſt often enough.

332

There is some little skill in this. It is composed of strophes of six lines, having two rhymes so arranged that the rhyme of the third and sixth lines in one strophe is repeated in the next at the first, second, fourth, and fifth. The likeness to Rabelais' Friar jumps to the eye in such an exchange as

> M. *Gens* . . .
>> B. *A dire: D'ond venez-vous?*
> M. *Francs.*
>> B. *Fins.*
>>> M. *Froidz.*
>>>> B. *Forts.*
>>>>> M. *Grans.*
>>>>>> B. *Gros.*
>>>>>>> M. *Escreuz.*

> M. The sort of men . . .
>> B. To say: Where d'you come from?
> M. Honest.
>> B. Subtle.
>>> M. Cool.
>>>> B. Strong.
>>>>> M. Tall.
>>>>>> B. Stout.
>>>>>> M. Enlarged.

But whether or not this and the Free Archer are Villon's will be ultimately revealed (the aged Sybil of Panzoult informs me) at the coming of the Cocqcigrues.

§ 4

Of his scattered irregularities, his obscurities, his occasional untidiness of syntax, his wilful carelessness, his one or two verses left helpless in the air, dangling their legs, his demi-assonances, like the rhyming of *Grenobles* with *Doles, peuple* with *seule,* and *enfle* with *temple,* to take three instances, there is no need to make a howl.[1]

---

[1] The *rime riche* Villon so often uses dropped out of English poetry after Chaucer. For example:

> The hooly blisful martir for to seke [seek]
> That hem hath holpen whan that they were seeke [sick].

Les poëtes font à leur guise, as the goddess says in the play; adding, with enormous truth and aptitude, so far as Villon is concerned,

> *Ce n'est pas la seule sottise*
> *Qu'on voit faire à ces messieurs-là.*

[That is not the only folly we perceive emanating from those gentlemen.]

But those who would make him a slovenly improviser, throwing off his song carelessly and tossing together his verses as he felt inclined, do him wrong. The most superficial examination of the planning of the *Grant Testament* [2] shows the arrangement of the whole work to be not haphazard, but, in spite of a few unimportant blemishes, rhythmic, subtle, and carefully studied: to take an example, that gradual crescendo of meditation on Death which rises a slow wave and bursts finally into the lovely melody of the Dead Ladies, falling back afterwards and dying in the Lament of the Belle Heaulmière, and her wailing for her lost youth; and again, that other slow lifting wave of religion and gratitude which swells and breaks in the Ballade to Our Lady; and once more, the mocking laughter of the Ballade of the Women of Paris, hardening and becoming harsh, and finally set in a bitter grimace as he passes to the Ballade of Fat Margot; and again, the first sad note, as of a passing-bell and the chant of *De Profundis,* in the song *"Au retour,"* deepening and growing more solemn and recollected thence to the end of the Testament and the Epitaph. A poet of Villon's stature could do no less. His finest and most ecstatic work is set in the mass of the Testament with all the anxiety of the medieval craftsman. Well did Huysmans call him *ciseleur inimitable, joaillier non pareil.* And if his best verse is required to pass an academic test, it still emerges triumphant, fulfilling at once Pater's condition that all high poetry aspires towards music, and the corollary of M. Henri Bremond [3] that all high poetry aspires towards prayer. As for his lesser flights, his gibes and fleers and mocks, Marcel Schwob, point-

---

[2] It is to be noted to begin with that the general form, as of the *Petit Testament* also, follows that of regular testaments, consistently, the testator beginning with the invocation to the Trinity and to Our Lady, and proceeding in order, soul, body, father, mother, friends, notaries, executors, etc.

[3] *Prière et Poésie,* 1926.

ing out that more than half Villon's butts are rich Parisian financiers, tax-farmers, usurers, and money-merchants, the Marchands, Cornus, St. Amants, Baubignons, Baillys, Trascailles, Raguiers, Tarannes, Hesselins, Colombels, Charruaus, Louvieux, Marbeufs, Marles, Culdoes, Laurens, Gossouyns, and Marceaus, argues thence that he deliberately intended his work for a social satire or pamphlet,[4] for at the latter part of the fifteenth century these financiers (and especially those of them who were usurers and speculators in food) were universally hated. But I do not think so much can be claimed for him, nor that he had anything more in his mind than personal dislikes and private hatreds. He was, like his ancestor the disreputable poet Eumolpus in Petronius, one of those men of letters *quos odisse divites solent,* and he obviously returned cordially and fivefold this dislike. If there were some secure proof for Marcel Schwob's theory, it would certainly give Villon's least gibes a political distinction.

We may grant him, then, his moments of slackness, and moments also when his bright genius sulked and left him plugging along merely a pedestrian rhymer. But for the greatest part there is in his verses a mastery, a sureness, a rhythm, a sharp clarity, a relief, and above all a vigour, a breeze of life, which stamps him great. In every page of his works there strikes upon the eye some subtle arrangement of words, some final clear-cut picture, some melody, some round perfection which enlarges and satisfies not only the eye and the ear, but the mind also.

For example,

> *Ou sont les gracieux gallans*
> *Que je suivoye ou temps jadis,*
> *Si bien chantans, si bien parlans,*
> *Si plaisans en faiz et en dis?*

and again:

> *Au moustier voy dont suis paroissienne*
> *Paradis paint, ou sont harpes et lus.*

and again:

> *Ryme, raille, cymballe, luttes,*
> *Comme fol, fainctif, eshontez;*

[4] Letter to Sidney Colvin, November, 1899. The theory is developed in Schwob's *Rédactions et Notes.*

335

> *Farce, broulle, joue des fleustes,*
> *Fais, es villes et es citez,*
> *Farces, jeux, et moralitez;*
> *Gaigne au berlanc, au glic, aux quilles:*
> *Aussi bien va, or escoutez!*
> *Tout aux tavernes et aux filles.*

and:

> *Venez a son enterrement*
> *Quant vous orrez le carrillon,*
> *Vestus rouge com vermillon.*

and once more:

> *Filles, amans, jeunes gens et nouveaulx,*
> *Danceurs, saulteurs, faisans les piez de veaux,*
> *Vifs comme dars, agus comme aguillon,*
> *Gousiers tintans cler comme cascaveaux . . .*

In all these there is a running song, playing among the printed words and perceptible to the inner ear, woven in and out and flowing and returning, repeated like a fugue, a perpetual undercurrent: like the liquid music one hears (Pater *duce et auspice* Pater) in gazing at the paint and canvas of Giorgione's *Concert*.

Sounds and sweet Ayrs, that give delight and hurt not.

I have chosen instances from the mass of his work. The three Great Ballades and some of the lesser are music absolute. Only a very great poet could have written any one of these three: the Ballade to Our Lady, like the rolling of minster organs at one of her feasts; the Ballade of the Hanged, which is like the *Dies Iræ*; the Ballade of Dead Ladies, a stringed symphony, shimmering and exquisite, heard afar off on a summer night, among the plashing of fountains.

Above all, there is his vigour. "It is all round him," says Mr. Belloc, "and through him, like a storm in a wood. It creates, it perceives. It possesses the man himself, and us also as we read him." [5] He bursts into a dying twilit world full of half-poets mumbling their worn-out formulæ, and creates the first modern poetry in Europe: modern, I mean, in that it is sharp and athrob

[5] *Avril.*

with frank self-searching, eager, moody, fed from the poet's own heart's blood. Had he, as Clément Marot wished, lived and been formed and polished in the courts of princes he would have become, most probably, a polite little, smug little, precious little Court versifier, rhyming his uninspired conceits and turning out his quaint enamelled confections to order, like so many others. But in place of the faded decorations like tapestries, full of stiffly-grouped knights and ladies, of these his predecessors and contemporaries, Villon creates the poetry of Paris and sets down her soul and the pageant of her streets. Where they used over and over again the stilted, pompous phrase, the formal courtesy, the decorative, lifeless pattern, Villon crams into his verse the noisy brawl of the Town, its sights and sounds and life, its slang, its thieves' patter, foreign oaths left over from the wars, Latin of the University and the Church, rude jokes of the tavern, the drone of the Schools, scraps of street-songs ("*Ma doulce Amour*"—"*Ouvrez vostre huys, Guillemette*"), country patois, the mincing affectations of the genteel. Just as in

> *Et quidam seros hiberni ad luminis ignes*
> *Pervigilat ferroque faces inspicat acuto;*
> *Interea longum cantu solata laborem*
> *Arguto conjunx percurrit pectine telas*

[Such a one works by night, by the light of his winter fire, cutting wood for torches with a sharp knife, while his wife, soothing her long labour with song, passes the noisy comb to and fro across the web.]

(*Vergil*, Georgics I)

the acrid scent of wood-smoke rises at once to the nostrils and there is heard the swish of the comb through the threads, the crackling of the log fire, the rhythmic chopping of the knife on wood, and over all the crooning of an old dreamy song, so in

> *Et aux pietons qui vont d'aguet*
> *Tastonnant par ces establis . . .*

[And to the foot-sergeants who go the rounds, groping past the stalls.]

there is heard the tramp of the Watch, the stumbling along the cobbles, the word of command, the rasp of halberds poked beneath

337

the ſtalls, the grunted exchanges; and over all the vaſt murmur of the Town. And once more:

Et Ysabeau qui dit:·"Ennél!"

For nearly five hundred years the girl Ysabeau, this cockney of medieval Paris, has been lisping *"Ennél!"*—"Reelly!": so that you can hear the very infleɛtion of her soft voice, and see the arched eyebrows, the cheap jewels, the pretty, silly, vapid face upturned to the mocking face of the poet. She is as alive as Galatea in the Bucolics, who so many centuries ago flung her apple at the shepherd Damoetas and fled to the willows. The apple (as a modern Vergil-iſt, M. Bellessort, has finely said) is ſtill rolling there, before our eyes. The willows are quivering; a girl's flushed, laughing face ſtill peeps behind. So Ysabeau is ſtill looking up and saying *"Ennél!";* the little affected fool. It is in the power of a poet to create, like this, a moment which is changeless, and to make Time ſtand ſtill.

Of the greatness of Villon, says Gaſton Paris, there is one supreme teſt. He wrote, in a French long ago obsolete and now sometimes barely intelligible, in an outmoded form, of an age long dead. The subjeɛt-matter of his verse loſt centuries ago any aɛtuality it had, and the values of his age have changed—though I may be excused for suggeſting, rather quaintly, that its vital essence, its faith, is of course indeſtruɛtible. Finally, some of his verse is concerned with persons or events so vague, so obscure, or so unpleasant that of themselves they would not arouse to-day the fainteſt intereſt. Yet his verse as you read it is alive, vibrant, as freshly coloured as when he firſt wrote it down, and ageless.

How true this is—and I have found it not possible to share all Gaſton Paris' judgments on this poet—one discovers by reading Villon as all good poetry should invariably be read: aloud. Such is the ecſtasy of his creative force, the life he has breathed into his work, that it is seen and felt to be poetry absolute, ſtirring the soul and the imagination like a fanfare of silver trumpets, fulfilling the mind, vibrating, awakening that inſtant response which is the mark of high poetry. This is a teſt no lesser verse can pass. Villon possessed *le Verbe,* the Word, and the magic formula (Rabelais has it,

338

too) by which words are changed into something beyond themselves and their arrangement transmuted into the language of another world; a language in which the very shape and size and colour and texture of words, their resonance, their position and significance, become as it were faëry, charged with tremendous, or mysterious, or ravishing music. Such music, I mean, as

> And we in dream behold the Hebrides,

and

> *Formosam resonare doces Amaryllida silvas,*

> [You teach the woods to resound with the name of lovely Amaryllis.]   (*Vergil*, Bucolics I)

and

> O western Wind, when wilt thou blow
> That the small rain down can rain?

and

> *Tuba mirum spargens sonum,*

> [Wondrous sound the trumpet flingeth.] (From the *Dies Iræ*.)

and of course—

> *Echo, parlant quant bruyt on maine*
> *Dessus riviere ou sus estan.*
> [Echo, more than mortal-fair,
> That, when one calls by river-flow
> Or marish, answers out of the air.]
>   (*Payne.*)

Such alchemy, the Trismegistan Arcana, only great poets know, and Villon is one. *"Quel magique ruissellement de pierres!"* cries J. K. Huysmans, adoring his genius, *"Quel étrange fourmillement de feux! Quelles étonnantes cassures d'étoffes rudes et rousses! Quelles folles striures de couleurs vives et mornes!"* *

There remains one final short thing to be said. He is a forerunner. "Through him first"—I quote Mr. Belloc again—"the great

---

*["What a magical stream of jewels!" cries J. K. Huysmans, adoring his genius, "What a strange clustering of fires! What astonishing rending of primitive, sunset-tinted fabrics! What fantastic striping of colors, vivid and gloomy!"]

⁵ *Le Drageoir aux Epices* (à Maître François Villon).

Town, and especially Paris, appeared and became permanent in letters. . . . Since his pen first wrote, a shining acerbity like the glint of a sword-edge has never deserted the literature of the capital. It was not only the metropolitan, it was the Parisian spirit which Villon found and fixed: that spirit which is so bright over the whole city, but which is not known in the first village outside; the influence that makes Paris Athenian."

This is a true judgment.

IV

THE CREAM OF THE TESTAMENTS

THE BALLADE TO OUR LADY

On the strong, simple tenderness and religious passion of this great Ballade there is no need to insist, beyond noting that the lines

Vierge portant, sans rompure encourir,
Le sacrement qu'on celebre a la messe,

sum up the Creed in a dozen words.

It is interesting to observe, in passing, how this noble salute and prayer to Our Lady, "Empress of the Infernal Marshes," is foreshadowed in English medieval poetry, so rich in devotion to Mary; strikingly in the opening of a Ballade by John Lydgate (1370-1451), of which Villon's opening might almost be an echo

Queene of Heaven, of Hell eke Emperess,
Lady of this world, O very Lodestar.

And again, in the beautiful anonymous *Queen of Courtesy:*

That Empress al Heaven hath
And Earth and Hell in her baily.

In modern English there is one lovely inspiration from Villon's chaunt:

Lady and Queen and Mystery manifold
And very Regent of the untroubled sky,
Whom in a dream St. Hilda did behold
And heard a woodland music passing by:
You shall receive me when the clouds are high
With evening, and the sheep attain the fold.
This is the faith which I have held and hold,
And this is that in which I mean to die.[1]

[1] Hilaire Belloc, *Ballade to Our Lady of Czestochowa.*

BALLADE

QUE VILLON FEIST A LA REQUESTE DE SA MERE, POUR PRIER NOSTRE DAME

DAME du ciel, regente terrienne,
Emperiere des infernaux palus,
Recevez moy, vostre humble chrestienne,
Que comprinse soye entre vos esleus,
Ce non obstant qu'oncques rien ne valus.
Les biens de vous, Ma Dame et Ma Maistresse,
Sont trop plus grans que ne suis pecheresse,
Sans lesquelz biens ame ne peut merir
N'avoir les cieulx, je n'en suis jangleresse:[2]
En ceste foy je vueil vivre et mourir.

A vostre Filz dictes que je suis sienne;
De luy soyent mes pechiez abolus;
Pardonne moy comme a l'Egipcienne,[3]
Ou comme il feist au clerc Theophilus,
Lequel par vous fut quitte et absolus,
Combien qu'il eust au deable fait promesse.
Preservez moy de faire jamais ce,
Vierge portant, sans rompure encourir,
Le sacrement qu'on celebre a la messe:
En ceste foy je vueil vivre et mourir.

Femme je suis povrette et ancïenne,
Qui riens ne sçay: oncques lettre ne leus.
Au moustier voy [4] dont suis paroissienne
Paradis paint, ou sont harpes et lus,
Et ung enfer ou dampnez sont boullus:
L'ung me fait paour, l'autre joye et liesse.
La joye avoir me fay, haulte Deesse,
A qui pecheurs doivent tous recourir,
Comblez de foy, sans fainte ne paresse:
En ceste foy je vueil vivre et mourir.

---

[2] *jangleresse* = trickster.
[3] *The Egyptian* is St. Mary of Egypt, penitent, whose story is given in *The Golden Legend*. The clerk *Theophilus,* Vidame of the church of Adana in Cilicia in the sixth century, being dispossessed of his office by the bishop, in order to regain possession of it sold himself to the Devil, and was redeemed by Our Lady. His story was a favourite one of the Middle Ages, and the Saxon nun Hroswitha, Gautier de Coincy, and Rutebeuf, among others, made a Morality from it. It is sculptured in high-relief in the tympanum of the North (Cloister) Door of Notre-Dame.
[4] *Au moustier voy:* The possibility of this minster being the Celestines' great church by the Bastille has been discussed elsewhere in this book.

THE BALLADE TO OUR LADY

Dante Gabriel Rossetti

Dame du ciel, Regente terrienne

Lady of Heaven and earth, and therewithal,
  Crowned Empress of the nether clefts of Hell,
I, thy poor Christian, on thy name do call,
  Commending me to thee, with thee to dwell,
  Albeit in nought I be commendable.
But all mine undeserving may not mar
Such mercies as thy sovereign mercies are;
  Without the which (as true words testify)
No soul can reach thy Heaven so fair and far.
  Even in this faith I choose to live and die.

Unto thy Son say thou that I am His,
  And to me graceless make Him gracious.
Sad Mary of Egypt lacked not of that bliss,
  Nor yet the sorrowful clerk Theophilus,
  Whose bitter sins were set aside even thus
Though to the Fiend his bounden service was.
Oh help me, lest in vain for me should pass
  (Sweet Virgin that shalt have no loss thereby)
The blessed Host and sacring of the Mass.
  Even in this faith I choose to live and die.

A pitiful poor woman, shrunk and old,
  I am, and nothing learn'd in letter-lore:
Within my parish-cloister I behold
  A painted Heaven where harps and lutes adore,
  And eke a Hell whose damned folk seethe full sore:
One bringeth fear, the other joy to me.
That joy, great Goddess, make thou mine to be—
  Thou of whom all must ask it, even as I;
And that which faith desires, that let it see.
  For in this faith I choose to live and die.

345

Vous portaſtes, digne Vierge, princesse,
Iesus regnant qu' n'a ne fin ne cesse.
Le Tout Puissant, prenant noſtre foiblesse,
Laissa les cieulx et nous vint secourir,
Offrit a mort sa tres chiere jeunesse;
Noſtre Seigneur tel eſt, tel le confesse:
En ceſte foy je vueil vivre et mourir.

O excellent Virgin Princess! Thou didſt bear
   King Jesus, our moſt excellent Comforter,
Who even of this our weakness craved a share
   And for our sake stooped to us from on high,
Offering to death His young life sweet and fair.
Such as He is, Our Lord, I Him declare
   And in this faith I choose to live and die.

THE BALLADE OF DEAD LADIES

ONE of the master-songs of the world, with its gentle rhymes in *-is*
and *-aine,* the exquisite ache of its music, caressing and soothing to
dreams, and its lovely refrain. Its melancholy inquiry and evocation
and its concern with Death are common to large masses of medieval
poetry: but it is incomparable.

Observe the rhyming of *moyne, essoyne, royne,* and *Saine.* This
was Parisian.

BALLADE

DES DAMES DU TEMPS JADIS

DICTES moy ou, n'en quel pays,
Est Flora [1] la belle Rommaine,
Archipiades,[2] ne Thaïs,[3]
Qui fut sa cousine germaine,
Echo parlant quant bruyt on maine
Dessus riviere ou sus estan,
Qui beaulté ot trop plus qu'humaine?
Mais ou sont les neiges d'antan?

Ou est la tres sage Helloïs,[4]
Pour qui fut chastré et puis moyne

---

[1] *Flora,* the celebrated Roman courtesan of Juvenal, *Sat.* ii. 9.
[2] *Archipiades* (or *Archipiada*) remains enigmas. It has been variously suggested that
Villon means the Greek courtesan *Hipparchia,* or perhaps Sophocles' mistress *Archippa.*
In 1896 M. Langlois, a professor at Lille, put forward the ingenious theory that it may
be *Alcibiades,* whose name Boëtius cites in praise of heroic beauty. This Villon may have
heard commented by a master in the Schools, and caught indistinctly.
[3] *Thaïs,* the Athenian courtesan who followed Alexander into Egypt; or perhaps the
Thaïs of Martial. The Middle Ages made the Egyptian Thaïs a penitent and a saint; the
composer Massenet and Anatole France, between them, a martyr.
[4] *Helloïs* and *Esbaillart* (Abelard) are well known. The site of their house is presumed to be at Number 9 of the Quai aux Fleurs. Until recently the reputed house of

THE BALLADE OF DEAD LADIES

Dante Gabriel Rossetti

Dictes moy ou, n'en quel pays

Tell me now in what hidden way is
    Lady Flora the lovely Roman?
Where's Hipparchia, and where is Thaïs,
    Neither of them the fairer woman?
    Where is Echo, beheld of no man,
Only heard on river and mere—
    She whose beauty was more than human? . . .
But where are the snows of yester-year?

Where's Héloïse, the learned nun,
    For whose sake Abeillard, I ween,

Pierre Esbaillart a Saint Denis?
Pour son amour ot ceſte essoyne.
Semblablement, ou eſt la royne
Qui commanda que Buridan [5]
Fuſt geté en ung sac en Saine?
Mais ou sont les neiges d'antan?

La royne Blanche [6] comme lis
Qui chantoit a voix de seraine,
Berte au grant pié,[7] Bietris, Alis,[8]
Haremburgis [9] qui tint le Maine,
Et Jehanne [10] la bonne Lorraine
Qu'Englois brulerent a Rouan;
Ou sont ilz, ou, Vierge souvraine?
Mais ou sont les neiges d'antan?

Envoy

Prince, n'enquerez de sepmaine
Ou elles sont, ne de ceſt an,
Que ce reffrain ne vous remaine:
Mais ou sont les neiges d'antan?

Canon Fulbert, the terrible uncle, was shown in the Rue Chanoinesse, on the north side of Notre-Dame, formerly part of the *Cloiſtre des Chanoines Noſtre-Dame*. Villon muſt have passed it often on his way to the house of Margot.

[6] *Buridan,* a celebrated professor of the University of Paris and a disciple of the Nominaliſt William of Ockham. In his youth, according to the tradition, he fell into the hands of the Queen of Burgundy, who is the centre of a Parisian legend exactly resembling that of Queen Thamar in the Russian folk-tale. The Queen lived in the Tour de Nesle (the weſt pavilion of the Palais Mazarin covers the site) and attracted into her bower any passer-by—ſtudents of the University especially—who pleased her fancy. When her caprice was satisfied she had her lovers thrown into the Seine: Buridan escaped by falling on a barge laden with ſtraw, towed under the Tower by his pupils. He ended his days towards 1360, aged over sixty. A pamphlet briskly entitled *Commentariolus hiſtoricus de adolescentibus Parisiensibus, per Buridanum, natione Picardum, ab illicitis cuiusdam Reginæ Franciæ amoribus retractis,* published at Leipzig in 1471, gives his ſtory; as also does the *Compendium* of Gaguin.

The Queen has been thought to be intended for Marguerite of Burgundy, wife of Louis x. ("*le Hutin*"). She was found guilty of adultery and executed by the King's order in 1314. There is no hiſtorical foundation for the Buridan legend.

[6] The *Queen Blanche* may be St. Louis' mother, Blanche of Caſtille, or a dream-figure of Villon's own.

[7] *Berte au grant pié,* Big-Foot Bertha, the tall wife of Pépin le Bref, and the mother, in the Epics, of Charlemagne.

[8] *Bietris* and *Alis* are from the Chanson de Geſte of *Hervi de Metz,* in the Lorraine Cycle, Bietris being the wife of Hervi de Metz, Alis his mother. Prompsault tries to identify them with Béatrix de Provence, wife of Louis viii.'s son Charles, and Alix de Champagne, wife of Louis le Jeune, dead in 1206; but this is pure pedantry. The poet may even have dreamed them.

[9] *Haremburgis* is Arembour, heiress of the Maine, wife of the celebrated Foulque v., Count of Anjou: d. 1126.

[10] *Jehanne* is of course St. Joan; burned in 1431. Domrémy, her birthplace, was then in the Duchy of Bar, part of medieval Lorraine.

Lost manhood and put priesthood on?
   (From Love he won such dule and teen)
   And where, I pray you, is the Queen
Who willed that Buridan should steer
   Sewed in a sack's mouth down the Seine? . . .
But where are the snows of yester-year?

White Queen Blanche, like a queen of lilies,
   With a voice like any mermaiden—
Bertha Broadfoot, Beatrice, Alice,
   And Ermengarde the Lady of Maine—
   And that good Joan whom Englishmen
At Rouen doomed and burned her there—
   Mother of God, where are they, then? . . .
But where are the snows of yester-year?

Envoy

Nay, never ask this week, fair lord,
   Where they are gone, nor yet this year,
Except with this for an overword—
But where are the snows of yester-year?

❀ ❀ ❀ ❀ ❀ ❀ ❀ ❀ ❀ ❀ ❀ ❀ ❀ ❀

THE EPITAPH, OR BALLADE OF THE HANGED

THIS superb, devout, and deadly earneſt exercise in the *macabré* needs little comment. Observe that the poet prophetically sees his body and those of his companions as if they had already been swinging and rotting for some time. The Montfaucon gibbet, as I have shown, was a place for junketting and night-parties. This faċt gives point to the imploring cry in the firſt ſtanza:

> *De noſtre mal personne ne s'en rie,*

and also that of the Envoi:

> *Hommes, icy n'a point de mocquerie.*

L'EPITAPHE

EN FORME DE BALLADE QUE FEIST VILLON POUR LUY & SES COMPAIGNONS, S'ATTENDANT ESTRE PENDU AVEC EULX

[*L'Epitaphe Villon.*]

FRERES humains qui après nous vivez,
N'ayez les cuers contre nous endurcis,
Car, se pitié de nous povres avez,
Dieu en aura plus toſt de vous mercis.
Vous nous voiez cy attachez cinq, six:
Quant de la char, que trop avons nourrie,
Elle eſt pieça devoree et pourrie,
Et nous, les os, devenons cendre et pouldre.
De noſtre mal personne ne s'en rie;
Mais priez Dieu que tous nous vueille absouldre!

Se freres vous clamons, pas n'en devez
Avoir desdaing, quoy que fusmes occis
Par juſtice. Toutesfois, vous sçavez
Que tous hommes n'ont pas bon sens rassis;
Excusez nous, puis que sommes transsis,

352

THE BALLADE OF THE HANGED

Algernon Charles Swinburne

Freres humains qui après nous vivez

Men, brother men, that after us yet live,
   Let not your hearts too hard against us be;
For if some pity of us poor men ye give,
   The sooner God shall take of you pity.
   Here are we five or six strung up, you see,
And here the flesh that all too well we fed
Bit by bit eaten and rotten, rent and shred,
   And we the bones grow dust and ash withal;
Let no man laugh at us discomforted,
   But pray to God that He forgive us all.

If we call on you, brothers, to forgive,
   Ye should not hold our prayer in scorn, though we
Were slain by law; ye know that all alive
   Have not the wit alway to walk righteously;
   Make therefore intercession heartily

Envers le Fils de la Vierge Marie,
Que sa grace ne soit pour nous tarie,
Nous preservant de l'infernale fouldre.
Nous sommes mors, ame ne nous harie;
Mais priez Dieu que tous nous vueille absouldre!

La pluye nous a buez et lavez,
Et le soleil dessechiez et noircis;
Pies, corbeaulx, nous ont les yeulx cavez,
Et arrachié la barbe et les sourcis.
Jamais nul temps nous ne sommes assis;
Puis ça, puis la, comme le vent varie,
A son plaisir sans cesser nous charie,
Plus becquetez d'oiseaulx que dez a couldre.
Ne soiez donc de nostre confrairie;
Mais priez Dieu que tous nous vueille absouldre!

ENVOI

Prince Jhesus, qui sur tous a maistrie,
Garde qu'Enfer n'ait de nous seigneurie: [1]
A luy n'ayons que faire ne que souldre.
Hommes, icy n'a point de mocquerie;
Mais priez Dieu que tous nous vueille absouldre!

[1] Longnon:

> Prince Jhesus, qui sur tous a maistrie,
> Garde qu'Enfer n'ait de nous seigneurie . . .

Thuasne:

> Prince Jhesus, qui sur tous seigneurie,
> Garde qu'Enfer n'ait de nous la maistrie . . .

With Him that of a Virgin's womb was bred,
That His grace be not as a dry well-head
   For us, nor let Hell's thunder on us fall;
We are dead, let no man harry or vex us dead,
   But pray to God that He forgive us all.

The rain has washed and laundered us all five,
   And the sun dried and blackened; yea, perdie,
Ravens and pies with beaks that rend and rive
   Have dug our eyes out, and plucked off for fee
   Our beards and eyebrows; never are we free,
Not once, to reſt; but here and there ſtill sped,
Drive at its wild will by the wind's change led,
   More pecked of birds than fruits on garden-wall:
Men, for God's love, let no gibe here be said,
   But pray to God that He forgive us all.

ENVOY

Prince Jesus, that of all art Lord and Head,
Keep us, that Hell be not our bitter bed;
   We have nought to do in such a maſter's hall.
Be ye not therefore of our fellowhead,
   But pray to God that He forgive us all.

THE BALLADE OF GOOD COUNSEL

TO THOSE OF NAUGHTY LIFE

THE nearest thing we have to this in English poetry as an evocation of medieval low life is, I think, Skelton's *Tunning of Elynour Rumming*; Skelton's picture being more convivial in a sluttish, boozy way and not professionally criminal.

The doctrine of this Ballade is admirable, and one sees the poet's wry grin as he writes it, drawing on his own rich experience. Henley's effective paraphrase in London thieves'-slang of the 'nineties appears in a later page of this book.

BALLADE DE BONNE DOCTRINE

A CEULX DE MAUVAISE VIE

[Ballade de bonne doctrine.]

"Car ou soies porteur de bulles,[1]
Pipeur [2] ou hasardeur de dez,
Tailleur de faulx coings,[3] tu te brusles
Comme ceulx qui sont eschaudez,
Traistres parjurs, de foy vuydez;
Soies larron, ravis ou pilles:
Ou en va l'acquest, que cuidez?
Tout aux tavernes et aux filles.

"Ryme, raille, cymballe, luttes,
Comme fol, fainctif,[4] eshontez;

[1] *Porteur de bulles:* An itinerant hawker of faked indulgences, such as throve on the strong devotion of the Middle Ages. A blood-brother to Chaucer's Pardoner. Jusserand, in his work on Chaucer, says of these impostors: "There is not a single stroke of satire in Chaucer's picture which cannot be justified by letters emanating from Papal or episcopal chancelleries." Yet they flourished.
[2] *Pipeur,* a dice-cogger.
[3] *Tailleur de faulx coings,* a coiner.
[4] *Fainctif,* a sneak-thief. Also a strolling player.

356

BALLADE OF GOOD COUNSEL

(Translation by John Payne)

Peddle indulgences as you may,
  Cog the dice for your cheating throws;
Try if counterfeit coin will pay,
    At risk of roasting at last, like those
    That deal in treason. Lie and glose,
Rob and ravish—what profits it?
    Who gets the purchase, do you suppose?
Taverns and wenches, every whit.

Rhyme, rail, wrestle, and cymbals play,
  Flute and fool it in mummers' shows;

Farce, broulle,[5] joue des fleuſtes;
Fais, es villes et es citez,
Farces, jeux et moralitez;
Gaigne au berlanc,[6] au glic,[7] aux quilles: [8]
Aussi bien va, or escoutez!
Tout aux tavernes et aux filles.

"De telx ordures te reculles,
Laboure, fauche champs et prez,
Sers et pense chevaux et mulles,
S'aucunement tu n'es lettrez;
Assez auras, se prens en grez.
Mais, se chanvre broyes ou tilles,
Ne tens ton labour qu'as ouvrez
Tout aux tavernes et aux filles."

ENVOI

"Chausses, pourpoins esguilletez,[9]
Robes, et toutes vos drappilles,
Ains que vous fassiez pis, portez
Tout aux tavernes et aux filles.

[5] *Broulle* may mean either to play in masquerades and farces or to practiſe sorcery. Compare *imbroglio*.
[6] *Berlanc*, a table game.
[7] *Glic*, a card game, resembling slightly the modern *bouillotte*. "Gleek, a game of cards, in which a *gleek* meant three cards alike" (Skeat).
[8] *Quilles*, skittles.
[9] *Pourpoins esguilletez*, tagged doublets.

358

Along with the strolling players stray
   From town to city, without repose;
Act mysteries, farces, imbroglios,
Win money at Gleek, or a lucky hit
   At the pins: like water, away it flows;
Taverns and wenches, every whit.

Turn from your evil courses, I pray,
   That smell so foul in a decent nose;
Earn your bread in some honest way,
   If you have no letters, nor verse nor prose,
   Plough or groom horses, beat hemp or toze,
Enough shall you have if you think but fit;
   But cast not your wage to the wind that blows;
Taverns and wenches, every whit.

Envoy

Doublets, pourpoints and silken hose,
   Gowns and linen, woven or knit,
Ere your wede's worn, away it goes:
   Taverns and wenches, every whit.

THE BALLADE AND PRAYER FOR THE SOUL OF
MASTER JEHAN COTART

AN admirable Bacchanalian thing, at once ironic, playful, and infused with real affection for a *rude beuveur*. Master Jehan Cotart was a lawyer of the Court of the Diocese of Paris, with the title *Procurator* or *Promotor Curiæ*. Villon mentions him early in the *Grant Testament,* and had obviously a friendship for him. The picture of old Fiery Face reeling up to Paradise, as he had so often reeled through the Quarter, hiccoughing and bellowing at the Gate,

BALLADE ET OROISON

PERE Noé, qui plantastes la vigne,[1]
Vous aussi, Loth,[2] qui beustes ou rochier,
Par tel party qu'Amours, qui gens engigne,
De voz filles si vous feist approuchier
(Pas ne le dy pour le vous reprouchier),
Archetriclin,[3] qui bien sceustes cest art,
Tous trois vous pry qu'o vous vueillez perchier
L'ame du bon feu maistre Jehan Cotart!

[1] *Pere Noé, qui plantastes la vigne.* Rabelais, who is so soaked in Villon's poetry, echoes this in the Prologue to the Second Book:
"*Noé le sainct homme, auquel tant sommes obligez & tenus de ce qu'il nous planta la vigne,*" etc.
[2] *Vous aussi, Loth.* The incident (in mentioning which the poet politely clears himself of any intent to carp) of Genesis xix.
[3] *Archetriclin,* the chief steward, *architriclinus,* of the marriage feast in Cana of Galilee:
"*Et autem gustavit architriclinus aquam vinum factam, et non sciebat unde esset,*" etc.
—St. John ii.
Villon uses the title as a proper name: a medieval habit.

360

and being admitted by the favour of Father Noë, Lot, and the Steward of Cana, all three ministers of the Sacred Vine, should have been painted by Rubens or Brauwer. The Procurator lives eternally in this Ballade. One can see his swagging belly, his jolly crimson face, and his great ruby nose, *diapré de bubelettes nacarat, boutonné d'améthystes troubles,* such a nose as Olivier Basselin's, in honour of which he wrote such a joyous *Vaux-de-Vire,* or the kind of superb nose belonging to the Canon Panzoult and Timber-Foot, Doctor of Angers, in the Second Book of *Pantagruel,* which resembled *la fluste d'un Alembic . . . pullulant, purpuré, à pompettes, tout esmaillé, tout boutonné, & brodé de gueulles;* and in the third stanza Villon has given an unforgettable glimpse of Master Cotart's progress home after an evening with the bottles, stumbling through the dark streets and bumping his head against a butcher's stall. The Procurator's tremulous old autograph last appears in a legal document of 1460. He died in January 1461.

In the Boozers' Breviary which Panurge might have compiled this ballade would certainly have been an Office Hymn.

BALLADE AND PRAYER FOR THE SOUL

(*1st verse*): Father Noë, who planted the Vine; you also, Lot, who drank in the grotto, in such fashion that Love, who mazes folks so, caused your daughters to approach you (I do not say this to reproach you!); Architriclinus, so learned in your art:—I pray you all three to receive on high the soul of the late good Master Jehan Cotart!

Jadis extraict il fut de vostre ligne,
Luy qui beuvoit du meilleur et plus chier,
Et ne deust il avoir vaillant ung pigne;
Certes, sur tous, c'estoit ung bon archier; [4]
On ne luy sceut pot des mains arrachier;
De bien boire ne fut oncques fetart.[5]
Nobles seigneurs, ne souffrez empeschier
L'ame du bon feu maistre Jehan Cotart!

Comme homme beu qui chancelle et trepigne
L'ay veu souvent, quant il s'alloit couchier,
Et une fois il se feist une bigne,[6]
Bien m'en souvient, a l'estal d'ung bouchier;
Brief, on n'eust sceu en ce monde serchier
Meilleur pyon,[7] pour boire tost et tart.
Faictes entrer quant vous orrez huchier [8]
L'ame du bon feu maistre Jehan Cotart!

ENVOI

Prince, il n'eust sceu jusqu'a terre crachier;
Tousjours crioit: "Haro! la gorge m'art." [9]
Et si ne sceust oncq sa seuf estanchier
L'ame du bon feu maistre Jehan Cotart.

---

[4] *C'estoit ung bon archier;* meaning that Master Cotart drew a good bow at a cask.
[5] *Fetart*, backward.
[6] *Bigne*, a bump, a blow.
[7] *Pyon*, a tosspot.
[8] *Huchier*, to bellow.
[9] *"Haro,"* etc.: "Hoi! My throat's afire!"

(2nd verse): For he was formerly of your own lineage, and ever drank of the beſt and deareſt, although he never was worth a brass penny. But truly he was the beſt of good topers, and no one could ever get the pot out of his grasp, nor was he ever backward at the bowl. Noble lords, do not suffer any impediment to the soul of the late good Maſter Jehan Cotart!

(3rd verse): Often have I seen him stagger and reel, having drink taken, when he went home to bed; and once, indeed, he banged his head—well I remember it—againſt a butcher's stall. In brief, you could not find anywhere in this world a better bottle-whacker, soaking early and late. Allow him, lords, to enter, when you hear a bellow from the soul of the late good Maſter Jehan Cotart!

(Envoy): Prince, he could scarcely spit on the ground for dry-ness! Forever he would roar: "Hoi! My throat's afire!" And never was he able to quench his thirſt—the soul of the late good Maſter Jehan Cotart!

⚜ ⚜ ⚜ ⚜ ⚜ ⚜ ⚜ ⚜ ⚜ ⚜ ⚜ ⚜ ⚜ ⚜

THE DOUBLE BALLADE

A FINE example of the swinging rhythm and verve of Villon in his more sardonic, clairvoyant mood.

DOUBLE BALLADE

Pour ce, amez tant que vouldrez,
Suyvez assemblees et festes,
En la fin ja mieulx n'en vauldrez
Et si n'y romprez que vos testes;
Folles amours font les gens bestes:
Salmon [1] en ydolatria,
Samson en perdit ses lunetes.[2]
Bien est eureux qui riens n'y a!

Orpheüs, le doux menestrier,[3]
Jouant de fleustes et musetes,
En fut en dangier du murtrier
Chien Cerberus a quatre testes;
Et Narcisus,[4] le bel honnestes,
En ung parfont puis se noya
Pour l'amour de ses amouretes.
Bien est eureux qui riens n'y a!

Sardana,[5] le preux chevalier,
Qui conquist le regne de Cretes,

[1] *Salmon* = Solomon.
[2] *Lunetes* = windows. Obvious slang for "eyes."
[3] *Menestrier* = musician. Villon got Orpheus no doubt out of Vergil, *Georgics* iv., that beautiful passage. Observe that he decorates Cerberus with four heads instead of the statutory three. This is for the sake of the metre.
[4] *Narcissus* did not die of the love of a woman, but of his own beauty. Nevertheless in verse as in lapidary inscriptions a man is not on his oath.
[5] *Sardana*. Possibly *Sardanapalus*, though Villon is wrong in attributing to him the conquest of Crete. *Saladin* has been suggested. The reference to spinning among the maidens recalls Achilles' behaviour when he hid at the court of Scyros in women's clothes, for love of his mistress Deidamia. Possibly Villon confused in his mind two or three heroes and invented a name, or took *Sardana* from some forgotten romance.

364

DOUBLE BALLADE

Now take your fill of love and glee,
 And after balls and banquets hie;
In the end you'll get no good for fee,
 But just heads broken, by and by;
 Light loves make beasts of men that sigh—
They changed the faith of Solomon,
 And left not Samson lights to spy:
Good luck has he that deals with none!

Sweet Orpheus, lord of minstrelsy,
 For this with flute and pipe came nigh
The danger of the Dog's heads three,
 That ravening at hell's door doth lie:
 Fain was Narcissus, fair and shy,
For Love's love, lightly lost and won,
 In a deep well to drown and die;
Good luck has he that deals with none!

Sardana, flower of chivalry,
 Who conquered Crete with horn and cry,

En voulut devenir moullier [6]
Et filler entre pucelletes;
David le roy,[7] sage prophetes,
Crainte de Dieu en oublia,
Voyant laver cuisses bien faites.
Bien eſt eureux qui riens n'y a!

Amon [8] en voulſt deshonnourer,
Faignant de menger tarteletes,
Sa seur Thamar et desflourer,
Qui fut inceſte deshonneſtes;
Herodes, pas ne sont sornetes,[9]
Saint Jehan Baptiſte en decola
Pour dances, saulx et chansonnetes.
Bien eſt eureux qui riens n'y a!

De moy, povre, je vueil parler:
J'en fus batu comme a ru toiles,[10]
Tout nu, ja ne le quiers celer.
Qui me feiſt maschier ces groselles,[11]
Fors Katherine de Vausselles? [12]
Noel le tiers eſt, qui fut la.
Mitaines a ces nopces telles,[13]
Bien eſt eureux qui riens n'y a!

Mais que ce jeune bacheler
Laissaſt ces jeunes bacheletes?
Non! et le deuſt on vif brusler
Comme ung chevaucheur d'escouvetes.[14]
Plus doulces luy sont que civetes;
Mais toutesfoys fol s'y fya:
Soient blanches, soient brunetes,
Bien eſt eureux qui riens n'y a!

---

[6] *Moullier* = woman. Lat. *mulier*.   [8] *Amon:* Ammon, son of David.
[7] *David le roy:* the Bathsheba incident.   [9] *Sornetes* = jests.

[10] *Batu comme a ru toiles:* beaten like washing in a ſtream. A vivid simile, as any one will perceive who has watched laundresses by a French river thumping their linen with the bat.

[11] *Maschier ces groselles:* chew such (sour) gooseberries.

[12] *Katherine de Vausselles* we know. Also Noël le Jolis.

[13] *Mitaines a ces nopces telles:* a reference to a country wedding cuſtom. After the ceremony the gueſts took off their gloves or mittens and playfully beat one another with them, using the formula: *"Des noces vous souviengne"*—"Remember this wedding!" In a similar fashion children's ears were once boxed in England at the passing of a royal procession. Rabelais in the Fourth Book of *Pantagruel* tells a long and extremely dull ſtory of the mock wedding at the house of the Seigneur de Basché, at which the butts of the party are so brutally thrashed in accordance with this cuſtom that they emerge from the ceremony half jellied.

[14] *Chevaucheur d'escouvetes:* a rider on broomſticks: a wizard.

366

For this was fain a maid to be
   And learn with girls the thread to ply:
   King David, wise in prophecy,
Forgot the fear of God for one
   Seen washing either shapely thigh:
Good luck has he that deals with none!

For this did Ammon, craftily
   Feigning to eat of cakes of rye,
Deflower his sister fair to see,
   Which was foul incest; and hereby
   Was Herod moved—it is no lie—
To lop the head of Baptist John
   For dance and jig and psaltery;
Good luck has he that deals with none!

Next of myself I tell—poor me!—
   How thrashed like clothes at wash was I
Stark naked, I must needs agree:
   Who made me eat so sour a pie
   But Katherine of Vausselles? thereby
Noël took third part of that fun;
   Such wedding-gloves are ill to buy;
Good luck has he that deals with none!

But for that young man fair and free
   To pass those young maids lightly by,
Nay, would you burn him quick, not he!
   Like broom-horsed witches though he fry,
   They are sweet as civet in his eye:
But trust them, and you're fooled anon;
   For white or brown, and low or high,
Good luck has he that deals with none!

                              (*Swinburne.*)

A BALLADE FROM THE JARGON

THE Jargon or Jobelin (*jobelin,* from the Patriarch Job, patron of beggars) of Villon's day was already a sealed language when Cl. Marot edited him in 1533. "Touching the Jargon," says Marot in his Preface, "I leave it to be exposed and explained by Villon's successors in the art of the crowbar and the jemmy"—*l'art de la pinse et du croq.* Guillaume Colletet, towards 1650, speaks of the existence in his time of a glossary of the Argot,[1] but disdains to use it to elucidate the Jargon; if indeed it did. The Jargon Colletet dismisses as *un recueil de mots dont se servoient les trucheurs et les couppeurs de bourses.* No honest man (adds Colletet) will feel any desire to comprehend this stuff, the property of the gentry of the bag and cord.

Since then Vitu, Francisque Michel, Lucien Schöne, Marcel Schwob, Jules de Marthold, Aug. Longnon, and above all Lazare Sainéan, have grappled with the Jargon, using the Dijon documents of 1455 as a basis; and although more than one of them claims to have understood and interpreted a large amount of it, the verdict of M. Sainéan, most qualified of all to speak, seems final: the Jargon remains, and will remain, for the greater part, undecipherable.[2] The Lexicon of the Jargon I have used is that of Longnon, compared with Sainéan. Fifty years hence scholars may be recoiling with equal despair from the slang of the *fortifs* which so embellishes

---

[1] This was apparently not the *Jargon ou langaige de l'Argot réformé,* many times reprinted since the end of the sixteenth century, but (thinks Lacroix) the *Dictionnaire en langage blesquin* published at the end of a volume of Lives of the Packmen, Mumpers and Bohemians, by an author signing himself "Pechon de Ruby, *gentilhomme breton.*" The date of this was 1596: printed at Lyons.

[2] Fewer than a hundred words, all told, are more or less explicable. Compare Dekker's "Canters Dictionarie" in *Lanthorne and Candle-Light,* 1608.

M. Francis Carco's studies of the modern Parisian underworld; for it is axiomatic that the criminal slang of any great city must change often and with great swiftness.

Many of the meanings given below are conjectural. I find this Ballade irresistible: the very sound and arrangement of the words is like a gambol of gargoyles and grotesque villainous shapes. The Envoi especially, though hardly a word in it can be deciphered with any assurance of accuracy, is an antic hay, danced in the Cour des Miracles.

LE JARGON OU JOBELIN

DE MAISTRE FRANÇOYS VILLON

BALLADE III

Spelicans,[1]
Qui en tous temps
Avancez dedens le pogois,
Gourde piarde,
Et sur la tarde,
Desbousez les povres nyois,
Et pour soustenir voz pois,
Les duppes sont privez de caire,
Sans faire haire,
Ne hault braire,
Mais plantez ilz sont comme joncs
Pour les sires qui sont si longs.

Souvent aux arques,[2]
A leurs marques,
Se laissent tous jours desbouser
Pour ruer
Et enterver
Pour leur contre, que lors faisons
La fée aux arques respons,
Et ruez deux coups ou trois
Aux gallois;
Deux ou trois
Nineront trestout aux frontz
Pour les sires qui sont si longs.

[1] *Spelicans*, light-fingered blades; *pogois*, cabaret; *gourde piarde*, good liquor; *desbouser*, to strip, rob; *caire*, money; *haire*, trouble; *braire*, squeak, yell; *joncs*, either the straw of prisons or the "long poles," or gibbet; *sires*, dupes.
[2] *Arques*, dice; *marque*, a trull; *enterver*, to hear or understand; *gallois*, ruffling fellows.

369

Et pour ce, benardz,[3]
Coquillars,
Rebecquez vous de la montjoye,
Qui desvoye
Vostre proye,
Et vous fera du tout brouer
Par joncher et enterver
Qui est aux pigons bien cher,
Pour rifler
Et placquer
Les angelz de mal tous rons,
Pour les sires qui sont si longs.

ENVOY

De paour des hurmes
Et des grumes,
Rasurez voz en droguerie
Et faierie,
Et ne soiez plus sur les joncs [4]
Pour les sires qui sont si longs.

---

[3] *Benardz*, ninnies; also a category of thieves unknown; *montjoye*, a signpost, possibly also a gibbet; *desvoyer*, lead astray; *brouer*, to run; *joncher*, to cheat; *rifler*, rifle, rob; *angelz*, Sergeants or Archers of the Watch.
[4] *Ne soiez plus sur les joncs* means "Look out for quod."

✿ ✿ ✿ ✿ ✿ ✿ ✿ ✿ ✿ ✿ ✿ ✿ ✿ ✿

FROM THE *PETIT TESTAMENT*

Most of these verses are already scattered through this book. I give them here again, the most vivid of them, together and in their order. By reading them thus their colour and rhythm are more amply tasted.

371

FROM THE *PETIT TESTAMENT*

[LES LAIS]

I   L'AN quatre cens cinquante six,
Je, Françoys Villon, escollier,
Considerant, de sens rassis,
Le frain aux dens, franc au collier,
Qu'on doit ses oeuvres conseillier,
Comme Vegece le raconte,[1]
Sage Rommain, grant conseillier,
Ou autrement on se mesconte . . .

II   En ce temps que j'ay dit devant,
Sur le Noel, morte saison,
Que les loups se vivent de vent
Et qu'on se tient en sa maison,
Pour le frimas, pres du tison,
Me vint ung vouloir de brisier
La tres amoureuse prison
Qui souloit mon cuer debrisier.

.   .   .   .

IX   Premierement, ou nom du Pere,
Du Filz et du Saint Esperit,
Et de sa glorieuse Mere
Par qui grace riens ne perit,
Je laisse, de par Dieu, mon bruit
A maistre Guillaume Villon,
Qui en l'onneur de son nom bruit,
Mes tentes [2] et mon pavillon.

X   Item, a celle que j'ay dit,
Qui si durement m'a chassié
Que je suis de joye interdit
Et de tout plaisir dechassié,
Je laisse mon cuer enchassié,
Palle, piteux, mort et transy:
Elle m'a ce mal pourchassié,
Mais Dieu luy en face mercy!

[1] *Comme Vegece le raconte:* The muddled edition of Galiot du Pré, 1532, gives a clue to this mysterious reference to Vegetius, the fourth-century author of a treatise, *De Re militari,* which contains no such moral lesson as Villon indicates. Du Pré reads *Valere* instead of *Vegece.* It is likely that *Valere,* Valerius Maximus, is the correct reading. To his *De dictis factisque memorabilibus* Villon is obviously alluding.

[2] *Mes tentes:* In the feudal ages the heir received from the dying head of the family his blazons and devices, and the pavilions (or standards) appertaining. G. Paris, as we have seen, suggests a double meaning here—*tantes,* referring to hypothetical relatives of the poet's.

FROM THE LITTLE TESTAMENT

(Payne)

I   This fourteen six and fiftieth year,
    I, François Villon, clerk that be,
    Considering with senses clear,
    Bit betwixt teeth and collar-free,
    That one must needs look orderly
    Unto his works (as counselleth
    Vegetius, wise Roman he),
    Or else amiss one reckoneth,—

II   In this year, as before I said,
    Hard by the dead of Christmas-time,
    When upon wind the wolves are fed
    And for the rigour of the rime
    One hugs the hearth from None to Prime,
    Wish came to me to break the stress
    Of that most dolorous prison-clime
    Wherein Love held me in duress.

     .   .   .

IX   First, in the Name of God the Lord,
    The Son and eke the Holy Spright,
    And in her name, by whose accord
    No creature perisheth outright,
    To Master Villon, Guillaume hight,
    My fame I leave, that still doth swell
    In his name's honour day and night,
    And eke my tents and pennoncel.

X   Item, to her who, as I said,
    So dourly banished me her sight,
    That all my gladness she forbade
    And ousted me of all delight,
    I leave my heart in desposite,
    Piteous and pale, and numb and dead.
    She brought me to this sorry plight:
    May God not wreak it on her head!

XIX   Et a maiſtre Jacques Raguier
       Laisse l'Abruvouër Popin,
       Pesches, poires, sucre, figuier,
       Tousjours le chois d'ung bon loppin,
       Le trou de *la Pomme de Pin,*
       Clos et couvert, au feu la plante,
       Emmailloté en jacoppin;
       Et qui voudra planter,[3] si plante.

       .   .   .

XXII   Item, au Chevalier du Guet,
       Le Hëaulme [4] luy eſtablis;
       Et aux pietons [5] qui vont d'aguet
       Taſtonnant par ces eſtablis,
       Je leur laisse deux beaux riblis,
       La Lanterne a la Pierre au Let.
       Voire, mais j'auray *les Troys Lis,*
       S'ilz me mainent en Chaſtellet.

       .   .   .

XXXI   Item, je laisse a mon barbier
       Les rongneures de mes cheveulx,
       Plainement et sans destourbier;
       Au savetier mes souliers vieulx,
       Et au freppier mes habitz tieulx
       Que, quant du tout je les delaisse,
       Pour moins qu'ilz ne couſterent neufz
       Charitablement je leur laisse.

       .   .   .

XL   Fait au temps de ladite date
       Par le bien renommé Villon,
       Qui ne menjue figue ne date.
       Sec et noir comme escouvillon,[6]
       Il n'a tente ne pavillon
       Qu'il n'ait laissié a ses amis,
       Et n'a mais qu'ung peu de billon
       Qui sera tantoſt a fin mis.

[3] *Planter,* in the laſt line, is a word of the Jargon used here in a moſt unseemly significance.

[4] *Hëaulme,* a closed helmet without visor or ventail, but with two side grilles. This made it difficult for the wearer to see in front of him. It was a common house and tavern sign in Paris, and figures in the papers concerning the University's action against the Provoſt in 1453.

[5] *Pietons,* the unmounted Sergeants of the Châtelet.

[6] *Escouvillon,* a maulkin, or baker's oven-mop.

XIX   Item, I leave to Jacques Raguier
The "Puppet" Cistern, peach and pear,
Perch, chickens, custards, night and day,
At the Great Figtree choice of fare,
And eke the Fircone Tavern, where
He may sit, cloaked in cloth of frieze,
Feet to the fire and back to chair,
And let the world wag at his ease.

      ·   ·   ·   ·

XXII   The Captain of the Watch, also,
Shall have the Helmet, in full right;
And to the crimps that cat-foot go,
A-fumbling in the stalls by night,
I leave two rubies, clear and bright,
The Lantern of the Pierre-au-Let,
'Deed, the Three Lilies have I might,
Hales they me to the Châtelet.

      ·   ·   ·   ·

XXXI   Unto my barber I devise
The ends and clippings of my hair;
Item, on charitable wise,
I leave my old boots, every pair,
Unto the cobbler, and declare
My clothes the broker's, so these two
May when I'm dead my leavings share,
For less than what they cost when new.

      ·   ·   ·

XL   Done at the season aforesaid
Of the right well-renowned Villon,
Who eats nor white nor oaten bread,
Black as a maulkin, shrunk and wan.
Tents and pavilions, every one
He's left to one or t'other friend;
All but a little pewter's gone,
That will, ere long, come to an end.

❀ ❀ ❀ ❀ ❀ ❀ ❀ ❀ ❀ ❀ ❀ ❀ ❀

FROM THE GRANT TESTAMENT

THESE nine verses, four early, one quaint conceit from near the end, and those leading to the Epitaph, I have chosen more for sincerity and spiritual depth than for the irony, anger, despair, or crackling laughter which are other notes of the Great Teſtament.

FROM THE *GRANT TESTAMENT*

[LE TESTAMENT]

LXXXIV   Ou nom de Dieu, comme j'ay dit,
Et de sa glorieuse Mere,
Sans pechié soit parfait ce dit
Par moy, plus megre que chimere;
Se je n'ay eu fievre eufumere,[1]
Ce m'a fait divine clemence;
Mais d'autre dueil et perte amere
Je me tais, et ainsi commence.

LXXXV   Premier, je donne ma povre ame
A la benoiſte Trinité,
Et la commande a Noſtre Dame,
Chambre de la divinité,
Priant toute la charité
Des dignes neuf Ordres[2] des cieulx
Que par eulx soit ce don porté
Devant le Trosne precieux.

---

[1] *Fievre eufumere,* the diurnal fever, or ague.
[2] *Neuf Ordres,* the nine Choirs of Angels.

376

FROM THE *GRANT TESTAMENT*

(Payne)

LXXXIV Now in God's name and with His aid
And in Our Lady's name no less,
Let without sin this say be said
By me, grown haggard for duress.
If I nor light nor fire possess,
God hath ordained it for my sin;
But as to this and other stress
I will leave talking and begin.

LXXXV First, my poor soul (which God befriend)
Unto the Blessed Trinity
And to Our Lady I commend,
The fountain of Divinity,
Beseeching all the charity
Of the Nine Orders of the sky,
That it of them transported be
Unto the throne of God most high.

377

LXXXVI   Item, mon corps j'ordonne et laisse
A noſtre grant mere la terre;
Les vers n'y trouveront grant gresse,
Trop luy a fait faim dure guerre.
Or luy soit delivré grant erre:
De terre vint, en terre tourne;
Toute chose, se par trop n'erre,
Voulentiers en son lieu retourne.

LXXXVII   Item, et a mon plus que pere,
Maiſtre Guillaume de Villon,
Qui eſté m'a plus doulx que mere
A enfant levé de maillon: [3]
Degeté m'a de maint bouillon,[4]
Et de ceſtuy pas ne s'esjoye,
Si luy requier a genouillon
Qu'il m'en laisse toute la joye;

.   .   .

CLXVIII[5]   Item, donne aux amans enfermes,
Sans le laiz maiſtre Alain Chartier,[6]
A leurs chevez, de pleurs et lermes
Treſtout fin plain ung benoiſtier,[7]
Et ung petit brin d'esglantier,
Qui soit tout vert, pour guipillon,
Pourveu qu'ilz diront ung psaultier [8]
Pour l'ame du povre Villon.

[3] *Maillon,* swaddling-clothes.
[4] *Degeté m'a de maint bouillon* seems to cry for our popular locution. "He has got me out of the soup a hundred times." *Bouillon* is from *tourbillon* = upheaval, scrape, mess.
[5] A dainty, finicking trifle, mingling sacred rites with profane love as Lydgate mingles them in his Mass to Venus. The Middle Ages had a vital enough faith to be able to do these things.
[6] *Alain Chartier* (c. 1386-1449), the mannered and prodigious dull Court poet about whose memory clings the ſtory of the Princess who kissed his lips as he sat asleep in the sun, on account of all the good words that had issued therefrom. This is the moſt poetic thing about Alain Chartier, a diplomat of sorts. The *laiz* Villon speaks of is, some think, the *Hospital d'Amours:* but Foulet hits the gold more precisely in tracing the allusion to *La Belle Dame sans Mercy:*

> *Je laisse aux amoureulx malades,*
> *Qui ont espoir d'allegement,*
> *Faire chansons, ditz et balades,*
> *Chascun en son entendement. . . .*

[7] *Ung benoiſtier,* a holy-water ſtoup, filled with their tears, into which the despairing lovers muſt dip their *guipillon,* or sprinkler, a sprig of fresh hawthorn. The conceit might be out of Herrick, or even the Yellow Book.
[8] *Ung psaultier,* a Book of Hours, psalter, *psalterium,* containing the whole of the Psalms, divided among the Offices of every day in the year—Matins, Lauds, Prime, Terce, Sext, None, Vespers, and Compline. It is hardly likely that Villon expeĉts the lovers, however desperate, to recite the whole Psalter for him. He means the Hours of one day.

LXXXVI   Item, my body, I ordain
Unto the Earth, our grandmother;
Thereof the worms will have small gain;
Hunger hath worn it many a year.
Let it be given ſtraight to her,
From earth it came, to earth apace
Returns; all things, except I err,
Do gladly turn to their own place.

LXXXVII   Item, to Guillaume de Villon,—
(My more than father, who indeed
To me more tenderness hath shown
Than mothers to the babes they feed,
Who me from many a scrape hath freed
And now of me heth scant liesse,—
I do entreat him, bended-kneed,
He leave me to my present ſtress.

     .   .   .   .

CLXVIII   To lovers sick and sorrowful,
As well as Alain Chartier's Lay,
At bedhead, a benature-full
Of tears I give, and eke a spray
Of eglantine or flowering May
(To sprinkle with) in time of green;
Provided they a Psalter say
To save poor Villon's soul from teen.

CLXXVI   Item, j'ordonne a Sainte Avoye,[9]
Et non ailleurs, ma sepulture;
Et, affin que chascun me voie,
Non pas en char, mais en painture,
Que l'on tire mon eſtature
D'ancre, s'il ne couſtoit trop chier.
De tombel? riens: je n'en ay cure,
Car il greveroit le planchier.

CLXXVII   Item, vueil qu'autour de ma fosse
Ce que s'ensuit, sans autre hiſtoire,
Soit escript en lettre assez grosse,
Et qui n'auroit point d'escriptoire,
De charbon ou de pierre noire,
Sans en riens entamer le plaſtre;
Au moins sera de moy memoire,
Telle qu'elle eſt d'ung bon follaſtre:

EPITAPHE

CLXXVIII   CY GIST ET DORT EN CE SOLLIER,[10]
QU'AMOURS OCCIST DE SON RAILLON,[11]
UNG POVRE PETIT ESCOLLIER,
QUI FUT NOMMÉ FRANÇOYS VILLON.
ONCQUES DE TERRE N'OT SILLON.
IL DONNA TOUT, CHASCUN LE SCET:
TABLES, TRESTEAULX, PAIN, CORBEILLON.
GALLANS, DICTES EN CE VERSET:

VERSET
[ou rondeau]

Repos eternel [12] donne a cil,
Sire, et clarté perpetuelle,
Qui vaillant plat ni escuelle [13]
N'eut oncques, n'ung brin de percil.
Il fut rez,[14] chief, barbe et sourcil,
Comme ung navet qu'on ret ou pelle.
Repos eternel donne a cil.

[9] *Sainte Avoye:* We have already seen that the nuns' chapel was on the firſt floor.
[10] *Sollier* = upper floor, chamber. Lat. *solerium*. Mid. Eng. *soler*.
[11] *Raillon*, the bolt shot from an arbaleſt.
[12] *Repos eternel*, etc.: a deliberate evocation of the Introit which begins the Mass for the Dead:
Requiem æternam dona eis, Domine, et lux perpetua luceat eis.
[13] *Escuelle* = bowl.
[14] *Il fut rez*, etc.: showing that the poet, by privations, by misery, by shaving in prison, or moſt probably by some malady, had become completely bald. Observe the "dying fall,"

CLXXVI   Item, my body, I ordain,
At Ste. Avoye shall buried be;
And that my friends may there again
My image and presentment see,
Let one the semblant limn of me
In ink, if that be not too dear.
No other monument, perdie:
'Twould overload the floor, I fear.

CLXXVII   Item, I will that over it
That which ensues, without word more,
In letters large enough be writ;
If ink fail (as I said before),
Let them the words with charcoal score,
So they do not plaſter drag:
'Twill serve to keep my name in ſtore
As that of a good crack-brained wag.

Epitaph

CLXXVIII   HERE LIES AND SLUMBERS IN THIS PLACE
ONE WHOM LOVE WREAKED HIS IRE UPON:
A SCHOLAR, POOR OF GOODS AND GRACE,
THAT HIGHT OF OLD FRANÇOIS VILLON:
ACRE OR FURROW HAD HE NONE.
'TIS KNOWN HIS ALL HE GAVE AWAY;
BREAD, TABLES, TRESTLES, ALL ARE GONE;
GALLANTS, OF HIM THIS ROUNDEL SAY:

Roundel

Æternam Requiem dona,
   Lord God, and everlaſting light,
   To him who never had, poor wight,
Platter, or aught therein to lay!
Hair, eyebrows, beard all fallen away,
   Like a peeled turnip was his plight.
Æternam Requiem dona,

Rigueur le transmit en exil
Et luy frappa au cul la pelle,
Non obstant qu'il dit: "J'en appelle!"
Qui n'est pas terme trop subtil.
Repos eternel donne a cil.

as in a plainsong chant, of this beautiful verse. In three MSS., and in Levet's first printed edition of 1489, the refrain is given as *"Repos"* simply; and this, I think, deepens its note of longing and finality.

Exile compelled him many a day
   And Death at last his breech did smite,
   Though "I appeal!" with all his might
The man in good plain speech did say.
Æternam Requiem dona.

❀ ❀ ❀ ❀ ❀ ❀ ❀ ❀ ❀ ❀ ❀ ❀ ❀ ❀

V

THREE ENGLISH VERSIONS

PRAYER OF THE OLD WOMAN, VILLON'S MOTHER

JOHN MILLINGTON SYNGE

MOTHER of God that's Lady of the Heavens, take myself, the poor sinner, the way I'll be along with them that's chosen.

Let you say to your own Son that He'd have a right to forgive my share of sins, when it's the like He's done, many's the day, with big and famous sinners. I'm a poor aged woman was never at school, and is no scholar with letters, but I've seen pictures in the chapel with Paradise on one side, and harps and pipes in it, and the place on the other side, where sinners do be boiled in torment; the one gave me great joy, the other a great fright and scaring; let me have the good place, Mother of God, and it's in your faith I'll live always.

It's yourself that bore Jesus, that has no end or death, and He the Lord Almighty, that took our weakness and gave Himself to sorrows, a young and gentle man. It's Himself is Our Lord surely, and it's in that faith I'll live always.

FROM THE LAMENT OF THE BELLE HEAULMIERE

Algernon Charles Swinburne

Advis m'est que j'oy regreter

MESEEMETH I heard cry and groan
    That sweet who was the armourer's maid;
For her young years she made sore moan,
    And right upon this wise she said:
    "Ha! fierce old age with foul bald head,
To spoil fair things thou art over-fain;
    Who holdeth me? who? would God I were dead!
Would God I well were dead and slain!

VI   "Where is my faultless forehead's white,
    The lifted eyebrows, soft gold hair,
Eyes wide apart and keen of sight,
    With subtle skill in the amorous air;
    The straight nose, great nor small, but fair,
The small carved ears of shapeliest growth,
    Chin dimpling, colour good to wear,
And sweet red splendid kissing mouth?

VIII   "A writhled forehead, hair gone grey,
    Fallen eyebrows, eyes gone red and blind,
Their laughs and looks all fled away,
    Yea, all that smote men's hearts are fled;
    The bowed nose, fallen from goodlihead;
Foul flapping ears like water-flags;
    Peaked chin, and cheeks all waste and dead,
And lips that are two skinny rags.

X   "So we make moan for the old sweet days,
    Poor old light women, two or three
Squatting above the straw-fire's blaze,
    The bosom crushed against the knee;
    Like fagots on a heap we be,
Round fires soon lit, soon quenched and done:
    And we were once so sweet, even we!
Thus fareth many and many an one."

VILLON'S STRAIGHT TIP TO ALL CROSS COVES

WILLIAM ERNEST HENLEY

Tout aux tavernes & aux filles

SUPPOSE you screeve? or go cheap-jack?
   Or fake the broads? or fig a nag?
Or thimble-rig? or knap a yack?
   Or pitch a snide? or smash a rag?
   Suppose you duff? or nose and lag?
Or get the ſtraight, and land your pot?
   How do you melt the multy swag?
Booze and the blowens cop the lot.

Fiddle, or fence, or mace, or mack,
   Or moskeneer, or flash the drag;
Dead-lurk a crib, or do a crack,
   Pad with a slang, or chuck a fag;
   Bonnet, or tout, or mump and gag;
Rattle the tats, or mark the spot:
   You cannot bag a single ſtag—
Booze and the blowens cop the lot.

Suppose you try a different tack,
   And on the square you flash your flag?
At penny-a-lining make your whack,
   Or with the mummers mump and gag?
   For nix, for nix the dibs you bag!
At any graft, no matter what,
   Your merry goblins soon ſtravag—
Booze and the blowens cop the lot.

ENVOY

It's up the spout and Charley Wag
With wipes and tickers and what not;
   Until the squeezer nips your scrag,
Booze and the blowens cop the lot.

VI

APPENDICES

APPENDIX A

THE EARLIER SCHOOLS

THE Lateran Council of 1179 ordered a school to be established in the precincts of every cathedral in Christendom, with at least one master: for clerks and poor students education was to be free. From these sprang a galaxy of great schools, the direct origin of the Universities of Europe. It is therefore well to be aware, in considering the rise of the University of Paris, as also of Oxford and the other thirteenth-century foundations, of their immediate forerunners, the abbatial and episcopal Schools of Europe.

The most important of these were:

England . The abbatial School of York, under Alcuin.

Low Countries The capitular Schools of Utrecht, Liége, and Tournai.

Germany . The abbatial Schools of Fulda, under Raban Maur; Salzburg, St. Gall, and Reichenau.

France . . The *Ecole Palatine,* with Alcuin, Raban Maur, and Erigen; the abbatial Schools of Tours (Alcuin taught here too), Corbie, Cluny (with St. Odo), Le Bec (with St. Anselm and Lanfranc), Fleury, and Auxerre. Also the episcopal Schools of Lyons, Reims, Laon (St. Anselm taught here), and Chartres (with John of Salisbury).

Paris . . The Cathedral School of Notre-Dame and the abbatial Schools of St. Geneviève, St. Germain-des-Prés, and St. Victor—this last notable for the famous four, Thomas, Hugues, Adam, and Richard de St. Victor, and also St. Thomas Becket.

For this list I am indebted to the *Initiation thomiste* of the learned French Dominican, Father Pègues.

APPENDIX B

VILLON-PANURGE

THÉOPHILE GAUTIER, round about 1832, firſt put forward the thesis that Rabelais drew Panurge in the main from Villon, of whose works Rabelais had such knowledge, and for whose memory such affection. I judge it of value to reproduce the portrait of Panurge from the Second Book of *Pantagruel*, Sir Thomas Urquhart's translation, 1653.

Poor Panurge bibb'd and bows'd most villainously, for he was as dry as a Red-Herring, as lean as a Rake, and like a poor lank slender Cat, walked gingerly as if he had trod upon Egges.—II. xiv.

Panurge was of a middle Stature, not too high, nor too low, and had somewhat an Aquiline Nose, made like the handle of a Rasor: he was at that Time five and thirty years old or thereabouts, fine to gild like a leaden Dagger; for he was a notable Cheater and Cony-catcher, he was a very gallant and proper Man of his Person, only that he was a little leacherous, and naturally subject to a kinde of Disease, which at that time they call'd lack of Money: it is an incomparable Grief, yet, notwithſtanding he had three-score and three Tricks to come by it at his Need, of which the moſt honourable and moſt ordinary was in manner of Thieving, secret Purloining and Filching; for he was a wicked lewd Rogue, a Cosener, Drinker, Royster, Rover, and a very dissolute and debautch'd Fellow, if there were any in Paris; otherwise, and in all Matters else, the best and most vertuous Man in the World; and he was ſtill contriving some Plot, and devising Mischief againſt the Serjeants and the Watch.—*Ib.*, xvi.

In brief, he had (as I said before) threescore and three Wayes to acquire Money, but he had two hundred and fourteen to spend it, beside his Drinking.—*Ib.*, xvii.

And with this he ran away as fast as he could, for Feare of Blowes, whereof he was naturally fearful.—*Ib.*, xxi.

At Pantagruel's firſt meeting with Panurge (II. ix.) Rabelais makes Panurge "a young Man of very comely Stature, and surpassing handsome in all the Lineaments of his Body." I conjecture, therefore, that he began to draw Panurge but vaguely, feeling his way, as it were; and that as he proceeded—it is five chapters more before he describes Panurge further, emphasising this time his leanness and cat-like tread—the Villon portrait gradually took shape and blossomed in his mind.

In the chapter (ii. xvi.) called "Of the Qualities and Conditions of Panurge" there seem clear echoes. For example:

> At one time he assembled three or foure especial good Hacksters and roaring Boyes, made them in the evening drink like Templers, afterwards led them till they came under St. Genevieve, or about the Colledge of Navarre, and at the houre that the Watch was coming up that way, which he knew by putting his Sword upon the Pavement, and his Eare by it, and when he heard his Sword shake, it was an infallible Signe that the Watch was neare at that instant: then he and his Companions took a Tumbrel or Dung-Cart, and gave it the Brangle, hurling it with all their Force down the Hill, and so overthrew all the poor Watchmen like Pigs, and then ran away, etc.

In this, in other japes and frolics of Panurge, and again in his squandering three years' revenues of his Lairdship of Salmygondin in fourteen days,

> in a thousand little Banquets and jolly Collations, keeping open House for all Comers and Goers; yea, to all good Fellows, young Girles, and pretty Wenches; felling Timber, burning the great Logs for the sake of the Ashes, borrowing Money before-hand, buying dear, selling cheap, and eating his Corn (as it were) whilst it was but Grass,

I see the Villon of the *Pet-au-Deable,* the *Repues Franches,* and the College burglary. Finally, Rabelais has not overlooked the poet's other dominant note:

> One day I found Panurge very much out of Countenance, melancholick and silent.—ii. xvii.

It is pleasant to believe that the author of *Pantagruel,* who shared with the Parisian poet, his spiritual ancestor, the magic formula, made him to some extent his model for Panurge, the *compère* of his gigantic work.

393

APPENDIX C

THE DOUBLE REMISSION

A LETTER OF REMISSION was generally granted for a delinquency on a petition presented by the *suppliant* himself, after having voluntarily handed himself over to Justice: but if he had, as the term went, "absented himself," either through fear or some other cause, his near relations, *parens & amis charnelz,* might apply for a Letter in his behalf. In this case they had to explain clearly all the circumstances in which the petitioner implored the *grace & misericorde* of the King; and attenuated them as much as they dared. The Letter, being granted, was obtained either from the Grande Chancellerie of the Great Seal or from the Petite.Chancellerie of the Lesser Seal; it was customary to apply to either, but not to both, especially if only one delinquent was concerned.

Villon, being an absentee, very daringly but prudently took advantage of the two names, Montcorbier, *dit* Villon and des Loges, by which he was known, to make sure of getting a Letter of Remission, 'through his relations, in one name at least: and applied to both Chancelleries. He therefore got two Letters, one from the Grande Chancellerie, addressed to "Maistre François des Loges, *autrement dit de Villon,"* in which he was said to be *s'absenté du pays,* and the other from the Petite Chancellerie, addressed to "Maistre François de Montcorbier," in which it was stated that it had been *contre luy procedé par banissement de nostre royaulme;* that is, he had been summoned, had not presented himself, *par contumace,* and was therefore automatically banished.

The subsequent procedure of *entérinement* or confirmation necessary to be observed by the holder of a Letter of Remission I have already described.

394

P. Lacroix, much confused and incornifustibulated over this double letter of Villon's, in order to account for it weaves out of it the hypothetical existence of a certain François de Montcorbier, a presumed fellow-student of Villon's, who had been an eye-witness of the killing of Chermoye and had been accused in Villon's stead, but nobly forbore to give the poet away. This is pure novelette.

APPENDIX D

THE ROAD TO ORLEANS

SINCE there is no means whatever of tracing the exact path of Villon's wanderings during the years 1456-60, from the St. Jacques Gate to Orleans Prison, but only his own scattered indications in the *Grant Testament,* the dates he himself gives, and one or two known historical facts chiming with his testaments, I have firmly avoided consulting any Authority whatsoever in my conjectural tracing of his route: for we all start equal. I have therefore reconstructed his exile, as far as it can be reconstructed, from the two principal sources, the *Grant Testament* and the map of France, and from my own travel, at the same time using certain assumptions based on experience and first principles. For example,

(*a*) A man with no settled plan of travel will readily follow the course of a river when he strikes one. Hence the probable mounting of the Loire to Orleans, and thence round the wide sweep of the river to Sancerre and Bourges, and thence, again, the following of the river down to Lyons and beyond.

(*b*) When a man is merely loafing to kill time he will not readily travel in zigzags involving the covering twice over of the same ground, when he can go straight on and lessen thereby the tedium of his days.

(*c*) In the autumn and winter rains and snows a man will not tramp the roads more than he can help; therefore Villon's stay at Blois and Moulins, the much longer stay at St. Généroux, and at Bourges and at Roussillon (provided he got there) occupied all together some considerable part of his four years.

And so forth.

APPENDIX E

THE BLAZON OF BEAUTY

In connection with the catalogue of vanished charms contained in the Lament of the Belle Heaulmière it may be of æsthetic interest to consider the Blazon of Beauty which Brantôme collected from the lips of a laughing lady of Toledo. The following thirty excellences (said the Spanish lady) are required to make a woman of perfect and absolute beauty:

> *Tres cosas blancas: al cuero, los dientes, y las manos.*
> *Tres negras: los ojos, las cejas, y las pestañas.*
> *Tres coloradas: los labois, las maxillas, y las uñas.*
> *Tres lungas: el cuerpo, los cabellos, y las manos.*
> *Tres cortas: los dientes, las orejas, y los pies.*
> *Tres anchas: los pechos, las frente, y el entrecejo.*
> *Tres estrechas: la boca, la cinta, y l'entrada del pie.*
> *Tres gruesas: el braço, el musto, y la pantorilla.*
> *Tres delgadas: los dedos, los cabellos, y los labios.*
> *Tres pequeñas: las tetas, la naris, y la cabeça.*

That is to say (I have already modified one series slightly, in deference to modern reticences):

> Three things white: the skin, the teeth, and the hands.
> Three black: the eyes, the eyebrows, and the eyelashes.
> Three rosy: the lips, the cheeks, and the nails.
> Three long: the body, the hair and the hands.
> Three short: the teeth, the ears, and the feet.
> Three broad: the breast, the forehead, and the space between the eyebrows.
> Three narrow: the mouth, the waist, and the instep.
> Three plump: the arm, the thigh, and the calf.
> Three fine: the fingers, the hair, and the lips.
> Three small: the paps, the nose, and the head.

APPENDIX F

Laudemus viros gloriosos . . .
　　　　　　　　　　—The Book of Wisdom, **xliv.**

Since this study of Villon and his environment is concerned with a gallows company for the most part, I have thought it equitable to balance and round off this fragment of Parisian life of the Fifteenth Century with some little indication of how better men than they conducted their affairs. The document which follows (Chancellery Registers, JJ 173, No. 580) I render straightforwardly from the Longnon collection. It concerns the foundation of a chantry in the Cluniac Priory of St. Martin-des-Champs at Paris in the year 1426 by a high minister of State and his wife, and is an invaluable illustration of the medieval mind. Though French in its accidents, its substance, combining strong devotion with a measured equity, is common to Christendom. In this document, so like a painting of the Burgundian School, Messire Philippe and his wife kneel in the shadow, heaving up their hands to the Blessed Trinity and Our Lady; yet a calm and honourable shrewdness is mixed with their devotion, and they have no intention of allowing the Prior and Community to play fast and loose with the bond.

The foundation was confirmed by Bedford, on behalf of Henry vi., and by the Parliament on the sixth of December 1426. Messire Philippe de Morvillier died in 1438: his statue, removed from his tomb when St. Martin's Priory was sacked and suppressed at the Revolution, is now in the Louvre. The Prior of St. Martin concerned in the agreement is the Dom Séguin at whose table our friend Master Guillaume de Villon was so often a guest.

These are the treaties, accords, promises, and obligations made, entered into, promised, and accorded between the sage and noble persons Messire Philippe de Morvilier, Counsellor of the King our Lord and First President in his Parliament, and Madame Jehanne du Drac, his wife, of the one part; and the religious and honourable persons the Prior and Community of the Church and Monastery of Monseigneur Saint Martin des Champs, in Paris, of the other part:

Firstly, the foundations and other acts hereinafter mentioned shall be made in the name and for the profit of the said Monseigneur the First President and Madame his wife, and for each. *Item,* the said founders, and each of them, shall be, if it seem good to them, interred and buried in the said Church and Monastery of Saint Martin des Champs, in the chapel of Saint Nicolas, near to Our Lady's chapel, on the left side, and shall erect there such representation in sculpture as may seem good to them. *Item,* there shall similarly be interred and buried in the said chapel of Saint Nicolas the children of the said founders, if it seem good to them, and all issue of these children in the direct line by loyal marriage, including the husbands and wives of the said children. *Item,* the said religious, Prior and Community, shall not suffer nor allow the interment and burial in the said chapel of any other persons without the agreement and consent of the said founders or of one of them, or of their said children after them. *Item,* on the feast of Monseigneur Saint Martin, in the winter of every year, when the custom is to hold the General Chapter, two religious shall be chosen from the Chapter, being of the said monastery and resident there, by whom, or by one of whom, during the said year and until the next feast of Saint Martin, in the following year, there shall be said a Mass every day between eight and eleven o'clock in the said chapel of Saint Nicolas for the said founders, and for each of them, their fathers and mothers and other predecessors and benefactors, and also their said children and other successors; and in addition the said two religious, and each of them, shall be bound to recite prayers and particular devotions for the said founders and each of them, their predecessors, successors, and benefactors. *Item,* that is to say, during the lives of the said founders the said Mass shall be the Office of the Day with a prayer or collect for the said founders; and after the said Mass the celebrant thereof, vested in alb and stole, shall recite an antiphon of Our Lady; that is, the *Salve Regina,* or some other antiphon of Our Lady and to her honour, with the versicle, prayer, or collect of Our Lady. *Item,* after the death of the said founders, or of each of them, the said Mass shall be of *Requiem* every day for the first year after the death of the said founder or founders, and after this Mass the celebrant shall proceed to the said tomb, being vested in alb and stole, and there say the *De Profundis* and *Pater Noster,* with the verses, prayers, and collects pertaining, with aspersion of holy water. *Item,* the said first year being past after the death of the said founders, or either of them, the said Mass shall be of the Day, and the celebrant shall be bound to proceed afterwards, as has been said, vested in

399

alb and ſtole, and recite on behalf of the said founders *De Profundis* and *Pater Noſter,* the verses, prayers, and collects pertaining, with aspersion of holy water. *Item,* the said founders shall have share and participation in all the orisons, prayers, and benefits of the Cluniac Order, and especially of the said Monaſtery of Saint Martin des Champs. *Item,* if the said two religious, or either of them, shall die during the said year, the Prior of the said Monaſtery, or his vicar, in the absence of the said Prior, shall be bound during the eight days after death to replace them by two others, or by another, until otherwise provided by the Chapter General. *Item,* in the case where the said two religious, or one of them, shall be hindered by illness or other reasonable impediment, the said religious, Prior and Community, shall be bound to have the said Mass celebrated by another, or two other religious, who shall perform all that the said religious would have performed if there were no such impediment. *Item,* each of the said founders shall have celebrated every year during his and her lifetime a Solemn Mass of the Holy Ghoſt, with deacon, subdeacon, and singer, the said Mass to be celebrated at the high altar of the choir of the said Church of Saint Martin; that is, the one Mass on the third day of July, the eve of the feaſt of the Translation of Monseigneur Saint Martin, or, if it fall on a Sunday, on the fifth day of July, the morrow of the feaſt; and the other Mass to be celebrated on the thirteenth day of November, or, if it fall on a Sunday, on the day following the said Sunday, the fourteenth day of November. *Item,* immediately following the said Masses of the Holy Ghoſt, and after each of them, there shall be made a solemn procession into the said chapel of Saint Nicolas, with the singing in procession of an antiphon of Our Lady, with the verse and prayer pertaining; and after this there shall be said in the said chapel an antiphon of Saint Nicolas, with the versicle, prayer, and collect of that saint; and returning there shall be said in procession an antiphon of Monseigneur Saint Martin, with the verse and prayer of that saint. *Item,* the said founders, and each of them, every year after their death, shall have, on the anniversary of their death, or as soon afterwards as is possible, if there be any impediment on the day, each an *Obitt,* that is, a vigil with nine psalms and nine lessons, and the next day a sung Mass, with deacon, subdeacon, and singer, the said Mass or Masses of *Obitt* to be celebrated at the high altar of the choir of the said Church of Saint Martin: and afterwards there shall be made a solemn procession to the said tomb, with the singing in procession of *Libera me, Deus,* with versicles; which done, there shall be recited *De Profundis* and *Pater Noſter,* with the versicles and prayers pertaining, with aspersion of holy water, and in returning there shall be said in procession an antiphon of Monseigneur Saint Martin, with verse, prayer, or collect. *Item,* every year on the eve of the feaſt of Monseigneur Saint Martin, in the morning before noon, there shall be presented to Monseigneur the Firſt President of the Parliament for the time being, by the senior of the said religious, the Prior and Community of the said Saint Martin, and by one other of the said religious, two bonnets with earpieces, one double and the other single, with the following words:

> "Monseigneur, Messire Philippe de Morvillier, during his life First President of Parliament, founded in the Church and Monastery of Monseigneur Saint Martin des Champs in Paris a perpetual Mass and other Divine services, and ordered that in memory and for the perpetuation of the said foundation there should be offered and presented every year on this day, to Monseigneur the First President of Parliament for the time being, at the hands of the senior of the said Community and another of the religious, this gift and present, which may it please you to accept and approve."

And the price of the said gift and present of the said bonnets shall be twenty sols Parisis, at the present rate. *Item,* with this there shall be made to the First Usher of Parliament for the time being. at the hands of the said senior and other religious, the gift of a pair of gloves and an inkhorn, with these words:

> "Sire, Messire Philippe de Morvillier, during his lifetime First President of the Parliament, founded in the Church and Monastery of Monseigneur Saint Martin des Champs in Paris a perpetual Mass and other Divine services, and ordered that in memory and for the perpetuation of the said foundation there should be offered and presented, every year on this day, to the First Usher of the Parliament for the time being, at the hands of the senior of the said Community and another of the religious, this gift and present, which may it please you to accept and approve."

Which words shall be recited from writing by the aforesaid senior and religious; and the price of the said gift and present of the said gloves and inkhorn shall be twelve sols Parisis, at the present rate. *Item,* and in order that these things and all of them shall be performed and carried out by the said Prior and Community of Saint Martin and all the goods of the said Church and Monastery, assigned, obliged, charged, and hypothecated, the said founders shall present and give to the said Church and Monastery of Monseigneur Saint Martin sixteen hundred livres Tournois in one sum, for and in place of sixty livres Tournois annual, perpetual, and amortised, which the said founders had intended to make over, present, and well and truly assign to the said religious, the Prior and Community and Monastery of Saint Martin des Champs, for the reason that the said religious declare and affirm several fine and notable buildings, edifices and ancient heritages of the said Church, which formerly produced a large and notable income every year, being well situate and convenient to the said Church, and capable of doing so again if they could be overhauled, repaired, and refurbished, to be at present in a state of such ruin and dereliction, owing to the wars which have now continued for twenty years, and still continue, that the said religious derive no income from them, or very little, and, what is worse, the said heritages, if they are not immediately put in order, will, it is understood, fall into complete ruin, the which would be an irreparable loss to the said Community and to their said Monastery. On which account they have held among themselves, with the assistance and advice af the counsellors and friends of their said Church and Monastery, several consultations with the object of saving the said heritages for the good of their said Monastery, and have come to the opinion that they can neither see nor expect any means of obtaining sufficient funds to remedy the ruinous condition of the said places, edifices and ancient heritages, which were of such value to the said Church of Saint Martin, seeing that the revenues of the said Church at the present are scarcely sufficient to provide for the maintenance of the said Community. On this account the said religious, Prior and Community, desiring fervently to preserve the said places and ancient heritages, and to amend their state, have, after long and mature deliberation, and for the evident good of their Monastery, in unanimity determined to accept and take charge of the said amount of sixteen hundred livres Tournois in one sum, for and in place of the said sixty livres Tournois annual, perpetual, and amortised, and to employ the said sum in repairing and rebuilding the said places and ancient heritages, so far as this sum may be so employed: to which decision the said founders have freely and willingly consented and agreed in behalf of the said Church, and have determined, if there be any residue of the said sixteen hundred livres Tournois, to lay the said residue out in behalf of the said Monastery as profitably as possible. *Item,* the said sum of sixteen hundred livres Tournois, with the consent and agreement of the said founders and the said Community, shall be placed in the care and keeping of Guillaume Sanguin, burgess of Paris, to be expended as has been decided. *Item,* the said founders and the said religious, Prior and Community, agree that Master Jehan Vivien, Counsellor to the King our Lord and President of Chamber of Inquests of his Parliament, with the Sub-Prior of the said Church and Monastery of Saint Martin des Champs, shall be delegated by the said founders and religious to decide on which of the said heritages the sum of sixteen hundred livres Tournois can be most usefully expended for the good of the said religious and their Monastery, and according to their advice and decision the said sum shall so be expended. *Item,* with this, the said founders shall give, bequeath, and assign to the said Church and Monastery of Saint Martin des Champs forty sols Parisis annual, perpetual, and amortised. *Item,* the said founders, over and above what is heretofore mentioned, and in order that the said religious shall be the more inclined and willing to pray God for the said founders and each of them, shall present and give to the Community of the said Monastery of Monseigneur Saint Martin the amount of one hundred livres Tournois in one sum, of which one-half shall be expended on the vestry of the religious of the said Community, of which there is great need and necessity, as they affirm, and the other half employed to the advantage of the said Community as they shall direct. *Item,* the said founders shall furnish and supply the said chapel of Saint Nicolas, where the aforesaid Masses shall be said, well and fittingly with a chalice, missal, and other requisites (which the said religious, Prior and Community, shall be bound to preserve, keep, repair, and replace when necessary), and shall also supply bread, wine, and lights for the celebration of the aforesaid Mass and other Divine services; the lights for the aforesaid Mass to be two tapers of wax, each of one livre and capable of burning during the celebration of the said Mass, and also one torch, to be lighted at the elevation of the Body of our Lord Jesus Christ. And when the said tapers are consumed they shall be replaced by two others of the same price, and thus shall be assured the lights for the said Mass, and for this purpose the said founders shall give and present to the said Church of Saint Martin, for the benefit of the sacristan of the said Church, forty sols Parisis annual, perpetual, and amortised. Item, if the said heritages, or any part of them, on which the said sum of sixteen hundred livres Tournois shall be expended, shall diminish or come to loss by reason of wars or the fortune of Time, or in any other manner whatsoever, nevertheless the said Monastery and all the goods thereof shall remain obliged, charged, and responsible for all the performances herein mentioned, without any diminution whatsoever. *Item,* and over and above all the things aforesaid, and in order that the said two religious and bedesmen shall be the more inclined, diligent, and willing to offer prayers and particular supplications for the good estate of the souls of the aforesaid founders, their predecessors, successors, and benefactors, the said founders shall give and assign to the said Church and Monastery of Saint Martin des Champs, and for the benefit of the said two religious, ten livres Parisis annual, perpetual, and amortised, which the said religious shall take and receive into their own hands: that is, one hundred sols Parisis each, over and above what the said two religious ordinarily receive from the said Church and Monastery of Saint Martin; and the said Prior and Community shall in no wise prevent or hinder their so doing. Nevertheless the said religious, Prior and Community, shall be bound to guard, preserve, and defend by Justice, at their own expense, the said income, in the same way that they are accustomed to guard and defend all other rights, heritages, and revenues of the said Church of Saint Martin; but if the said income of ten livres Parisis shall diminish or fail by reason of wars, the fortune of Time, or otherwise, by no fault of the said religious, Prior and Community, then the said Community shall not be held responsible to make it good nor to pay it to the said two religious and bedesmen, but the said two religious shall be content to take and receive what is left for them: but this notwithstanding, the said religious, Prior and Community, shall remain bound to celebrate the aforesaid Masses and other Divine services in the manner already set forth. *Item,* all these presents and all contained therein the said religious, Prior and Community, shall take up and cause to be agreed, confirmed, ratified, approved, and authorised by Monseigneur the Abbot of Cluny, with his letters engrossed and duly signed with his seal, and to this end the said Monseigneur the First President shall show all diligence in any way possible, if need arise. *Item,* all these presents, treaties, accords, agreements, and obligations shall be presented to the Court of Parliament, and the said parties, and each of them, shall be ordered by the said Court to observe and perform them. Made and presented to the Parliament by Dom Jacques Séguin, Prior, and Jehan de la Bretonniere, Sub-Prior, in their own persons, and by Master Jehan Paris, Procurator to the said Prior and Community of Saint Martin, by virtue of the procuration hereto attached and incorporated, of the one part; and by the aforesaid Messire Philippe de Morvillier and Dame Jehanne du Drac his wife, also in their own persons, of the other part: the which parties the Court of the said Parliament has, at their request and consent, ordered by decree to observe, accomplish, and perform this present agreement and all therein contained and set forth; this fourth day of December, 1426.

APPENDIX G

BIBLIOGRAPHY

I. Biographical and Critical

Of critical editions of Villon's text the three best are those I have used for this book and describe below: Longnon, Foulet, and Thuasne. I have not taken into any consideration the numerous editions with a modernised text: any man of sensibility ranks such things with *The Girls' Shakespeare*.

It is madness to attempt comprehension of Villon, his verse, or his background without some acquaintance with, among others, the following authorities:

Belloc, Hilaire.—*Avril;* Essays on the Poetry of the French Renaissance. London, 1904.
> The essay on Villon sums up the poet in half a dozen fine pages.

Champion, Pierre.—*François Villon, sa Vie et son Temps*. Paris, 1913.
> A splendid work, continuing and completing the research of Marcel Schwob. The biographical notes on Villon's companions and legatees are monumental.

Foulet, Lucien.—*François Villon: Œuvres*. Paris, 1923. (Third Edition.)
> A revision of Longnon's text of 1892.

Lacroix, Paul.—*Œuvres de François Villon*. Paris, 1877.
> An edition frequently reprinted, now in the *Editions Jouaust*. Later research has left it behind, but some of the notes are still good. The text is that of the Arsenal MS., since superseded as a base.

Longnon, Auguste.—*Etude biographique sur François Villon*. Paris, 1877.
> The work which inspired Stevenson's essay. It is still a classic, though later discoveries have demolished parts of it.

Longnon, Auguste.—*Œuvres complètes de François Villon*. Paris, 1892.
> The base of all subsequent critical editions of the text.

PARIS, GASTON.—*François Villon (Les grands Ecrivains Français)*. Paris, 1901.

A compact and for the most part reliable study.

SCHWOB, MARCEL.—*François Villon; Rédactions et Notes*. Paris, 1912.

Notes on the Coquillards, the Jargon, and various episodes in Villon's career, fully documented.

THUASNE, LOUIS.—*François Villon: Œuvres: Edition critique*. Paris, 1923.

The last word (apparently) on the text.

Note.—Longnon's text is based on thirteen manuscripts and printed editions; Foulet's founded on this, with emendations; and Thuasne's derived from three sources—the Stockholm MS. of 1470, the MS. Fr. 20041 of the Bibl. Nationale, and Levet's printed text of 1489. All three authorities, though they differ in many readings, agree that the two last are the best of the ancient sources of Villon's text extant.

II. HISTORICAL AND TOPOGRAPHICAL

BAINVILLE, JACQUES.—*Histoire de France*. Paris, 1924.

BELLOC, HILAIRE.—*Paris*. London, 1900.

DENIFLE, (LE P).—*Documents relatifs à la Fondation de l'Université*. Soc. Hist. Paris, 1883.

DE ROCHEGUDE (MARQUIS) and DUMOLIN, MAURICE.—*Guide pratique à travers le vieux Paris*. Revised, 1923.

The standard handbook to Old Paris.

DUBECH, LUCIEN, and D'ESPEZEL, PIERRE.—*Histoire de Paris*. Paris, 1926.

EVANS, JOAN.—*Medieval France*. Oxford Univ. Press, 1926.

LEBEUF (L'ABBÉ).—*Histoire de la Ville et du Diocèse de Paris*. Paris, 1890.

The master-work, revised by Augier and added to by Bournon, of the learned abbé who in 1745-1760 published the history of each of the 450 parishes in the old Diocese of Paris. It is still authoritative.

LEMOINE, HENRI.—*Manuel d'Histoire de Paris*. Paris, 1925.

A sketchy work, by an Archivist of the Seine.

III. FIFTEENTH-CENTURY PARISIAN LIFE, ETC.

CHAMPION, PIERRE.—*Liste des Tavernes de Paris, d'après des documents du XVᵉ siècle*. Soc. Hist. Paris, 1912.

DE LA SALE, ANTOINE.—*Les Quinze Joyes de Mariage, 1464*. (Ed. Jouaust.)

A profound and celebrated satire.

GÉROLD, THÉODORE, D. es L.—*Le Manuscript de Bayeux: Publications de la Faculté de Lettres de l'Université de Strasbourg*. 1921.

406

One hundred and three popular songs, words and music, of the fifteenth century: historical, political, satirical, pastoral, amorous, Bacchanalian, derisive, and *grivoises,* transposed from the Bayeux MS. into modern notation. An anthology of extreme value.

LONGNON, AUGUSTE.—*Paris pendant la Domination anglaise: Documents extraits des Registres de la Chancellerie de France,* 1420-1436. Paris, 1878.

I have quoted largely from this volume of first-hand evidence.

PETIT DE JULLEVILLE, L.—*Les Comédiens en France au Moyen Age.* Paris, 1885.

Note.—There are a dozen publications of the Société de l'Histoire de Paris, mainly contemporary papers (*e.g.* the *Journal d'un Bourgeois de Paris*) which throw light on Villon's time; also many volumes on medieval French art, manners, and life which are valuable—for example, those large illustrated volumes published in the seventies by Firmin-Didot; if so be you can find one.

IV. TRANSLATIONS

Villon has been translated entire into English three times at least: by John Payne, 1892, H. de Vere Stackpoole, 1913, and J. Heron Lepper, 1924. Separate Ballades and Rondeaux have been done into English from time to time by Rossetti, Swinburne, Wilfred Thorley, and half a dozen other poets.

[THE END]